LOTUS DOMINO ADMINISTRATION IN A NUTSHELL

A Desktop Quick Reference

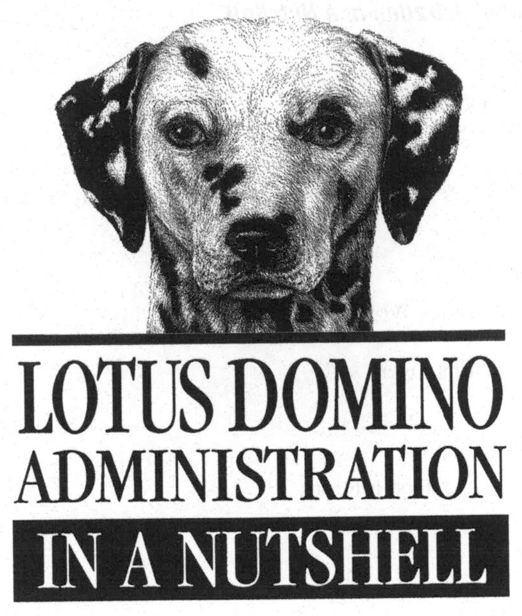

LOTUS DOMINO ADMINISTRATION IN A NUTSHELL

A Desktop Quick Reference

Greg Neilson

O'REILLY®

Beijing • Cambridge • Farnham • Köln • Sebastopol • Tokyo

Lotus Domino Administration in a Nutshell

by Greg Neilson

Published by O'Reilly & Associates, Inc., 101 Morris Street, Sebastopol, CA 95472.

Editor: Robert Denn

Production Editor: Nancy Wolfe Kotary

Cover Designer: Hanna Dyer

Printing History:

August 2000: First Edition.

Library of Congress Cataloging-in-Publication Data

Neilson, Greg.
Lotus Domino Administration in a nutshell : a desktop quick reference / Greg Neilson.-- 1st ed.
p. cm.
Includes index.
ISBN 1-56592-717-6
1. Lotus Domino. 2. Web sites--Authoring programs.

HF5548.4.L673 N44 2000
005.7'13769--dc21 00-057987

ISBN: 978-1-565-92717-9
[LSI] [2010-09-30]

Table of Contents

Preface

Lotus Domino usage is skyrocketing in the marketplace. Lotus Notes, Domino's client software, sold 22 million licenses in 1999, with 8.5 million of those in the fourth quarter, and is still winning industry awards from the likes of *PC Magazine* and others. The first version was launched over 10 years ago (a long time ago in IT terms), and yet the basic ideas behind the product—which created the concept of groupware—are as relevant today as they were back then.

The latest version, Domino R5, was released in early 1999, and there have been many small areas of improvements as well as a number of bug fixes released since then. So with the threat of Y2K behind us, many IT managers will be considering an upgrade to or installation of Domino R5 in their environments.

Domino would be impressive enough if it were only an enterprise mail server and workflow application environment, but it has come into its own as a secure application and web server. In many cases, applications written for the Notes client have been transformed on the fly into HTML web pages and sent to browsers. The mature replication technology within Domino that allows any of the multiple distributed copies of a database to be updated and then propagates the updates throughout the network is yet to be equaled.

This book provides a quick reference for Domino system administrators who pretty much know the basics but need a reference to get the detail that they need to do their work.

Other Resources

It is a source of wonder and amazement to me how few Domino R5 resources are available to system administrators—even more than a year after the launch of R5. For many other current technologies, the walls of bookshops are lined from one end to the other with new books, but this is not the case for Domino administration. However, there are two main resources with which you should be familiar. First, the product documentation for Domino (now, don't laugh!) is becoming much better. The documentation folks at Lotus have done a pretty good job with the new R5 administration documentation, so this is a fine place to start. You can download it from *http://notes.net/doc*, or view it from an installed R5 server as *help\help_admin.nsf*. These "yellow books" (named for their yellow cover) can also be ordered in hard copy separately or as a set.

IBM has also produced a number of "redbooks" (yes, they do have a red cover) on Domino, which are written by experts in the technology and describe in depth how to work with specific areas of Domino functionality. You can search *http://www.redbooks.ibm.com* for redbooks on Domino technology and download them in PDF format. You can also order these in hardcopy from *www.fatbrain.com*. In particular, there are redbooks on migrating and upgrading to R5 and implementing Domino R5 on the RS/6000 and AS/400 platforms, and I understand that many more will be available by the time you are reading this.

In Appendix F, *Web Links*, I have also listed a number of web sites that contain Domino information.

Organization of the Book

This book consists of fourteen chapters and seven appendixes, as follows:

Chapter 1, *Notes and Domino Overview*, covers the history of Notes and Domino, explains some key concepts used in the product, then concludes with the steps involved in a sample implementation.

Chapter 2, *Domino Directories*, takes a detailed look at the Domino Directory and the main types of documents found within it. It also discusses the roles of Directory Assistance and Directory Catalogs, then concludes with coverage of the LDAP support for the Domino Directory.

Chapter 3, *Domino Databases*, covers the main database properties of interest for system administrators, as well as database Access Control Lists (ACLs).

Chapter 4, *Mail*, covers the Domino messaging environment in detail. This chapter discusses the mail routing process, access from Internet clients, and calendaring and scheduling.

Chapter 5, *Domino as a Web Server*, examines the configuration of Domino's HTTP web services.

Chapter 6, *Domino Administration Tools*, looks at the new R5 Domino Administrator, user registration with a text file, using the Web Administrator, and the Administration Process (AdminP) task.

Chapter 7, *Monitoring Domino*, discusses many of the options available for system administrators to monitor the health of their Domino network—statistics and events, probes, log files and databases, and mail tracking.

Chapter 8, *Supporting the Notes Client*, covers the new R5 features, explains how the client is configured for LAN and dialup access, then discusses the new Notes Minder applet and synchronizing Notes with the PalmPilot using EasySync.

Chapter 9, *DECS*, covers a new feature that provides real-time access to backend data sources from Domino databases.

Chapter 10, *Domino for Microsoft IIS*, discusses another new R5 feature that allows Domino to run as an add-in task for Microsoft's Internet Information Server, which now comes with Windows NT/2000.

Chapter 11, *Internet Cluster Manager (ICM)*, discusses the new R5 feature that adds failover and load balancing for web clients to Domino application-level clustering. This chapters covers the basics of Domino clustering, how the ICM works and the different ways it can be employed, and how to configure it.

Chapter 12, *R4/R5 Coexistence and Migration*, outlines the main factors to consider when planning an R5 upgrade, then discusses the recommended upgrade sequence.

Chapter 13, *Domino Server Tasks and Console Commands*, covers all of the Domino server tasks and the commands available at the Domino server console.

Chapter 14, *NOTES.INI*, lists many of the common parameters in the *NOTES.INI* configuration file, which is used by both Notes and Domino.

Appendix A, *Domino/Windows NT Integration*, looks at the specific features in Domino and Notes to integrate with the Windows NT platform. The appendix also includes a discussion of Lotus's plans for supporting Windows 2000.

Appendix B, *Using InstallShield's Silent Installation Option*, is a brief discussion of how to perform batch installs of Domino and Notes code on Windows 95/98/NT/2000.

Appendix C, *Domino for AS/400*, covers the specific Domino features that are used to integrate with the AS/400 platform.

Appendix D, *Domino on Linux*, discusses the current state of support for Domino on the Linux platform, then briefly covers the installation process for Domino.

Appendix E, *TCP/IP Ports*, discusses the standard ports used by the Domino server tasks and how to change these. The appendix finishes with an overview of the NotesConnect tool, which can be used to check connectivity.

Appendix F, *Web Links*, lists some interesting web sites for further information on Domino.

Appendix G, *Domino Updates: QMRs and QMUs*, discusses how Lotus periodically releases updates to the Domino and Notes versions.

The book closes with a *Glossary* of common Domino terminology.

Conventions Used in This Book

The following typographical conventions are used in this book:

`Constant width`
: Indicates command-line or server console commands and syntax.

`Constant width italic`
: Indicates user-defined elements in examples.

Italic
: Indicates URLs, variables, or user-defined files and directories.

We'd Like to Hear from You

The information in this book has been tested and verified, but you may find that features have changed (or you may even find mistakes!). You can send any errors you find, as well as suggestions for future editions, to:

O'Reilly and Associates
101 Morris Street
Sebastapol, CA 95472
(800) 998-9938 (in the United States and Canada)
(707) 829-0515 (international/local)
(707) 829-0104 (fax)

There is a web page for this book, where we list any errata, examples, and additional information. You can access this site at:

http://www.oreilly.com/catalog/domino/

To ask technical questions or comment on this book, send email to:

bookquestions@oreilly.com

For more information about our books, conferences, software, Resource Centers, and the O'Reilly Network, see our web site at:

http://www.oreilly.com

Acknowledgments

My deepest thanks go to my wife Sue, who displayed an enormous amount of patience while I was locked away in another room writing this book on evenings and weekends. And to my two "assistants," Timothy and Matthew, Daddy is looking forward to be able to spend a lot more time with you both now.

To the editor of this book, Robert Denn, thanks for your attention to detail, your sense of humor and your vision.

To Tim O'Reilly, thanks for giving me the sense of purpose in what I needed to be writing about.

I am very grateful to those who performed technical reviews of this book and provided helpful input:

- Libby Ingrassia Schwarz, Domino Professional Magazine Contributing Editor and Independent Trainer/Consultant
- Stefan Auerbach, Navigant Consulting
- Michael White, MicroAge Consulting Services

Thank you all for your suggestions for improvement and corrections. Of course, all errors and omissions are mine and mine alone.

—Sydney, Australia

CHAPTER 1

Notes and Domino Overview

This chapter contains a brief description of the product and its architecture, and defines some key concepts. (A glossary at the end of the book defines many other Domino terms.) There is an overview of the history of Notes and Domino and what each of these products does. This section is followed by a quick overview of the new features in the Domino R5 release compared with the previous release, Domino 4.6.

The chapter concludes with a medium-sized example of a sample Domino R5 implementation intended to illustrate what may be required for a simple rollout.

Until a few years ago, Lotus Notes was the name used for both the server and client components, so you will often hear users and IT Managers refer to the server product as "Notes" instead of "Domino" out of habit (and I admit that sometimes I have to stop myself from saying that too). Nevertheless, Notes is the client and Domino is the server, and the next few sections will show you how they work together.

The Basics

The R5 Reviewer's Guide from Lotus describes Domino as an enterprise server platform for messaging, collaboration, and Internet and intranet applications. It runs on a broad range of server platforms: Windows NT, Windows 2000, Linux, AIX, HP-UX, Solaris (SPARC and Intel), OS/2 Warp Server, OS/400, and OS/390.

Domino has evolved over the years, growing from a proprietary groupware server product that provided a secure network replication infrastructure for running collaborative applications into an open web application server that supports a great many Internet technologies (Java, JavaScript, HTML, XML, IIOP, POP3, IMAP, SMTP, NNTP, and LDAP).

The Notes client is used to access the applications (including mail) from the Domino server, and it too has changed drastically over the past few years. Its interface is more browser-like, and now includes support for HTML, JavaScript, and Java applets. It also can integrate with your web browser (Microsoft Internet

Explorer or Netscape Communicator), and support accessing of other mail sources by POP3 and/or IMAP, sending mail with SMTP, accessing newsreader servers by NNTP, and using LDAP to correctly address Internet mail.

Domino is often referred to as a single product, but there are currently four versions available. In ascending order of feature levels, these are as follows:

Domino Mail Server
: Supports mail, calendaring, and discussion databases.

Domino Application Server
: Supports Mail Server functionality and the typical custom application features typically associated with Notes/Domino.

Domino Enterprise Server
: Supports Application Server functionality; application-level clustering for Notes and web clients, together with partitioning; and the ability to run multiple instances of Domino, each appearing as a distinct Domino server.

Domino Advanced Enterprise Server
: Supports the Enterprise Server functionality for the high-end AS/400s using the P40 and P50 processor groups.

Key Concepts and Architecture

In order to work effectively with Domino, there are a number of key terms and concepts that need to be understood by system administrators, and these are discussed below. Figure 1-1 is a conceptual view of Domino's architecture in operation.

Databases

The heart of the Domino server comprises the databases, which contain both data and application elements. For example, my mail in Domino is found in a dedicated database that stores my sent and received mail documents as well as many forms, views, and other design elements.

Domino uses the following terms:

Templates
: Sample applications included with Domino; these can be used as is to create databases, or can be customized using the Domino Designer product to fit individual requirements.

Documents
: Contain the actual stored data within the database.

Forms
: Are used to control the graphical layout during document creation and display.

Views
: Are used to list the documents that fit given criteria.

Agents
: Programmed tasks within the database that can run on either the server or the client as needed.

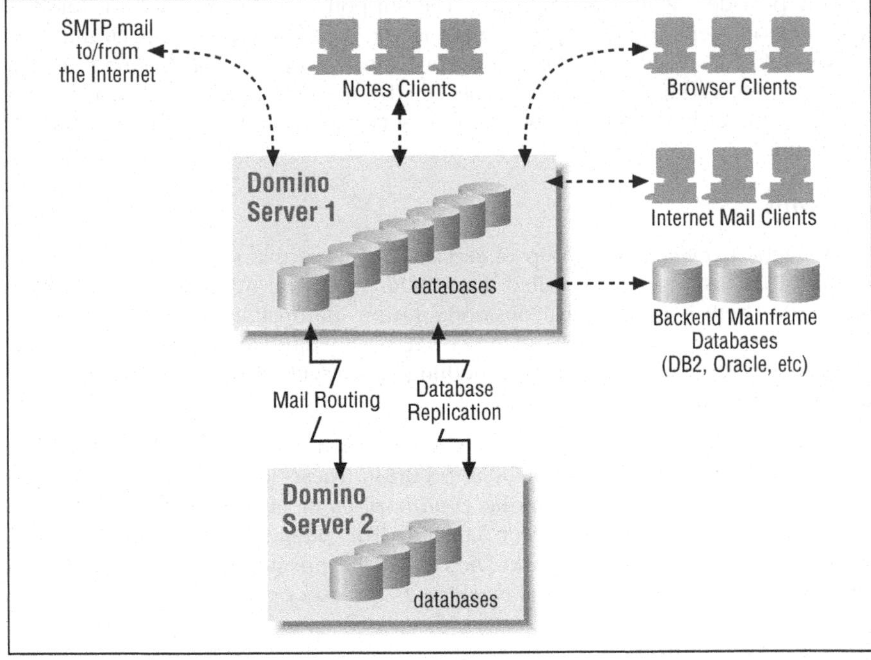

Figure 1-1: Domino architecture

Replication engine

The key to Domino's functionality is its mature replication engine, which allows multiple updateable copies of the databases to be distributed across a network. Changes in both data and program design are periodically replicated to the other copies. This has always been one of Notes' key strengths, and the field-level replication introduced in R4 allows you to send only the changes across the network, rather than requiring you to replicate the entire changed document.

Mail and messaging

Mail is probably the most critical application supported within Domino, and mail routing within Domino is a separate process from database replication. For servers within the same *Domino Named Network (DNN)*—these are servers using the same network protocol in a constant connection (not dialup) within the same domain—mail routing is immediate and does not need to be configured.

Since Domino supports custom applications and is also a messaging server, it is most often used to create mail-enabled applications that support automated workflow for an enterprise.

Support for Internet standards

Support for a great number of Internet standards has been progressively added to Domino, though this has not been a major architectural change, since in most cases, the Internet standards have been a subset of the functionality that Domino already provided. POP3, IMAP4, and SMTP support have been added for Internet mail support; perhaps the biggest change in the past few years has been the integration of the HTTP stack and the functionality to convert Domino design elements into HTML for browser clients on the fly. Other technologies have also been added, such as NNTP for newsreader server support and LDAP for directory integration.

Domains

In Domino, a *domain* is a group of servers and users that use the same *Domino Directory* (which used to be called the Public Name and Address Book in earlier releases). There is a great deal of configuration information within this Domino Directory, but its main purpose is the correct addressing and distribution of mail. (This use of the word "domain" has nothing to do with Windows NT domains or with DNS domains.)

To identify servers and users within an organization, Notes/Domino uses public/private key-pair technology from RSA Security. These keys are generated from special certifier IDs that represent the *Organization* or *Organizational Unit* under which the user or server has been created. The public key for each user and server is stored within the Domino Directory. The private key is stored in an ID file that must be on the same local machine as the user or server.

Hierarchical naming

Hierarchical names for servers and users (which have existed since R3) are based on the X.500 naming standard. A name can comprise:

- An optional Country name (C). This is not often used in practice.
- An Organization name (O). This is compulsory.
- Up to four Organizational Units (OU).
- The Common Name (CN) of the server or user.

The full hierarchical name of an object is its common name, followed by the complete path up the tree, separated by a forward slash. For example, a server might have the name *CN=ServerA/O=ALAMEDA* and a user might have the name *CN=Greg Neilson/OU=Admins/O=CompanyA*.

Typically, most companies use a single domain and a single organization. However, larger companies have had to use multiple domains and/or organizations for a variety of reasons. First, there were scalability issues with earlier versions of Notes databases, meaning that early implementers may have needed to use multiple domains (and thus multiple address books). Similarly, these companies may have totally separate *production* and *test* Notes/Domino environments, so that the development teams producing new and updated applications are not interfering with the operation of the production network.

When users and servers are descendants of a common organization—and thus a common certifier—they automatically trust each other's identity. However, when they are from different organizations, a process known as *cross-certification* must be involved, so that they can be sure that users or servers are who they say they are. This process keeps a copy of the public key of the other ID as a reference in the Domino Directory or the Personal Name and Address Book.

Product Background and Version History

It in order to understand what Domino is and where it may be going in the future, it is instructive to understand where it came from.

The story of Notes/Domino goes back to the early 70s, when the Computer-based Education Research Laboratory (CERL) at the University of Illinois released *PLATO Notes*. This product was a secure mail system intended to handle bug reports. Subsequent versions expanded the messaging functionality of the system with the release of PLATO Group Notes in 1976.

Ray Ozzie worked on this PLATO system in the late 70s, and with the subsequent birth of the PC, he began considering a PC-based version. He managed to convince the founder of Lotus, Mitch Kapor, to fund the development of this product, and in late 1984, Ozzie founded Iris Associates, Inc., to develop the product. Lotus bought the rights to Notes in 1987 and Lotus later bought out Iris in 1994.

Release 1.0 of Notes shipped in 1989. This version contained the key features of the basic product: replication of database content across servers, encryption and signing of document updates, discussion databases, dialup support, and the @formula language for application development (which was based on the macro language then used in Lotus 1-2-3).

Release 2.0 shipped in 1991 and included support for a C API, rich text fields, and larger databases.

Release 3.0 shipped in 1993 with many new features, including full-text searching, selective replication, and a hierarchical naming scheme. There were also scalability improvements that enabled support for up to 200 concurrent users per server.

In July 1995, IBM acquired Lotus, mainly for the Notes technology. At the time, there was great disagreement as to whether this was a good idea. IBM's OS/2 2.x had seemingly gone nowhere and was unable to compete against the growth of Windows NT. Notes was seen by many as a "cool" product that at the time was still not widely used; at the same time, the threat of the Internet appeared to make this type of product obsolete. In retrospect, it seems like a brilliant move for the IBM team to understand how Notes could integrate backend data sources with emerging Internet standards, and I believe also that the command to make IBM "eat its own dog food" in moving from OfficeVision/VM to Notes mail internally in 1997 played a part in adding scalability and functionality to Notes' enterprise messaging infrastructure.

Release 4.0 came out in early 1996. It offered a myriad of new features that made it more enterprise-ready. It introduced support for LotusScript, a Visual Basic–like programming language that enabled more serious application development than the existing @formula language would allow. It introduced field-level replication and the passthru concept, which enables access to a server via another Notes server. It also included new design elements, such as navigators and action bars.

As Internet technologies grew more pervasive, Lotus released an add-on product called InterNotes Web Publisher, which ran on a schedule to produce static HTML documents from documents in Notes databases. However, a web server was still needed to serve this HTML to browser clients. The next generation of this add-on was called Domino and caused a great deal of excitement. It had its own HTTP stack, and would convert Domino documents to HTML on the fly for web clients, in many cases requiring little or no programming changes.

Release 4.5 in December 1996 was a major new version. The server product now included the Domino add-on and was renamed as *Domino* (the full name being "Domino 4.5, Powered by Notes"), and the client was now called *Notes*. This rebranding effort was to emphasize that the old "proprietary" Notes server had undergone a metamorphosis into an open Internet applications server. It added calendaring and scheduling, POP3 support, and the SMTP and cc:Mail MTAs. By now, Windows NT had surpassed OS/2 as the preferred server of choice, and new releases were developed on NT first. A number of NT integration features (single sign-on, Performance Monitor support, event monitor support, User Manager add-in, and Domino as a service) were also added in this release.

The 4.5 release also included the Advanced version of Domino, which contained three new features for general use. These features had formerly been part of a special version of Notes 4.0 called Notes for Public Networks, which was intended for telephone companies such as AT&T and Australia's Telstra to host Notes public mail services. The new features were:

- The Billing feature, which allowed administrators to monitor server usage in a number of areas in order to determine usage information (and thus billing information as well).
- Partitioning, which meant that multiple instances (or "partitions") of Domino could run independently on one server, all sharing the same code.
- Clustering—specifically, an application-level clustering that allowed Domino to create clusters of up to six heterogeneous servers. A new type of replication, which was event-driven rather the typical schedule-driven replication normally used in Domino, was used to keep database replicas in synchronization across the cluster. Failover support built into the Notes client meant that if a replica copy within a cluster could not be opened, the client would be able to find other replicas of that database within the cluster and open one of them.

The release of Domino 4.6 in September 1997 added Java classes for Domino server objects as well as support for Java Servlets. Support for IMAP, NNTP, and LDAP was also added.

Check out *http://www.notes.net/history.nsf* for a more detailed history of Notes and Domino.

Domino R5 New Features

R5 has been driven by a number of goals, which include:

- Improved support for Internet standards, including changes to make the client UI more browser-like as well as support for browser technologies (JavaScript, frames, etc.). The web server in Domino has been extended to support IIOP, application-level clustering, and access control of flat files.

- Improvements in ability to access backend data sources, as part of IBM's strategy to provide browser access to backend data sources (mainframes, midrange, PC servers) via a Domino server.

The new features of R5 include the following:

Native Internet mail
: The distinction between Domino mail and Internet mail no longer exists. MIME and SMTP are supported natively and users can use Internet address formats. These include both the RFC 821 and RFC 822 formats: *user@foo.com* and "My User" <*user@foo.com*>, respectively.

    This topic is discussed in further detail in Chapter 4, *Mail.*

IIOP support
: IIOP, or Internet Inter-ORB Protocol, allows writing of Java applets for web browsers that can access Domino Server objects transparently directly via CORBA.

Internet Cluster Manager
: Application-level clustering for Domino web clients is now supported. The new ICM task monitors the status of the servers within the cluster and then generates a URL for a given client request to be redirected to a server within the cluster.

    This topic is discussed in further detail in Chapter 11, *Internet Cluster Manager (ICM).*

Access control for flat files
: The Domino security model is extended to support flat files (HTML, etc.) served by the Domino web server.

Support for Microsoft IIS
: R5 can run as an add-on to Microsoft IIS on the Windows NT/Windows 2000 platform instead of using its own HTTP stack.

    This topic is discussed in greater detail in Chapter 10, *Domino for Microsoft IIS.*

Transactional logging
: Database updates can now be written to the sequential transaction logs, which are then written in the background to the correct database. This provides three main benefits: performance, fast startup after server failures, and data integrity of Domino databases. The performance benefit is that the sequential updates to the logs are quicker than the updates of each database. The fast startup comes from the way the server restarts after a failure; without the logs, it had to check the integrity of suspected open databases before they could be opened. With transaction logging in place, the logs can be replayed from the last commit point and the server can then restart. Data integrity means that the logs can be used (assuming you have a backup program that is able to work with the transaction logs) to restore a given database and then updates can be rolled forward from the transaction logs, so no data is lost.

    Transaction logging is turned on at the server, although specific databases can disable this feature if it is not needed.

    This feature is covered in more detail in Chapter 2, *Domino Directories.*

Improvements in server monitoring

There are a couple of ways that this feature has been addressed. First, probes can be configured to check regularly that servers and the services on them are available. Second, the monitoring facilities of the Domino Administrator client allow graphical real-time monitoring of tasks and statistics on specified servers.

Domino Administrator is discussed in more detail in Chapter 6, *Domino Administration Tools*, and probes are discussed in more detail in Chapter 7, *Monitoring Domino.*

Message tracking

Message tracking keeps records of mail traffic on Domino servers, so that users can monitor the delivery of their own mail and system administrators can track any mail passing through the servers. Once this data is collected, usage reports can be run to track mail usage.

This feature is discussed in more detail in Chapter 7.

Database size limitation changes

R5 introduces a new version of the internal database format that removes the old 4GB database limit. The new supported limit is 64GB, and this limit will increase as testing continues, since the theoretical limit is nearly infinite.

The implications of this new feature are covered in Chapter 3, *Domino Databases.*

DECS

DECS is a technology available for download for R4.6.3 onwards and bundled as part of R5. It enables transparent real-time access to back end databases from Domino with a little programming effort.

This topic is covered in more detail in Chapter 9, *DECS.*

A Sample Implementation

This simplified example is based on an R5 implementation I recently completed for approximately 1300 users. The intention here is to provide a feel (or more likely, a reminder) for the way that Domino and Notes operate and what is involved in deploying these products. This is in keeping with the main purpose of the book, which is to act as a quick reference for Domino system administrators who understand the basics but often need something to refer to for the details. It is very common nowadays for the same staff to have to manage many products such as Windows NT, Domino, Novell Netware, and maybe Linux or Solaris as well. Therefore, we can't always be expected to remember every detail of every product.

Figure 1-2 shows the Domino design to be implemented.

The steps involved in performing the implementation are:

1. The first Domino server—AMRSFO1—is installed. This creates the organizational certifier that will be used to create to create all child ID files (OUs and users), this server ID file, and the ID file for the first administrator for the domain. It also creates the Domino Directory for the new domain XYZ. The hierarchical name of the server is AMRSFO1/XYZ.

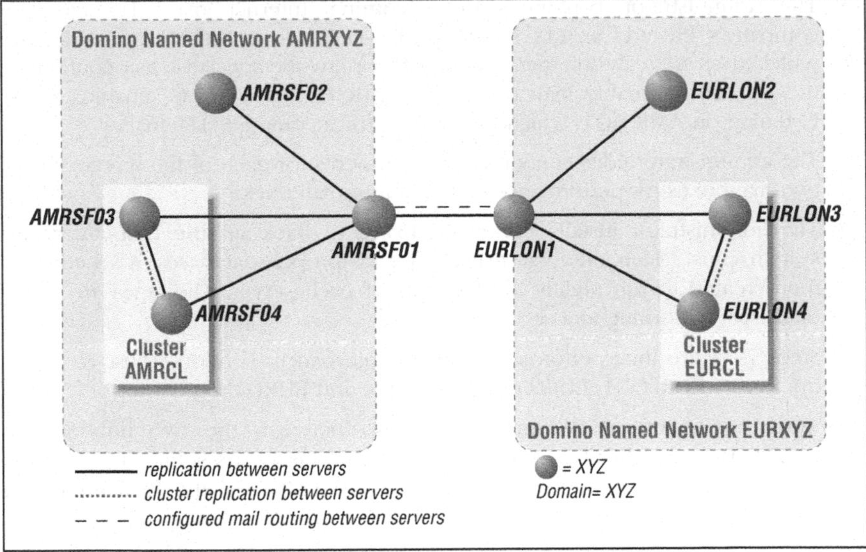

Figure 1-2: Domino architecture for XYZ Corp.

2. The administrator installs the Domino Administrator client on his machine.
3. The certification log database (*CERTLOG.NSF*) is manually created on AMRSFO1 from the template on this server.
4. The administrator registers all of the subsequent servers. This creates Server documents within the Domino Directory, and ID files for each under the certifier used to create them. He then creates the OUs AMR/XYZ and EUR/XYZ, both as children from the XYZ certifier. He adds his ID to the recovery information for these certifiers. These certifiers and their passwords are then kept in a safe place, since with them, anyone can create their own users and servers.
5. The administrator creates three groups: XYZ_Admins for the Domino Administrators, and then AMR_ALL and EUR_ALL, to which all of the created users will be added. He adds himself to the XYZ_Admins group.
6. The administrator sets the security for the Domino Directory. He changes the Default access to None and adds the Person Groups AMR_ALL and EUR_ALL with reader access. He then uses Domino Administrator to grant Manager access to all databases on the server to the group XYZ_Admins.
7. The administrator installs servers AMRSFO2, AMRSFO3, and AMRSFO4. All four AMR servers are configured to be part of the same Domino Named Network: AMRXYZ. This means that mail routes automatically among all four servers. To make name resolution simple, the IP addresses for all four servers are added to the company DNS. All client PCs are already configured to use these DNS servers.
8. The administrator configures replication. AMRSFO1 will the "hub" server and the other three servers will be the "spoke" servers. So he creates three Connection documents from AMRSFO1 to each of the other three servers. The replication schedule is every 15 minutes between 12:01 A.M. and 11:59 P.M.

9. The administrator configures the incoming Internet mail. He has the company's ISP add an MX record to the DNS for *XYZ.COM* for AMRSFO1, which uses a "real" Internet address. The network specialist has configured the firewall to enable mail to pass to AMRSFO1. Finally, he enables SMTP Listening on AMRSFO1, which then listens for incoming SMTP mail.
10. The administrator edits configuration documents for each of the servers, using two mailboxes for performance and enabling mail tracking.
11. The administrator installs backup software to back up the base operating system, plus a Domino agent that can back up open databases. A schedule is then created to run nightly full backups of each server. The tapes are taken offsite each morning to a secure site.
12. Steps 7–11 are then performed by his counterpart in London. These steps set up servers EURLON1, EURLON2, EURLON3, and EURLON4.
13. Another Connection document is set up between the two hub servers AMRSFO1 and EURLON1. In addition to replication, this setup must include mail routing, since the servers are on a different NNN and mail routing is therefore *not* automatic.
14. The administrator sets up the clustering of the application servers in each of the geographies. AMRSFO3 and AMRSFO4 were both installed with Domino Enterprise Server. They also have an additional network adapter installed and configured so that the cluster replication can be between these two adapters on a private network and thus avoid having an impact on client network performance. He creates the replica copies of the key database applications on both of the servers. He then creates a cluster, AMRCL, and adds both AMRSFO3 and AMRSFO4 to it. He runs the Cluster Analysis7 tool to ensure that everything is set up correctly, and the same process is repeated in the EURCL cluster for servers EURLON3 and EURLON4. Regular replication is also configured between these two servers and scheduled to occur every ten minutes. This ensures that the contents of the databases are kept closely synchronized even if the cluster replication is manually stopped by an administrator for any reason.
15. Lists of users to be created are prepared as text files (from a spreadsheet or via a Perl script) so that the users can be created in batches by importing these text files into Domino Administrator. This creates the Person records in the Domino Directory, as well as their mail databases and their ID files. These ID files are stored on a network drive so that they are more secure than they would be in the Domino Directory. Each of the users is created with a profile (for either LON or SFO), containing several bookmarks of interest to the users in the location: the Domino Directory, the Directory Catalog, and some key business applications.
16. The Notes R5 client is installed by an SMS job that uses the silent installation process. The NT Domain logon scripts are altered to include a one-time copy of the ID files from a shared LAN location to the user's hard disk. Users are issued hardcopy instructions on how to set up their Notes client: the location and name of their ID file, their initial password, and their home server (which contains their mail database). They are also instructed on how to change their ID passwords.

17. NT RAS/DUN is used for remote access. Therefore, dialup support does not need to be configured in the Notes clients or Domino servers. A local replica of the Directory Catalog and the user's mail database is created on his laptop. A Location document is created in the user's Personal Name and Address book, so that she will be able to work offline using the regular Office location to connect to the Domino Server when dialed up via RAS.

International Versions of Domino

Domino uses encryption technology from RSA Security, and the U.S. government currently restricts certain encryption levels from being exported to other countries. This has led to the current situation in which there are three main types of Domino code (leaving aside all of the different language versions), and two types of IDs that can be used with Domino.

The North American version of Domino code uses 64-bit encryption keys. However, the maximum exportable key is 40 bits, so Lotus has an International version that uses a special U.S. government 24-bit key. This effectively gives the International user 40 bits of key in the whole 64-bit key. However, the French government was not pleased by this change, so a special 40-bit encryption scheme was used in the French version. When looking for the correct version of code to install, typically look for the words "North American", "International", or "40-bit" to denote each of the versions.*

Along the same lines, there are two types of user license that can be created as part of the ID file in Domino: North American and International. The French version uses International IDs. As you would expect, typically we create the ID to match the version of code being installed. For example, when using North American code, we use a North American license type for the user ID being registered. Be careful when mixing these—the North American client code can use an International ID, but the International client code cannot use a North American ID. The user license type is entered when the user ID file is created, so keep in mind what this can mean if not selected correctly.

In early 2000, the U.S. government relaxed its export encryption laws. The 5.0.4 QMR release in mid-June was the first to take advantage of this, creating a single Global release equivalent to the former North American version. The Domino Administrator dialogs still allow the creation of North American/International IDs and are yet to be changed. This doesn't change the situation with France and China, which have import regulations on encryption. Existing implementations with lower encryption levels can interoperate with this newer version. Expect to hear more about this in future Domino QMRs.

* I must admit I did once make a mistake with this myself by using the wrong code to install at a client site (yes, the one mentioned in the case study earlier)—I had the 40-bit Domino code instead of the International version that was actually needed. At 10 P.M., it's not much fun, I'm afraid, having to backout a server installation and download the correct version. : - (

CHAPTER 2

Domino Directories

In this chapter, I will explain the Domino Directory structure and related features. The Domino Directory is the heart of the Domino server; in it is stored a great deal of information about the resources within the domain, and also much of the server configuration. The directory catalog and directory assistance features complement the Domino Directory by easing the task of using multiple directories with Notes and Domino. At the end of the chapter, I will discuss the LDAP support offered by Domino and the new *ldapsearch* tool, which checks that LDAP server results are as expected.

Domino Directory

The Domino Directory stores server and user information (such as username, email address, public keys, department information) and makes it accessible to servers and users within the same domain. Its main purpose is the correct addressing and transfer of mail; it also contains a great deal of server configuration information. Table 2-1 lists the document types stored within the Domino Directory.

Table 2-1: Document Types Within the Domino Directory

Document	*Purpose*
Group	Defines groups of users and servers for use with access control and/or mail distribution lists. There are two groups created by default in a new domain: LocalDomainServers and OtherDomainServers. As new servers are created in the domain, they are automatically added to the LocalDomain-Servers group. Groups created with the group type of Deny List Only do not appear in the Groups view of the Domino Directory; they appear under the Server\Deny Access Groups view.

Table 2-1: Document Types Within the Domino Directory (continued)

Document	*Purpose*
Location	Performs no real purpose for a server. This once was useful for storing information if a replica of the Domino Directory was kept locally rather than in a Personal Name and Address Book. However, with the advent of the Domain Catalog as an alternative way to keep that information locally, this is probably no longer desirable. Another alternative is to keep some skeleton location documents here that users can copy into their Personal Name and Address.
Person	Defines the configuration for authenticated web and Notes users.
Configuration	Defines further configuration for all servers, a group of servers, or a specified list of servers. This includes LDAP, ROUTER/SMTP mail processing, and some of the main *NOTES.INI* parameters.
Certificate	Contains the public key information for certifier IDs, cross-certified IDs for this domain, and also the public key information from many of the well-known Internet Certificate Authorities.
Connection	Contains information about connecting to other servers for routing mail and for database replication, including the scheduling information and what to replicate.
Domain	Defines another domain to which Domino can route mail. The different types of domain available are: foreign, nonadjacent, adjacent, foreign X.400, foreign SMTP, foreign cc:Mail, and Global.
External Domain Network Information	Used to allow clients to access resources in other domains without having to explicitly create Connection documents within the client's Personal Name and Address Book.
File Identification	Defines MIME content types served by the Domino web server.
Holiday	Contains the master set of holiday documents that users can download to their mail databases to automatically schedule company holidays. There are a number of default holidays for each country that come with the Domino server.
Mail-in databases and resources	Configured to be able to receive mail. These are typically used in workflow applications. Resources are special mail-in databases used for calendaring and scheduling.
Program	Allows the server to schedule to run utility programs on a seven-day schedule.
Server	Contains much of the configuration for a server within the current domain.
Setup Profile	Contains client configuration information that is used for new users to customize their Notes workstation environments. (These are discussed in more detail in Chapter 8, *Supporting the Notes Client*.)

Document	*Purpose*
V3 Stats and Events	Contains obsolete statistic and event monitors from R3. These are now kept in the Statistics and Events database (*EVENTS4.NSF*).
Web Configurations	Contains information for definition of file-level access, realms, and virtual servers for the web server component of Domino.

The four most important types of documents are the Person, Connection, Program, and Server documents, so these will now be discussed in greater detail.

Person Document

The Person document holds a great deal of information, but not all of it is of interest to the system administrator. For example, the Work/Home tab contains reference information for other users, and you may or may not elect to populate it. The Basics tab and the Mail tab are the most interesting sections for administrators.

The Basics tab

The Basics tab of the Person document contains user identification information, as shown in Figure 2-1.

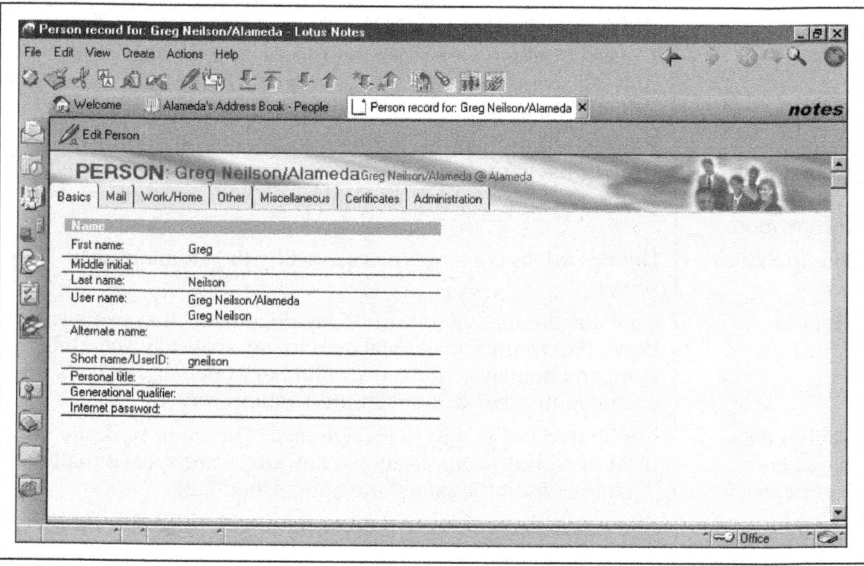

Figure 2-1: The Person document Basics tab

The "User name" field consists of one or more names that correspond to this user; mail sent to any of these names is sent to this user. The username does not have to be a variant of the first name/last name/organization—it could be an alias such as *postmaster* or *helpdesk*. If the "User name" field contains such an alias, mail sent to the alias will be delivered to this user.

The "Internet password" field is used to authenticate web users—the password here must match what is entered by the client in the browser. It is stored in a hashed format, so it cannot be read once this value has been entered into the Person document. Unless you write a custom application, there is no way to automatically update the contents of the password field—it must be entered manually in this Person document. Note that when web users are authenticated, only the first value in the "User name" field for this Person document is checked against each database ACL to confirm that the user has sufficient access to perform the desired task.

The Mail tab

The Mail tab of the Person document is used to define the mail configuration for this user, as shown in Figure 2-2.

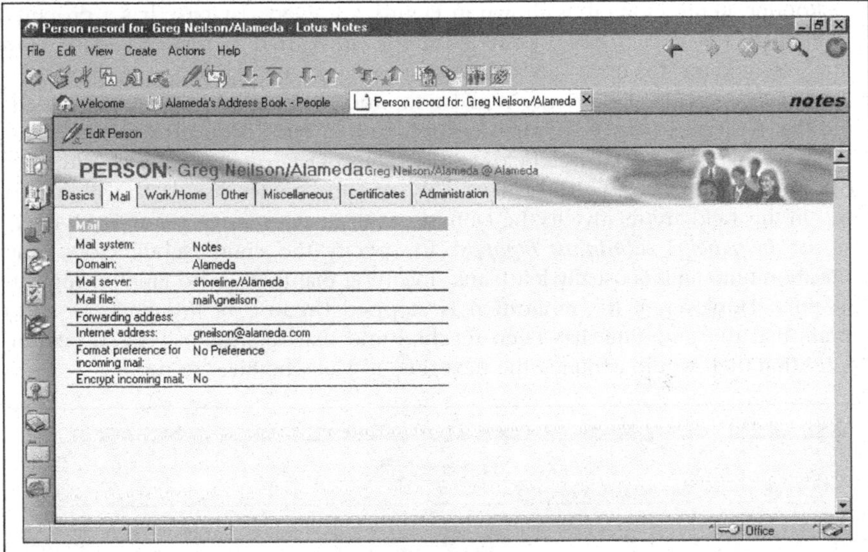

Figure 2-2: The Person document Mail tab

Typically, the "Mail system" field is set to Notes, indicating that this is a Notes user. Other options are POP or IMAP (for use with POP3/IMAP clients), or Other Internet Mail (when mail for this user will not be kept within Domino).

Information entered in the "Domain," "Mail server," and "Mail file" fields tell Domino where to route mail intended for this user.

The "Forwarding address" field is used to send mail for this user to another address. This other address can be that of another Notes user, or an Internet address such *userxyz@hotmail.com*. A value must be entered here when the "Mail system" field is set to Other Internet Mail.

The field "Format preference for incoming mail" is useful when dealing with mixed R4/R5 environments. The default is No Preference, which is fine for R5 Notes clients, but to ensure fidelity of messages for R4 clients this value should be set to Prefers Notes Rich Text, and for Internet mail users, to Prefers MIME. Otherwise, attachments can appear corrupted when message formats are not converted properly for the different client types.

Connection Document

The Connection document is used to configure database replication and/or mail routing between two servers. The Basics tab allows you to specify the Source Server and the Destination Server, and the network Port(s) to communicate between the two. The Destination Server can be a group of servers, which can greatly simplify the creation of Connection documents. When a group of servers is used, the server performs database replication and/or mail routing with all servers that are members of the group.

The Routing/Replication tab

The Routing/Replication tab is shown in Figure 2-3. Every database has a property that defines the replication priority used for replication of that database—the default is medium priority. This means that you can configure specific mission-critical databases for high-priority replication, and then create a connection document that replicates only these databases. When the "Files/Directories to Replicate" field is left blank, all databases below the Domino Data directory are checked for replication. You can (optionally) have only specific entries listed. The filenames listed in this field are relative to the Domino Data directory—for example, *NAMES.NSF*, or *help\help5_admin.nsf bigapps* to specify the entire subdirectory. The replication time limit is usually left blank, meaning that there is no limit on replication time. However, if the replication is stopped because of this limit, Domino reports that the time limit has been reached and that replication was successful. Replication then would continue the next time it was scheduled to run.

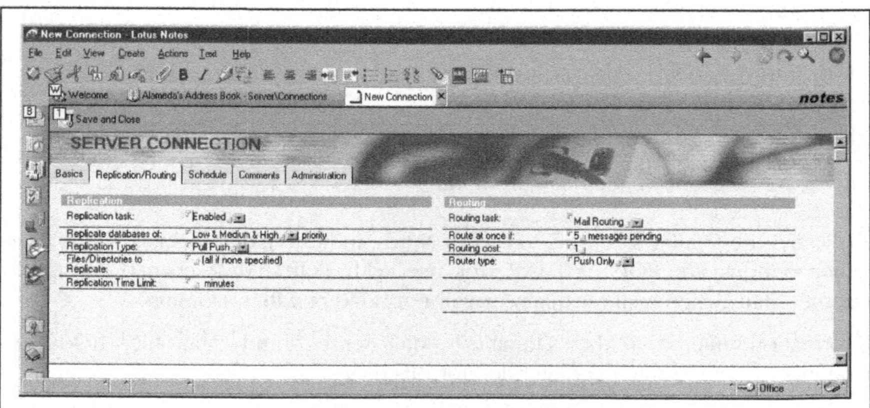

Figure 2-3: The Connection document Replication/Routing tab

The replication type can be one of four types:

Pull Pull
: The source server pulls database changes from the destination server, then the destination server pulls database changes from the source server.

Pull Push (default)

The source server pulls database changes from the destination server, then pushes changes to the destination server.

Pull only

The source server pulls database changes from the destination server only.

Push only

The source server pushes database changes to the destination server only.

The replication type selected in each of the Connection documents should match the replication design for the domain. For example, in a typical "hub and spoke" design, there would be Connection documents for the "hub" server to perform Pull Push replication for each of the "spoke" servers.

Mail routing is a little simpler to configure, because of the power of the *Notes Named Network (NNN)* concept. This feature means that between servers in the same domain running the same protocols and same NNN, mail routing is done automatically and does not need to be explicitly configured. However, you will often need to route mail to servers outside the same NNN or domain.

The default "Routing Task" field entry is Mail Routing, unless you are communicating with X.400, R4 servers sending SMTP mail, or cc:Mail. The "Route at once if" field is used to determine how many medium priority mail messages must be accumulated before being routed by the server. The delivery priority is set by the user. High-priority mail messages are always routed immediately. The "Routing cost" field is used for multiple connections between two points—for instance, when you have a dialup line and a permanent network and you wish to prioritize your preferred mail route. A connection with the lowest number is the preferred mail route.

There are four options available for the "Router type" field:

Push/Wait

The server waits until another server contacts it, then pushes all messages to the other server.

Push Only (the default)

The server pushes its messages to another server.

Pull Push

The server pushes its messages to the other server, and then the other server will push any messages to this server.

Pull Only

The server contacts another server and has that server push messages to this server.

The Schedule tab

The Schedule tab is used to determine which days of the week to run the program, what time to run it, and optionally whether to keep running it every *x* minutes. The Schedule tab also contains an option to enable or disable the running of the scheduled program. The default is to run the replication and routing between 08:00 and 22:00 each day, with a repeat interval of 360 minutes.

Keep in mind that this repeat interval is calculated from the *end* of the last replication and routing activity, not the start.

Program Document

The Program document in the Domino Directory provides another option for scheduling server tasks instead of the `ServerTasksAtX=` lines in *NOTES.INI*. You have more control here over the schedule—you can schedule a task to run at any time during the week or schedule it to repeat at a given interval. And you can also disable a task from running without having to edit *NOTES.INI* to remove it and then later replace it. Figure 2-4 shows the Program document.

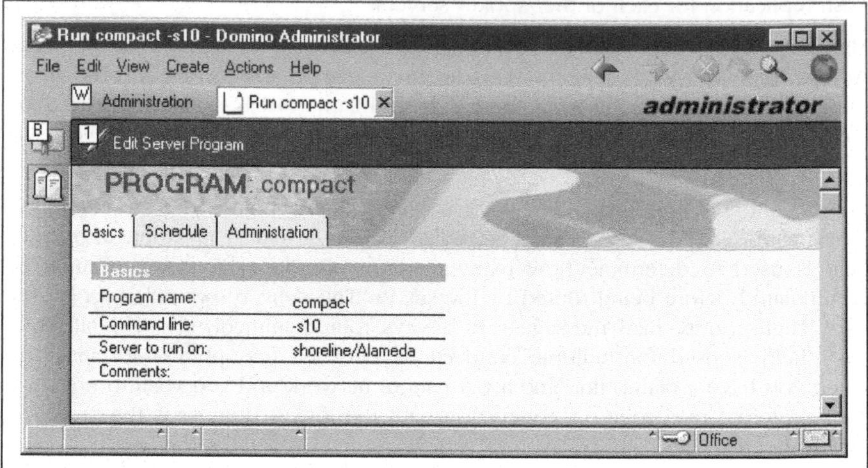

Figure 2-4: The Program document Basics tab

The Basics tab

The Basics tab allows you to specify the name of the task to schedule in the "Program name" field and enter any parameters in the "Command line" field. In addition to Domino tasks, you can use this document to run any command file or program on the server.

The Schedule tab

The Schedule tab allows you to specify which days of the week to run the program, what time to run it, and optionally whether to keep running it every *x* minutes. The Schedule tab also contains an option to enable or disable the running of the scheduled program.

Server Document

The Server document contains much of the configuration information for the server.

The Basics tab

The Basics tab contains general information about the server, much of which is automatically created when the server is registered; information such as server build number and operating system level is maintained by the AdminP process. One item of interest is the SMTP listener task, which, if enabled, automatically starts the SMTP task to listen for incoming Internet mail.

The Security tab

The contents of the Security tab (shown in Figure 2-5) greatly affect the security of your Domino server, particularly if the server is exposed to Internet users.

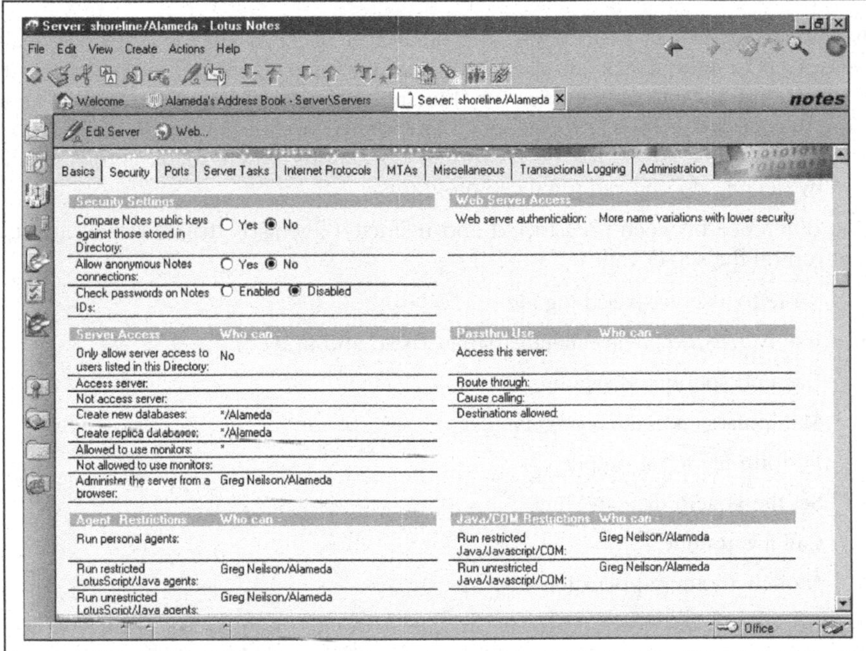

Figure 2-5: The Server document Security tab

The majority of these fields are cached in server memory when the server starts, so if you change an entry, you must stop and restart the server for the changes to take effect. Since this is not desirable, the alternative is to list groups, rather than individual usernames, in these fields. This way, you can move users between the groups as needed and have these security changes take effect.

When the value for "Allow anonymous Notes users" (in the "Security Settings" section) is set to No, all web users must be authenticated before they can access any system resources.

The default for "Access server" is anyone, so often administrators use a group name here that includes all users and servers within the organization. Similarly, it is usual to create a "Deny access" group for former employees and to add this group name to the "Not access server" field. The defaults for "Create new databases" and "Create replica databases" allow no one to do this, so you will probably add the administrator names and/or groups that are allowed to perform these tasks. You may also want to add the names of the servers at this point, so that the servers themselves can create new databases and replicas. Typically the default group LocalDomainServers works well here. (Many of the fields in the "Server Access" section have an equivalent *NOTES.INI* parameter, as discussed in Chapter 14, *NOTES.INI*.)

By default, none of the functionality under the "Passthru Use" section is enabled, so should you want to involve this server in passthru, either as a destination server or to have users route through this server. This specification should be explicitly configured.

In the section "Agent Restrictions," the default blank entry for the "Run personal Agents" field means that all users can run personal agents on the server. In contrast, the default blank entries for "Run restricted LotusScript/Java agents" and "Run unrestricted LotusScript/Java agents" mean that no one can run these types of agents. The same is true for the Java/COM restrictions, where blank entries mean that by default, no one can run these programs.

The difference between unrestricted and restricted agents is that restricted agents that run on the server can:

- Write to a server-based log file
- Use *NOTES.INI* environment variables (read and update)
- Use encryption and signing
- Manipulate embedded objects
- Perform file input/output
- Set the system date and time
- Call a C routine
- Launch another application

If your Notes users need to activate the Out of Office notification feature, which runs a LotusScript agent on their home server each night, these users need access to run Restricted LotusScript/Java agents.

The Ports tab

In the Ports tab, you configure the Notes Network Name for the enabled network ports and enable/disable the various Internet ports (HTTP, HTTPS, LDAP, NNTP, POP3, IMAP, SMTP, IIOP), or optionally change them from their usual well-known values. If SSL is used, its configuration is also specified here.

The Server Tasks tab

The Server Tasks tab allows you to configure a number of the server tasks: Administration Process, Agent Manager, Domain Catalog, Directory Catalog, Internet Cluster Manager, and Web Retriever.

The Internet Protocols tab

The Internet Protocols tab is primarily for configuring the Domino web server and the news server options. This includes logging options and standard web server directory mappings.

The Transactional Logging tab

The Transactional Logging tab (shown in Figure 2-6) is a new feature in R5. Transactional logging changes the way that Domino writes updates to its databases. The changes are written and committed in the transaction logs first, and then, in the background, the changes are applied to the Domino databases. This offers a performance improvement, as it is quicker to write the updates to the sequential log files than to the Domino databases themselves. It also offers better data integrity, since changes can be reapplied from the logs after a database is restored—otherwise, these changes would have been lost. Another important advantage is that during a server restart following a failure, the logs can be automatically rolled forward so that the server will be ready to process requests. In the past, the server needed to determine which databases were open at the time of a failure and then check the integrity of each (by running the *fixup* task against them all) before users were allowed access.

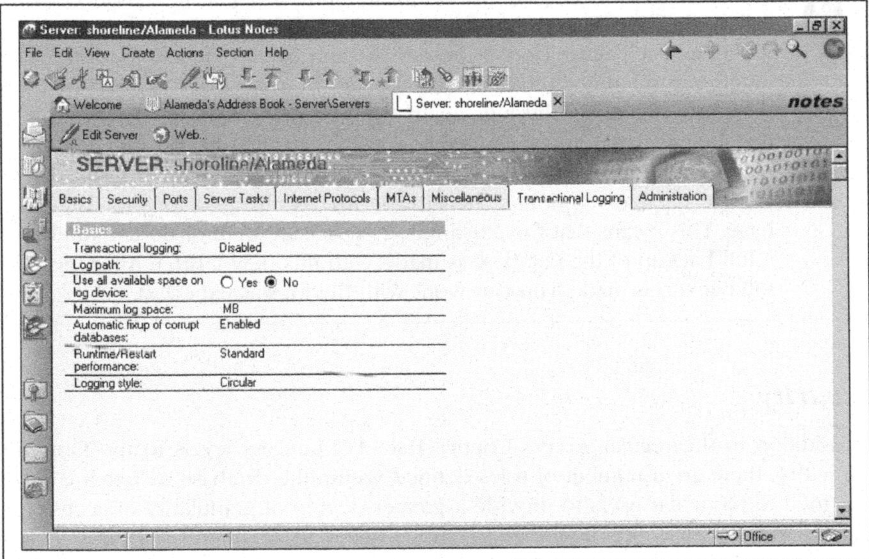

Figure 2-6: The Server document Transaction Logging tab

Once enabled, transaction logging applies to all databases on the server, although there is a database property to disable it on a per-database basis. To make best use of this, I suggest that the logs be written to a different drive than the Domino databases, and that for maximum availability, this drive be mirrored. After all, if a drive containing both the databases and the logs fails, then little has been gained.

There are two types of logging available: circular and archival. *Circular logging* reuses log files as needed and is used primarily for performance reasons. This improves server write performance (in that it is quicker to write to a sequential log file than to a Domino database), and also improves server restart performance, since after a failure, the server can quickly replay the last committed transactions and restart. Previously, the server had to check each database that was open at the time of failure before the database could be used.

Archival logging keeps all log files since the last backup, thus enabling these logs to be replayed at a later time if a database has to be restored. The log files are purged automatically during the backup process. In order to make best use of these log files and transactional logging in general, you need to install backup software that has been written to work with Domino transactional logging. IBM's Tivoli product (which used to be called ADSM) can now do this. Many of the main Domino backup products should soon also be able to work with logging. When using archival logging, the database restore process is changed to a two-step process. The first step is to restore the database to its state as of the last full backup. Then the log files are applied to the database up to a specific point in time as needed.

For transactional logging, Domino R5 introduces a new concept called the *database instance ID* (DBIID). This number uniquely identifies each database on the server, and is used in transactional logging to reference the database affected by each log entry. This is then used to replay the logs against the correct database. Be aware that if you make any changes to a database that change the database's physical layout (such as running a `COMPACT` against it to change database options), then the DBIID is changed for the database. This means that the existing log entries are then of no use until a full backup of the database is made with this new DBIID. After the full backup is made, you can work with the logs as expected.

Security

In addition to the regular Access Control List (ACL) access levels to the Domino Directory, there are a number of roles defined within the database ACL that can be assigned to particular users to provide a greater degree of granularity of access for administration. ACLs are described in more detail in Chapter 3, *Domino Databases*. Note that these creator roles aren't really a security feature, since they apply to the GUI only; they can be bypassed by using a program to create the documents. In contrast, the modifier type roles are a security measure. The available roles are:

GroupCreator
: Permits users with "Create document" access to create new Group documents via the Create menu.

GroupModifier

Permits users with "Author" access to the database to edit Group documents. Users with "Delete documents" access are also allowed to delete Group documents.

NetCreator

Permits users with "Create document" access to create documents (except the Group, Person, and Server documents) via the Create menu.

NetModifier

Permits users with "Author" access to the database to edit documents (except the Group, Person, and Server documents). Users with "Delete documents" access are also allowed to delete these documents.

ServerCreator

Permits users with "Create document" access to create new Server documents via the Create menu.

ServerModifier

Permits users with "Author" access to the database to edit Server documents. Users with "Delete documents" access are also allowed to delete Server documents.

UserCreator

Permits users with "Create document" access to create new User documents via the Create menu.

UserModifier

Permits users with "Author" access to the database to edit User documents. Users with "Delete documents" access are also allowed to delete User documents.

A further option for access control within the Domino Directory is to add a username within the Administrator field on only the individual documents that this user is then allowed to edit. The user must have Author access to the database in order for this to work.

Maintaining the Domino Directory

Changes made to the Domino Directory do not take effect immediately for a couple of reasons. First, most of the Domino Directory lookups use views, which need to be rebuilt after documents are created/updated in the database. In particular, two hidden views—*($Users)* and *($ServerAccess)*—are of interest here. The *($Users)* view matches all of the permutations of username and short name available from the Person documents in the database to the full hierarchical username. The *($ServerAccess)* view lists the group membership for each Domino user. Of course, over time the indexes for these views will be updated, but you can force this to occur immediately by entering the following console commands:

```
updall names.nsf -t "($ServerAccess)" -r
updall names.nsf -t "($Users)" -r
```

Secondly, group membership information for the Notes user is cached after the first access of the Domino server. To update this, users must press F5 to *unlock* their ID file (this is similar to logging off), then reaccess the server, which again prompts for the password. The new updated group membership information is now cached.

Directory Catalog

The Directory Catalog provides summary information optimized for quick searching, as a sort of aggregate cross-domain address book. This information can be either a smaller copy of the Domino Directory used by remote laptop users to address mail correctly, or smaller copies of the secondary directory information used by Domino servers for searching. (Secondary directories are any other directories used on a Domino server other than the Domino Directory for that domain.) Each record in a Directory Catalog is about 100 bytes, in contrast to a full Person record, which can be about 4K in size.

Directory Catalogs are created from the *DIRCAT5.NTF* template; the *dircat* server task maintains the contents of the Directory Catalog. The Directory Catalog needs a full-text index in order to be searched. The Server Tasks Directory Cataloger tab on the Server document in the Domino Directory can be used to schedule automatic updates of the Directory Catalog, which eliminates the need to add the *dircat* task to *NOTES.INI*. If the Directory Catalog databases are required on multiple servers, it is more efficient to make replica copies on the other servers and replicate the changes rather than having every server maintain its own Directory Catalog.

Figure 2-7 shows the configuration for a Directory Catalog, which is a document within the Directory Catalog database. Here you can specify which fields and groups are included and the sort order used for entries.

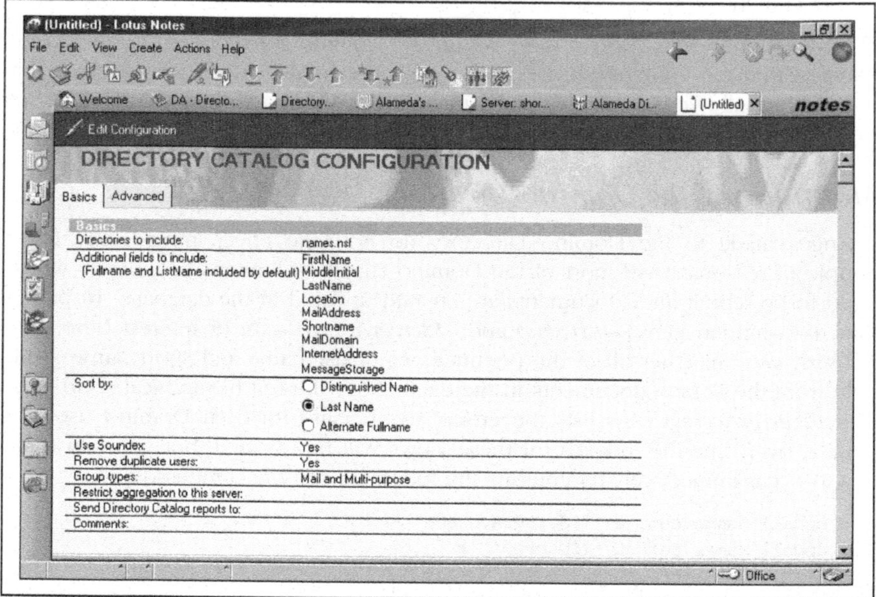

Figure 2-7: Directory Catalog configuration

The basic concepts are the same for both types of Directory Catalog (server and mobile). However, there are small differences in the setup required for each. Both types can exist on a server, and the actual name of the database used is unimportant.

For a server Directory Catalog, the directory database(s) specified in the configuration document are the secondary, or other, directories used for searching. There are two places to specify these directories: in the Profile document in the Domino Directory, which configures the name of the Directory Catalog for the entire domain. This can be overridden by specifying the Directory Catalog name in the Server field in the Server document.

For a mobile Directory Catalog, the primary Domino Directory is included, as well as any secondary directories needed for correct mail addressing. The client then keeps a local replica of this database on a laptop for use when not attached to the server. The Location document in Personal Name and Address Book on the client then specifies the name of the local replica of this database in the "Local address books" field on the Mail and News Preferences tab of the User Preferences dialog box. The database name is thus added to the **NAMES=** entry in *NOTES.INI* on the client machine.

Directory Assistance

Directory Assistance allows Domino to refer to Domino Directories in other Domino domains and other LDAP directories. The Directory Assistance database is created from a template (*DA50.NTF*) and specifies which directories are to be included in the reference. (This feature was previously known as Master Address Book.) A specified secondary Domino Directory need not be necessarily associated with another domain. For instance, a common Domino web application allows users to register themselves, which creates Person records in the Domino Directory with a background agent. In many cases, administrators elect to have this registration application update a totally separate Domino Directory database to protect the integrity of the primary Domino Directory database, *NAMES.NSF*.

An older technique known as *cascaded address books* should no longer be used, since this method is now considered obsolete by Lotus. This updated the **NAMES=** entry on the server with additional name and address books to use for lookup, with the limitation being that no more than 16 directories could be used, and the length of the **NAMES=** parameter could not exceed 256 characters.

The sequence to enable the use of Directory Assistance is as follows:

1. Create the Directory Assistance database from the Directory Assistance template (*DA50.NTF*).
2. Configure the Directory Assistance database to use secondary Domino or LDAP directories. (This will be described in detail shortly.)
3. Create replicas of this Directory Assistance database on all servers that require it. This is usually every server in the domain. Ensure that the replication topology in place is set to replicate changes to this database; otherwise, you will need to set up the appropriate connection documents.

4. Set each Server document within the Domino Directory to use Directory Assistance by filling out the "Directory Assistance database" field for each document.

To configure the Directory Assistance database, open the database and press the "Add Directory Assistance" action button to create a Directory Assistance document. This document has three tabs:*

Basics
: The naming information for this directory. For LDAP directories, you can select a directory to be used for group member expansion. You can also specify the relative search order of this directory as opposed to the other Directory Assistance sources.

Rules
: In the Rules tab (as shown in Figure 2-8), you may specify up to five rules that define the X.500 hierarchical names available for searching with this directory. Each level of the hierarchy in these rules can have either a name, a wildcard (*) that matches all names at this level, or a space or null character that excludes names at this level. For example, an entry of `*/*/*/*/*/*` represents all entries in the directory.

  The "Trusted for Credentials" option allows you to specify whether that rule can be used for authentication purposes.

Replicas (for Notes assistance)
: Under Replicas, you can either paste up to five database links or specify up to five replicas (server name and database name) of the directory on the network.

LDAP (for LDAP assistance)
: Under LDAP, you can specify the connection details to the LDAP server and whether this directory is for use by Notes/web clients and/or LDAP clients (see the following section).

LDAP Support

LDAP support was first added to Domino 4.6, and now with R5 the support for LDAP has been extended even further. LDAP v3 is now supported, which means that the Domino Directory can be now updated by LDAP. You can also refer to other LDAP servers for authentication. Another useful addition in R5 is the *ldapsearch* tool to check that the LDAP task is running and returning the expected results.

LDAP Configuration

LDAP configuration is done within a Configuration document in the Domino Directory for All Servers for the domain. Figure 2-9 shows the LDAP tab within the Configuration document. Once this is configured, the LDAP Domino server task services the LDAP queries.

---

* Note that the third tab will be either Replicas or LDAP, depending on which type of Directory Assistance document (Notes or LDAP) you choose to create. This selection is made on the Basics page in the field "Domain type."

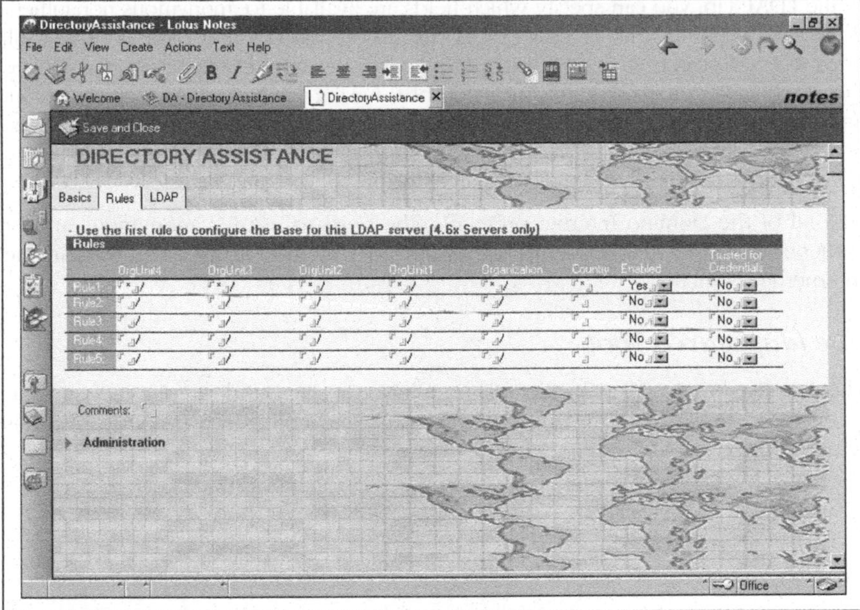

Figure 2-8: Directory Assistance configuration Rules tab

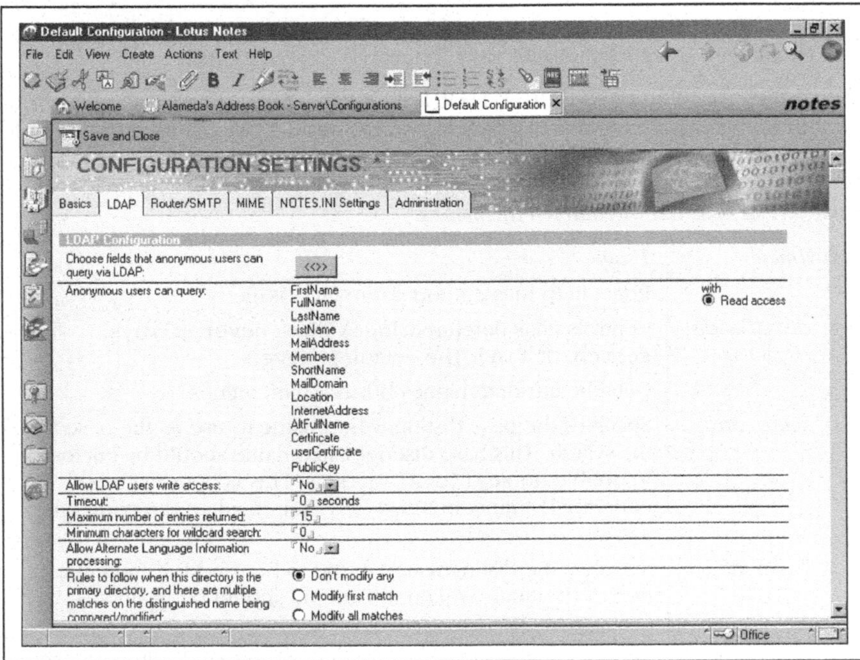

Figure 2-9: LDAP configuration tab in the Configuration document, within the Domino Directory for All Servers

In the LDAP tab, you can specify which fields are available to anonymous nonauthenticated LDAP users, whether LDAP users can update the Domino Directory (they still need ACL access in order to do this), and a limit to the amount of entries returned and the LDAP server timeout. A timeout value of 0 means that there is no server timeout and that the query runs to completion. The last value in the document (shown at the bottom of Figure 2-9, "Rules to follow when . . . ") controls what happens when an LDAP query update matches multiple names within the Domino Directory.

Like all of the Domino Internet protocols, the ports to use for anonymous and/or authenticated user LDAP queries are configured in the Server document, in the Internet Ports section.

The ldapsearch Tool

This tool is now installed by default on all Notes client and Domino server platforms. It ensures that the LDAP task is running and configured properly, and has returned the expected results.

The syntax for using the tool is:

```
ldapsearch parameters filter [attributes]
```

where:

- `parameters` is the list of parameters for the LDAP search (see Table 2-2).
- `filter` is the search filter used to determine which entries are returned.
- `attributes` optionally specify which attributes are returned for each entry. The default is for all attributes to be returned.

The results are returned in LDIF (LDAP Data Interchange File) format. This tool can be run against a non-Domino server, and the results redirected into a text file and used in migration to create Domino users.

Table 2-2: ldapsearch Available Parameters

Parameter	*Usage*
`-?`	Prints help message on parameter usage.
`-a derefence`	Controls alias dereferencing. Values: `never`, `always`, `search`, or `find`. The default is `never`.
`-A`	Gets the attribute names but not their values.
`-b base dn`	Specifies the base distinguished name to use as the base for the search. This base distinguished name should be enclosed in double quotes (`"o=Alameda"`). This is optional when querying Domino, but may be required when querying other servers.
`-D bind dn`	Specifies the distinguished name to be used for authentication of the query. Again, this name should be in quotes (`"cn=Greg Neilson/o=Alameda"`).
`-f filename`	Specifies the filename that contains the search filters to use for the query.
`-h hostname`	Specifies the hostname of the LDAP server to query. This parameter is required.

Table 2-2: ldapsearch Available Parameters (continued)

Parameter	*Usage*
`-l` *`timeout`*	Specifies the maximum time to wait in seconds for a response for a LDAP query. The default is 0, which means that it will wait indefinitely, or until the server reaches its time limit.
`-n`	Tells ldapsearch not to run the query but to provide information as to how the search will be carried out.
`-p` *`port`*	Configures a port to use instead of the default LDAP port of 389.
`-s` *`scope`*	Used with the `-b` option; specifies the scope of the search. The available values are: **`base`** (search only the hierarchical level specified); **`onelevel`** (search one child level of the hierarchical level specified); and **`subtree`** (search the entire subtree below the hierarchical level specified; this is the default).
`-S` *`attribute`*	Sorts the results set by the values of this attribute.
`-z` *`size limit`*	Specifies the maximum number of entries to return. The default is 0, which means that an unlimited number of entries can be returned. Like the `-l` parameter, the LDAP server may be configured to have a maximum number of entries to return that may override this.
`-u`	Specifies that the user distinguished names are returned in a "user-friendly" format. This is the name and organizational information with the hierarchical name types removed—for example, `"cn=Greg Neilson/o=Alameda"` in this user-friendly format is `"Greg Neilson, Alameda"`.
`-v`	Runs query in verbose mode, which can help determine why queries are not returning the expected results.
`-w` *`password`*	Specifies the password to use when using authentication in the query with the `-D` parameter.

The LDAP Schema Database (*SCHEMA.NSF*) can be used as a reference for the various object classes and attributes provided by the Domino Directory—particularly if the Domino Directory schema has been customized. This database can be created by issuing the console command **`tell ldap exportschema`** or alternatively, maintained by the design task running on the server. For example, typical classes found here include *dominoPerson, dominoServer, dominoGroup, dominoOrganization,* and *dominoOrganization.* The most prevalent attributes for these classes is the **`cn`**, or common name (which is not part of *dominoOrganization* or *dominoOrganizationalUnit*). The *dominoGroup* class has a member attribute that defines each member of the group.

The following code shows some sample queries of the Domino Directory using the ldapsearch tool. The final example demonstrates how many attributes are returned using an authenticated query rather than an anonymous query:

```
ldapsearch -h shoreline.alameda.com objectclass=dominoServer

CN=shoreline,O=Alameda
cn=shoreline
```

```
objectclass=top
objectclass=dominoServer
certificate=03002E02 C71183ED 09G01616 G00267FB

CN=westline,O=Alameda
cn=westline
objectclass=top
objectclass=dominoServer
certificate=03002D02 ABD1196E 09G01615 G002D566

ldapsearch -h shoreline.alameda.com  cn=greg*
CN=Greg Neilson,O=Alameda
cn=Greg Neilson
shortname=gneilson
uid=gneilson
mail=Greg_Neilson/Alameda%Alameda@alameda.com
objectclass=top
objectclass=person
objectclass=organizationalPerson
objectclass=inetOrgPerson
objectclass=dominoPerson
certificate=03003102 44BB3CAE 09G01619 G00271F5
givenname=Greg
sn=Neilson
maildomain=Alameda

ldapsearch -h shoreline.alameda.com -b "o=Alameda" -D "cn=Greg Ne
ilson/O=Alameda" -w password cn=greg*

CN=Greg Neilson,O=Alameda
cn=Greg Neilson
shortname=gneilson
uid=gneilson
mail=Greg_Neilson/Alameda%Alameda@alameda.com
objectclass=top
objectclass=person
objectclass=organizationalPerson
objectclass=inetOrgPerson
objectclass=dominoPerson
mailsystem=1
messagestorage=1
encryptincomingmail=0
certificate=03003102 44BB3CAE 09G01619 G00271F5
creatorname=CN=Greg Neilson,O=Alameda
clienttype=0
checkpassword=0
availablefordirsync=1
passwordchangeinterval=0
passwordgraceperiod=0
givenname=Greg
sn=Neilson
userpassword=(355E98E7C7B59BD810ED845AD0FD2FC4)
maildomain=Alameda
mailserver=CN=shoreline,O=Alameda
mailfile=mail\gneilson
```

CHAPTER 3

Domino Databases

Databases

Domino databases are very much the heart and soul of the system. Nearly everything of interest is stored within one of these databases: the directories, the custom applications, the user mail, and the majority of configuration information. You have already seen in detail the contents of the Domino Directory in Chapter 2, *Domino Directories*, which is probably the most important database on the server.

Each database is an individual file on the server filesystem, typically with an extension of *.NSF* (for Notes Storage Facility). They usually reside underneath the *Domino Data* directory on the server, although you shall soon see that there are methods available to make these databases only appear as though they reside under the this directory.

Database Templates

Databases are created and updated from the design contained within a database template. Domino comes with a number of these templates by default, and custom applications (or modifications to the standard Domino databases) are usually created from a database template. Templates use the file extension of *.NTF* (for Notes Template Facility).

The DESIGN task runs by default on the Domino server at 1:00 A.M., then propagates template changes to the databases that were created from them. This can also be done manually by selecting File → Database → Refresh Design or File → Database → Replace Design in the Notes or Domino Administrator. The difference between these two options is that the refresh option uses the existing link established between a database and its template, and the replace design option asks you to select the template to use to update the database design.

When creating a new database (File → Database → New...), you can select from a number of list database templates. These templates are listed by name, and those templates marked as "advanced" do not appear in this list by default. In order to use these advanced templates, the Show Advanced Templates checkbox must be selected. See the New Database window in Figure 3-1. (There is an option to create a blank database, but this is of most use for application developers, not administrators.)

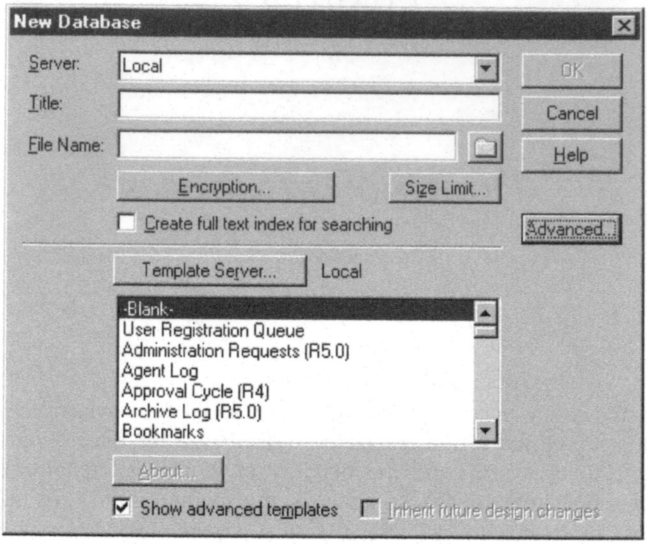

Figure 3-1: New Database window

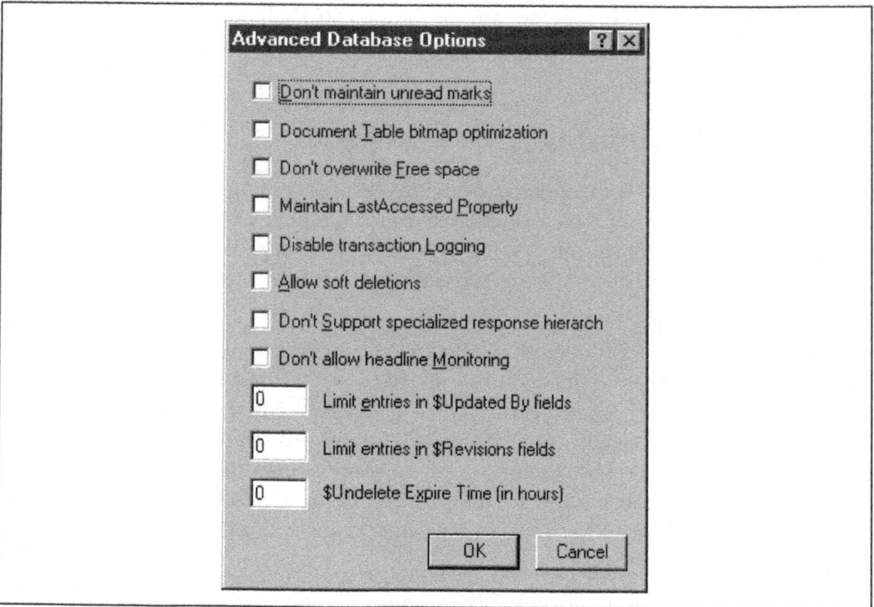

Figure 3-2: Advanced options available when creating a new Domino database

There are also some advanced database options available when creating a new database under the Advanced option on this window. These advanced options correspond to those in the Advanced tab in the Database Properties, as explained in the next section of this chapter. See the Advanced Options window in Figure 3-2. The Template name is what appears on the Info page of the template database; for example, StdR4AdminRequests. Databases that are configured to accept design changes from this template will use this name, not the template title.

Table 3-1 lists the database templates provided by Domino. Those with a "yes" in the "Advanced?" column are visible only when creating a new database if the Show Advanced Templates option is selected. In many cases, these databases are created for you by Domino; however, there are times when you need to manually create your own databases and use these templates. For example, the templates are useful when creating a certification log database after a new domain is created, or when creating a discussion database.

Table 3-1: Domino System Templates

Template Title	*Template Filename*	*Template Name*	*Advanced?*
Administration Requests (5.0)	*admin4.ntf*	StdR4AdminRequests	Yes
Agent Log	*alog.ntf*	StdR4AgentLog	Yes
Archive Log	*archlg50.ntf*	StdR50ArchiveLog	Yes
Billing	*billing.ntf*	StdR4Billing	
Bookmarks	*bookmark.ntf*	Bookmarks	
Catalog (R5)	*catalog5.ntf*	StdNotesCatalog	Yes
Certification Log	*certlog.ntf*	StdNotesCertificationLog	Yes
Cluster Analysis	*clusta4.ntf*	StdR4ClusterAnalysis	
Cluster Directory (R5)	*cldbdir4.ntf*	StdR4ClusterDirectory	Yes
Database Analysis	*dba4.ntf*	StdR4DBAnalysis	
Database Library	*dblib4.nsf*	StdR4DatabaseLib	
Decommission Server Reports	*decomsrv.ntf*	StdNotesDecommission-Server	Yes
DECS5 Adminis-trator Template	*decsadm.ntf*	DECS Administrator Template	Yes
Design Synopsis Template	*dsgnsyn.ntf*	DesignSynopsis	
Directory Assistance	*da50.ntf*	StdMasterAddressBook4.5	
Directory Catalog	*dircat5.ntf*	Lightweight Directory	
Discussion—Notes & Web (R5.0)	*discsw50.ntf*	StdR50Disc	
Doc Library –Notes & Web (R5.0)	*doclbw50.ntf*	StdR50WebDocLib	
Domino Adminis-trator (R5)	*domadmin.ntf*	StdAdminDatabase	Yes

Table 3-1: Domino System Templates (continued)

Template Title	*Template Filename*	*Template Name*	*Advanced?*
Domino Directory	*pubnames.ntf*	StdR4PublicAddressBook	Yes
Domino LDAP Schema	*schema50.ntf*	StdDominoLDAPSchema	Yes
Domino Mail-Tracker Store	*mtstore.ntf*	MailTrackerStore	
Domino R5 Certificate Authority	*cca50.ntf*	StdNotes50SSLAuth	Yes
Domino Web Administrator	*webadmin.ntf*	StdWebAdminDatabase	Yes
Domino Web Server Configuration (R5.0)	*domcgf5.ntf*	StdR5DominoWebServer-Configurat	
Domino Web Server Log	*domlog.ntf*	Domino Web Server Log Template	
Extended Mail (R5.0)	*mailex.ntf*	Ext50Mail	
Local Document Cache	*cache.ntf*	NotesDocCache	
Local Free Time Info	*busytime.nsf*	BusyTime	Yes
Lotus SmartSuite Library (5.0)	*doclbs5.ntf*	SmartSuiteDocLibR5	
Mail Router Mailbox (R5)	*mailbox.ntf*	StdNotesMailbox	Yes
Mail (IMAP)	*imapcl5.ntf*	StdR50IMail	Yes
Mail (R5.0)	*mail50.ntf*	StdR50Mail	
Mailing List (R5)	*maillist.lst*	StdNotesMailingList	Yes
Microsoft Office Library (R5.0)	*doclbm50.ntf*	StdR50DocLibMS	
News Articles (NNTP)	*nntpcl5.ntf*	StdR50NNTPClient	Yes
NNTP Cross-Post	*nntppost.ntf*	StdR46NNTPPostBox	
NNTP Discussion (R5.0)	*nntpdi50.ntf*	StdR5.0NNTPDisc	
Notes Log	*log.ntf*	StdNotesLog	Yes
Notes Log Analysis	*loga4.ntf*	StdR4LogAnalysis	
NT/Migrating User's Passwords	*ntsync.ntf*	StdNotesNewUserPass-words	Yes
Personal Address Book	*pernames.ntf*	StdR4PersonalAddressBook	
Personal Journal (R5.0)	*journal5.ntf*	Std50Journal	
Personal Web Navigator (R5.0)	*perweb50.ntf*	Std50PersonalWebNavi-gator	

Table 3-1: Domino System Templates (continued)

Template Title	*Template Filename*	*Template Name*	*Advanced?*
Reports (R5)	*reports.ntf*	StdReportsDatabase	Yes
Resource Reservations (5.0)	*resrc50.ntf*	Std50ResourceReservation	
Search Site	*srchsite.ntf*	StdNotesSearchSite	
Server Certificate Admin	*csrv50.ntf*	StdNotes50SSLAdmin	Yes
Server Web Navigator (R5.0)	*pubweb50.ntf*	StdR50WebNavigator	
Server.Planner: Analyst	*dspa.ntf*	Server.Planner: Analyst	Yes
Server.Planner: Decision Maker	*dspd.ntf*	Server.Planner: Decision Maker	Yes
Server.Planner: Vendor	*dspv.ntf*	Server.Planner: Vendor	Yes
Site Registration 5.0	*siregw50.ntf*	StdSite50Reg	
Statistics and Events	*events4.ntf*	StdR4Events	Yes
Statistics Reporting (R5)	*statrep5.ntf*	StdR5StatReport	Yes
Subscriptions	*headline.ntf*	StdNotesHeadlines5.0	
TeamRoom (5.0)	*teamrm50.ntf*	Std50TeamRoom	
User Registration Queue	*userreg.ntf*	(not marked as a template!)	

Database Properties

Many of these database properties are inherited from the design template used to create and/or update them. However, many others are configured by administrators to change their operational characteristics. In this section, we will examine only elements of the database properties that are of interest to Domino system administrators.

The properties of an open database can be viewed by selecting File → Database → Properties from Notes or Domino Administrator menus, or by selecting the Properties SmartIcon of the open database (if SmartIcons are enabled). This SmartIcon appears by default on the far left, directly underneath the File menu. Hitting Alt-Enter will also launch the database properties window for the current open database.

This type of property window is known in Domino as an Infobox. It is used to look at the database properties, the form properties, the document properties, or the design element properties. (These other properties are mostly of interest to developers.)

Database Basics Tab

The Basics tab, as shown in Figure 3-3, provides many important pieces of information about the database. As a system administrator, this and the Advanced tab are the two main tabs you will be interested in.

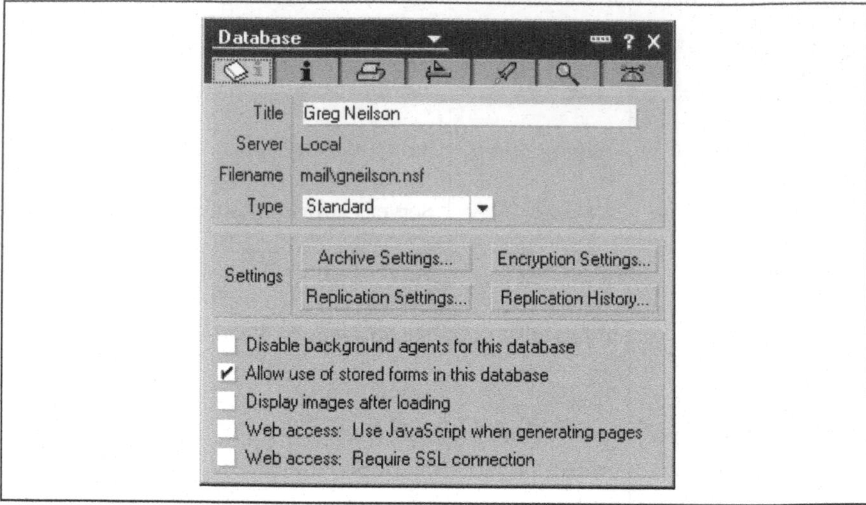

Figure 3-3: Database Basics properties tab

Title
: The title is the name of the database that is displayed in the database icon on the user's Notes bookmarks. It is also the name used within the Database Catalogs; it is editable.

Server
: This field is the name of the server that contains the database. "Local" means that the database resides on the local filesystem of the client.

Filename
: This is the physical filename of the database on the server.

Archive Settings
: This setting is typically used for handling users' mail database. It archives documents that have not been read or accessed for *x* days, and/or not modified or updated for *x* days, and/or marked as expired into a designated database on the user's local machine.

Replication Settings
: This setting enables an optional feature known as *selective replication*, whereby only a subset of the database content is replicated to other servers. This can be used for both design elements (forms, agents, access control lists) as well as documents selected by a formula, or those from selected views and folders only. (This feature is discussed in detail later in this chapter.)

Encryption Settings

These settings, used on client workstations (particularly with laptop users), can encrypt the local database with the user's ID file. If the laptop is stolen, the database cannot be read unless the reader knows the password to the ID file.

Replication History

If the database has been involved in replication activity, then this field will record in detail the last time and with whom the database was successfully replicated with a server. This is used during subsequent replication activity to determine the changes that need to be replicated. This history can be cleared by those with Manager access to the database, which causes the replication task to review the entire database contents.

Allow use of stored forms in this database

When this option is selected and the form design is stored with each document as it is created, the resulting database is much larger; if the form design is later changed, this change is not propagated to the stored forms. However, this option does ensure that every document will always display correctly.

Info Tab

The Info tab, as shown in Figure 3-4, provides some additional basic information about the database, such as its size, replica ID, and ODS version.

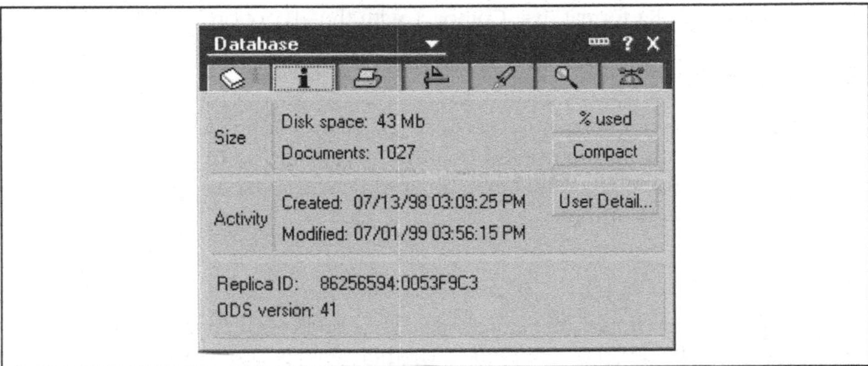

Figure 3-4: Database Info properties tab

Size

Displays the size of the database in MB, and also the number of documents contained within the database. The *% used* button calculates how much of the physically allocated database is currently used. This can be used to determine whether there will be a significant amount of unused space returned by running the `COMPACT` task against the database. The *Compact* button starts the compaction process immediately on the database.

Activity

Shows when the database was first created and last accessed. The *User Detail . . .* button tracks user access to this database, which is not enabled by default. If this option is enabled, then it shows a list of user accesses to the database. There is no programmatic way to later access this activity information—it can only be cut and pasted from this window.

Replica ID

Shows the Replica ID of the database, a hexadecimal number. This ID is important, since only databases with identical Replica IDs will be able to replicate.

ODS version

ODS stands for *On Disk Structure*, which defines the internal architecture used in Domino databases. The number here denotes the version of Notes/Domino from which the database was created. This field was not visible in Notes clients before R5. It is also visible in Domino Administrator, in the Files tab. The current versions of ODS are:

- R5 (ODS version 41)
- R4 (ODS version 20)
- R3 (ODS version 17)
- R2 (ODS version 16)

In R5, the new version of ODS provides functionality for in-place database compaction, database sizes greater than 4GB, and transaction logging. This capability is of interest mostly for sites that are upgrading to R5 from previous versions of Notes/Domino. The Compact process automatically updates the database format the first time it runs after an upgrade, unless the database has been renamed with an NS4 extension. If a backout is required to convert an R5 database to R4 format, use Compact with the –R option.

Printing Tab

This tab is mostly self-explanatory. Its settings allow the header and footer to be defined when documents are printed from the database. The five buttons provided allow for the page number, date, time, tab, and database title to be included in the text of the header and/or footer.

Design Tab

The Design tab, as shown in Figure 3-5, has a number of entries, but of main interest are the fields that determine whether this is a database template or whether this database inherits design changes from a template.

The first line of text tells us whether the database design is hidden. The regular templates shipped with Domino do not hide their design, but third-party custom application vendors often hide their design. Not being able to see how the design works acts as a security measure and also a way to protect the intellectual property of the vendor. If the design is hidden, you cannot make modifications to the database design.

Options and selections on the Database Design tab include:

Inherit design from template

If this option is selected, you can list the template name that the design is inherited from. You can also temporarily uncheck this box to disable the subsequent inheritance of an updated template design.

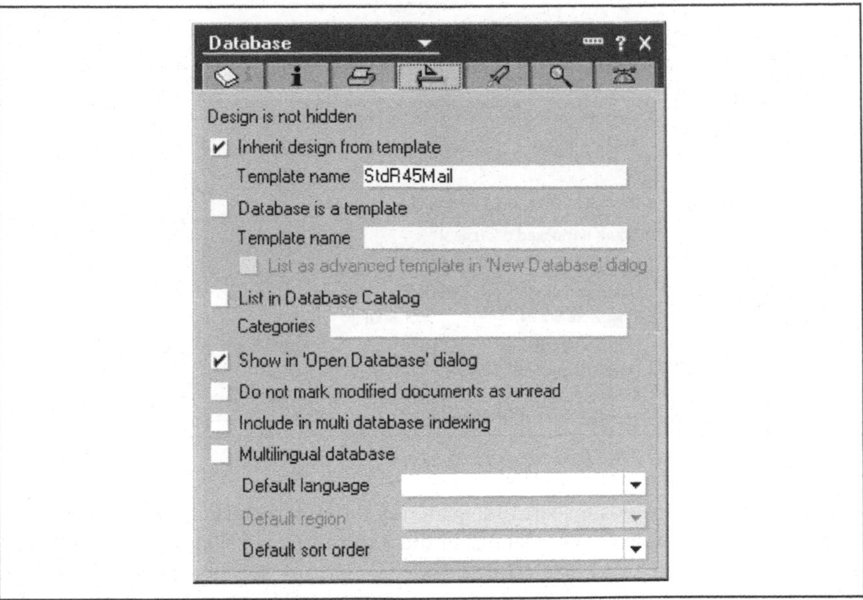

Figure 3-5: Database Design properties tab

Database is a template
: If this checkbox is selected, the database is a template. It also needs a template name. The regularly scheduled *Design* task uses this and the previous field for each database to determine whether to update the design and which template to use.

List in Database Catalog
: This option allows you to specify whether this database is listed in the database catalog. Typically, special purpose administration databases and user mail databases are not listed in this catalog.

Show in "Open Database" dialog
: This property is used to hide databases from being listed in the Open Database dialog. This does not prevent them from being opened, but the user must know and enter the name of the database manually in order to access it. For example, the *MAIL.BOX* database on the Domino server is not shown in the Open Database dialog.

Launch Tab

This tab is used by programmers to define what users see when they open the database from a Notes client or a browser.

Full Text Tab

The Full Text tab, as shown in Figure 3-6, specifies whether the database has a full text index, and if so, configures how the database is indexed.

Databases

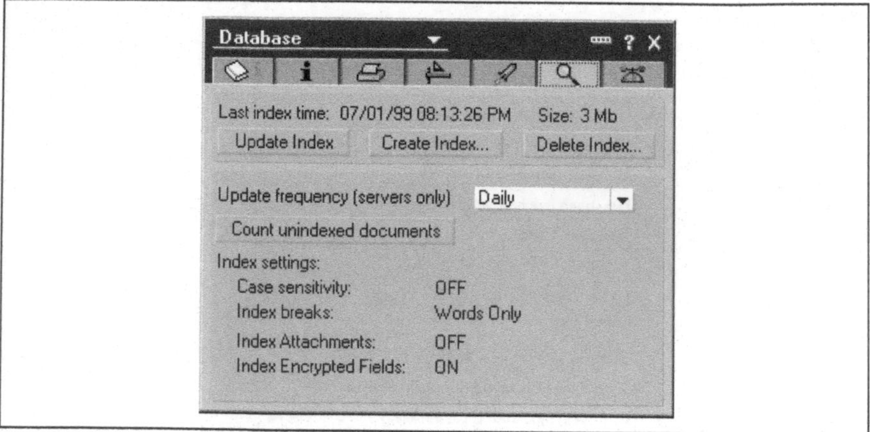

Figure 3-6: Database Full Text properties tab

A full text index provides for fast text searches through the database documents. If no full text index exists for the database, the top of this tab will read: "Database is not full text indexed," and only "Create Index . . ." and "Delete Index . . ." will be available on this tab.

If a full text index is created, a subdirectory is created below the current location of the database. If the database was called *TESTDB.NSF*, then the subdirectory will be *TESTDB.FT*. The full text index is then located in this created subdirectory.

If a full text index exists for the database, the last index time will be displayed, together with the current size of the index. The index can be 50–75% of the size of the source database, so keep this in mind when planning server disk space and determining whether a full text index is required.

Other options and settings on the Full Text tab include:

Update frequency (servers only)
: This can be set to daily, scheduled, hourly, or immediate.

Count unindexed documents
: This button will return either the count of the unindexed documents in the database, or if all have been indexed, "All are indexed."

Index settings
: This section displays the current index settings, which were determined when the index was created. Of course, the more indexing activity selected, the more useful it will be, but the resulting index will be larger, and also more server processing time will be required to create and maintain the index. The settings available at creation include:

    - Index attached files (raw text only or binary attachments)
    - Index encrypted fields
    - Index sentence and word breaks
    - Enable case-sensitive searches
    - Index frequency

The best advice here is to select all of these options, which makes the full text search ability as powerful as possible. However, you could elect to not enable some of these options (particularly if the database uses large attachments that you know are not searched on) once you understand the document content within the database and the way your users access and use the database. Currently, Lotus is touting the Knowledge Management features of Notes/Domino, and your users can't make the most use of Domino content if the documents aren't indexed correctly. Keep in mind that indexing encrypted fields means that the index is not encrypted and thus may be a security exposure.

Advanced Tab

The Advanced tab properties, shown in Figure 3-7, are all new to R5. They are used to increase Domino server performance by eliminating unnecessary maintenance work on the Domino database and reducing its size. Note that these advanced properties are available only if the database is in the new R5 format: ODS version 41.

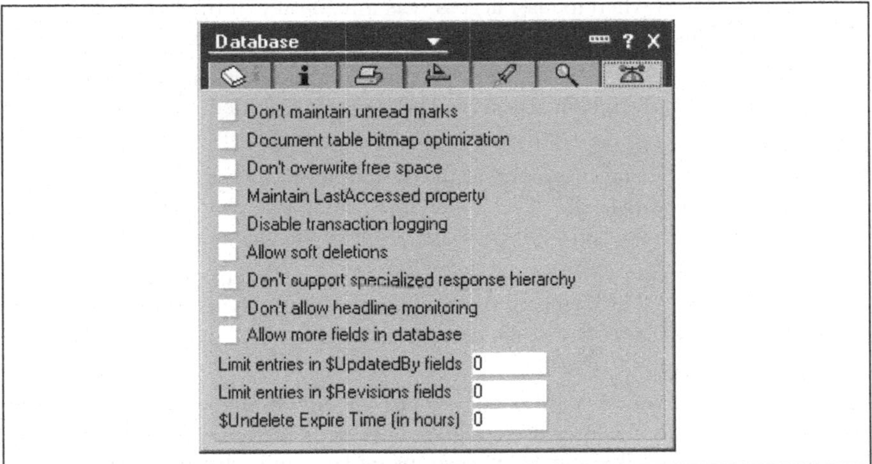

Figure 3-7: Database Advanced properties tab

The options and settings on the Advanced tab include:

Don't maintain unread marks

This option is for databases in which keeping track of documents that have been accessed by a user is not needed. There is a performance benefit from the server not having to maintain these unread marks. After this setting has changed, the compact utility must be run against the database to make the change effective.

Compact with the –U option enables this property and –u disables it. As well as changing the database property, the Compact utility then rebuilds the database so that the change takes effect.

Document table bitmap optimization

This is a performance improvement that makes view updates quicker by maintaining a table of which documents are in which view. Updating this table to offset the quick view updates involves some cost as documents are changed within the database. After this setting has changed, the Compact utility must be run against the database to make the change effective.

Running Compact with the `-f` option disables this property and `-F` enables it. As well as changing the database property, the Compact utility then rebuilds the database so that the change takes effect.

Don't overwrite free space

This property controls whether Domino overwrites free space within a database to ensure that the deleted data cannot be accessed by the filesystem on the server. There is an overhead cost in doing this, so if the server is already physically secure or security for the database is not important, this option can be enabled.

Maintain LastAccessed Property

This controls whether the database maintains the last accessed date for each document, even when the last access was a read-only. If the last access was a write, then this date is still updated in the document regardless.

If document archiving is selected for this database, this property should be selected so that document access date is correctly recorded.

Disable transaction logging

If transaction logging is enabled at the system level, this option can turn it off at the individual database level. After this setting has changed, the Compact utility must be run against the database to make the change effective.

Running Compact with the `-t` option disables transaction logging, and `-T` enables it. As well as changing the database property, the compact utility then rebuilds the database so that the change takes effect.

Allow soft deletions

Soft deletion allows deleted documents to be shown in a special view and to be undeleted by the user as required. It is particularly useful for mail databases, since as mail volumes increase, users have more to process (and store or delete after reading it), and often find later that they need to reference a deleted email.

To see the documents that have been soft deleted, you must create a special view in the database of type "Shared, contains deleted documents."

Don't support specialized document hierarchy

Typically, documents keep information about parent or child documents. This specialized document hierarchy is used when views within the database use `@AllChildren` and `@AllDescendants` view selection formulas. If a database does not need this information (and you'll need to confer with the developers of the application to find out), there is a performance gain in selecting this option. After this setting has changed, the Compact utility must be run against the database to make the change effective.

Running Compact with the `-h` option disables the maintenance of this document hierarchy, and `-H` enables it. As well as changing the database property, the Compact utility then rebuilds the database so that the change takes effect.

Don't allow headline monitoring
Notes clients can create headline items on Domino server databases, and this checking of the database contents by many clients can adversely load the Domino server. Checking this option stops clients from monitoring this database from their headlines database.

Allow more fields in database
This feature allows more fields in the database. Without this option selected, the total length of all field names concatenated together must be under 64KB, which is approximately 3,000 fields in the database. If this option is enabled, up to 64,000 fields can be used in the database, but Lotus warns that full text indexing of this database may not work correctly.

Limit entries in the $UpdatedBy fields
Each document in the database keeps an `$UpdatedBy` field that contains the user and server names that last updated the document. Keeping all of this information requires server disk space and CPU to maintain it. If you don't need to keep a detailed track of who made changes to the database for auditing purposes, using this option provides a performance benefit by limiting the requisite resources. To enable this feature, enter the number of `$UpdatedBy` entries to keep in each document. Lotus currently recommends you keep at least 10 as a minimum. The default value of 0 means that a complete edit history is maintained.

Limit entries in $Revisions fields
By default (with a value of 0) this can contain the date and time of up to the last 500 revisions in each document, and is used when replicating updates across servers. This can consume quite a lot of disk space and server CPU to maintain this information. To make use of this option, enter the desired number of `$Revisions` entries to keep in each document. Lotus currently recommends you keep at least 10 as a minimum.

$Undelete Expire Time (in hours)
If the soft delete function is enabled, this allows the configuration of how many hours the deleted notes can be available for restoration by users.

Updating Properties for Multiple Databases Using Domino Administrator

Now that we have covered the advanced properties, it is time to demonstrate how these can be changed on multiple databases with Domino Administrator. Working with multiple databases is shown in Figure 3-8. After selecting the Files tab, select the databases you wish to work with. This can be an individual database, or you can include others by holding down the Ctrl key and selecting multiple databases, or you can hold down the Shift key and use the Up and Down arrow keys. Then select Advanced Properties . . . from the Tools → Database menu, and right-click with the mouse, or choose Files → Advanced Properties to get this window. As you might expect, this works only for databases that you have Manager access to.

There are two steps to making these changes. First, select which properties you wish to change on the far lefthand side. Then, for each of those properties you want changed, either enable or disable them by clicking (to enable) or leaving blank (to disable) the property. As you have seen from the previous section, many of these advanced properties require the Compact process to physically rebuild the database to make the changes active. For more information about Domino Administrator, refer to Chapter 6, *Domino Administration Tools*.

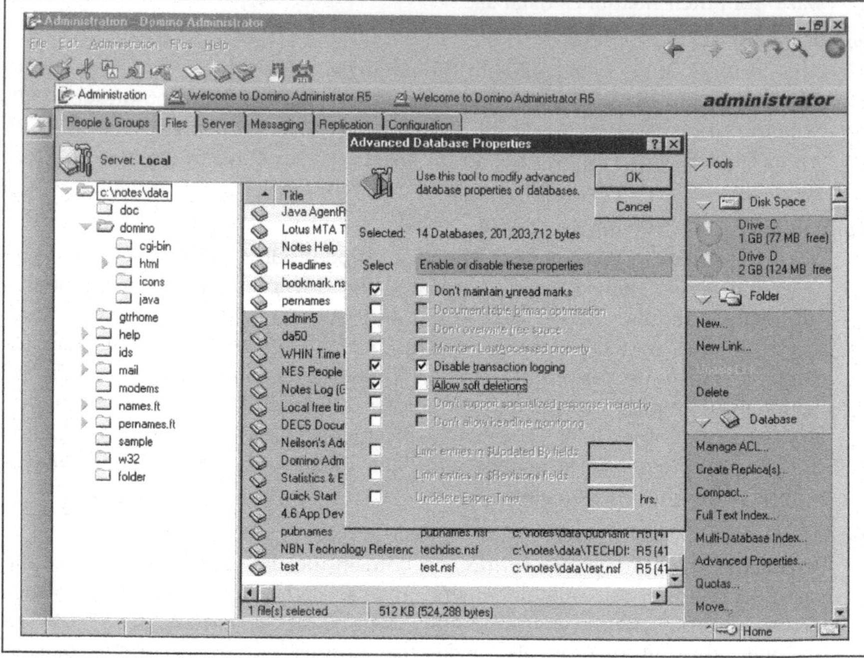

Figure 3-8: Working with multiple databases in Domino Administrator

Selective Replication

Selective replication is used to temporarily disable design replication to other servers while still ensuring data is replicated, to reduce the size of databases on laptop machines, and also as a security measure so that a user or company gets only replicated documents that relate to it.

These replication settings are available for the currently open database, through the File menu of the Notes and Administration clients under the File → Replication → Settings option, or under the Replication Settings button on the Info page of Database Properties.

Although the next four figures show "Replication settings for Greg Neilson" as the title, keep in mind that the usage of my name here is because that is the title property of my mail database, not because this relates to all databases for this user.

Space Savers tab

The Space Savers tab, as shown in Figure 3-9, provides some basic configuration of selective replication. (The Advanced tab enables a more granular configuration of selective replication between specific servers and/or users and servers.)

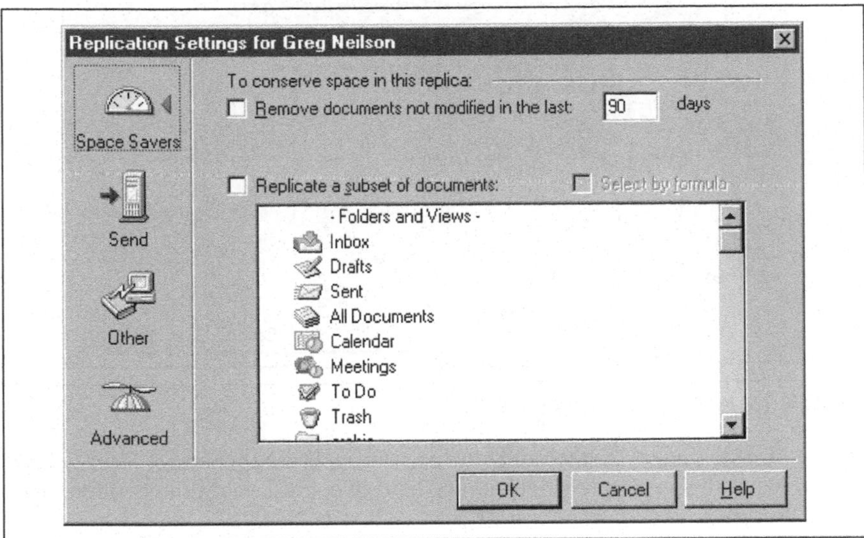

Figure 3-9: Replication settings Space Savers tab

In the Space Savers tab, you have the option to remove documents not modified in the past *x* days by checking the box next to "Remove documents not modified in the last *x* days." Be aware that if you check this box and enter 0 as the number of days, it deletes all documents within the database.

This numeric value is also used to create the *purge interval*, which is how often the database is checked for deletion stubs that need to be removed. Documents that are deleted in the database are not actually deleted immediately. A deletion stub is created, so that the deletion of the document can be propagated across all replicas of the database. The purge interval is calculated as 1/3 of this value, so the default value is 30 days, since it's 1/3 of the number of 90 days value for this field. Setting this value to 0 (without checking the box) then removes all deletion stubs in that replica immediately, so be careful when using this in databases that have multiple replicas; otherwise, the deletions may not be propagated as expected.

You can also select documents from one or more folders for replication, leaving the remainder ignored. Lastly, you could use a formula to select the documents for replication.

Send tab

This tab, as shown in Figure 3-10, allows configuration of specific types of changes that this replica will not send to others during replication.

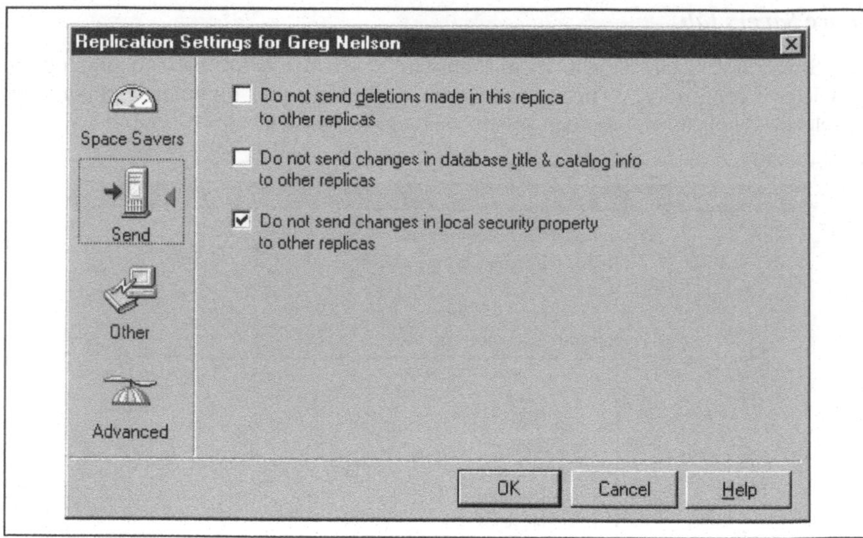

Figure 3-10: Replication settings Send tab

The Send page gives you the ability to prevent replicating changes from deleted documents in this replica, changes in database title and catalog information, and/or local security.

Other tab

The Other tab, as shown in Figure 3-11, features an assortment of selective replication settings that don't fit on any of the other tabs.

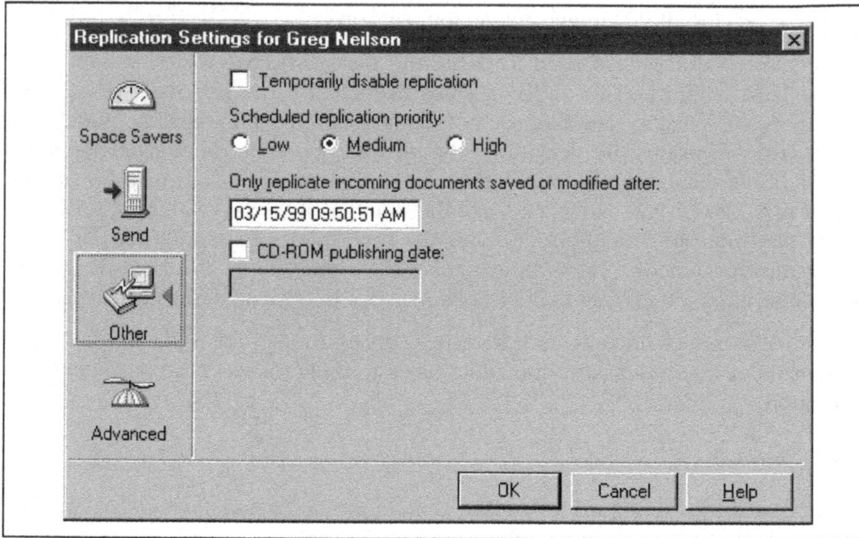

Figure 3-11: Replication settings Other tab

Here you have the option to temporarily stop replication for this database. You can set the replication priority (high/medium/low) for the database. The server connection document that has replication configured can have different replication settings for different priority databases. You can also replicate only documents created or modified after a given date. Lastly, if publishing a database on a CD-ROM, you can set the publication date.

Advanced page

The Advanced page, as shown in Figure 3-12, allows configuration of specific selective replication options between a server and other servers and users.

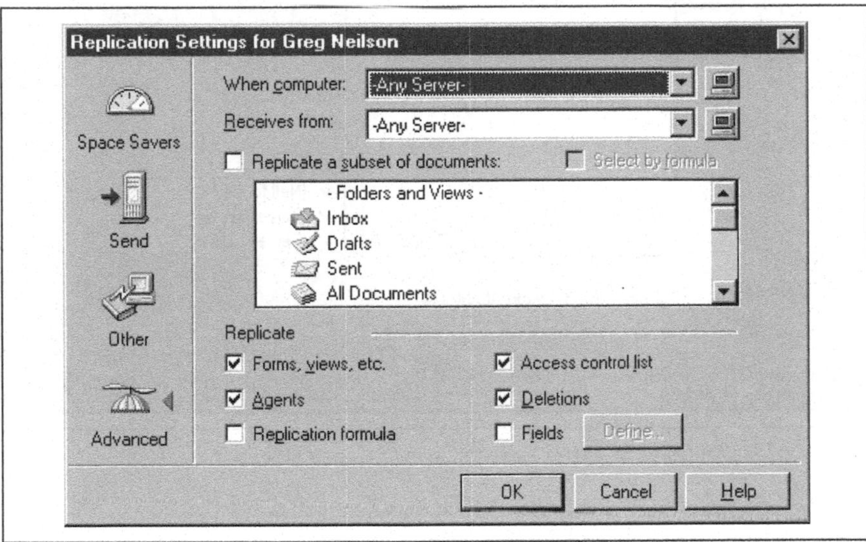

Figure 3-12: Replication settings Advanced tab

In the Advanced settings, you can configure what is sent between all servers and any servers. You can choose documents from any of the folders as before, or you can use a formula to select the documents. You can also optionally select which (if any) design elements are replicated between these servers. For example, during a mixed R4 and R5 Domino network, you may not wish to replicate design elements, since the R5 design elements are not recognized by R4 clients although the document updates in the database need to be replicated. The view selection formula `Select @All` enables all documents in the database as eligible for replication. Alternatively, `Select Form = "Memo"` replicates only documents that have the value of Memo in a field called Form in them, and ignores the other documents.

Database Access Control Lists (ACLs)

Each database has an Access Control List (commonly referred to as an ACL) that determines which users and servers are allowed to work with the database and what they are permitted to do within it. The database ACL pages can be accessed from the File → Database → Access Control menu option from the Notes or Domino Administrator.

Access Control Basics page

Here you can set the access levels for users and servers to the database. Figure 3-13 shows an example of this page.

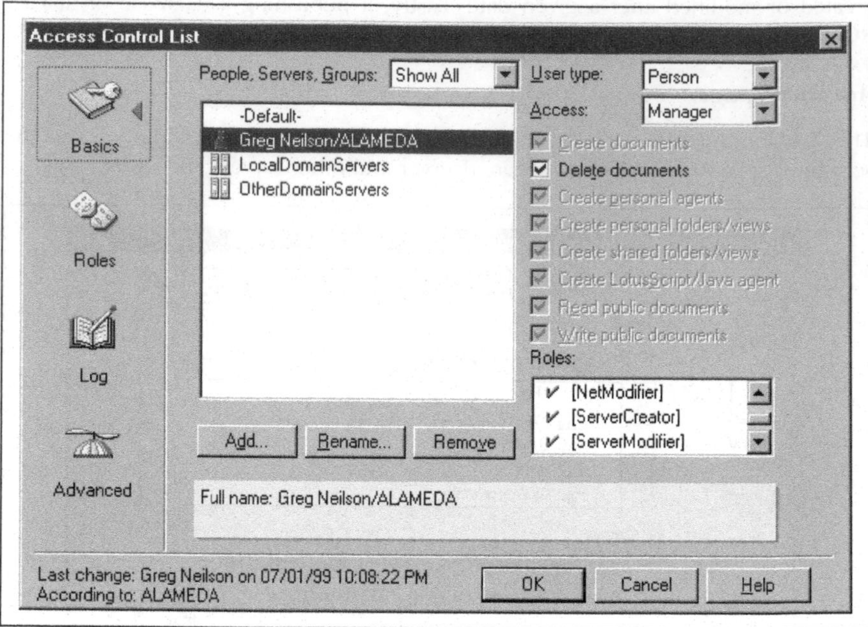

Figure 3-13: Database ACL Basics page

The default entries for a newly created database are:

- -Default- has Designer access.
- The database creator has Manager access.
- The LocalDomainServer and OtherDomainServer groups have Manager access.

ACL entries can be left in the database template and thus added to the new database when created. To do this, the named ACL entries must be enclosed in square brackets; for example, `[Greg Neilson/ALAMEDA]`.

An entry for Anonymous can be added to the ACL; this applies to unauthenticated web users. Otherwise, the Default level of access applies to them.

Entries can be for users and groups from the Domino Directory, either as the Common Name only (`Greg Neilson`), or the full hierarchical name (`Greg Neilson/ALAMEDA`). The hierarchical name is needed if the user and server are part of different organizations. Wildcard entries can also be used to denote all users in a given container (`*/ALAMEDA`). For more information about the X.500 naming scheme used in Domino, refer to Chapter 1, *Notes and Domino Overview*.

For each user, additional roles can be assigned as appropriate in order to provide application developers with additional levels of security above the standard Domino security model.

The following levels of security are available within a database. Within each level, various access privileges are automatically assigned and others can be optionally assigned. These privileges are listed down the lefthand side of the Basics window:

Manager
: Can edit others' documents, modify database design, change replication settings, and change the database Access Control List. The Manager can also delete the database.

Designer
: Can edit others' documents, create a full text index, and modify design elements in the database.

Editor
: Can create documents in the database and edit others' documents.

Author
: Can create documents in the database and review own documents.

Reader
: Can view documents in the database.

Depositor
: Can create documents in the database but cannot view them.

None
: Has no access to the database, and cannot create even a bookmark or workspace entry with this database.

Within each ACL level, there are some privileges that are assigned automatically, and others available that can be optionally assigned. Table 3-2 lists these.

Table 3-2: Automatic and Optionally Assigned Privileges for Each ACL Level

	none	*Depositor*	*Reader*	*Author*	*Editor*	*Designer*	*Manager*
Create documents[a]		A		O	A	A	A
Create personal agents			O	O	O	A	A
Create shared folders/views					O	A	A
Create personal folders/views			O	O	O	A	A
Read public documents	O	O	A	A	A	A	A
Write public documents	O	O	O	O	A	A	A
Delete documents				O	O	O	O
Create LotusScript/Java agents			O	O	O	O	A

[a] "A" denotes that this right is automatically assigned; "O" denotes that this right can be optionally assigned.

For each ACL entry, a user type can and should be assigned. Available options are:

- Unspecified
- Person

- Server
- Mixed group
- Person group
- Server group

These user types are used to ensure that only the correct resource type (user or server) can make use of these ACL entries. For example, if an administrator is attempting to use a server ID interactively to make changes on the database, having the correct user type in an ACL would ensure that the ID spoofing will not be successful.

Access Control Roles page

On the Access Control Roles page, roles can be added, deleted, or renamed for the database. This function is intended for application developers to provide additional granularity of security access to their application over the standard levels of security that Domino provides. Each role name must be surrounded by square brackets—for example, `[MyTestRole]`. There is an architectural limit of 256 defined roles in a database.

Access Control Log page

The Access Control Log page provides an audit log of all changes to the database ACL, so you can easily see not only what changes have been made, but also who made them.

Access Control Advanced page

The Access Control Advanced page, as shown in Figure 3-14, contains a number of advanced options to control access to this database.

This last page of the ACL properties is a collection of unrelated yet very important and powerful features:

Administration Server
: This setting optionally sets an Administration Server to maintain the ACLs on the database as accounts are deleted and/or renamed. If not enabled, select None. It is a good idea to make use of an Administration Server, since this does some of our administration work for us for free, using the `AdminP` server process.

Do not modify Reader or Author fields
: If you have enabled the Administration Server, you can then have this server update the reader and author fields within the database as user accounts are removed and/or renamed. Reader fields and Author fields are an additional security measure available in Domino at the document level to further refine the database ACL.

Reader fields, if present in a document, allow only those listed in this field to read that document. Note that these people must already have at least Read access to the database as well. This means that even those with Manager access to the database cannot access the document if it's not listed here, so it is important that these fields are kept updated as users and servers are

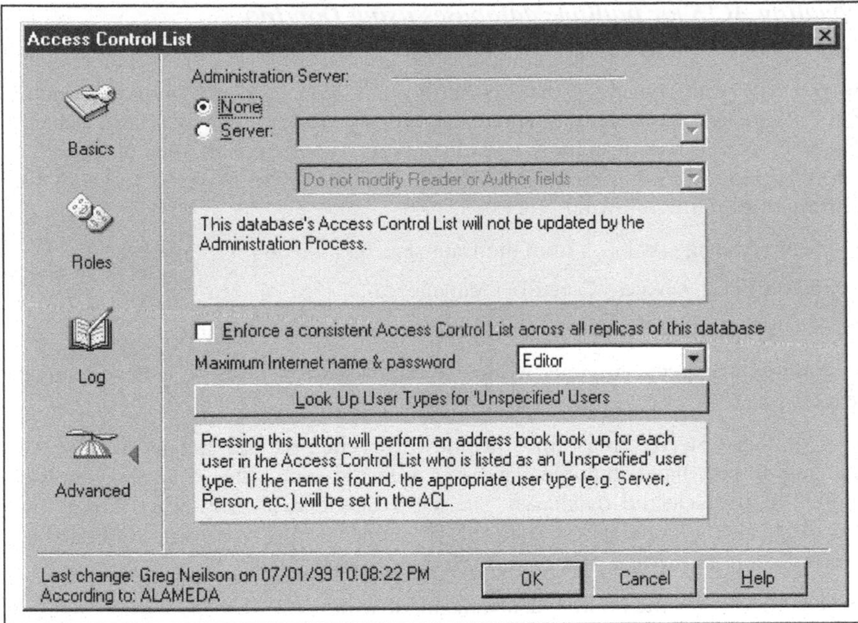

Figure 3-14: Database ACL Advanced page

renamed. A common problem with reader fields is a server name is not listed in the reader field of documents in the database. When that server attempts to replicate with this database, it is not able to read these documents and thus these documents are not replicated to that server.

Author fields, if present in a document, allow only those listed in this field who already have Author ACL access to the database to edit the document. It does not affect users with Editor access to the database or higher.

Enforce a consistent Access Control List across all replicas of this database
This setting ensures that all servers and clients that replicate this with database have an identical ACL on each replica copy. If this option is selected, and replication is attempted with a replica database that has a different ACL, then replication will fail. It also ensures that when users access this database via a local file system (as opposed to via a Domino server), the ACL entries are enforced.

Maximum Internet name and password
This option sets the maximum access available for this database to browser users, and can be anything from Manager to None. The default is Editor. This setting does not apply to browser users accessing the database via SSL. For example, when this option is set to Editor, even those with Manager access to the database have only Editor access when using a browser to do this.

Lookup User Types for "Unspecified" Users
This checks the ACL entries where the user type is "Unspecified," and looks up the known Domino Directories for a user type (server or user). This helps to tighten up the ACL so that a Server ID cannot be used to access the database via a Notes Client and vice versa.

Updating ACLS for multiple databases using Domino Administrator

As you saw with advanced database properties, you can use Domino Administrator to make changes to multiple databases at once. You can also select a database, copy its ACL entries, and then paste them into another database. As before, in the Files tab, select all of the databases you wish to modify, then perform one of the following processes:

- Select Manage ACL . . . from the Database Tool menu
- Select Files → Access Control → Manage
- Right-click with the mouse and select Access Control → Manage

As you might expect, this only works for databases for which you have Manager access.

Each of these steps brings up a window for entering the details for the ACL changes. If you have multiple databases selected, enter the changes you want applied to the selected databases. The View Single ACL drop-down box allows you to check the contents of each ACL by name. If you have only one database selected, then its existing ACL entries are displayed.

See Figure 3-15 for the Multi-ACL Management window.

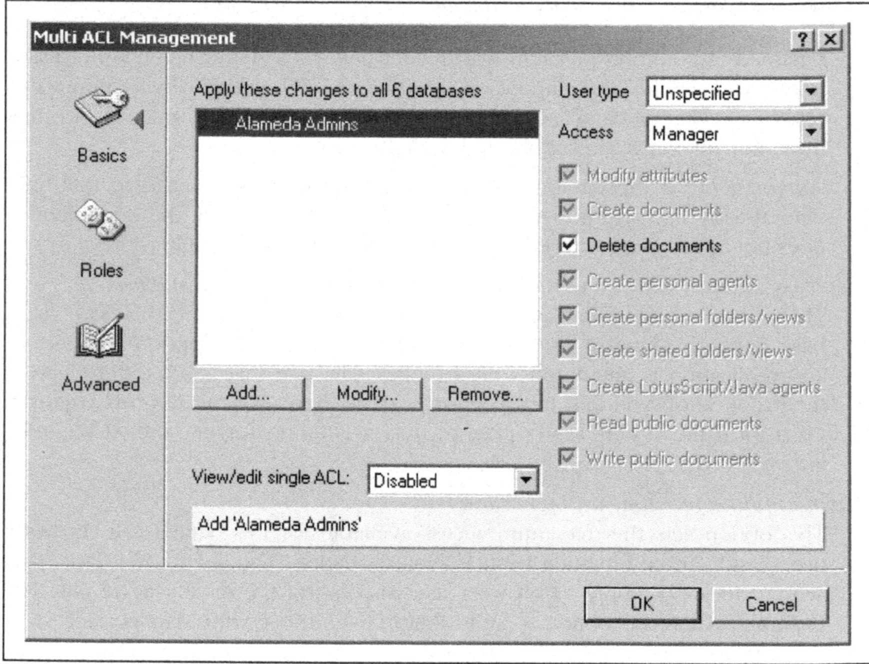

Figure 3-15: Working with database ACLs for multiple Domino databases

Directory and Database Links

Domino databases on a server are usually located within the *DATA* directory, though it is not always possible to find databases at this location on the server file-system. Directory and database links provide a way to "virtualize" directories and individual databases from other locations so that they appear to reside under the *DATA* directory hierarchy.

A *database link* is a text file with an *.NSF* extension. The first line contains the real physical location of the file. Subsequent lines in the file determine who can access this link: a link called *MYTEST.NSF* might consist of the following lines:

```
D:\LOTUS\DOMINO\DATA\MYTEST.NSF
Greg Neilson/ALAMEDA
Trusted Friends/ALAMEDA
Sue Neilson/ALAMEDA
```

Databases

Note that if there is no list of users and groups to specify who can access the link, the default is to allow everyone access.

A *directory link* is a text file with a *.DIR* extension. Similar to the database link, it consists of the actual physical location of the directory, and then optionally lists users and groups who can use this link. A directory link called *MINE.DIR* might consist of the following line:

```
E:\DOMINO
```

As before, when no users are explicitly specified, all users have access to use this link.

Domino Administrator contains a way to create these link files automatically via a GUI. In the Files tab, you can select New Link . . . from the Folders Tools menu, Files → New → Link . . . , or right-click with the mouse and select New → Link . . . . This then creates either the directory link or database link file via the data entered (see Figure 3-16).

NotesPeek

NotesPeek is a free downloadable tool obtainable from the IRIS web site at *http://notes.net/sandbox.nsf/Download* (see Figure 3-17). It was written by Ned Batchelder, an IRIS employee, for his own use, and has become a useful support tool. There are two versions currently available—one for R5.x databases and another for 4.x, so make sure you have the current version for the version of Domino you are running.

NotesPeek allows us to look inside each database and view individual entries, which are called *notes* (this is how the Notes product was first named). You can see the database properties, ACL, design details, data and document deletion stubs. NotesPeek is useful both to better understand the contents of Domino databases and also as a problem-solving tool. For developers, it is a great way to check the actual contents of the database against expectations, and since it uses the C API, it can be used to verify the results obtained via their programs that also use this API. For system administrators, the most useful feature is to view the deletion stubs—documents marked for deletion that are still present within the database, since there is no other way to view these.

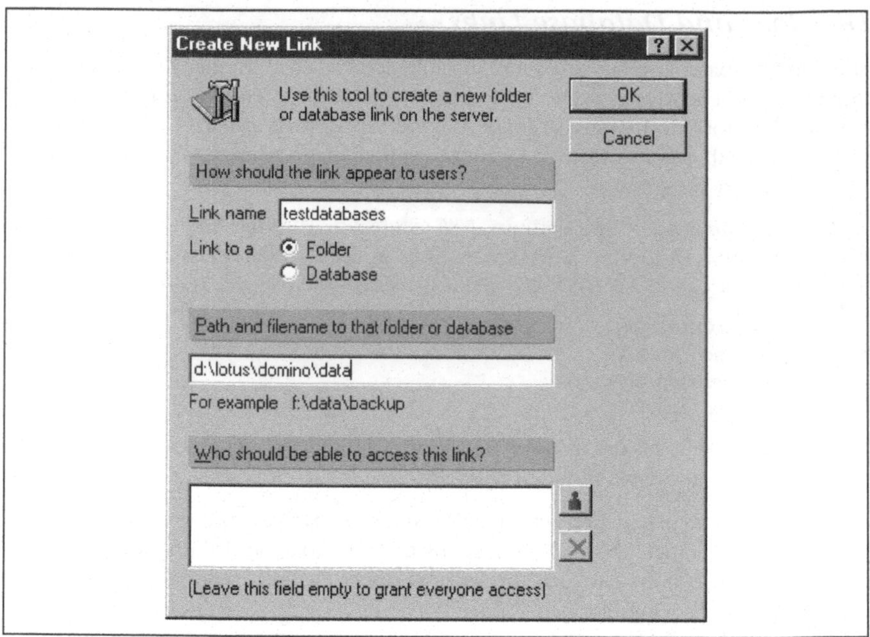

Figure 3-16: Creating a link in Domino Administrator

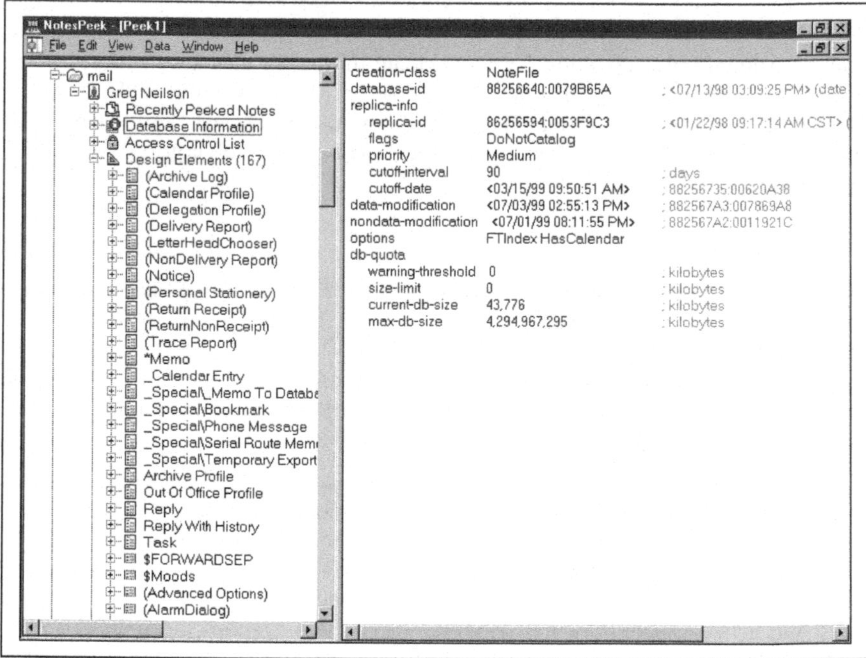

Figure 3-17: Viewing a database in NotesPeek

CHAPTER 4

Mail

Mail

Mail is usually the main mission-critical application on the Domino platform, so here I'll briefly discuss the architecture of mail processing within Domino. I'll also look at some of the alternative ways of accessing mail instead of using the Notes client, and lastly look at the shared mail function that can be used to provide single instance object storage for each Domino server.

Domino Mail Architecture

The Domino Named Network, as discussed in Chapter 1, *Notes and Domino Overview*, is a group of servers using the same network protocol in a constant connection within the same domain. Mail routing is immediate and does not need to be configured for servers within the same DNN.

The Domino Mail architecture is shown in Figure 4-1. In larger mail environments—particularly those with multiple DNNs defined within them—the most typical Domino mail routing design is the familiar "hub and spoke" model you have already seen with database replication. This model lets you control which servers are trying to communicate across WAN links and how often mail traffic is routed. As you saw in Chapter 2, *Domino Directories*, mail routing in Domino is configured by Connection documents within the Domino Directory.

A special database on each server (called *MAIL.BOX*) is used for mail delivery. When sending mail, Notes clients deposit mail into the *MAIL.BOX* database on the server that contains their own mail database (their "home" server). The `ROUTER` task then checks the Domino Directory to determine what to do with the mail. If the recipient is on the same server, the document is moved to the recipient's mail database. If the recipient's mail database is on another server within the same DNN, it is transferred by the router task immediately to the other server's *MAIL.BOX*, and the destination server moves the document to the recipient's mail database. Otherwise, if a Connection document is defined between this server and the recipient's server, mail is routed according to the rules defined within this Connec-

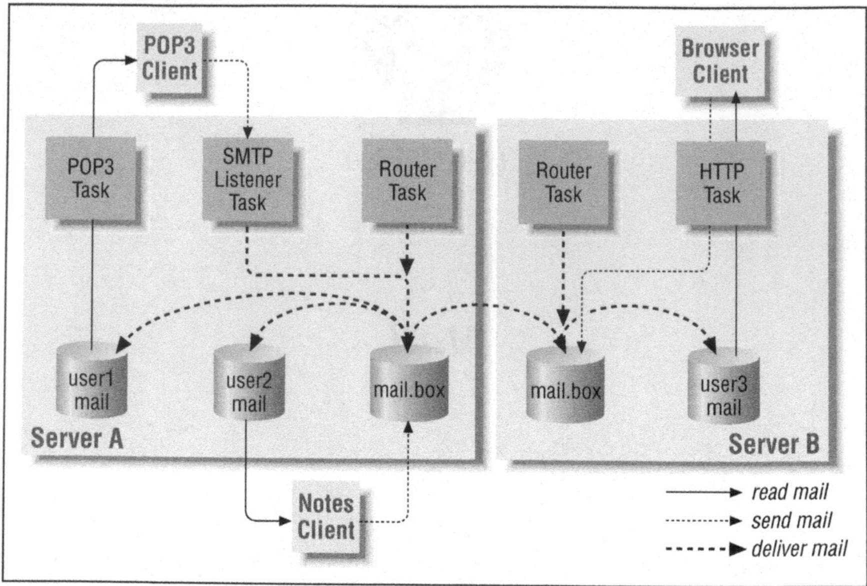

Figure 4-1: Domino Mail architecture

tion document. If there is no Connection document defined, the ROUTER task uses a dynamic mail routing table held in memory to determine which intermediate server to transfer the mail message to.

R5 introduced a feature to optionally enable multiple mailboxes—*MAIL1.BOX* and *MAIL2.BOX*, for example—but the concepts involved in their usage has not changed. Configuring multiple mailboxes is enabled in the "Number of mailboxes" field on the Router/SMTP tab of the Configuration document in the Domino Directory. In tests performed by Lotus, having two mailbox databases provides a performance boost, but the performance benefit declines with each additional mailbox.

Domains and Addressing

As explained in Chapter 1, the word *domain* is used for servers and users that share a common Domino Directory. An *adjacent domain* is another domain that can be directly accessed from this domain by a network connection. The Connection document specifies which server contacts which other server in order to send the mail between the two domains. Adjacent domain documents are created only when you need to restrict mail traffic to this adjacent domain—you can specify in the document which domains may send mail to this adjacent domain and/or which domains are prevented from sending mail to it.

A *nonadjacent* domain is another domain that cannot be accessed directly from your domain and must be routed via an intermediate domain. For example, to reach domain C from nonadjacent domain A, create a nonadjacent domain document for domain A that routes messages for domain C to domain B, which already has a connection to domain C set up.

A *foreign domain* is used for fax, pager, cc:Mail messages, and other gateways. Create a foreign domain document in the Domino Directory that specifies the server and database where messages destined for this domain are to be sent. For example, I might send a message to *5551111@MyFax*, where *MyFax* is the name of the Fax server foreign domain, and *5551111* is the fax number for sending the message.

When sending mail in Notes, the name of the domain is appended to the addressee, and preceded by an @ symbol; for example, *Joe Sixpack/ACME@DomainC*, where *DomainC* is the name of the Notes domain. A user can force the sending of mail to a nonadjacent domain when none has been configured by the administrator by addressing the mail to *Joe Sixpack/ACME@DomainC@DomainB*, assuming a defined connection to *DomainB* exists. However, this is not often used in practice. R5 now understands Internet mail addressing, so it is able to determine that *Joe Sixpack/ACME@DomainC* is the same user as *j_sixpack@acme.com*, and either addressing format now works.

SMTP Mail Processing

R5 can now process SMTP mail natively, whereas R4 needed dedicated server(s) in the network running the `SMTPMTA` task to send and receive Internet mail and also to convert mail to and from the MIME format to the Notes CD format. This means that potentially every Domino server can receive SMTP mail from the Internet and send SMTP to the Internet. (Whether this is desirable depends on your network environment.) You can also select whether to use SMTP routing or the regular Domino NRPC (Notes RPC) between servers. This setting is made from Domino Directory → Configuration document → Router/SMTP basics tab → "SMTP allowed within the local Internet domain field." This field can be set to "Disabled," "MIME messages only," or "All messages to use SMTP routing." This last option means that the Notes mail message must be converted to MIME format before being sent.

Delegation

Users can use delegation to allow others to work with their mail; this does not require any action by an administrator. This can be enabled by selecting Tools → Preferences → Delegation tab → Mail Delegation. This selection makes changes to the mail database ACL, as shown in Table 4-1.

Table 4-1: Mail Delegation: Changes Made to the Mail Database ACL

Delegation Action	*Mail Database ACL Change*
Allows to read mail, calendar, and To Do documents	Adds name to ACL and grants Read access
Allows to read mail, calendar, and To Do documents and sends mail on your behalf	Adds name to ACL and grants Author access with the Create Documents right
Allows to read, send, and edit mail, calendar, and To Do documents	Adds name to ACL and grants Editor access
Allows to delete mail, calendar, and To Do documents	Adds name to ACL and grants Author access with the Create Documents and Delete Documents right

Calendars and Scheduling

At first glance, Calendaring and Scheduling would appear to have little to do with mail processing; however, on the client, this functionality is built into the user mail database. A calendar is just a special type of view within this database. The `CALCONN` (Calendar Connector) and `SCHED` (Schedule Manager) server tasks, combined with the Free Time database (*BUSYTIME.NSF*, or *CLUBUSY.NSF* for clustered mail servers), perform the server-side functionality for calendaring and scheduling.

The Schedule Manager looks on the Domino server for mail databases that have a Calendar profile. This profile defines who owns the mail database. For every mail database found on the server with a Calendar profile, the Schedule Manager creates an entry in the Free Time database on the server for that user and also includes the dates and times of calendar entries that the user has defined. This means that another user can check whether this user is available at a given time and can then invite him to a meeting, but cannot see exactly what appointments the other user has unless he has explicitly been granted calendar delegation rights. The clustered version of the Free Time database means that other users can check whether someone is available at a given time, even when that user's mail database (and thus his Free Time database) is located on a server that may be unavailable.

The Calendar Connector is used when you wish to schedule a meeting with someone whose mail database is not on the same mail server as yours. This task then refers to the Domino Directory to find the Calendar server for that user's Person Document, and asks that server directly for the Free Time information for that user.

Meeting invitations are sent as mail messages to the invited users. When a user accepts the invitation, the meeting is added to his calendar and an acceptance message is sent to the inviter.

The Free Time database by default is accessible only by the server, and users and system administrators don't have access to this database. However, you can use the `TELL SCHED SHOW` *`username`* server console command to check the entries for a given user. As users add new entries to their schedule, these entries are added to the Free Time database. Refer to Chapter 13, *Domino Server Tasks and Console Commands*, for other console commands that can be used with the `SCHED` and `CALCONN` server tasks.

As an administrator, you can also create a Resource Reservation database to allow users to schedule resources such as meeting rooms for their meetings. This is created from the Resource Reservations Template (*RESRC50.NTF*). You then need to determine who can create site profiles and resources within the database and add them to the database ACL with the `[CreateResource]` role. There must be a minimum of one site profile created before a resource can be created. After a resource is created in the database, the `AdminP` task creates an entry in the Domino Directory for this resource so that users can perform lookups for it. Users can then either explicitly create a reservation document in this database for that resource, or alternatively include the resource when sending a meeting invitation.

Users can use delegation to allow others to work with their calendar; this does not require any action by an administrator. This option is enabled by selecting Tools → Preferences → Delegation tab → Calendar Delegation. It changes the mail database ACL as shown in Table 4-2.

Table 4-2: Calendar Delegation—Changes Made to the Mail Database ACL

Delegation Action	*Mail Database ACL Change*
Allows anyone to read calendar	Gives the existing -Default- ACL entry the Read Public Documents right (this works even when -Default- has an access level of None)
Allows only the following people to read calendar	Adds name to ACL and grants access level of None with the Read Public Documents right
Allows anyone to create and edit entries in calendar	Gives the existing -Default- ACL entry the Write Public Documents right (this works even when -Default- has an access level of None)
Allows only the following people to create and edit entries in calendar	Adds name to ACL and grants access level of None with the Write Public Documents right

Internet Mail Clients (POP3, IMAP)

POP3 and IMAP are Internet protocols that allow clients to retrieve email from a server. Netscape Communicator and Outlook Express (part of Microsoft's Internet Explorer web browser) are common email clients that be configured to work with these protocols. IMAP is more advanced than POP3, and is able to work with folders in the user's mail database. In both cases, the SMTP protocol is used by the clients to send mail.

The `POP3` task must be running on the Domino server in order for it to serve POP3 clients. Similarly, the `IMAP` task is needed for IMAP client support. When SMTP listening is enabled on the Basics tab of the Server document for your server, the `SMTP` task is automatically launched at server startup.

Internet mail clients require two things before they can access the server:

- A Person document in the Domino Directory that contains their name, the location of their mail database, and their Internet password.
- A mail database that can be created from the regular *MAIL50.NTF* mail template. For a mail database to be used by an IMAP client, it must have been created with the *MAIL50.NTF* template and you must run `LOAD CONVERT -M` ***`maildatabasename`*** command against it.

When a regular Notes user is created, these two things are done automatically, and all that is necessary is to enter an Internet password in the Person document. So a regular Notes user could switch to use a POP3/IMAP client, provided that these tasks are running on the server. Otherwise, you must manually create a mail database and Person record for each user who will be accessing their mail via either POP3 or IMAP.

WebMail

WebMail is a client for accessing user mail databases via HTTP. Like Internet mail clients, this also requires a Person document in the Domino Directory that contains the user's name, the location of his mail database, and his Internet password; it also requires creation of a mail database. The **HTTP** task must be running on the server.

The URL that a user must enter is based on a combination of:

- The hostname of the server containing the mail database
- The location of the mail database relative to the Domino data directory
- The name of his mail database

As you might expect, there is a tradeoff here in usability, as opposed to using a full Notes client. This provides only a subset of traditional Notes mail client functionality and doesn't include calendaring and scheduling. Interestingly, Domino 5. 0.2 introduced the functionality to include contact information within the mail database for WebMail users; this is a change from Notes clients, which store this information in their personal name and address book (*NAMES.NSF*) on the client.

In the example shown in Figure 4-2, the mail database is located in the *\mail* subdirectory below the Domino Directory, so the full URL is *http://servera\mail\sneilson.nsf*.

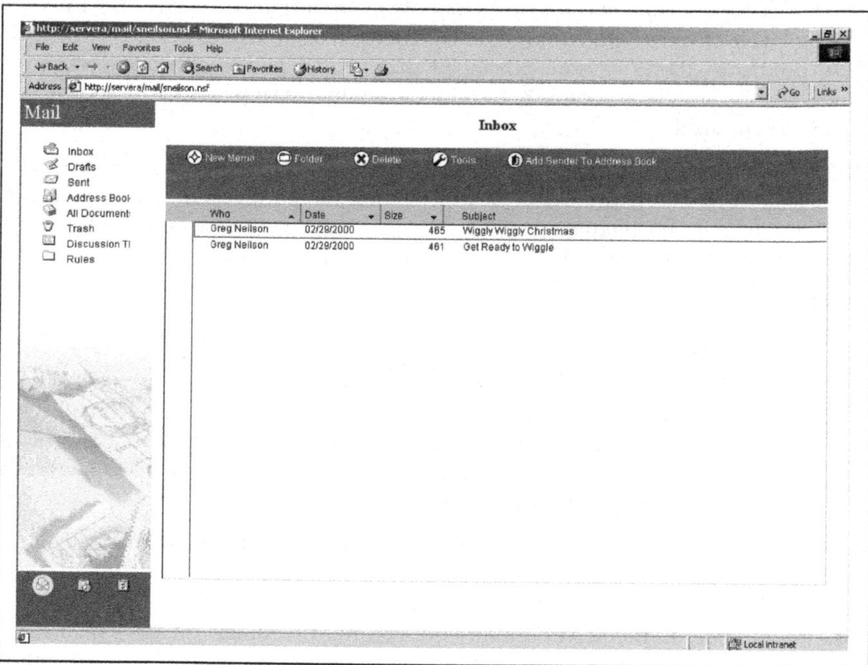

Figure 4-2: WebMail example

Shared Mail

Notes R4 introduced a new feature called Shared Mail, which enabled mail databases to share a single mail database for mail addressed to multiple users on the same server. In practice, this feature was not widely implemented. I believe there are several reasons for this:

- The initial implementations were buggy. This is probably no longer the case, yet the war stories that emanated from those versions are well-known, and administrators are not willing to now take the risk that all is well, given that this feature potentially affects every mail user on the server.
- This feature does require some monitoring of the size of the shared mail database. As this fills up (and recall that the old R4 size limit was 4GB, not 64MB and growing as today), the administrator must prepare another shared mail database for use by the server.
- As the cost of disk drives has fallen drastically over the last few years, the savings in disk usage don't warrant the effort required in working with shared mail.

When this feature is implemented, it works as follows:

- When an incoming message is addressed to more than one user on the server, the mail message is split into two—the body of the message is written to the shared mail database, and the to/from/subject header information and a pointer to the body are stored in the user mail database.
- The user opens her email normally, and there is no apparent difference from mail without this feature. As messages that have the body stored in the shared mail database are opened, the server transparently retrieves them. If the user has a local replica of his mail database, it contains both the header and body information of all of the messages.
- As users delete messages that use the shared mail database, only the header information in their own mail databases is deleted. When all of the users who had been using a given shared message have deleted all links to it, the shared message is deleted from the shared mail database when the `OBJECT COLLECT` task is next run. By default this is scheduled to run at 2:00 A.M.

To start using shared mail, issue the console command `TELL ROUTER USE` *`SHARED.NSF`* (where *`SHARED.NSF`* is the name of the shared mail database you wish to use). This creates the database specified, adds the line `SHARED_MAIL=2` to *NOTES.INI*, and creates a database link called *MAILOBJ.NSF* that points to the current shared mail database in use.

Refer to Chapter 13 for all of the options available to work with the `OBJECT` task. These can be used to configure specific mail databases to use or not use the shared mail database. Refer to Chapter 14, *NOTES.INI*, for the possible values and their meanings for the *SHARED_MAIL* parameter in *NOTES.INI*.

Mail

CHAPTER 5

Domino as a Web Server

Another of Domino's abilities is that of web server. To this end, the `HTTP` server task does the work needed for users to send URL requests that access Domino resources. It receives the incoming requests and sends the resulting HTML to the user. In order to do this, it parses the incoming URL to determine what Domino resources are being requested and what Domino command is being requested for that object. Each Domino object type has an internal method to render itself as HTML; these methods are called when the URL is being processed.

Domino also has a series of Java applets that are included in the delivered web pages as appropriate, to simulate the Notes user interface for web browser users. For example, there are applets to display views and to edit Rich Text fields within documents. These applets are added automatically by Domino and don't require intervention by either application developers or system administrators.

All the while, the Domino security model is maintained. A special ACL entry on each database ACL called Anonymous defines the access available for unauthenticated web users (if the Anonymous entry is not present, the -Default- entry applies). When users are authenticated, they are authenticated against the Password field in a Person document in the Domino Directory.

The `HTTP` task is thus a fully functional web server that can serve static HTML, Java applets, and graphic files (GIFs and JPEGs); it can also run CGI programs, such as Perl scripts.

In this chapter, I'll cover the configuration of the `HTTP` task and the special Domino URL commands. Keep in mind that to make any configuration changes effective for a running `HTTP` task, you must issue the server console command `TELL HTTP RELOAD` to enable the changes.

Configuration

There are several places where configuration information is kept:

- In the Server document for the server in the Domino Directory.
- In virtual server, URL redirection, file protection, and realm documents in the Domino Directory (web configuration documents).
- In the custom error messages and login forms in the Domino Configuration Database (*DOMCFG.NSF*) on that server.
- In the text file *HTTPD.CNF* on that server. However, Lotus will support the addition of only MIME types to this file. For example, to add the correct type for ShockWave Flash files, add this line to the *HTTPD.CNF* file:

  ```
  AddType .swf application/x-shockwave-flash binary 1.0 # Shockwave Flash
  ```

  MIME types are used to tell the browser about the content being served so that it can respond appropriately; for example, to process it with a given plug-in.
- In the text file *DOMINO.CNF*. This file is created dynamically from the settings in the Server document, so you should not update it directly.

These first three sources of configuration will be discussed further in this chapter.

Server Document

Two pages in the Server document are relevant to the HTTP task. Figure 5-1 shows the Internet Protocols → HTTP page. Figure 5-2 shows the Internet Protocols → Domino Web Engine page.

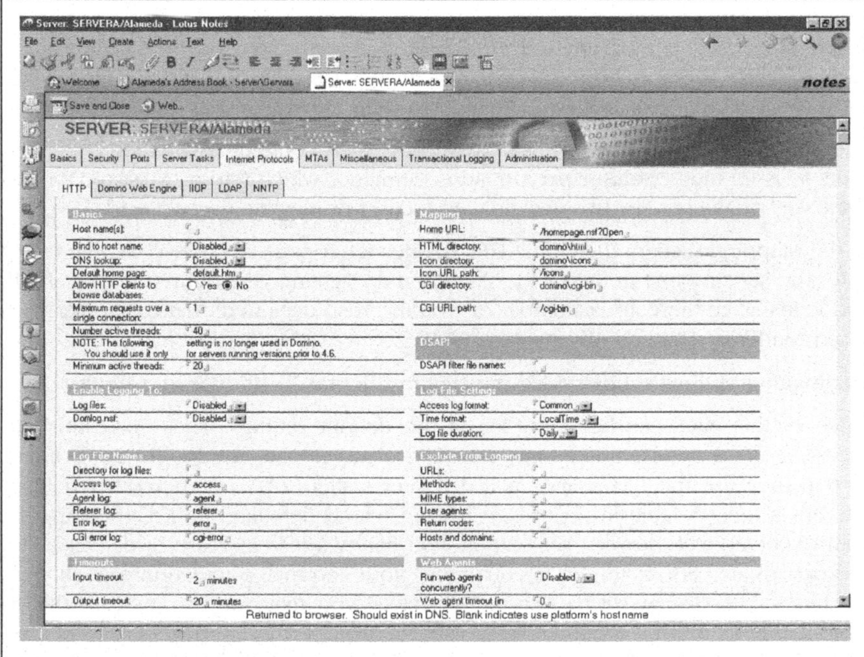

Figure 5-1: Server document → Internet Protocols → HTTP page

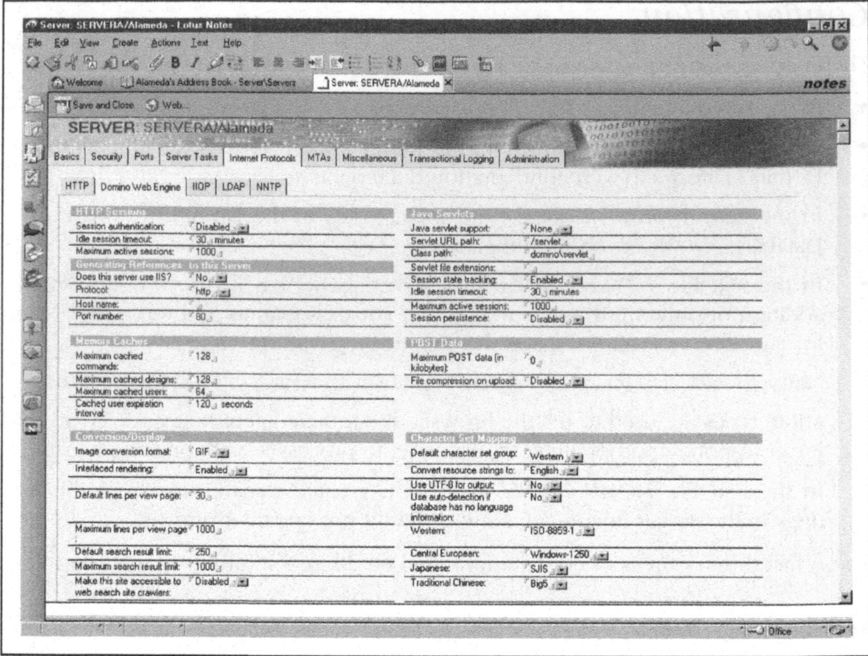

Figure 5-2: Server document → Internet Protocols → Domino Web Engine page

In the Basics section, the "Host name(s)" field defaults to blank, which means that Domino uses the hostname from the underlying operating system. The "Bind to host name" field, when enabled, means that the server can use alias host server names. When DNS Lookup is enabled, a DNS lookup is performed on the client making each request. This can be resource-intensive, but can also mean that any logging done on client requests can use the name returned rather than just an IP address.

The "Allow HTTP clients to browse databases" field configures whether you allow users to issue the `?OpenServer` Domino command, which returns a list of Domino databases on the servers. In some circumstances, this may be a security risk.

In the Mapping section, the Home URL defines what page the user sees when they enter the server name in their URL. You shouldn't change the definitions for HTML and icons since there are a number of Domino resources here that the server uses when rendering Domino objects into HTML.

The logging options are discussed in detail in Chapter 7, *Monitoring Domino*.

Much of this page can be safely left at the default settings. The "Make this site accessible to web search site crawlers" field changes generated URLs for Domino so that they use the `!` character as a delimiter instead of `?`. Also, another field of interest is the "Default lines per view" page, which defaults to 30. Depending on your expected web browser population, you may want to increase or decrease this as appropriate. For example, if you know your intranet population has all new machines with display set to 1024 × 768 pixels, you may want to increase this to 50 to make use of the additional screen space available.

Web Configuration Documents

These documents are very straightforward, and are defined for each Domino server. Interestingly, when the Domino Directory is opened, these documents are created by browsing the Server/Servers view, selecting the "Web action" button, and specifying the type of configuration you wish to create. These completed documents can then be viewed and edited under the Server/Web Configuration view. The four types of documents that can be created are:

Virtual server documents.
: Allow you to define multiple virtual servers within one Domino web server; for example, *www.xyz.com* and *www.acme.com*. Each virtual server must have a dedicated IP address assigned to it.

URL mapping documents
: Allow you to map URLs to Domino server resources; for example, creating virtual directories that can exist anywhere on the server filesystem. For instance, you could map *www.acme.com/level* to the *F:\WEBFILES* directory on the server. Alternatively, this can be used to redirect users that request a specific resource to a URL that resides on another server.

File protection documents
: New in R5; provide access control for files served by Domino that are not in Domino databases; for example, HTML files and icon files. You can give access to a drive, directory, or file to designated Domino users. The access levels available are None, Read, and Execute (`HTTP GET`), and Write, Read, and Execute (`HTTP PUT`).

Realm documents
: Give a name to a specific file path on the Domino server. When users are prompted by their browser for a user ID and password to access a resource underneath this file path, they are given the name of this Realm on their login screen. The realm should therefore be a more meaningful name that would make sense to the user. Otherwise, if a realm hasn't been defined, the user is given the pathname of the resource, which in many cases may not be meaningful.

The last three document types can be created for a specific virtual server or for all Domino web servers defined for that server.

Domino Configuration Database

Configuring this database is entirely optional. You must first create a new database called *DOMCFG.NSF* on the server from the Domino Web Server Configuration template.

In Domino 4.x, this database also contained virtual server and URL redirection documents, but as we have just seen, these have been moved in R5 to the Domino Directory. When a server is first upgraded to R5, these documents will be automatically moved to the Domino Directory.

You can create a custom error message document, either for each web server defined on that server, or for all servers. You are given the option to specify the form name and the database name you wish to be displayed, in case of the following situations:

- Authentication failure
- Authorization failure
- Document deleted OK
- General error

The forms themselves will most likely be created for you by an application developer. If you do not specify a custom error page, Domino supplies one for you.

If you are using session-based web authentication, you can specify a custom login form and database to be used for each web server, or for all web servers defined on that server.

Domino URLs

Domino has special URL syntax rules that are used to access Domino resources via a web browser. Creating URLs that use this special syntax is better left for application developers; however, it is you, as the system administrator, who developers will come to when their finished application doesn't work as they had intended. In this case, you must be able to examine a Domino URL and understand what resources in what database the request is attempting to access.

Domino URLs have the form:

```
http://servername/Database/Object?Action&Arguments
```

The *servername* can be the IP address of the server or server host name. *Database* is the name of the Domino database being referenced. The location of the database on the server in this URL is relative to the Domino data directory. Instead of the name of the database, the replica ID of the database can be used. *Object* is a Domino database object such as a navigator, form, or view. It can be specified by name, universal ID, or NotesID. Since the NotesID can be different across different database replicas, you should use the universal ID. There are also a set of special object names called *$defaultView*, *$defaultForm*, *$defaultNav*, *$searchForm*, *$file*, *&icon*, *$help*, *$about*, and *$first*, which are self-explanatory. When Domino dynamically creates URLs, they usually use the universal ID, which means that the URLs tend to look like:

> *http://servera.alameda.com/mail/gneilson.nsf/*
> *bd053b46b119c67a8525643000742b16/*
> *682b277898c5e95cca2568c80055e4d7?OpenDocument*

Action is the type of request you want performed on the object. For example, this could be *?OpenDatabase*, *?OpenView*, or *?EditDocument*. The action is commonly unspecified, since the default action for each object type is the *?Open* type. For example, if a view name is the object, an *?OpenView* is the default action. There is a parameter in the server document to enable use of ! characters; for example *!OpenDatabase*. This parameter enables web crawlers to continue to trawl and index your site; without this setting they would stop at the first encounter with a ? in an URL.

Arguments are optional but relate to the type of action requested. For example, an *?OpenView* URL may have the additional arguments *Count=20* and *Start=100*, which tell Domino to list 20 records in the view on the next form, starting at the 100th document in the view. The argument *&Login* forces user authentication, instead of waiting until the user attempts a resource he doesn't have access to.

URLs must be less than 1024 bytes long. Replace any spaces in the URL (for example, in a database view called The Big View) with a "+" sign (The+Big+View).

The available Domino URL commands are listed in Table 5-1.

Table 5-1: Domino URL Commands

URL Command	*Meaning*
?OpenServer	Produces a list of server databases on the server.
?OpenDatabase	Opens the database. The returned information varies based upon the option selected for the "When opened in a Browser" database property field.
?OpenView	Returns the database view.
?OpenAbout	Returns the Help → About This Database document for the database.
?OpenHelp	Returns the Help → Using This Database document for the database.
?OpenIcon	Return the database icon.
?OpenFrameset	Returns the specified frameset.
?OpenAgent	Runs the specified agent and returns the output.
?OpenForm	Returns the specified form.
?OpenNavigator	Returns the specified navigator.
?ReadForm	Returns the specified form without any editable fields.
?CreateDocument	Creates a document of the specified type.
?DeleteDocument	Deletes the specified document.
?EditDocument	Edits the specified document.
?OpenDocument	Opens a specified document.
?SaveDocument	Saves the updates to a specified document.
?OpenPage	Returns a web page.
?OpenElement	Returns an attachment, image file or OLE object.
?SearchDomain	Performs a domain search for a given text string and returns the results.
?Redirect	Redirects the user to another web resource, which can be on the same server or a different server.
?SearchSite	Performs a search using the specified search site database and returns the results.
?SearchView	Performs a search against all the documents in a given view and returns the results.

CHAPTER 6

Domino Administration Tools

In this chapter, I'll cover the administration tools provided by Domino: the 32-bit Windows Domino Administrator and the web administrator client. I'll also discuss registration of users and the operation and configuration of the Administration Process, a Domino task that automates many administration functions.

In R5, the Notes client was separated from the Domino server code, and these are installed now as separate products into separate directories. Previously, these were installed together, meaning that when you installed the server on Unix, OS/2, or Windows NT, you also installed the client, which had functionality to administer the server as well. Domino Administrator runs only on Windows 95/98/NT and 2000. Lotus does not recommend installing Domino Administrator on the Domino server, and it is certainly preferable in most cases to administer the servers from a separate machine. However, you might want to consider installing Domino Administrator on Windows NT Domino servers for "just in case" when you need to access the server databases locally.

If you have set up and configured your Domino server on the Windows NT platform, you have seen the "Setup Client" that Lotus ships with the server to run the Setup application. You can use this client code on the server to access databases locally, although this use is *not* documented or supported by Lotus. To start this program, run *\LOTUS\DOMINO\NLNOTES.EXE*. (Thanks to Ben Malekzadeh from *Domino Professional* for this tip!) Note that this process uses the Server ID file, so use the *NOTES.INI* statement `KeyFileName` to define the location of the user ID you wish to use at the server and ensure that the Server-KeyFileName entry points to the Server ID file. I am not advocating that you use this on a running production server, and I would suggest you use this facility only in an emergency.

Domino Administrator

One of the major new features in R5 was the creation of the Domino Administrator, which runs only on 32-bit Windows clients. In previous releases, the administration options were on a menu within the Notes client. Domino Administrator pulls together a lot of server information in one central place, and can also be configured to graphically monitor and display the status of specific tasks on a number of Domino servers.

Domino Administrator Preferences

The location of the basic configuration settings for the Domino Administrator client is File → Preferences → Administration Preferences from either the Notes or Domino Administrator client. Figure 6-1 shows the Administration Preferences dialog box.

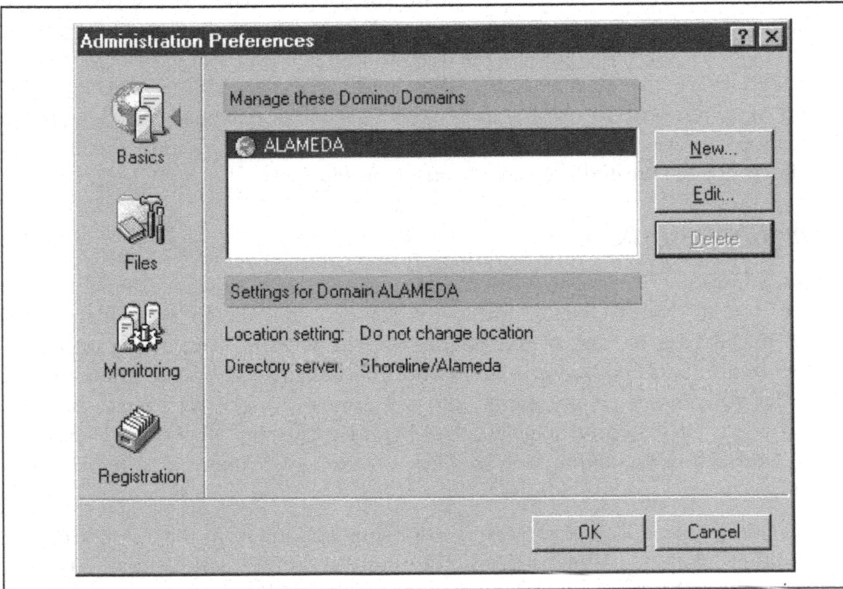

Figure 6-1: Domino Administrator Preferences dialog box

The available options are:

Basics
: Configures which domain(s) you will be managing with Domino Administrator, the directory server used by default for each domain, and the Location document to use within your Personal Name and Address Book on the client for this domain. Location documents are discussed further in Chapter 8, *Supporting the Notes Client*. You can change the actual directory server used at any given time later by a simple selection from a dropdown list on the Configuration tab.

Files
: Configures which database properties columns are displayed as columns (and in what order) within the Files tab. The available options are Title, Filename,

Physical Path, File Format, Size, Max Size, Quota, Warning, Created, Last Fixup, and Is Logged.

Monitoring

Configures how the Server → Monitoring tab works. Specify here the maximum amount of the monitoring data to retain in memory (4—99 MB), whether to automatically monitor all servers within the bookmark bar, and for each Location document defined within the Personal Name and Address Book, whether to collect the database statistics by the Domino Administrator client or use a defined server running the Collect task. There are also options that define the polling interval for each server and specify whether to automatically monitor servers as the Domino Administrator is started (or instead wait until the administrator goes to that tab within the Domino Administrator).

Registration

Sets the defaults for the registration of new users. This includes Registration Server (the server you'll use to update the Domino Directory with the new Person record for the user); the Certifier ID (used to create the public/private key pairs for the user ID file, which also defines the hierarchical name of the created user); the Mail System (Notes/IMAP/POP/Other/None), Mail Server, and Mail Template to use for the created user mail database; the default file locations to store ID files for users, servers, and certifiers; and the Internet domain for the created user and the user profile.

Server Bookmarks

Domino Administrator also uses the new Bookmark user interface element introduced in the R5 Notes client. The lists of servers available to be managed are selected by clicking on one of the buttons on the lefthand side; these include a Favorites button and one button per domain that is managed by the Administrator client. The domain servers are sorted into categories to make it easier to find the server you are interested in managing: All Servers, Clusters, Networks, Hierarchy, Release, and Server Operating System. Click on the server name to administer the server of choice.

You can add to these lists of servers by choosing options from the Administration menu within Domino Administrator. The Refresh Server List option has two choices, Current Domain and All Domains. As you would expect, these update the list of servers from the current domain and all domains specified in the Administrator Preferences, respectively. You can also add a server to your favorites list by specifying the name under Administration → Add Server to Favorites.

There is also a menu option for selecting the Domino server to administer: choose File → Open Server, then enter the name of the server.

People and Groups Tab

This tab administers control of users and groups in the Domino Directory and is shown in Figure 6-2.

The five options here—People, Groups, Mail-In Databases, Setup Profiles, and Certificates—are views from the Domino Directory. From here, you can select one

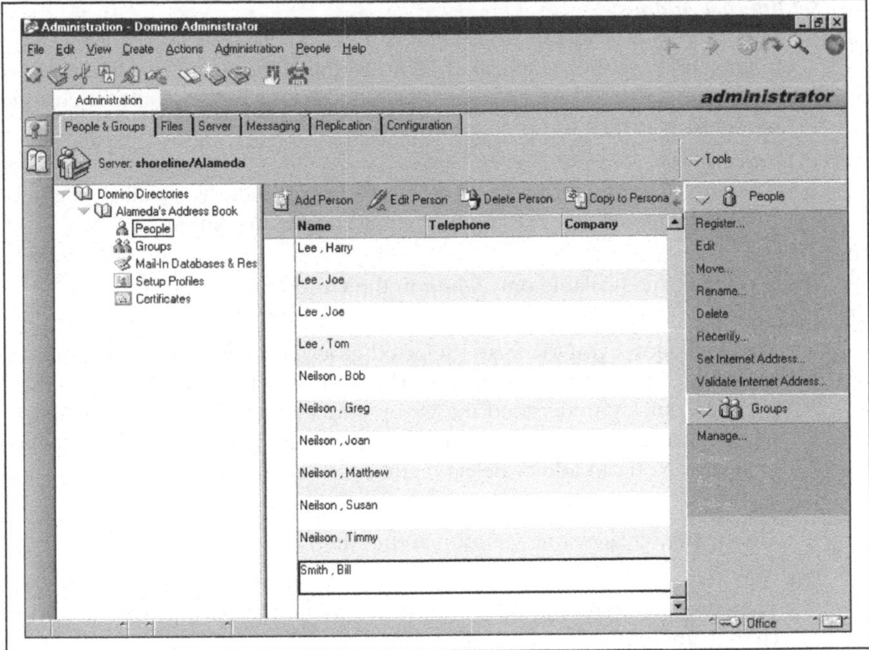

Figure 6-2: Domino Administrator People and Groups tab

or more usernames and make changes to them all. The available tools menu options are:

People

The following options are available only when in the People view:

Register

This option registers new Domino users. (This is a large topic and is covered in the next section of this chapter.)

Edit

This option edits the currently selected Person document.

Move

This option automatically moves the selected user mail databases from one server to another using the Administration Process task.

Rename

This option renames the username, using the Administration Process task.

Delete

This option deletes the selected users. It also prompts to ask whether their mail files should be deleted as well. Again, the Administration Process may perform this work if you elect to have the mail file deleted in the background.

Recertify

This option recertifies a user ID file that may have already expired or may be about to expire. The Administration Process then performs this task in the background.

Set Internet Address

This option sets the Internet address field for all selected People documents in the format specified. For example, you can configure "first name+underscore+lastname" or "firstinitial+lastname" or whatever custom standard you wish to use in your Domino implementation.

Validate Internet Address

This tool can run across the current Domino Directory (or all configured directories) to ensure that the Internet addresses are unique.

Groups

These options are available only when in the Group view:

Manage

This tool allows you to expand selected group types to show hierarchies of nested groups and their members. This is a very powerful way by which you can quickly understand the group structure of an unfamiliar Domino environment. It can also be used to confirm that the group structure is as expected. You can add or delete members from groups here as well.

Create

This option creates a new Group within the Domino Directory.

Edit

This option opens the selected Group in edit mode so that you can change any of the group details.

Delete

This option deletes the Group from the Domino Directory.

You can also create, view, edit, or delete Setup Profiles here. These are used to customize the users' Notes environments, and are further discussed in Chapter 8.

Files Tab

This tab allows you to work with databases on the Domino server, as shown in Figure 6-3. The options here will not work unless you have Manager access to each database.

In Figure 6-3, the Show Me option (above the file list in the center of the screen) configures what is displayed in the database list on the right side of the screen. The available options are Databases only, Templates only, Mail Boxes only, All database types, All files, Database links only, or Custom (where you choose which file types and/or file extensions you want to view). Also, next to this is a box that toggles what is displayed in this option. You can have either a Windows Explorer-type display (the default), which shows the server data directory hierarchy on the lefthand side together with the contents of the selected directory on the righthand side, or displays all files at once. This option allows more columns of information to be displayed across the screen without needing to scroll. Recall that the Files tab of the Domino Administrator Preferences screen configures which columns are displayed here and the order in which they are displayed. Double-clicking a database displayed in the list opens it.

The available tools within this tab are:

Disk Space

Graphically displays all configured drives on the server, with both used and unused space on each highlighted.

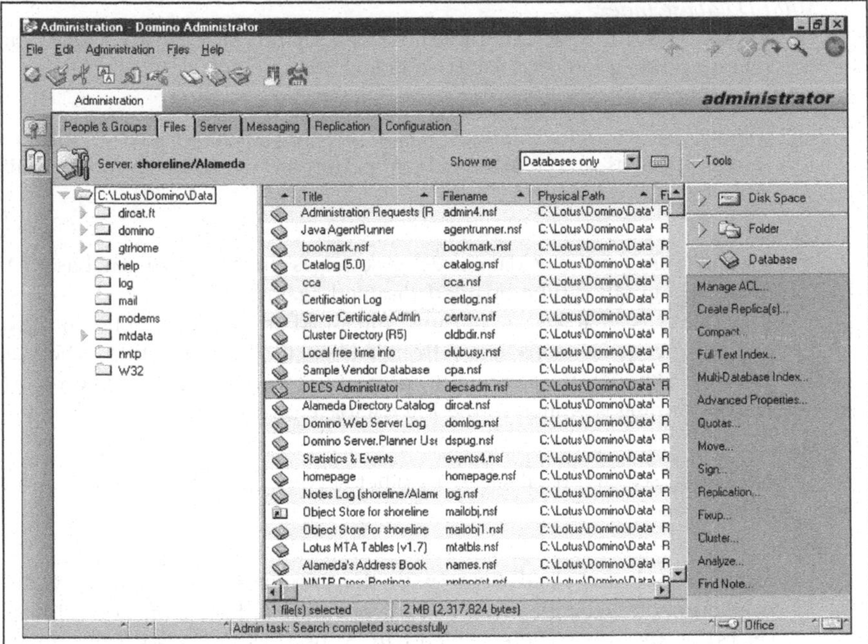

Figure 6-3: Domino Administrator Files tab

Folder

New

Creates a new folder (subdirectory) below the current selected location in the filesystem underneath the Domino data directory.

New Link

Creates a new database or directory link on the server. (These links are described in detail in Chapter 3, *Domino Databases.*)

Update Link

Updates the selected database or directory link definition.

Delete

Deletes the selected folder.

Database

Manage ACL

Enables you to make the same ACL change to multiple selected databases.

Create Replica(s)

Creates replicas of the selected databases on specified servers.

Compact

Runs the Compact task (with selected options from the GUI) against the selected databases.

Full-Text Index

Allows you to update the full-text index properties of multiple selected databases, and to update/delete these indexes now.

Multi-Database Index

Allows you to select multiple databases and have them added or removed from a multiple database index.

Advanced Properties

Allows you to make changes within the Advanced Properties for the selected databases. The advanced properties are discussed in more detail in Chapter 3.

Quotas

Typically used on mail databases to set sizes on their mail databases. A quota size in MB can be enabled/disabled against the selected databases. If a quota is enabled, a warning threshold in MB can optionally be added. The quota stops users from adding to their mail files when at capacity, although they continue to receive incoming mail and can read it. The warning is written to the log database on the server.

Move

Moves the selected database(s) to other servers, using the Administration Process task.

Sign

Signs the selected database(s) with the current ID file in use by the Administrator. Signing is used in conjunction with Execution Control Lists (ECLs) on the Notes client, which can be used as protection from unauthorized (or unsigned) changes on their workstation by rogue Notes applications.

Replication

Enables/disables replication for the selected database(s).

Fixup

Runs the `Fixup` task (with selected options from the GUI) against the selected databases.

Cluster

Works with the selected databases within a Domino cluster, by making them available, unavailable, or pending delete.

Analyze

Reports on changes to the selected database over a selected period. By default, produces a report in a database called *DBA4.NSF* on the local machine. This report can consist of changes in data, design, user reads and writes, and replication. Typically, you would use this tool only when unexpected changes or out-of-sequence changes are being made to the database and you need to understand what has happened with the database.

Find Note

Finds a specific Note (or record) within a database. Often when you see error messages in the Domino console or the Log database, it reports problems with Databases by listing the particular NoteID that may be corrupt. Here you can query the database by the given NoteID to find the document properties in question.

Server Tab

The four tabs located under the Server tab provide options to monitor the health of Domino servers within your network. Figures 6-4 and 6-5 show two of these screens.

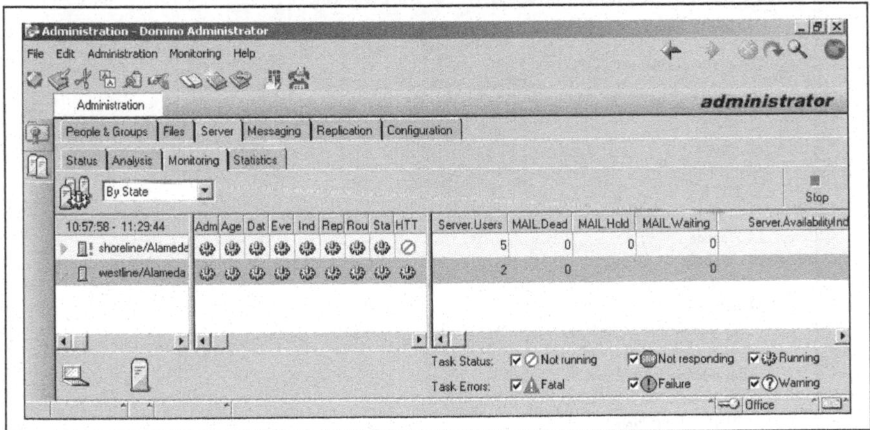

Figure 6-4: Domino Administrator Server page Monitoring tab

The Server → Status tab shows the status of the running tasks and connected users on the server—equivalent to the output from the `SHOW TASKS` and `SHOW USERS` console commands. (If you check the server console after you change to this page, you'll see that these commands are executed on the server and redirected into a temporary text file so that the information can be displayed on this tab.) You can also open a session to the Domino console from here, enter commands, and check the output. (Chapter 13, *Domino Server Tasks and Console Commands*, covers the console commands in more detail.) There is also a Tools menu on this tab, which simplifies entering commands to the Domino console—select the command and any option you wish to enter. The commands available are:

Task commands

Tell

Issues the `TELL` *<task>* command to the selected task running on the server. This also includes the relevant options available for each task, which means you don't also need to remember the syntax for each and every command.

Start

Starts a server task from a list.

Stop

Issues the `STOP` *<task>* command to the selected task running on the server.

User commands

Broadcast Message

Issues a broadcast command to the selected user or to all connected server users.

Drop

Drops the selected user connection or all connected users from the server.

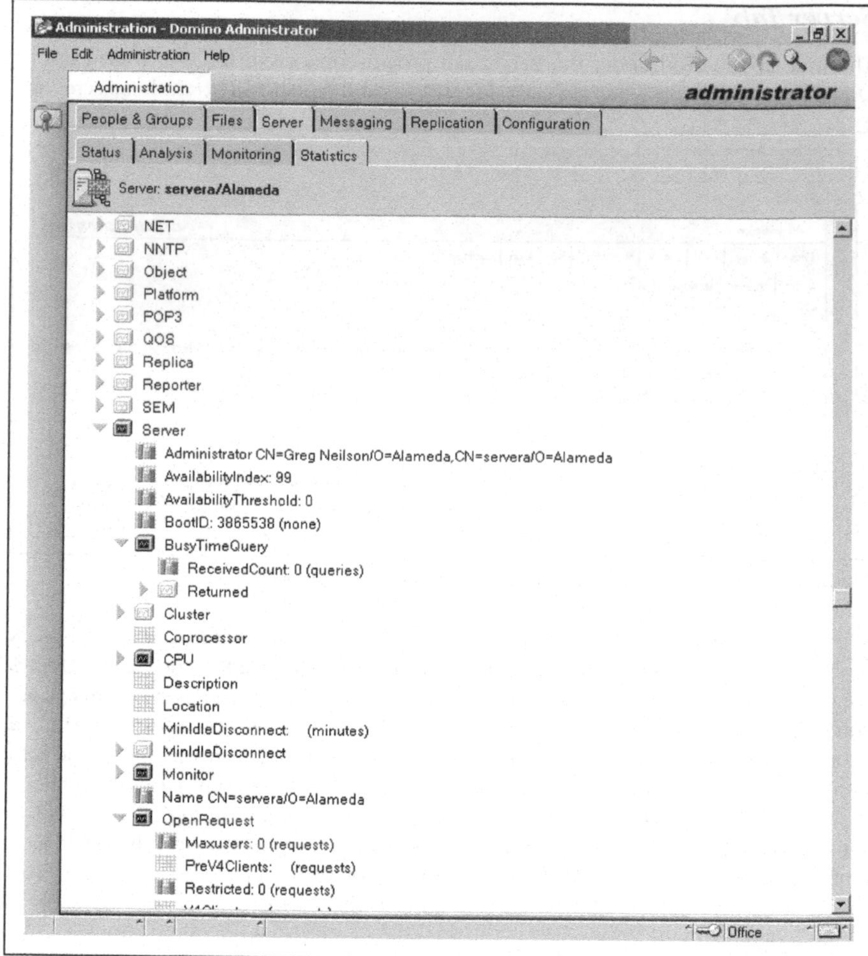

Figure 6-5: Domino Administrator Server page Statistics tab

Server commands

Replicate

Performs immediate database replication with a selected server.

Route Mail

Routes mail to a selected server.

Setup Ports

Configures and activates or deactivates server ports.

Secure Console

Allows you to set a password that must be used when working with the Domino server console.

Stop Port

Stops the selected network port on the server.

Shutdown

Shuts down the Domino server.

The Server → Analysis tab collates server information from a number of sources into a single place. This includes a list of views from the Log database, the Statistics Reports database, and the Administration Requests database on the server being monitored. (The Log database and Statistics Reports database are covered in more detail in Chapter 7, *Monitoring Domino*. The Administration Requests database is covered in the Administration Process section later in this chapter.)

The Server → Monitoring tab allows you to monitor the health of a number of servers within your Domino network. Here, by choosing options from the Monitoring menu, you can select the servers, the tasks, and any particular statistics you want to monitor. If you have a large number of servers to monitor, you should consider setting up a dedicated server management console that is always available to be visually checked periodically for any problems with any of the servers being managed. Refer to the configuration options in the Domino Administrator Preferences that control how monitoring operates.

The Server → Statistics tab shows a snapshot of the values of server statistics. Since these are shown graphically in a hierarchical manner, it is simple job to find the value of any statistic. The server console command `SHOW STATISTICS` provides the same information, but is a long list of statistics and values that must be scrolled though.

Messaging Tab

The two tabs underneath the Messaging tab provide information about the health of mail delivery in Domino as well as further information that can be used to determine the cause of any problems identified. Figure 6-6 shows the Messaging → Mail tab.

The Messaging → Mail tab contains the following options:

Mail Users
: Displays the Mail Users view from the Domino Directory, which contains the users categorized by their mail server.

Routing Mailboxes
: Shows the server mailbox(es) and their contents. For example, if multiple mailboxes are not configured, this selection shows a view of the contents of *MAIL.BOX*. Alternatively, if multiple mailboxes are configured (and this is defined within a Configuration document within the Domino Directory), it lists *MAIL1.BOX*, *MAIL2.BOX*, etc., and shows a view of each. Here there may be dead mail or mail waiting to be transferred to other servers, and while you cannot open the mail messages, you can delete messages from here; for example, any dead mail, which means neither the recipient or the sender can be found. Make sure you grant your Administrators Manager ACL access to the server mailbox(es) or else they will have only the default (Depositor) access and not be able to see anything there, let alone delete dead mail.

Shared Mail
: Shows the shared mail usage reports from the Log database. (Shared Mail is covered in detail in Chapter 4, *Mail*.)

Admin Tools

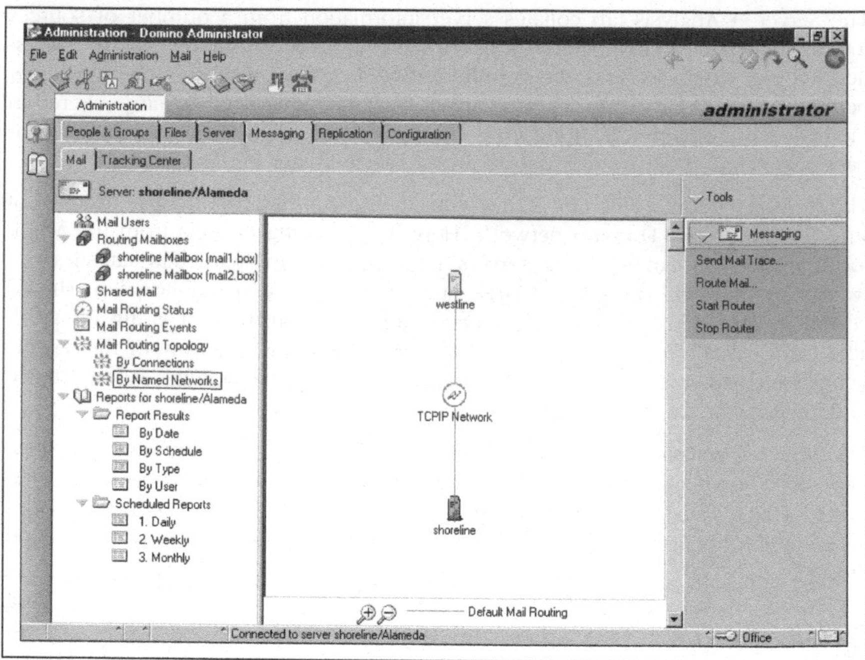

Figure 6-6: Domino Administrator Messaging page Mail tab (mail routing topology)

Mail Routing Topology

Offers two graphical modes: Connections or Named Networks. This information is extracted from the Domino Directory by the `MAPS` task and graphically displayed here. Two options are provided, since there are two ways to configure mail traffic between servers. When servers within a domain use the same network protocol and configure the network ports with the same Named Network (the default name is Network1), mail routing is performed automatically between all of the servers within that same Named Network. The alternative is to create connection documents that define the schedule for mail routing between servers. Figure 6-6 shows an example of mail routing topology.

Reports

Shows both the mail usage reports scheduled to be run as well as the mail usage report output. (Mail usage reports are discussed in detail in Chapter 7.)

Mail Status

Shows the dead mail and mail waiting to be transferred on the server in a graphical "dashboard" format.

The Tools menu on this tab provides a few options to work with mail processing on the server currently being administered:

- Send a Mail Trace to a given server. This feature is used to test that mail can be transferred successfully.
- Route mail immediately to a given server. This selection is the same as issuing the `ROUTE` *`<server>`* command at the server console.

- Stop the router task. This selection is the same as issuing the TELL ROUTER QUIT command at the server console.
- Start the router task. This selection is the same as issuing the LOAD ROUTER command at the server console.

The second tab here is the Tracking Center, which is used to track the location and status of user mail messages. This functionality is described in Chapter 7.

Replication Tab

This tab, as shown in Figure 6-7, provides information about the configured replication between servers and whether that replication has actually taken place. Thus an administrator can quickly determine whether everything is fine with replication on the server, and if not, check the relevant log entries to determine the cause of any problems.

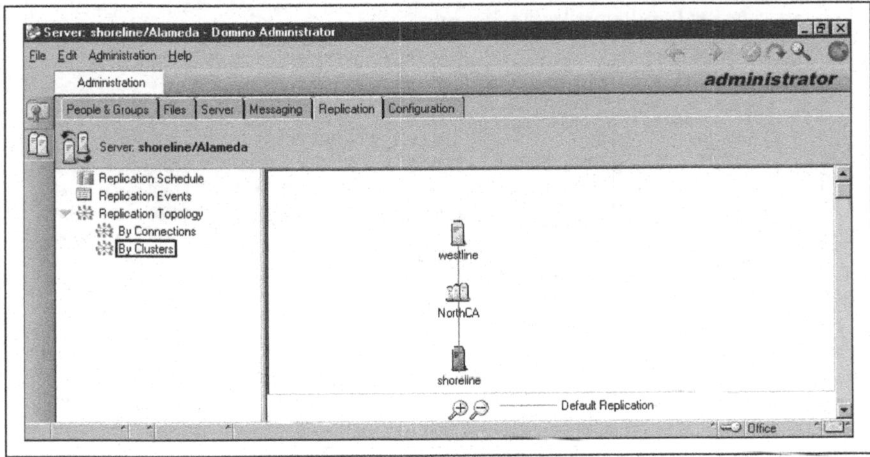

Figure 6-7: Domino Administrator page Replication tab

The Replication tab contains the following options:

Replication Schedule
: Shows a graphical representation of the replication schedule of this server with others. It lists each server this server is scheduled to replicate with, and uses colors to represent whether replication has been successful with these servers. In this way, the administrator can graphically see if any of this scheduled replication requires any further attention to determine why replication is not occurring as intended.

Replication Events
: Shows the Replication Events view of the Log database on the server in question. Here the administrator can check into the details of why scheduled replication may not be occurring, as illustrated by the Replication Schedule option listed previously.

Replication Topology

Offers two selections (By Connections and By Clusters) to graphically show the configured replication topologies. The information here shown graphically is extracted from the Domino Directory on the server by the **Maps** task.

Configuration Tab

The Configuration tab contains an assortment of configuration options, as shown in Figure 6-8—mainly in the Domino Directory, but also including configuration options from the Directory Catalog database, the Directory Assistance database, Statistics and Events database, and the DECS Administrator database.

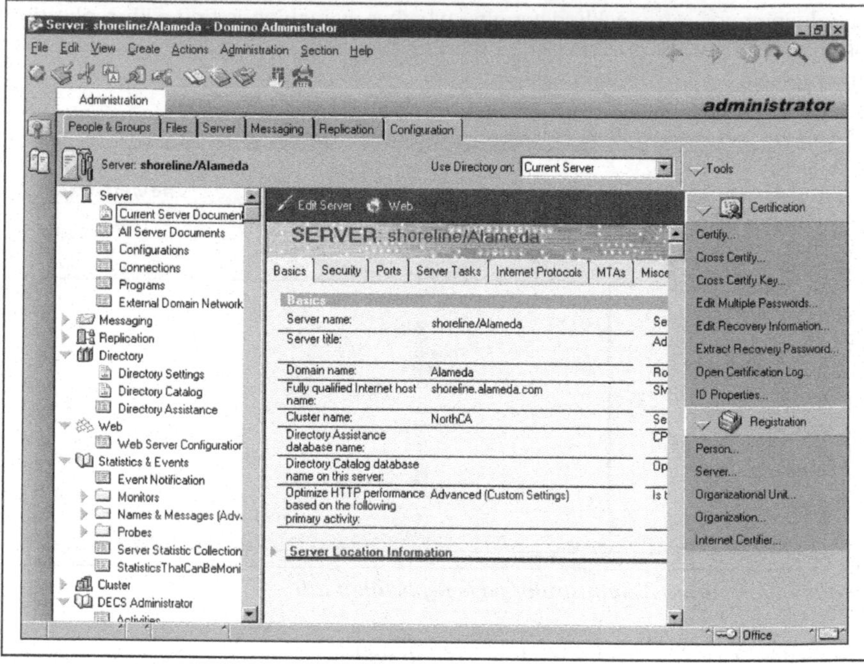

Figure 6-8: Domino Administrator page Configuration tab

The Configuration tab contains the following options:

Server

Lists a few key documents from the Domino Directory: the current Server document as well as all Server documents, the Configuration Connection, and Program and external Domain Network Information documents that refer to the current server being administered.

Messaging

Lists a number of documents from the Domino Directory that relate to messaging. These include Domain documents, Connection documents, and Configuration documents.

Replication

Lists Connection documents from the Domino Directory.

Directory

Shows a number of configuration documents relating to directories: the LDAP configuration for the Domino Directory, the configuration document from the Directory Catalog (if it exists), and the configuration document from the Directory Assistance database (if it exists).

Web

Shows web configuration documents from the Domino Directory: realm, virtual server, and virtual directory configurations.

Statistics and Events

Shows the contents of the Statistics and Events database: monitors, probes, and statistics for collection documents. (This feature is discussed in greater detail in Chapter 7.)

Cluster

Shows views relating to management of Domino clusters, and is displayed even if you don't have any clusters defined.

DECS Administration

Shows the connection and activity definitions from the DECS Administrator database. DECS is discussed in greater detail in Chapter 9, *DECS*.

Miscellaneous

Shows a few views from the Domino Directory that don't belong anywhere else: the Certificates view, the Licenses view, and the Holidays view.

There are a number of tools here that are mainly used to work with certifiers.

Certification

This area deals with the certifier ID files and the user ID files Domino uses for public key/private key authentication and contains the following options:

Certify

Used to recertify an ID that is about to expire, or to change the password quality information or the alternate language information. Specify the certifier you wish to use for the ID, and enter the password for this certifier, then the name of the ID file to recertify. Then select which options of the ID file to change.

Cross-Certify

Used to cross-certify an ID with another so that the identity of the other organization/organizational unit/server/user being cross-certified can be trusted.

Cross-Certify Key

Used to cross certify an ID without actually receiving a copy/safe copy of the ID. Here you enter the fully qualified name of the ID you are cross-certifying as well as the public key of that ID, and this is added to the Server → Certificates view in the Domino Directory.

Edit Multiple Passwords

Used to add multiple passwords to a certifier, which is used when the security of the certifier is paramount. Each Administrator who can access the ID is added to the ID, and they must enter a password for this ID. You can also specify how many of these administrators must be available to open the certifier.

Admin Tools

Edit Recovery Information

After you select the certifier file you wish to update, you can add administrators to the certifier who are able to perform ID recovery for user ID files that are subsequently created with this ID.

Extract Recovery Password

Used as part of the ID recovery process. Select this option, then select the copy of the ID file you are recovering, then enter your administrator password. This displays a special administrator password used to unlock the ID.

Open Certification Log

Opens the certification log (*CERTLOG.NSF*) on the server.

ID Properties

Allows any ID (certifier, user, or server) to be opened—you must know the password—and the properties displayed. Among the many options available here are the ability to create a safe copy for use with cross-certification or to change the password.

Registration

This area contains the following options:

Person

Launches the User Registration dialog, in the same way that the Person → Register tool does. (User Registration is covered in the next section of this chapter.)

Server

Creates the Server document for the new server and an ID file for the server using a given certifier (which you must select first). Multiple servers can be entered at once; when finished, you select the register button and they are all created at once.

Organizational Unit

Creates an organizational unit certifier underneath a given organization or organizational unit certifier.

Organization

Creates an entirely new organization certifier. You must use cross-certification between resources in each organization in order for them to trust each other.

Internet Certifier

Creates x.509 certificates for clients from your trusted Certificate Authority key ring file.

User Registration

User Registration is the process by which you create users, either by entering them one by one manually within the Registration dialog, by the Import Text file option (covered in the next section), or by the migration agents from Exchange, cc:Mail, or GroupWise by selecting the Migrate People option. I am assuming that you have entered the data within the Registration panel (reached by Domino Administrator → People and Groups tab → People → Register, or Domino Administrator → Configuration → Register → Person.

There are either Basic or Advanced options available for user creation. Here, we're using the Advanced options. At the end of this section, I'll cover which of these are available for the Basic option.

After you select the option, you are asked for the password for the most recently used certifier (which is stored as the entry `CertifierIDFile=` within *NOTES.INI* on the Administration Client machine). If you want to use a different certifier, select Cancel, then select the certifier from the Select File dialog presented. Again, in this case you will be asked for the certifier password before you can proceed to register a user.

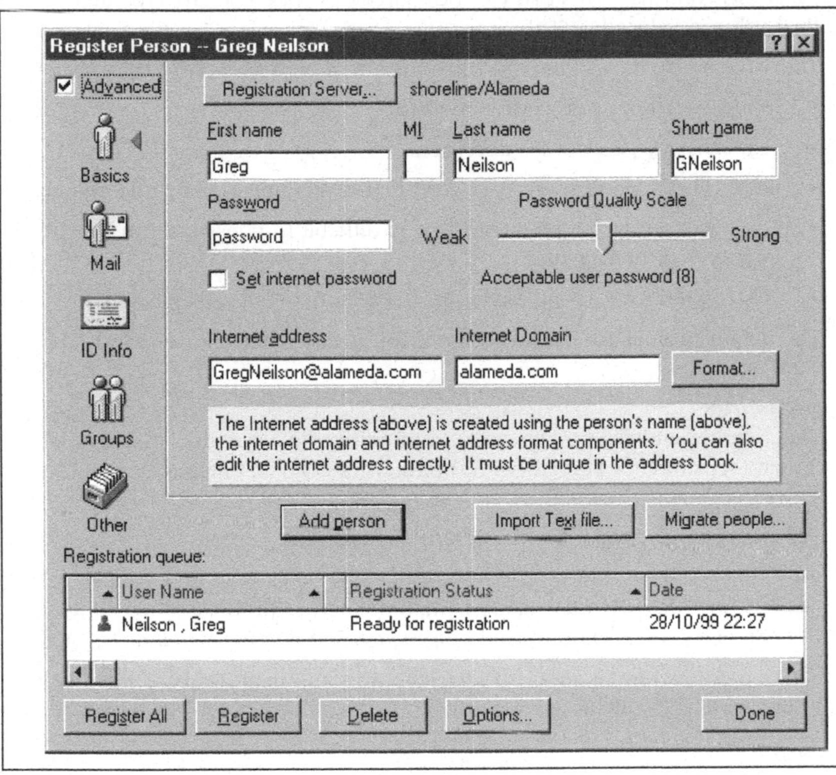

Figure 6-9: Registration option Basics tab

The Basics tab is shown in Figure 6-9. The fields are as follows:

Registration Server
: The server on which the Domino Directory will be updated for the created Person record.

First name, Middle initial, Last name, Short name
: Defaults to first initial+last name. Change this field if the default is not suitable. The short name must be unique within the Domino Directory.

Admin Tools

Password

Specifies the initial password for the created ID. It must be suitable for the selected password quality scale value used; otherwise, the user creation will fail.

Password quality scale

A value between 0 and 16 that defines how unique the password must be for this ID. Knowledge Base article 175962 describes how this value is calculated. The starting value of a password is its length, and then a bonus of 25% is added if the password includes any one of mixed case, numbers, and punctuation. A bonus of 50% is added if there are two or more. Then, if the password contains words that can be searched by a dictionary-type attack, the final value is reduced.

The same article draws these conclusions about the password quality scale:

- 0 means that no password is required.
- 1 means any password is accepted.
- 2–6 will produce a weak password that can be guessed by trial and error.
- 7–11 will produce a password that is difficult to guess but can be vulnerable to a dictionary attack.
- 12–16 produce a strong password the user may not remember.

The defaults values for password are 0 for a server, 8 for a user, and 10 for a certifier.

Internet address

The Internet address for the user, combining the username in the selected format (see entry for Format) with the Internet Domain entered.

Internet domain

The domain name to be used to create the address.

Format

Defines how the Notes username is manipulated to produce an email address (for example, Greg Neilson could be *greg.neilson, gneilson, neilson_g,* etc.).

The Mail tab (shown in Figure 6-10) specifies how the mail database for this user should be created. The fields are as follows:

Mail Server

Specifies on which server the mail database will be created.

Mail system (Lotus Notes/Other Internet/POP3/IMAP/Other/None)

Defines whether a mail database is created at all. For the Other Internet and Other options, a forwarding address is specified and no mail database is created. For the None option, no mail database is created. Otherwise, a mail database is created for the user. The default Mail System type is Lotus Notes.

Mail file template

Specifies which mail template to use for the created mail database. The default is *MAIL50.NTF.*

Mail file name

The default is to create it under the mail subdirectory and use the user short name as the database name. Use this field if you wish to use something different from the default.

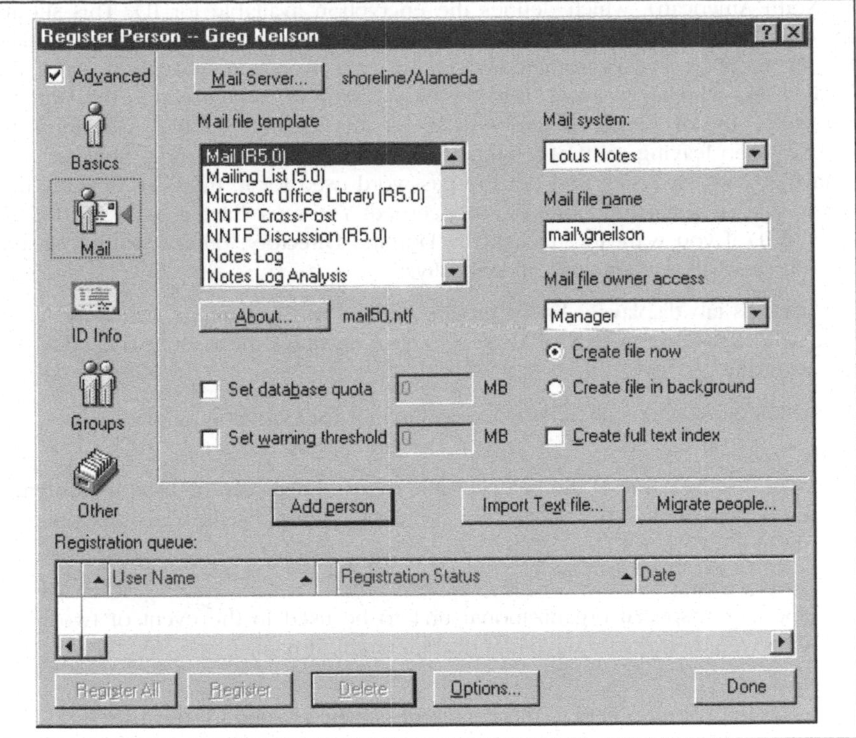

Figure 6-10: Registration option Mail tab

Mail file owner access
: Determines what access will be added to the Database Access Control List for the user. The default is Manager. However, you may want to change this because the default means that the user can delete their own mail database.

Create file now/Create file in background
: Controls when the mail database is created. If you create it now it will take longer, and this is particularly noticeable when many users are created at once. The background option uses the `AdminP` task, which is described in more detail at the end of this chapter.

Create full text index
: Creates a full text index on the mail database.

Set database quota (in MB)
: Sets the maximum allowable size of the mail database before the user can no longer make updates, although mail can still be received.

Set database threshold (in MB)
: Specifies when warnings will be issued to the log database indicating that the mail database is approaching the quota.

In the ID Info tab, you can specify which certifier to use for the creation of the user (this should be correct, since you specified this when you launched the Registration dialog). You can also specify the security type for the user ID (International or North American), which defines the encryption available for ID. This should match the type of Notes client that user has installed. The default expiration date for the ID is two years from today. Lastly, you are asked what to do with the created ID—whether to attach it to the new Person document within the Domino Directory, and/or which directory to create the created ID file. You must be careful when leaving an ID file attached to the Domino Directory—any user can detach it, and once they find out the password used for it, they can become that user, as far as Notes and Domino is concerned. You must have a password for the created ID if you want to attach it the Domino Directory; otherwise the registration process will not complete successfully.

The Groups tab displays a list of groups defined in the Domino Directory. From here you can select which of these groups you want the user to be added to automatically.

The Other tab contains miscellaneous options for user creation:

Setup Profile
: Specifies the name of the Setup Profile to use. These can be used to configure the setup of the user Notes environment. (Setup Profiles are described in detail in Chapter 8.)

Unique Org unit
: Specifies a special organizational unit to be used in the event of two users who would otherwise have identical hierarchical names.

Location
: Adds the Location field to the Person document created for this user.

Local Administrator
: Adds the Administrators field to the Person document, and the person specified (if he has author access to the Domino Directory) then has update access to the created Person document.

Comment
: Added to the Comments field in the created Person document for this user.

Alternate name language
: Creates an alternate (non-English) language name for the user. This specifies the language to be used. This field and also the alternate name and alternate org unit can be used only if the certifier ID being used to create the user has been defined with an alternative language.

Alternate name
: Specifies the alternate name for the user in the native language.

Alternate org unit
: An OU level to distinguish between two users who have the same name and are created by the same certifier.

Windows NT user name
: Use this field if you want the NT username created at the same time you register the Domino user.

Add this person to Windows NT group
: If you are creating a new NT user, this option allows you to add the created user to this NT group.

The Basic option has only two tabs, Basics and Groups. The Groups option is identical to that from the Advanced option. The Basics tab requires only the selection/entry of:

- Registration Server
- First Name
- Middle Initial
- Last Name
- Short Name (defaults to first initial + last name)
- Password

User Registration from a Text File

There are two ways to create users via a text file. The first is the Person → Register From File option from the menus of Domino Administrator. This provides a GUI dialog that can be used to set the common details of all of the created users:

- Registration Server
- Set internet password
- Password Quality Scale
- Setup Profile
- Internet domain
- Address name format
- Mail server
- Mail template
- Mail file directory
- Mail file owner access
- Set database quota
- Create file now/Create file in background
- Set warning threshold
- Create full text index
- Certifier ID
- Security type (North American /International)
- Certificate Expiration Date
- Alternate name language
- Store user ID in address book and/or in directory
- Assign users to groups
- Local administrator
- Add NT User account(s)
- Windows NT group name

The second method is Domino Administrator → Registration panel → Import Text File. Here all the values must be entered in the text file or else these values take on their default value. You can edit the entries for each person and resave them into the registration queue, or confirm that the import file has been interpreted as expected and the file values are displayed correctly in the correct field on the screen. From here, some or all of the users can be created at once.

The *NOTES.INI* variable **BatchRegFile=** can be used to specify the default location of the text file on the Administration client machine, although you have the option to use a different file when you start either method. The default separator between each field is a semicolon. You can change this by adding an entry for **BatchRegSeparator=** to *NOTES.INI* on the Domino Administrator client machine.

When using the Registration panel option, those users not created and having errors are left within the queue, with an error message that can help determine what the problem was.

See Table 6-1 for a list of **BatchRegFile** fields.

Table 6-1: Text File Fields

Parameter Order	*Parameter*	*Comments*
1	Last name	Required.
2	First name	Optional user first name.
3	Middle initial	Optional user middle name.
4	Unique OU	Special OU to be added to the hierarchical name for this user to distinguish between two users with the same name.
5	Password	Required
6	ID file directory	The default is to attach the ID to the created Person record within the Domino Directory. This is considered by many to be a security exposure, since anyone can detach that ID and impersonate that user if they know the password.
7	ID file name	The default is the user's short name.
8	Mail server name	The server that will contain the mail database.
9	Mail file directory	The default is *\mail.*
10	Mail file name	The default is the user's short name.
11	Location	Added to the Location field, which is on the Work/Home tab, Work page on the created user's Person document. This entry is displayed to the user when addressing mail to users with the same name.
12	Comment	Added to the Comments field, which is on the Misc tab on the created user's Person document.

Table 6-1: Text File Fields (continued)

Parameter Order	Parameter	Comments
13	Forwarding address	Added to the Forwarding Address field within the Mail tab of the created Person document. The forwarding address automatically forwards all intended for this user to this designated forwarding address.
14	Profile name	The name of the setup profile used for creation and maintenance of the user environment.
15	Local adminis-trator	Added to the Administrators field within the Administration tab of the created Person document. If this person has author access to the Domino Directory, they can update this Person Document.
16	Internet address	Internet mail address for user.
17	Short name	Defaults to the user's first initial plus last name, up to a maximum of 8 characters, and must be unique within the domain. Therefore, in most environments you will probably want to make an entry here, since this is also used as the filename for the created mail file.
18	Alternate name	Used when creating a user with an alternate name in another language (this can only be used if the certifier being used to create the ID has an alternate language added to it).
19	Alternate OU	An OU level to distinguish between two users who have the same name and are created by the same certifier.
20	Mail template filename	Defaults to *MAIL50.NTF* if not entered.

Be careful when using the Mail template filename option. It is probably a bug and may be fixed in future releases; using the 5.0.1a Admin client, the mail files were created with an ACL entry granting the user No Access (and therefore you need to correct their ACL access manually later!). You should also add your Domino Admin groups to each created database manually after creation. Recall Domino Administrator provides the ability to select multiple databases to make an ACL change.

Admin Tools

Web Administrator

When the **HTTP** task is run on the Domino server for the first time, it automatically creates the Web Administration database (*WEBADMIN.NSF*) from a template. This database can be used by authorized administrators to manage the Domino server from a web browser. It deliberately uses a different replica ID on each server so that it cannot be replicated across servers. During creation of this database, the contents of the Administrator field of the Server document determine who has manager access and can access this Web Administration database to work with the server. If for any reason this database is deleted, the HTTP task recreates it next time it is started on the server.

This database application can be invoked by opening *http://servername/webadmin.nsf* from your Java-enabled browser. The application consists of a number of Java applets that allow you to manage the server; this is the main limitation of using this tool, which was first introduced with version 4.6. If you attempt to use this tool to manage the server, you will often find stability problems with the Java virtual machine used within the browser. In many cases, this causes the browser to crash. Unfortunately, like all client-side Java applications, this is an area that Lotus has no control over. Figure 6-11 shows the Web Administrator as launched.

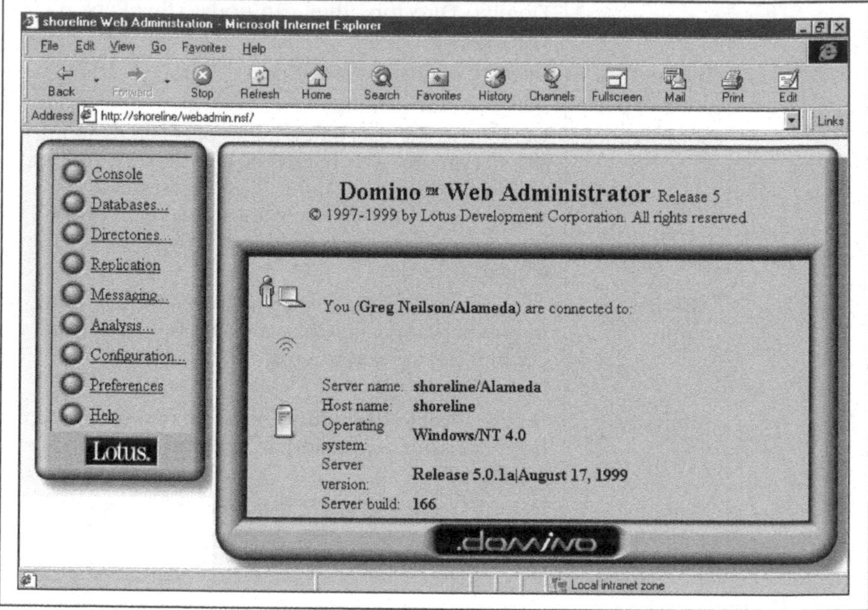

Figure 6-11: Domino Web Administrator at startup

The options listed down the lefthand side allow you to perform the following tasks:

Console
: Display the Domino server console in real time, and allows you to enter console commands.

Databases
: Create a new database from a template, look at database usage and size information, run database maintenance tools against a database, change the database ACL, browse the database catalog, and view clustering information.

Directories

Add/edit People documents or group documents within the Domino Directory. This does not mean you can register users with this tool, which is probably its greatest limitation.

Replication

Look at replication events from the server's log database.

Messaging

View the current status of messaging on the server, look at past routing activity from the log database, check the shared mail status, view a mail status report, or issue an ad-hoc mail tracking request.

Analysis

Work with the contents of the server's log database, statistics and events, and alerts.

Configuration

Create or edit documents from the Domino Directory including Server documents, Connection documents, Program documents, Web Configuration documents, and Domain documents. Also, browse or edit text files on the server.

Preferences

Set the preferred Domino Directory, as well as the type of user interface (dropdown, button, or plain) used for the web administration tool. The interface type defines how the various configuration options are presented to the user. The *button interface* option is shown in Figure 6-11, with the options shown as buttons down the lefthand side within a frame. The *dropdown interface* presents the options in a dropdown list at the top lefthand side of the screen. The *plain interface* simplifies the dropdown interface by not using frames and having the dropdown list as another field within the screen. You can also view the environment information from the server and client, as shown in the following code, which is a sample of the information returned here, and which would appear to be of most use to the IRIS developers for debugging, but could also be useful to determine what information is being passed from the browser to the server (browser type and version and MIME types that are accepted):

```
Template revision: 104
Tool revision: 104
Tool status: Up to date
Server software: Lotus-Domino/5.0.1
Server protocol: HTTP/1.1
Server port: 80
Server name: shoreline
Remote_User: CN=Greg Neilson/O=Alameda
Remote_Host:
Remote_Addr: 10.0.0.2
Path_Info: /webadmin.nsf/$shared/preferences?OpenDocument&ExpandSection=1
HTTP_User_Agent: Mozilla/4.0 (compatible; MSIE 4.01; Windows NT)
HTTPS: OFF
```

```
HTTP_Accept: application/vnd.ms-excel, application/msword, application/
vnd.ms-powerpoint, image/gif, image/x-xbitmap, image/jpeg, image/pjpeg,
*/*
Auth_Type: Basic
```

Help
: Launches the Domino Administration Help option in a separate browser window. You can view topics in order, via the Index, or perform searches.

There are a number of roles defined within the Web Administrator database that can be used to selectively grant access to specific parts of this client. By default all of these roles are granted to Server Administrators within the Domino Directory. These are:

ServerAdmin
: Enables all the Console, Analysis, Messaging, and Directories options. All Configuration options are available except access to text files on the server.

ServerMonitor
: Enables the Messaging, Replication, and all Analysis options, except viewing `AdminP` requests.

DatabaseAdmin
: Enables all of the Database options and the people and groups parts of the Directories option.

FileRead
: Enables the ability to read text files from the Configuration option.

FileModify
: Enables the ability to read text files from the Configuration option.

Using the Administration Process (AdminP Task)

The Administration Process automates many administrative tasks and greatly simplifies life for the administrator. This tool is used by Domino to perform tasks such as:

- Creating, moving, and deleting user mail files
- Renaming users and groups and recertifying IDs
- Updating server documents with build and network port information

Databases have an *Administration Server* property that can point to any server within the domain. This is defined on the Advanced tab of the Database ACL property page; it is the server on which the `AdminP` task manages this database. In particular, the correct configuration of the Administration Server for the Domino Directory is very important, since much of the work `AdminP` does relates to this database.

You must have hierarchical IDs to use `AdminP`. It doesn't work with flat IDs created with Notes 2.x and older versions, although it can be used to recertify a flat organization with a hierarchical one.

By default, the first server in the domain is the *Administration Server* of the Domino Directory, although you may wish to later change this to another hub server within your replication design. The main database used for the Administration Process is the *Administration Requests (R5.0)* database (*ADMIN4.NSF*). As other servers are added to the domain, when the **AdminP** task is run on these servers, a replica copy of this database is created on the server.

To make use of the **AdminP** function to do recertifications and name changes, you need to create the *Certification Log* database (*CERTLOG.NSF*) before you register the users. This database keeps a record of each created user and the certifier used to create the user's ID file, and should be originated on the server used to register the users.

All databases on every server should have the Administration Server configured on them, although you might want to make exceptions for databases such as the Domino help and release notes databases, since these are not updated in general use. You can check which databases have the Administration server configured by issuing the **tell adminp show databases** command on each server console in the domain. The following code is an abbreviated example of the output from this command. We are particularly interested in those databases under the heading "These databases have no Administration Server designated." Recall from the Domino Administrator discussion that you can select multiple databases within Domino Administrator in the Files tab and make a change to all selected databases by using the "Manage ACL option" to configure an Administration Server. (Note that the linebreaks in the following code example are not actual, but occur here artificially due to the width of pages in this book.)

```
> tell adminp show databases
10/05/99 09:07:43 PM  These databases have shoreline/Alameda designated as
    their Administration Server.
10/05/99 09:07:48 PM  Title: cca File name: cca.nsf
10/05/99 09:07:48 PM  Title: Certification Log File name: certlog.nsf
10/05/99 09:07:48 PM  Title: Alameda Directory Catalog File name: dircat.nsf
10/05/99 09:07:48 PM  Title: Notes Log (shoreline/Alameda) File name: log.nsf
10/05/99 09:07:50 PM  Title: Greg Neilson File name: mail\gneilson.nsf
10/05/99 09:07:55 PM  Title: Matthew Neilson File name: mail\mneilson.nsf
10/05/99 09:07:56 PM  Title: Susan Neilson File name: mail\sneilson.nsf
10/05/99 09:07:56 PM  Title: Timmy Neilson File name: mail\tneilson.nsf
10/05/99 09:07:57 PM  Title: Object Store for shoreline File name: mailobj.nsf
10/05/99 09:07:57 PM  Title: Object Store for shoreline File name: mailobj1.nsf
10/05/99 09:07:57 PM  Title: Alameda's Address Book File name: names.nsf
10/05/99 09:07:57 PM  Title: Reports for shoreline/Alameda File name: reports.
    nsf
10/05/99 09:07:57 PM  Title: Object Store for shoreline File name: shared.nsf
10/05/99 09:07:58 PM  These databases have specified that the Administration
    Process maintain the names in their Readers and Authors fields.
10/05/99 09:07:59 PM  These databases have no Administration Server designated.
10/05/99 09:07:59 PM  Title: Administration Requests (R5.0) File name: admin4.
    nsf
```

There are a number of changes **AdminP** can make that require approval by an Administrator before they can be processed. Therefore, you must check the Pending Administrator view daily for requests requiring approval. Approvals are

Admin Tools

needed for accepting administration requests from other domains, deleting databases, deleting shared calendar resources, moving users to a different organization hierarchy, and deleting private design elements when the user who created them has been deleted. You should also check the "All Errors by Date" and "All Errors by Servers" views regularly for any errors encountered by `AdminP`.

Chapter 13 lists a number of options available in the `TELL ADMINP` console command to control the processing of `AdminP` on a server.

Cross-Domain Administration

This is a new feature that allows you, as an Administrator, to create administration requests for another domain, which are mailed to the Administrative Server of the other domain. This feature requires that both Administration Servers be running Domino 5.x.

There are two parts to the configuration required to enable this function. The first part is to update/create the Domino Directory Profile. The last field on this profile lists the administrators who are able to make Cross-Domain Configuration documents within the Administration Requests database. Then, in the Administration Requests database (*ADMIN4.NSF*), you must create and configure a Cross-Domain Configuration document. This document specifies whether requests can be inbound and/or outbound, who can make requests, who can approve requests, what requests are allowed, and what domains can be used to send requests to/from. The types of requests that can be completed across domains are:

- Create database replica
- Delete person in the Domino Directory
- Delete server in the Domino Directory
- Move database replica
- Rename person in the Domino Directory
- Rename server in the Domino Directory

CHAPTER 7

Monitoring Domino

In this chapter, I discuss the various methods Domino provides for system administrators to monitor the health of their Domino networks. These methods can be used to proactively monitor the system and advise when action is needed as well as review the server activity history to understand what happened and when.

Several different types of activity can be monitored, such as database ACL changes, database activity and space usage, replication success or failure, and Domino server statistics. When one of these monitored activities occurs, you have a number of methods to notify the administrator that action may be required. A new R5 feature called *probes* extends this set of tools to include periodic checks that a specific server resource is available.

With R5, you can also now monitor the delivery of mail. Therefore you can query whether a specific mail message was delivered and summarize this data to provide administrators with information about mail usage on the server.

There are also the various log databases and files that show in detail the Domino server activity history. Some of these are not enabled by default; you can use settings in *NOTES.INI* to control the amount of the log output for the specific components within the server, as described later in this chapter.

Domino Administrator, described in Chapter 6, *Domino Administration Tools*, also has a number of options to graphically monitor the status of the servers within your Domino server network.

Statistics and Events

A *statistic* is defined in Domino to be the status of a server component, which is continuously updated as the server runs. For example, the number of current users on the server is a statistic called Server.Users. In Domino, an *event* is defined as occurring when something happens on the server, an example of which is replication with another server. (See "Events," later in this chapter.)

Monitors

Domino provides the ability to advise administrators that things have happened (or worse—not happened!) on the server. You can configure Domino to monitor changes in database ACLs, replication status, database usage information, and when Domino statistics have reached a configured threshold.

Figure 7-1 illustrates the architecture of how Domino works with statistics and events.

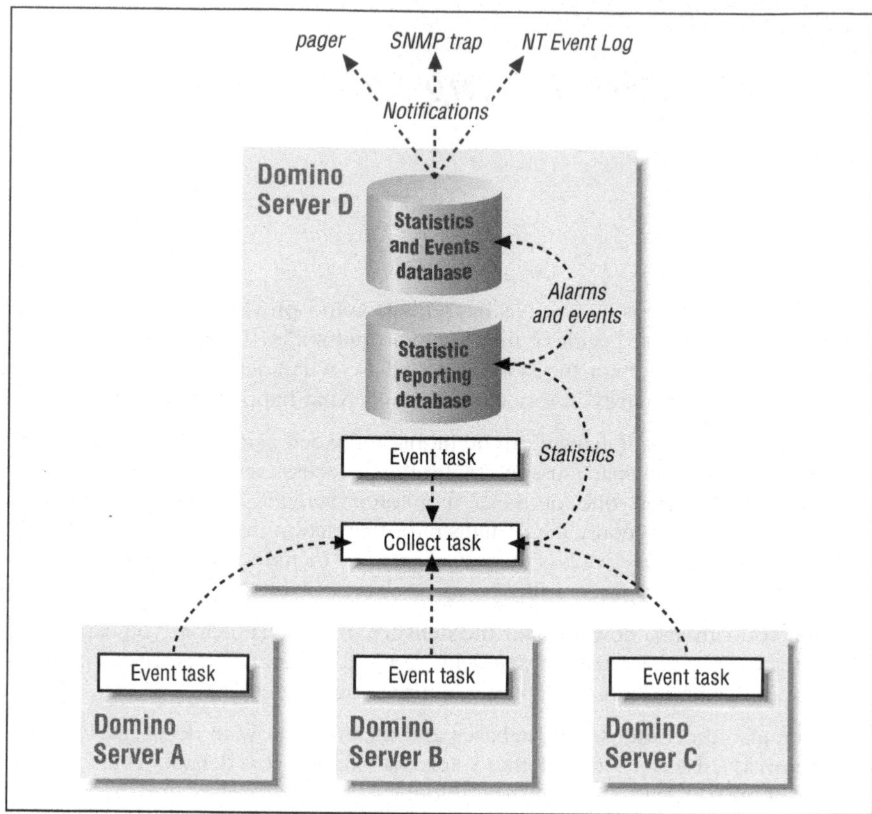

Figure 7-1: Statistics and events architecture

The `Event` task is run on each Domino server to be monitored. Then, on a server designated to collect statistics, a *Server Statistic Collection* document is created within that server's *Statistics and Events* database (*EVENTS4.NSF*). The `Collect` task runs on this server, collecting the server statistics from the defined server(s) within the domain and periodically writing the data into the *Statistics and Reports* database (*STATREP.NSF*).

Within the Statistics and Events database are any defined statistic monitors, which are the configured thresholds for any of the server statistics. If any of these thresholds are crossed, an *alarm* is created within the Statistics and Events database. The first time an alarm is created for a particular statistic, it generates an *event*, which can be configured to notify the system administrator via a number of methods (pager, SNMP trap, NT event viewer, and so forth). Until the alarm is cleared (for example, the statistic falls below the configured threshold), an event is created daily, also within the Statistics and Events database.

When you create a *Server Statistic Collection* document, you specify which server in the domain is to collect the statistics from this document. Then you can elect to have it collect from all servers in the domain, from all servers that are not already listed to be configured, or for specific named servers.

Options also define the statistic collection behavior. By default, Domino doesn't log statistics to a database, so you must enable this feature in the document in order to have the statistic monitoring operational for these servers. Then you can select the name of the mail-in database to send the statistics to (the default is *STATREP.NSF*, and you shouldn't need to change it). The two other options allow you to change the intervals between statistic report collections and each statistic alarm to be generated. In both cases the default is 60 minutes, and the minimum value available is 15 minutes.

You can produce several different reports and graphs within the Statistics Reports database. Figure 7-2 shows a statistic report from a server at a specific collection time. The entire report scrolls down over five screens to show the status of everything on the server at the time the statistics were collected. Figure 7-3 shows a graph of system loads for the two servers being monitored by this server.

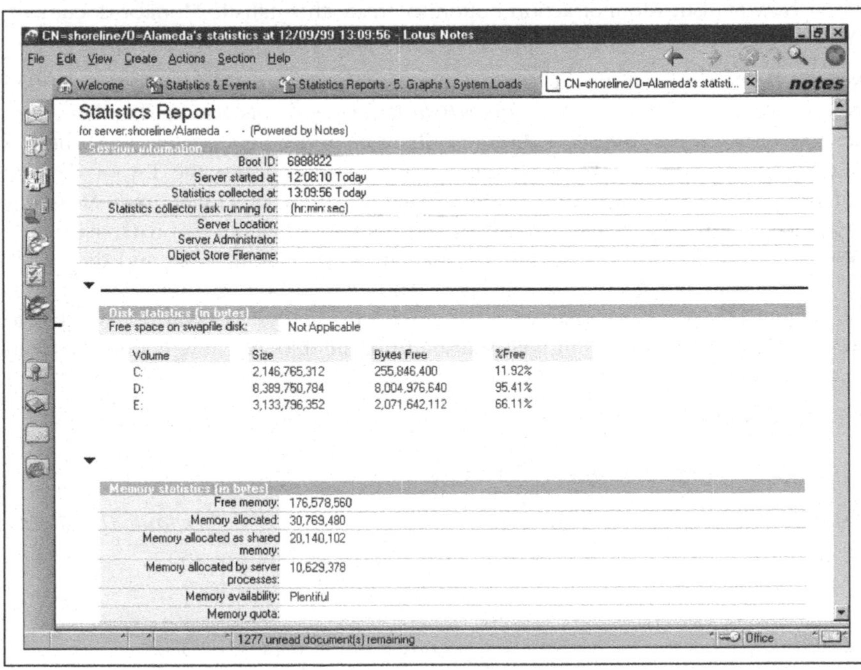

Figure 7-2: Statistic report

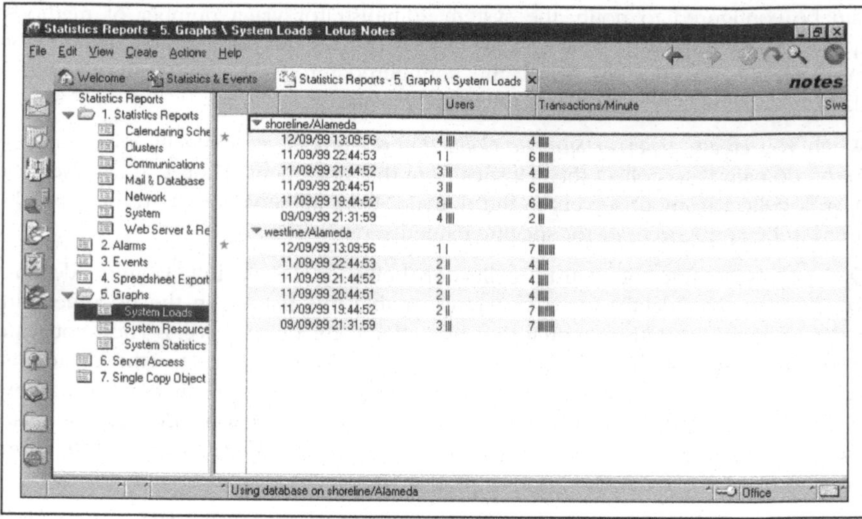

Figure 7-3: Graph of system loads for servers collected

Now that the server statistics have been collected, you can specify the statistics to monitor and set the threshold for each. This configuration is done within the Statistics and Events database on the monitoring server. Select Monitors → Statistics → New Statistic Monitor action button to create the Statistic Monitor document. (You can also choose Create → Monitor → Statistic from the menus.)

Not all the defined statistics within Domino can be monitored—some are defined as templates, such as *NET.<Portname>.BytesReceived*; others have a flag that signifies that they are not useful for statistic collection; and others contain text, such as Domino.BuildName and Domino.BuildVersion. You can see the list of defined statistics in the Statistics and Events database under Names and Messages (Advanced) → Statistic Names. However, a hidden view within this database called ($Statistics) filters out the template statistics, those containing text, and those that are classified as not useful for collection. Therefore, if any changes are made to the defined statistics, or if new ones are added manually, you will not be able to create a Statistic Monitor using that statistic until this hidden view within the database is rebuilt.

Table 7-1 lists the default Domino server statistics that can be monitored.

Table 7-1: Statistics Available to be Monitored

Statistic	*Meaning*	*Default Threshold*
Comm. NumOldSessionsClosed	Number of sessions closed by the server to accommodate new users	>50
DataBase.DbCache. CurrentEntries	Number of entries in the database cache	>300
DataBase.DbCache. MaxEntries	Maximum number of entries in the database cache	>100

Table 7-1: Statistics Available to be Monitored (continued)

Statistic	*Meaning*	*Default Threshold*
Disk.C.Free	Percentage of available space on C: drive	10%
Disk.D.Free	Available space on D: drive in bytes	<10,000,000
Disk.E.Free	Available space on E: drive in bytes	<10,000,000
Disk.F.Free	Available space on F: drive in bytes	<10,000,000
Disk.G.Free	Available space on G: drive in bytes	<10,000,000
Disk.H.Free	Available space on H: drive in bytes	<10,000,000
Disk.I.Free	Available space on I: drive in bytes	<10,000,000
Disk.J.Free	Available space on J: drive in bytes	<10,000,000
Disk.K.Free	Available space on K: drive in bytes	<10,000,000
Disk.L.Free	Available space on L: drive in bytes	<10,000,000
Disk.M.Free	Available space on M: drive in bytes	<10,000,000
Disk.Swapdisk.Free	Available space on drive with swap disk	<10,000,000
Disk.SYS.Free	Available space on NetWare server SYS volume in bytes	<10,000,000
Disk.Vol0.Free	Available space on NetWare server volume 0 in bytes	<10,000,000
Disk.Vol1.Free	Available space on NetWare server volume 1 in bytes	<10,000,000
Disk.Vol2.Free	Available space on NetWare server volume 2 in bytes	<10,000,000
Disk.Vol3.Free	Available space on NetWare server volume 3 in bytes	<10,000,000
Domino.Command.Login	Count of Login URLs processed by Domino	>100
Domino.Command.OpenDatabase	Count of OpenDatabase URLs processed by Domino	<300
Domino.Requests.Per1Day.Peak	Peak number of Domino requests over the past day	>1000
Domino.Requests.Per1Day.Total	Total number of Domino requests over the past day	>1000
Domino.Requests.Per1Hour	Number of Domino requests over the past hour	>1000

Table 7-1: Statistics Available to be Monitored (continued)

Statistic	*Meaning*	*Default Threshold*
Domino.Requests. Per1Hour.Peak	Peak number of Domino requests over the past hour	>1000
Domino.Requests. Per1Hour.Total	Total number of Domino requests over the past hour	>1000
Domino.Requests. Per1Minute	Number of Domino requests over the past minute	>25
Domino.Requests. Per1Minute.Peak	Peak number of Domino requests over the past minute	>1000
Domino.Requests. Per1Minute.Total	Total number of Domino requests over the past minute	>1000
Domino.Requests. Per5Minute	Number of Domino requests over the past five minutes	>150
Domino.Requests. Per5Minute.Peak	Peak number of Domino requests over the past five minutes	>1000
Domino.Requests. Per5Minute.Total	Total number of Domino requests over the past five minutes	>1000
Domino.Requests.Total	Total number of Domino requests received	>150
Mail.Dead	Count of undeliverable mail in the server's mail boxes	>5
Mail.Delivered	Count of mail delivered to other servers and users	>1000
MailTotalRouted	Count of mail delivered to other servers	>2000
Mail.TransferFailures	Count of mail that the server was unable to transfer to other servers	>10
Mail.Transfer	Count of mail that the server has attempted to transfer to other servers	>1000
Mail.Waiting	Count of mail that the server is still to transfer to other servers	>5
Mail.WaitingRecipients	Count of mail that the server is still to move to mail boxes on the server	>300
Mem.Allocated	Memory in bytes allocated to the server	>24,000,000
Mem.Allocated.Process	Non-shared memory in bytes allocated by server processes	>10,000
Mem.Allocated.Shared	Memory in bytes allocated as shared memory	>20,000
Mem.Free	Memory available in bytes free to be allocated to the server	<5,000,000

Table 7-1: Statistics Available to be Monitored (continued)

Statistic	*Meaning*	*Default Threshold*
Mem.SwapFileSize	Size of system swap file in bytes	>20,000,000
MTA.ccMail.Dead	Count of undeliverable mail within the cc:Mail MTA inbound and outbound queues	>10
MTA.ccMail. TransferFailures	Count of transfer failures by the cc:Mail MTA	>10
MTA.Smtp.Dead	Count of undeliverable mail within the SMTP MTA inbound and outbound queues	>10
MTA.Smtp. TransferFailures	Count of transfer failures by the SMTP MTA	>10
MTA.X400.Dead	Count of undeliverable mail within the X.400 MTA inbound and outbound queues	>10
MTA.X400. TransferFailures	Count of transfer failures by the X.400 MTA	>10
NNTP.Articles.Posted	Count of NNTP articles posted	>100
NNTP.Articles.Sent	Count of NNTP articles sent	>100
NNTP.Bytes.Received	Count of bytes received via NNTP	>10,000
NNTP.Bytes.Sent	Count of bytes sent via NNTP	>10,000
NNTP.Pull.Articles. Failed	Count of articles that failed to transfer during pull feeds of NNTP	>20
NNTP.Pull.Articles. Offered	Count of articles available during full feeds of NNTP	>1,000
NNTP.Pull.Articles. Requested	Count of articles requested during pull feeds of NNTP	>1,000
NNTP.Pull.Articles. Transferred	Count of articles transferred during pull feeds of NNTP	>1,000
NNTP.Push.Articles. Failed	Count of articles that failed to transfer during push feeds from NNTP	>20
NNTP.Push.Articles. Offered	Count of articles available during push feeds from NNTP	>1,000
NNTP.Push.Articles. Requested	Count of articles requested during push feeds from NNTP	>1,000
NNTP.Push.Articles. Transferred	Count of articles transferred during push feeds from NNTP	>1,000
Replica.Docs.Added	Count of documents added from replication	<<1
Replica.Docs.Deleted	Count of documents deleted from replication	>1000

Table 7-1: Statistics Available to be Monitored (continued)

Statistic	*Meaning*	*Default Threshold*
Replica.Docs.Updated	Count of documents updated from replication	<<1
Replica.Failed	Number of replication attempts that were unsuccessful	>3
Replica.Successful	Number of replication attempts that were successful	<<1
Server.Sessions.Dropped	Count of user sessions dropped mid-session	>5
Server.Users	Count of users currently using the server	>300
SMTPMTA.ConvFailures	Count of SMTP conversion failures	>10
SMTPMTA.Dead	Count of dead SMTP messages	>10
SMTPMTA.TransFailures	Count of SMTP transmission failures	>10
Web.Retriever.URLs. Failed	Count of URLs that the web retriever failed to retrieve	>10

Creating a statistic monitor is straightforward. In the Basics tab, select the server(s) to monitor and the statistic to be monitored (Table 7-1). Then, on the Thresholds tab, select the threshold number and choose whether to monitor the statistic above, below, or times a multiple of the entered threshold.

On the Other tab, you can enable or disable the monitoring of this statistic, set the severity of this statistic monitor, and set up the event notification profile for this event. The available severity levels for the monitor are Normal, Warning (low), Warning (high), Failure, and Fatal. (See "Events," later in this chapter.)

The other monitor types are even simpler. They are created in the same way as the Statistic Monitor and all have an Other tab, like the Statistic Monitor. The ACL Monitor document lists the file name of the database to monitor and the server on which it is to be monitored. The Replication Monitor document lists the servers to monitor, the file name of the database to be replicated, which servers they are supposed to replicate with, and a replication timeout (the default is 24 hours).

The File Monitor can monitor user activity and/or unused space within the specified database. On the Basics tab, specify which servers within the domain to monitor and the filename of the database to be monitored. Select whether to monitor for unused space within the database or user inactivity. One or both of these must be selected. As each is selected, the appropriate configuration tab—Unused Space or Unused Activity—is created for display in the document.

When the check for unused space is enabled, the Unused Space tab is created within the File Monitor document. Here you can specify the percentage of unused space within the database at which to trigger the monitor and whether you want the `Compact` task to run against the database automatically when this unused threshold is reached. In practice, it would be better to run `Compact` as a regularly scheduled task overnight on the server. Otherwise, **Compact** could potentially be triggered at any time during the day, perhaps slowing the response time for all users on the server. If the database uses the R4 ODS format (using an .NS4 file extension, as discussed in Chapter 3, *Domino Databases*), users will be locked out from accessing this database until the **Compact** task is completed.

When the check for user inactivity is enabled, the User Inactivity tab is created within the File Monitor document. Here you can set the cycle time for monitoring user activity on the database (day and/or week and/or month) and how many sessions with the database must be established at each interval for the event to be triggered. This can be used to detect underused or unused databases on the server that might be candidates for deletion after further analysis is undertaken.

Probes

Probes, another new R5 feature, enable you to check regularly that the Domino servers in your network are still available and functioning correctly. If the configured probe is not able to access the desired server resource, an Event is created. In this way, you can actively manage your Domino network, and not wait for users to inform you of any problems. Probes also maintain response time information for server access; this information is kept as server statistics.

Probes can be created to check periodically whether:

- A Domino server can be accessed or a specific database can be opened.
- Mail can be sent to a mailbox on a remote Domino server. Domino servers can also be configured to self-probe a local mailbox.
- A server (which doesn't have to be a Domino server) can be accessed by any or all of the DNS, FTP, HTTP, IMAP, LDAP, NNTP, POP3, and SMTP ports. (Domino doesn't by default provide FTP services, but this is part of the NetObjects Fusion Connector, if installed.) For HTTP and NNTP, there is also the option to fetch a URL (HTTP) or send a command to execute (NNTP) as well.

To use probes, you must have the **RunJava ISpy** task running on the server, so ensure that this task is listed in the **ServerTasks=** line in *NOTES.INI*.

Probes are configured in the Statistics and Events database (*EVENTS4.NSF*) on the Domino server. There is a Probe wizard available when the database is opened, or a new probe document can be created and the information manually entered. The only advantage to using the wizard is it launches the Event Notification Wizard after the probe has been created, thus ensuring your newly created probe is acted upon accordingly if an event is created because of a failure to access the desired network resource. Alternatively, when creating the probe manually, you can create a new notification profile by pressing the button called "Create a new notification profile for this event," which then launches the Event Notification Wizard.

Table 7-2 lists the server response time statistics available from each type of probe.

Table 7-2: Probe Statistics Created for Server/Resource Access

Probe Type	*Option*	*Resulting Statistic*
Domino Server	N/A	Server.*probeserver.destserver*
Mail	Self-probe	QOS.Mail.ISpy on *server*.ResponseTime
	Mail on other server	QOS.Mail.*recipient*.ResponseTime
TCP	DNS	QOS.DNS.*server.event*.ResponseTime
	FTP	QOS.FTP.*server.event*.ResponseTime
	HTTP	QOS.HTTP.*server.event*.ResponseTime
	IMAP	QOS.IMAP.*server.event*.ResponseTime
	LDAP	QOS.LDAP.*server.event*.ResponseTime
	NNTP	QOS.NNTP.*server.event*.ResponseTime
	POP3	QOS.POP3.*server.event*.ResponseTime
	SMTP	QOS.SMTP.*server.event*.ResponseTime

Following is a sample of the statistic output from a test Domino server. You can see the canonical names for servers and the recipient for testing Domino mail are used. The response times are reported in milliseconds, and the event number is the same as that for the defined probe that tests for the availability of that network resource. A value of –1 means that the probe was unsuccessful. If you are running Domino on the NT platform, these statistics are available for charting in NT's Performance Monitor. Appendix A, *Domino/Windows NT Integration*, discusses the Performance Monitor in more detail. The statistical output sample follows:

```
QOS.DNS.CN=westline/O=Alameda.GNEN-4BGQ3J.ResponseTime = -1
QOS.FTP.CN=westline/O=Alameda.GNEN-4BGQ3J.ResponseTime = -1
QOS.HTTP.CN=shoreline/O=Alameda.SHOE-4A95T4.ResponseTime = 70
QOS.HTTP.CN=westline/O=Alameda.GNEN-4BGQ3J.ResponseTime = 251
QOS.IMAP.CN=shoreline/O=Alameda.SHOE-4A95T4.ResponseTime = 60
QOS.IMAP.CN=westline/O=Alameda.GNEN-4BGQ3J.ResponseTime = 110
QOS.LDAP.CN=shoreline/O=Alameda.SHOE-4A95T4.ResponseTime = 50
QOS.LDAP.CN=westline/O=Alameda.GNEN-4BGQ3J.ResponseTime = 80
QOS.Mail.CN=Greg Neilson/O=Alameda.ResponseTime = 5
QOS.Mail.ISpy on shoreline.ResponseTime = 0
QOS.NNTP.CN=shoreline/O=Alameda.SHOE-4A95T4.ResponseTime = 60
QOS.NNTP.CN=westline/O=Alameda.GNEN-4BGQ3J.ResponseTime = -1
QOS.POP3.CN=shoreline/O=Alameda.SHOE-4A95T4.ResponseTime = 10
QOS.POP3.CN=westline/O=Alameda.GNEN-4BGQ3J.ResponseTime = 10
QOS.SMTP.CN=shoreline/O=Alameda.SHOE-4A95T4.ResponseTime = 20
QOS.SMTP.CN=westline/O=Alameda.GNEN-4BGQ3J.ResponseTime = -1
Server.CN=shoreline/O=Alameda.CN=shoreline/O=Alameda = 10
Server.CN=shoreline/O=Alameda.CN=westline/O=Alameda = 10
```

Probes are most useful in a multiserver Domino environment. In this way, you can set up automated checks to ensure that all managed Domino servers are up and functioning. In a single-server environment, it is likely that if the server crashed, then so too would the function to run these probes.

Events

Now that you have configured your monitors and probes, you should configure how you want to be notified when a particular `event=` occurs. We've seen that there is an enormous range of what can be monitored, but you must first determine what Domino services are important enough to monitor. These might include specific web services (HTTP or POP3), whether mail can be accessed on the server, or whether replication of specific databases occurs within a desired interval. Otherwise, you can waste significant system resources to collect all of this information, and even worse, be notified of so many events from the server that you are unable to determine what exactly is important or what can be ignored.

Three types of events are available for notification:

- An event that matches a criterion, such as one specifying a given message, a given priority, or a specific type.
- A built-in task or task event. There are several thousand defined system events available from the Statistics and Events database within the Names and Messages (Advanced) → Events Messages by Text view.
- Information from a specified custom monitor or probe (as defined in the previous sections of this chapter).

Event notification is configured within the Statistics and Events database (*EVENTS4.NSF*). You can select Create → Event Notification from the menus, or you can select the Event Notification view → New Event Notification action button.

The Basics tab defines the type of event trigger. The types of events available relate to discrete components of Domino server function, which can be Unknown, Comms/Net, Security, Mail, Replica, Resource, Misc, Server, Statistic, Update, Database, Network, Compiler, Router, Agent, Client, Addin, Adminp, Web (HTTP, HTTPS), News (NNTP), FTP, and Directory (LDAP).

When the event notification is set to match a built-in task or event, the Event tab looks like Figure 7-4. The option available here is to select any message, or alternatively a specific message, from the list.

When the event notification is set to match a custom probe or monitor, the Event tab contains a dropdown list of all available probes or custom monitors defined within the database for you to select from.

The last tab, the Action tab, is the same for all types of event notifications. Table 7-3 lists the available notification methods and their uses. Note that you also have the option to enable/disable notification and to enable notification only during specific hours, which you may wish to correspond to your scheduled support hours.

Having covered statistics, probes, and events, it is worth briefly discussing the wizards available with the Statistics and Events database.

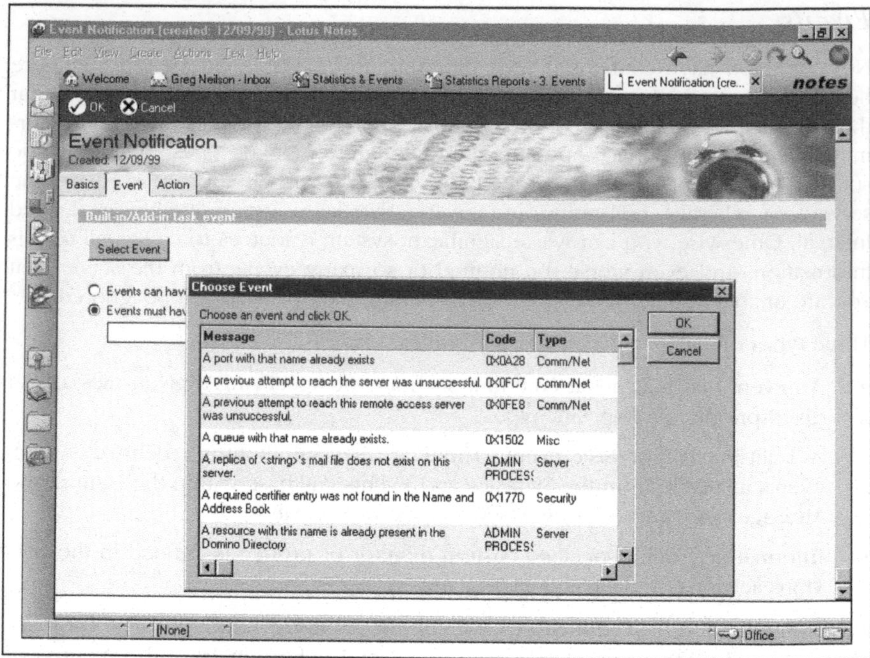

Figure 7-4: Event Notification page Event tab (when matching a built-in task or event)

Table 7-3: Event Notification Methods

Notification Type	*Use*
Broadcast	Broadcasts a message to all connected users or to a list of specified users.
Log to a database	Logs to a specified database on the server on which the event occurred, or to a specified server. Typically this would be to *STATREP.NSF*.
Mail	The name of the user(s) or mail-in databases to send the message to.
Log to NT Event Viewer	When running Domino on Windows NT, this method can write events to the NT Application Log, so that the events can be seen using NT's Event Viewer.
Pager	The alphanumeric address to send a pager message to.
Run program	Runs the specified program on the server on which the event occurred, or to a specified server.
Relay to another server	The name of the server within the same domain and using a common network protocol to relay the event to and have it write to the *STATREP.NSF* database.
SNMP trap	The name of the network management machine used to send an SNMP trap to.
Log to Unix system log	Writes the events to the Unix system log.

Wizards

Figure 7-5 shows the database opened with the Statistics and Events Setup Wizards view.

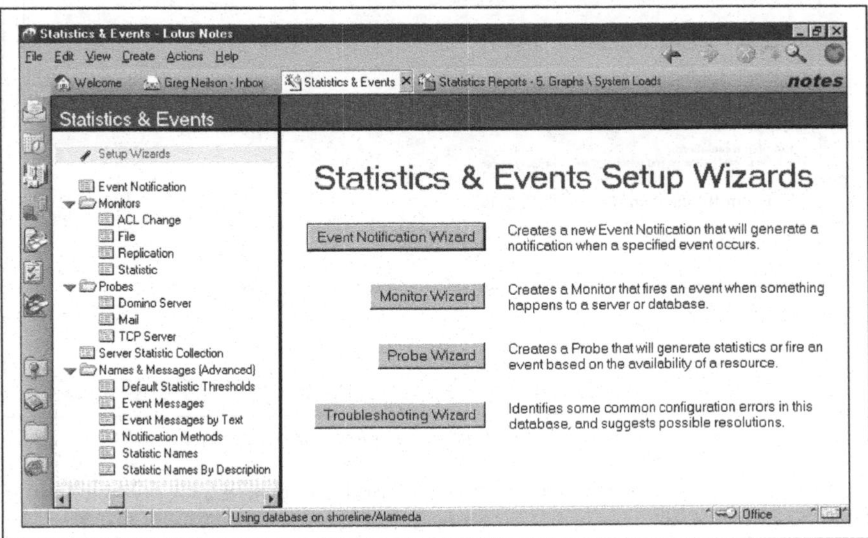

Figure 7-5: Statistics and Events wizards view

In most situations, these wizards are not particularly useful. You must understand the basic concepts involved in order to set them up, and all the wizards do is present a series of dialog boxes that guide you through the creation of the appropriate document. In all cases, when there is a list of options to select, the choices are the same for both options, so you do not gain a great deal.

The one wizard worth running after you have created all of your monitors, probes, and event notifications is the Troubleshooting Wizard. This wizard checks all the documents you have entered and cross-checks them against one another where appropriate. This can be a big help in avoiding potential problems in the future. Figure 7-6 shows some sample results from this wizard after I deleted some custom statistic monitor documents but not their event notifications.

Mail Tracking

Mail Tracking is a new feature introduced with R5. It keeps track of the work of the server `Router` task, and at a configured interval, records this information to the Mail Tracking Store database (*MTSTORE.NSF*). This database is generally not accessed directly by users or administrators, but the data held here can used in three ways:

- A user can elect to track the status of a message he is sending.
- An administrator can track the status of any message.
- An administrator can create a mail usage report to summarize mail activity on the server.

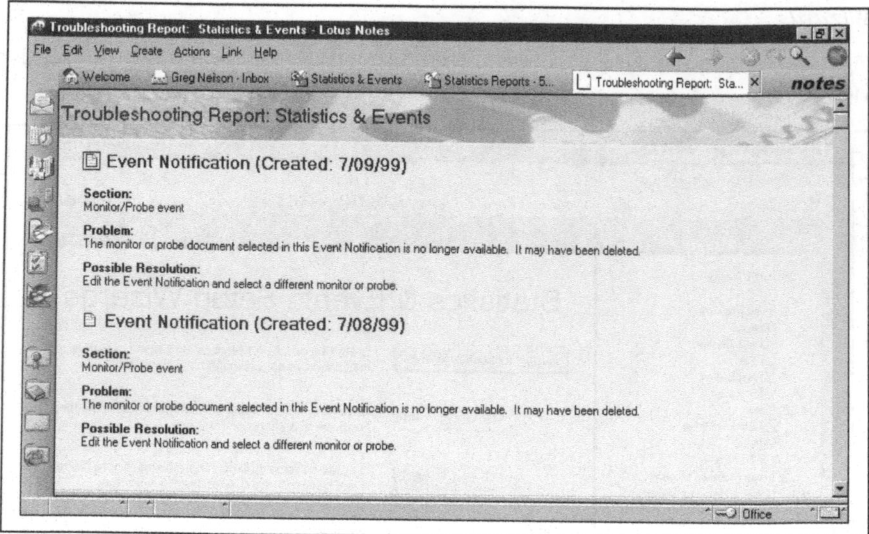

Figure 7-6: Statistics and Events database: Troubleshooting wizard results

Since this is a Domino feature, it can be used to track mail only within the Domino network. Internet mail, for example, can be traced only until the message leaves the last Domino server.

Keep in mind that mail *tracking* is not the same as mail *tracing*. Mail tracing is done to ensure that mail can be sent successfully to a given destination by a given user, but says nothing about whether a given piece of mail was able to reach the destination.

Enabling Mail Tracking

Disabled by default, Mail Tracking is enabled via a Configuration document in the Domino Directory. This document can be created for all servers within the Domino Domain, for a particular group of servers, or for any particular server. However, if you do enable this feature, you should do so for all servers that route mail within the enterprise; otherwise, tracking requests will not be able to track all mail successfully across the enterprise.

Figure 7-7 shows the appropriate section of the Configuration document (under the Router/SMTP tab).

When message tracking is enabled, it takes effect next time the `Router` task is started, which automatically launches the `MTC` (Message Tracking Collector) task on the server. By default, every 900 seconds (15 minutes), router activity is logged to *MTSTORE.NSF*. Also, keep in mind that no one can query the status of a message until its details have been logged in the message tracking store database. When this monitor is enabled and running on a server, you can find out how long until the collected tracking information will be written to the database by issuing the `Show Tasks` (`SH TA`) command at the Domino console; this command will issue the following information:

```
MT Collector Idle, collection interval is 900 seconds, next collection in
350 seconds.
```

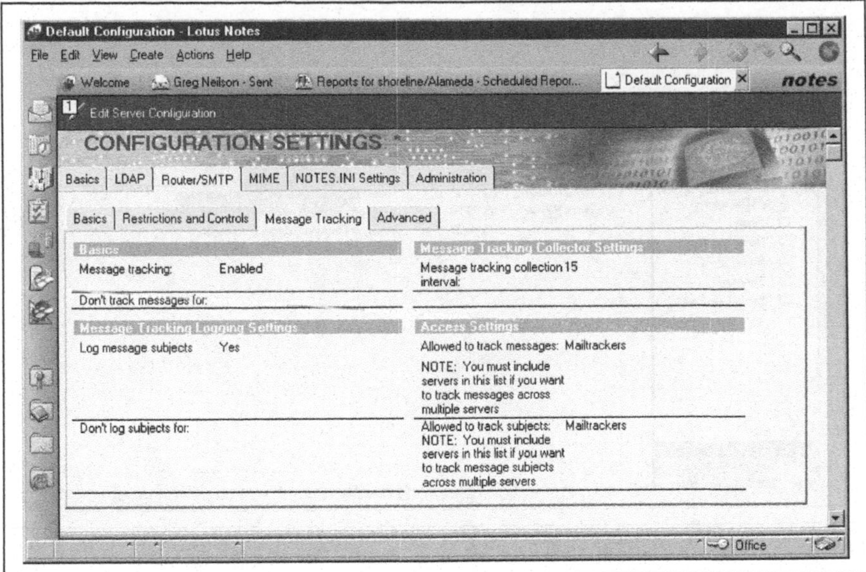

Figure 7-7: Enabling Mail Tracking via a Configuration document

You can use the Domino console command **TELL MTC PROCESS** to force the collected information to be written to the tracking database now.

You can elect whether to log the message Subject information, which is more information to track, but can make it easier to locate particular messages later.

When using mail tracing across multiple servers, you must configure the access settings for those allowed to track message and subjects; otherwise, users can track the status of messages on their home server only, which is not very useful. In these two fields, you can specify group names or the names of individual users who are permitted to track messages and subjects.

User-Requested Mail Tracking

Once this is enabled, users can track the status of mail they have sent. When the mail database is opened at the Sent view, you can select a message, and from the Tools menu, select the option to Send a Tracking Request, as shown in Figure 7-8.

The user is then presented with a short dialog box in order to select how the message tracking is to operate. The user must select the recipient of the message to track (if the message was sent to more than one recipient, then all recipients will be listed and available for selection). The user can also elect to receive only information about delivery status, which is the default, or he can trace the entire path from the user's mail server to the recipients'. Typically, users will be interested in ensuring only that the message was delivered to the recipient, not in tracing the message through each server within the path.

The user receives his answer via a mail message. If he elected to trace the entire path, the message will look something like the following example. You can see

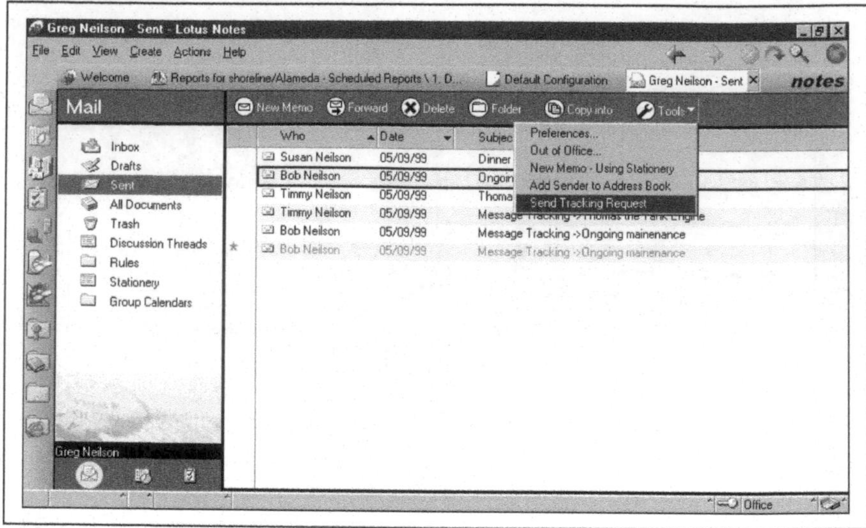

Figure 7-8: User-Requested Mail Tracking

that the message was transferred from *SHORELINE* to *WESTLINE* and that the message has not been read by the user:

```
Tracking response information:
Tracking Response - SHORELINE/ALAMEDA - 5/09/99 16:46:05
    Message to: Bob Neilson/Alameda@alameda Transfered WESTLINE/ALAMEDA
at: 5/09/99 15:52:10
Tracking Response - WESTLINE/ALAMEDA - 5/09/99 16:46:07
    Message to: Bob Neilson/Alameda@ALAMEDA Viewing Status: Unread  at:
5/09/99 15:50:46
```

If the user elected for delivery status only, he will receive a message that contains only the following:

```
Tracking response information:
Tracking Response - WESTLINE/ALAMEDA - 5/09/99 16:02:45
    Message to: Bob Neilson/Alameda@ALAMEDA Viewing Status: Unread  at:
5/09/99 15:50:46
```

Mail Tracking with Domino Administrator

Administrators can trace any message on their servers, and if they are enabled to trace mail across servers, they can track the entire path of a message within the Domino environment.

To start a mail tracking request, in the Messaging tab of Domino Administrator, select Tracking Center → New Tracking Request button. This will bring up a dialog box shown in Figure 7-9.

Here the only information you must enter is how far back to search for tracked messages. The available options are Today, Yesterday, Last week, Last 2 weeks, Last month, and All times. The other fields are optional, but can reduce the number of sent messages returned by this query. Otherwise, even on the most

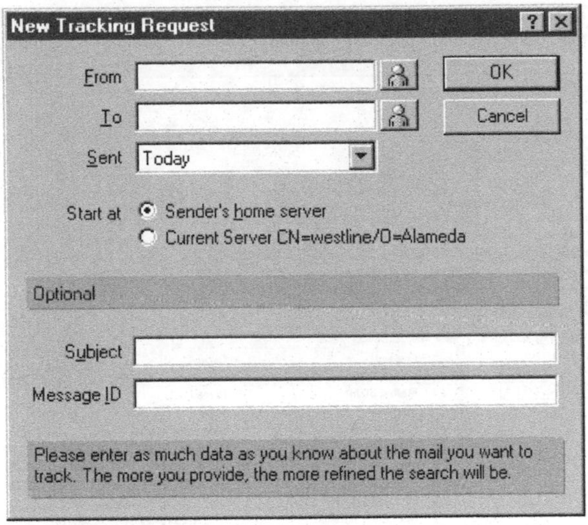

Figure 7-9: New Tracking Request

lightly loaded mail server, you can have hundreds of messages returned. Also, if you enable mail probes, then all of these messages are recorded by the mail tracking collector task and will appear in this list.

After the selection criterion has been entered, you are presented with a list of messages in the top list in this screen. Then, you can select a message from that list for more detailed tracking information (by selecting the Track Selected Message button), which returns the information displayed in the bottom two panels. Each server in the delivery path will be listed in the bottom lefthand panel, and when you select a server from this list, you will see the detailed status information for the message at that server. The display in Figure 7-10 shows that the message in question has been delivered but not yet opened by the recipient.

Mail Usage Reporting

Once the mail tracking information has been stored, you can elect to run scheduled reports that summarize the mail usage for a server. These reports are configured and the report results are stored within the Reports database (*REPORTS.NSF*). By default, any configured and enabled reports run at midnight. Weekly reports run on Saturdays, and monthly reports run on the first of the month.

Before you set up any reports to run, you should confirm that the background Java agents in the Reports database are actually enabled to run. To do this, you will need access to Domino Designer, the programming client for Domino. Open the Reports database and select the menu option View → Agents, which launches Domino Designer at the Agents view for this database. Figure 7-11 shows this view. In order for daily, weekly, and monthly reports to be run, these agents need to be enabled. If these agents are not enabled, click on the checkmark to enable them and save your changes.

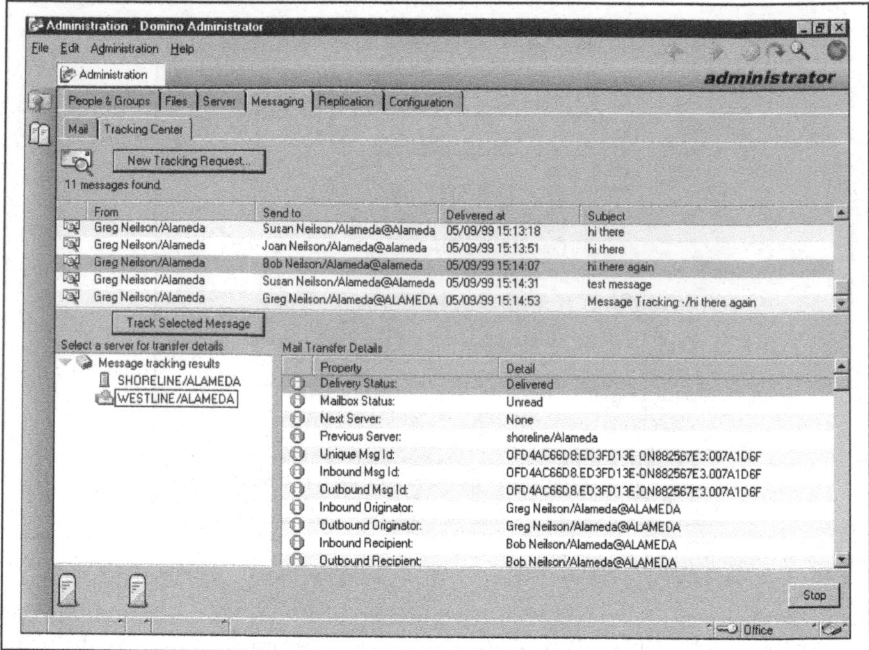

Figure 7-10: Tracking Request results

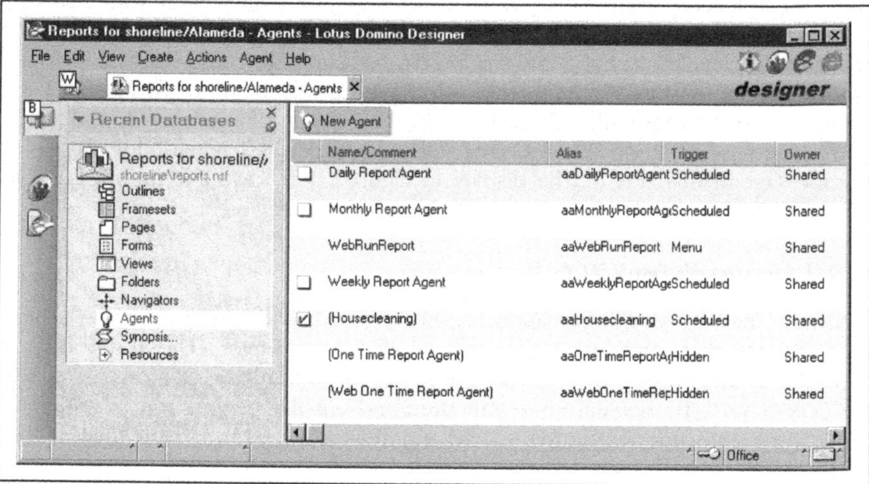

Figure 7-11: Reports Database, Agents View

By default, there are five reports that have been created but not enabled to run. These are:

Daily message status summary

For the previous day, this report graphs the number of messages sent by their status (delivered, not delivered, being processed).

Weekly message volume summary
This report is a day-by-day breakdown of the total number of bytes and messages sent.

Weekly 25 largest messages
This report identifies the sender, recipient, and size of the 25 largest messages from the previous week.

Monthly message volume summary
This report provides the same information as the daily message volume summary, but covers the last month.

Monthly message status summary
This report provides the same information as the daily message status summary, but covers the preceding month.

There are many other reports that can be created to run on the server. The available report types are:

- Top 25 users by count
- Top 25 users by size
- Top 25 senders by count
- Top 25 senders by size
- Top 25 receivers by count
- Top 25 receivers by size
- Top 25 most popular next hop
- Top 25 most popular previous hop
- Top 25 largest messages
- Message Volume Summary
- Message Status Summary

These reports can be used to identify the largest mail users on the server, and can help determine whether you are being subjected to large amounts of spam from Internet sources. You can then use the sender address details to block these senders from the Server by creating a Configuration Document in the Domino Directory. You can enter the domain name to be blocked in the "Deny messages from the following internet addresses/domains" field on the SMTP Inbound Controls page, under the Restrictions and Controls area of the Router/SMTP page.

You can create a custom report out of one of the basic types listed previously. It can be scheduled to run once, daily, weekly, or monthly. Like the Domino Administrator facility to search for messages, you can specify whether to report on data from today, yesterday, over the past week, over the past two weeks, over the last month, or on all available information. The completed report can also be configured to be written to the reports database ("Saved") and/or sent as a mail message ("Sent") to a specified user.

On the Conditions tab, you can specify that the report include only a given sender or recipient, a given delivery status (delivered, not delivered, or being processed), or messages greater than a given size. Mail that is not delivered represents a problem in your Domino environment. Many of the conditions, particularly the sender and recipient options, are more likely to be used to run ad hoc reports to better understand the mail usage on the Domino server. The status report information can be used to discover any problems in transferring mail within the Domino environment.

These reports can be a useful tool to understand the mail usage on the server and the growth in the number and size of messages. However, unless you intend to monitor the output from these reports, you are wasting both your time in setting them up and the system resources to produce and store these reports.

Log Databases and Files

The following sections describe how Domino handles the storage and display of log records.

Log Database

Domino server activity is logged in the log database, which usually has the name *LOG.NSF*. There are a number of *NOTES.INI* variables (listed in Chapter 14, *NOTES.INI*) that can control the amount of activity logged on the server. The defaults are fine for normal operation, but when you need to resolve an issue for a component of Domino (such as replication or mail routing) that is not operating as you would expect, you can change the appropriate values in *NOTES.INI* to produce more detailed diagnostic information.

The `LOG=` statement defines the name of the log database to use and how long to keep past log records. A number of other parameters are available to change the level of log activity for the different parts of Domino operation. These are:

- `Console_Loglevel`
- `Log_AgentManager`
- `Log_Dircat`
- `Log_MailRouting`
- `Log_Replication`
- `Log_Sessions`
- `Log_Tasks`
- `Log_Update`
- `Log_View_Events`
- `Passthru_LogLevel`
- `PhoneLog`
- `RTR_Logging`

These parameters are all described in Chapter 14.

The log database has a number of views available that categorize the information held in the database. These are:

Database sizes
: Lists all databases on the server sorted by size. Within each database document is the size of each view, a list of those with Manager access to the database, and the details of the database activity.

Database usage
: Lists database usage in date order for each database on the server.

Mail Routing Events
: Contains details of mail routing activity on the server.

Miscellaneous Events
: Contains everything that doesn't appear anywhere else. It also contains all of the Domino server console output.

NNTP Events
: Contains details about server connections and newsfeeds accessed if NNTP is running on the server.

Object store usage
: Contains details for each shared mail database about how many messages each user has within it, if shared mail is enabled.

Passthru connections
: Contains information about passthru sessions that are accessing this server.

Phone calls by date
: Contains phone call information (by this server and to this server) sorted by date.

Phone calls by user
: Contains phone call information (by this server and to this server) sorted by date.

Replication events
: Contains the details of the replication activity of this server with other servers, sorted by server and then by date. Each document in the view has details on what database were replicated, how many changes were made, and whether any problems were encountered.

Sample Billing
: Lists usage summary information by user and by date.

Usage By Date
: Details user database activity from each session, sorted by date and by user.

Usage by User
: Details user database activity from each session, sorted by user and by date.

Figure 7-12 through Figure 7-14 show the main types of log information you will likely be interested in using to solve any problems in your Domino network. These are Mail Routing, Replication, and Miscellaneous Events. Since most of the useful work that your Domino server does relates to mail routing or database replication, any analysis you do to understand what has or hasn't occurred within these areas will need to done by checking the log for Mail Routing and/or Replication events. Similarly, the Miscellaneous Events logs contain console output, the details of any console commands entered by administrators, and warning and error messages as they occurred at the server.

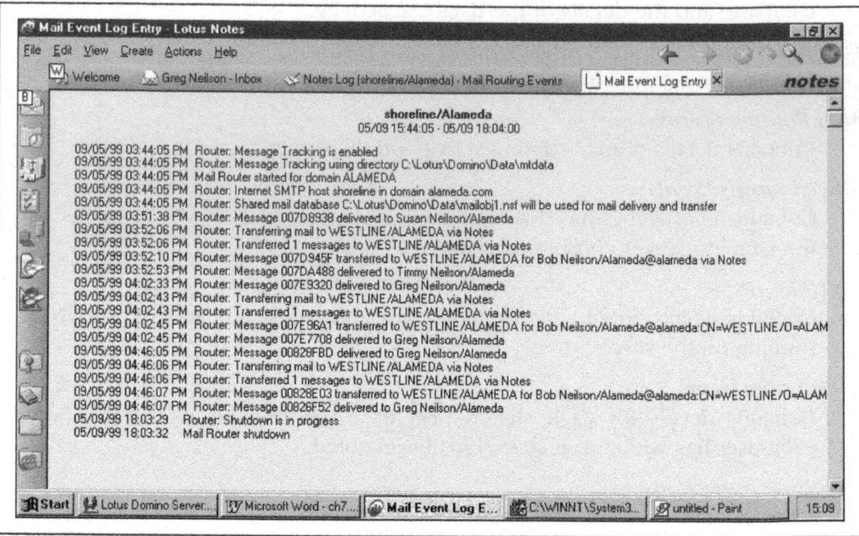

Figure 7-12: Domino Log database mail routing event

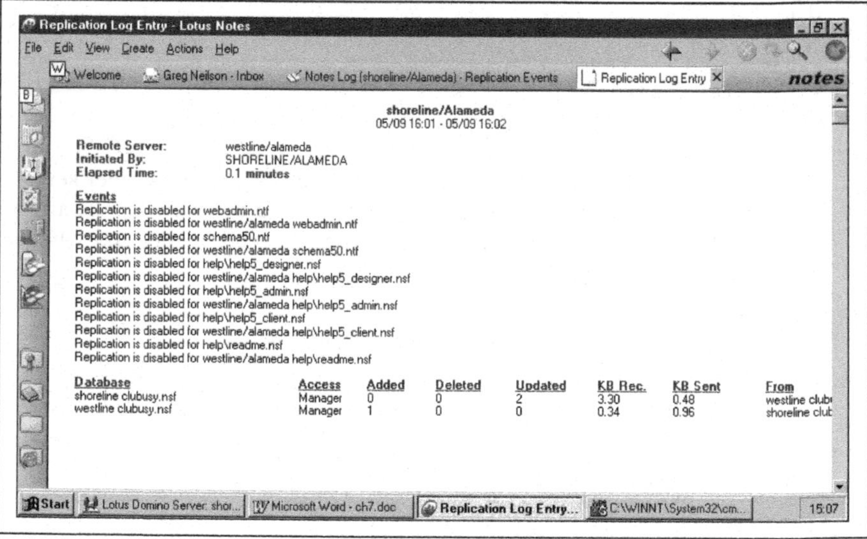

Figure 7-13: Domino Log database replication event

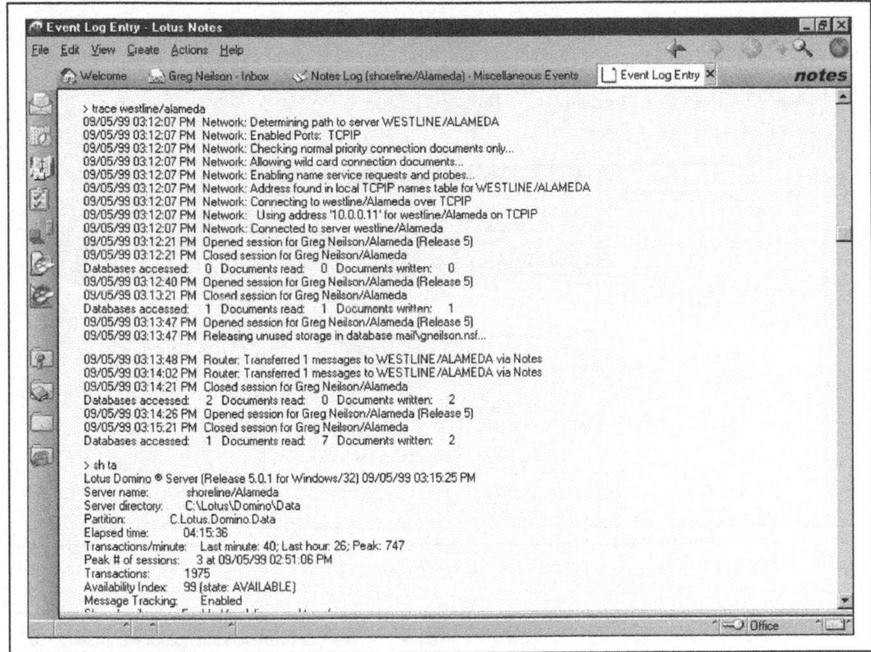

Figure 7-14: Domino Log database miscellaneous event

Domino provides a Log Analysis tool with Domino Administrator to enable fast searching of the log database. The output is typically written to the Log Analysis database (*LOGA4.NSF*) on the client machine used to create the query. To use this tool, select the Server tab of Domino Administrator → Tools → Analyze Log. Figure 7-15 shows the selection criteria for entries of interest within the Log database. Figure 7-16 shows the results within the Log Analysis database.

In this example, I am checking for logged events that relate to the Domino Directory (*NAMES.NSF*). In the analysis database, I find a list of events relating to this database in chronological order. We can see when replication was and wasn't able to complete with this database, and also error messages that were encountered due to access control problems.

Logging Domino HTTP Activity

Domino HTTP activity, if logged at all, is logged to totally different locations than is all other server activity. Logging for HTTP activity is by default disabled, but it can be configured to write to a database (*DOMLOG.NSF*) or to text files. This is configured under Domino Directory → Server document Internet Protocols tab → HTTP page, as shown in Figure 7-17.

The option to log to text files enables later processing by Perl scripts to summarize the information (count of hits, load distribution, and so forth) within the log files, and offers a performance benefit over logging to a Domino database. You

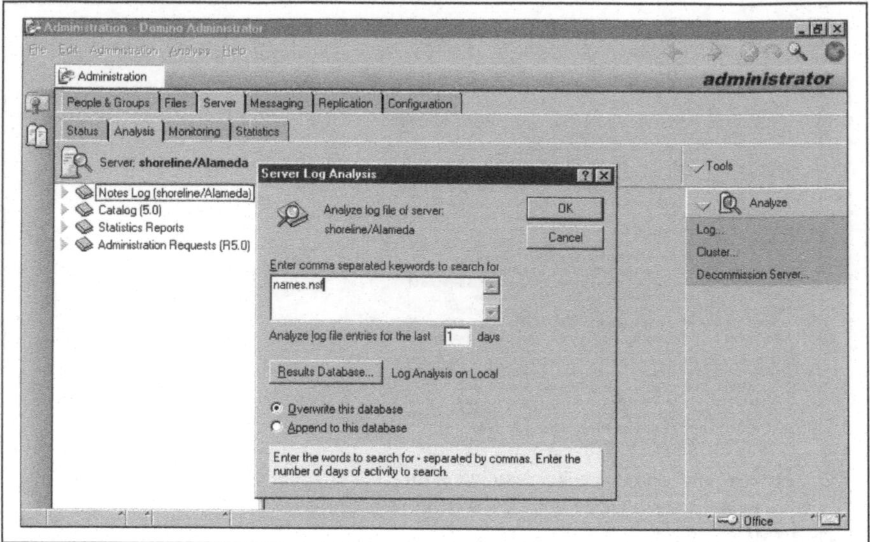

Figure 7-15: Server Log Analysis—creating the query

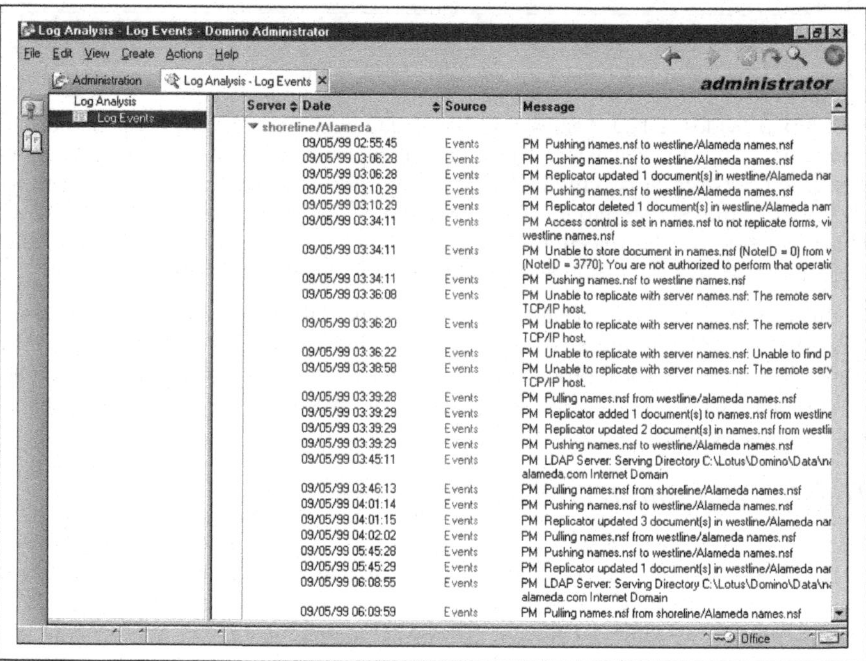

Figure 7-16: Server Log Analysis—viewing the output

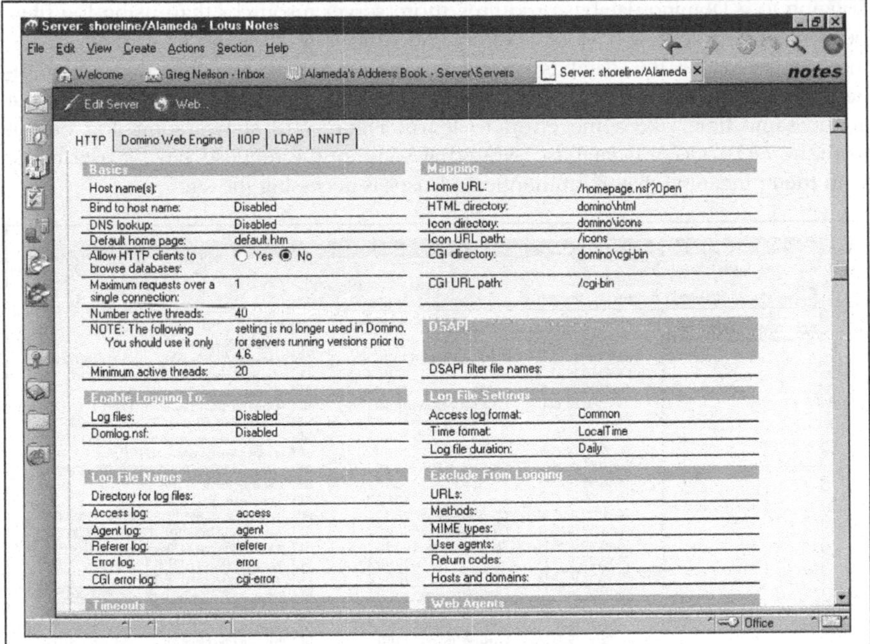

Figure 7-17: Server document—configuring HTTP logging

should log this information only if you need to keep and extract it later; otherwise it is better not to log HTTP activity at all. For example, at an intranet site, you are probably not overly interested in the number of hits, but at an Internet site, you are probably interested in hits and whether you have been subjected to any attempts to break into your site.

The log file directory name you enter on the Server document is created underneath the Domino data directory. The Agent and Referrer logs are created only when you use the Common access log format (as opposed to Common Extended). The default is to create new log files each day, so the log files have the file name of the filename prefix type (log, access, agent, referrer, error or cgi-error) plus *mmddyyyy.log*; for example, *access09061999.log*. Other options are weekly (*access_ _wwyyyy.log*), monthly (*access_ _mmyyyy.log*), or always use the same file (*agent.log*).

The error log is particularly useful since it can help resolve any issues that your clients have experienced. The CGI error log records the standard error output of any CGI programs executed on your Domino server.

To reduce the amount of HTTP activity that is logged, the Server document allows you to filter out requests based on given URLs, methods, MIME types, user agents, return codes, or hosts and domains. The domains to be excluded can be of the format **.mil*, **.company.com*, or *202.92.1.**.

Logging to a Domino database requires more server resources than using log files, but it does enable agents to be written and run within Domino to summarize the information within this database. Scripting languages such as Perl that are traditionally used for processing text files from web server logs are very powerful, but at the same time take some effort to learn. Figure 7-18 shows some log output from the *DOMLOG.NSF* database. Note that some of the requests have a user name with them, meaning that an authenticated user is accessing the site.

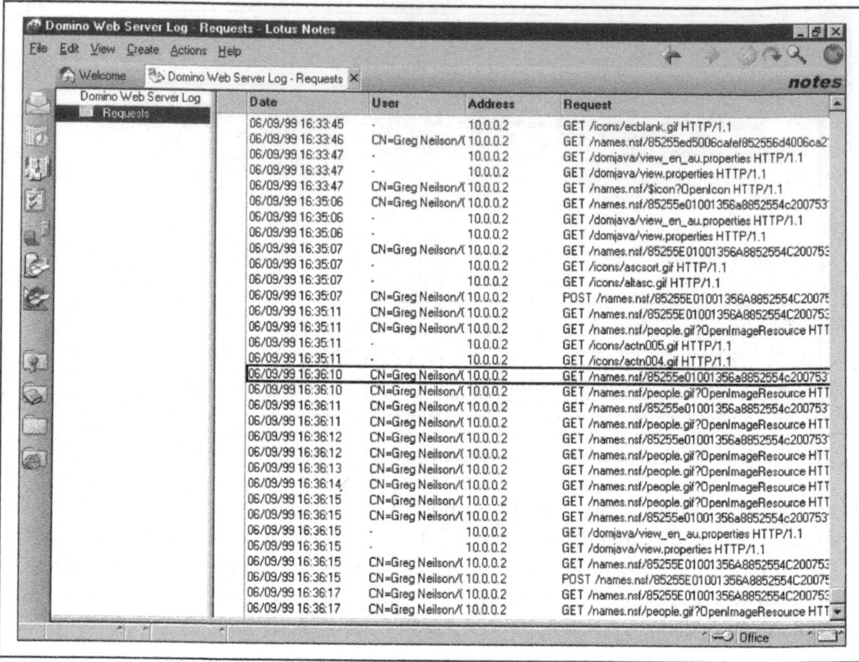

Figure 7-18: Logging HTTP activity to DOMLOG.NSF

CHAPTER 8

Supporting the Notes Client

In this chapter, I'll discuss how the Notes client works and how to configure it. Despite all your great work in designing, implementing, and supporting a Domino server infrastructure, if everything doesn't come together at the Notes client end, then your users will consider it all a failure. Your users will also generally expect you to know more about working with the Notes client than they do—something that may not be as easy as it sounds!

The new R5 Notes client runs on Windows 95/98/NT/2000 or PowerPC Macintoshes. In R5, the Domino Designer and Domino Administrator are installed separately, whereas previously these were a part of the old Notes client and installed at the same time. Both Domino Designer and Domino Administrator must have the Lotus Notes client installed on the same machine in order to function.

The New R5 Design

Two main design goals appear to have driven the Notes R5 feature additions: making using the Notes UI more browser-like, and matching/beating Outlook as a messaging client.

The importance of the Outlook client and its integration with Exchange cannot be overstated: in many cases, users are very resistant to Notes R4 clients after having worked with Outlook. Also, since Outlook was bundled with Office 97 and now Office 2000, users may already have it installed and may resist installing more client software, regardless of the power and features of R5 and its backend server infrastructure. At Lotusphere 2000, Lotus made the exciting announcement that they are working in partnership with Microsoft to provide Outlook clients with access to Domino resources, which they have called "iNotes." This client strategy looks very impressive and is something that many of us will follow with great interest.

Some of the most noticeable changes are:

- The old Notes desktop has been replaced by a customizable Welcome page, as shown in Figure 8-1 (see the section "Customizing the Welcome Page Interface," later in this chapter). This Welcome page can be a frameset containing three to five frames. The contents of each frame can be individually configured to hold a web page or Notes element such as the inbox, schedule, or ToDo list. This configuration information is stored within the new *BOOKMARK.NSF* database on the client. Change the configuration by selecting the Options button on the top righthand side of the screen. This presents a tabbed dialog box. The first tab contains the selectable number and arrangement of frames within the Welcome page. The second page is shown in Figure 8-2, where you select the contents of each frame from the options available.

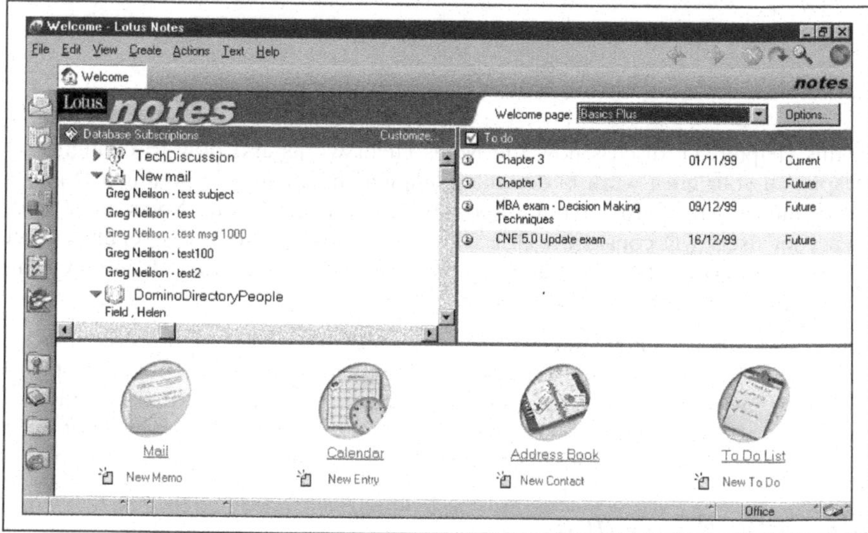

Figure 8-1: Notes R5 client Welcome page (customized)

- A new feature called *database subscriptions* allows the user to check for new and updated documents in databases. An example of this is shown in the top lefthand side of Figure 8-1. For each subscription, the user can select some or all documents of interest, pick a subset of documents, or use a formula to select documents. The subscriptions can be displayed in one of the frames on the Welcome page. Subscriptions are created with the new Create → Subscription menu option within each open database. The subscription information is stored within the new *headlines.nsf* database on the client. Select the Configure option on the Welcome page to change, delete, or disable any of the database subscriptions. This feature can use a lot of server resources in the client polling for database updates, so recall from Chapter 3, *Domino Databases,* that a new advanced database property is available to turn off headline monitoring.

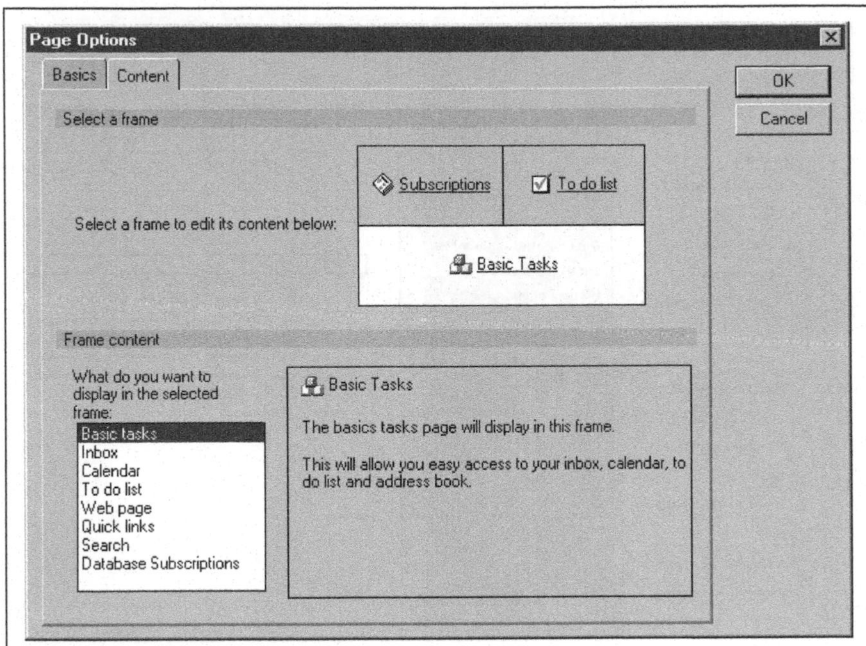

Figure 8-2: Selecting Welcome page content

- Bookmarks are now used to denote databases of interest to the client. When an existing client is upgraded to R5, all existing databases icons from the Notes desktop are upgraded to bookmarks in R5. Note that in R5, you must select each database to be bookmarked individually (an option in the Database Open dialog). This is a change from R4, where an icon was automatically created on the current workspace page when a database was first opened. You have the option (by clicking on the pin icon) to keep each set of bookmarks always open in the Notes client. Figure 8-3 shows bookmarks in action on a Notes client.
- The desktop file is now called *DESKTOP5.DSK*. It is still essential for Notes to function properly. For example, if Notes crashes or you kill the running process without stopping Notes properly, you still get the familiar message saying "Unable to open desktop file. Notes may been terminated in an earlier session. Please logoff or shutdown the operating system before running Notes again." You can also open a workspace in the R4 format if you choose. This feature is available under the first option under the Databases button.
- As part of the move to integrate the Notes client with more Internet technologies, JavaScript support has been added. This means that applications can now be written with common client-side scripting for both Notes and web browser clients. Also, the Notes client now supports HTML 4.0 and MIME natively.
- Notes now has the ability to create rules to process newly arrived mail. (This feature will probably sound familiar to Outlook users, and this is not a coincidence.) This feature is described in more detail later in this chapter, but for

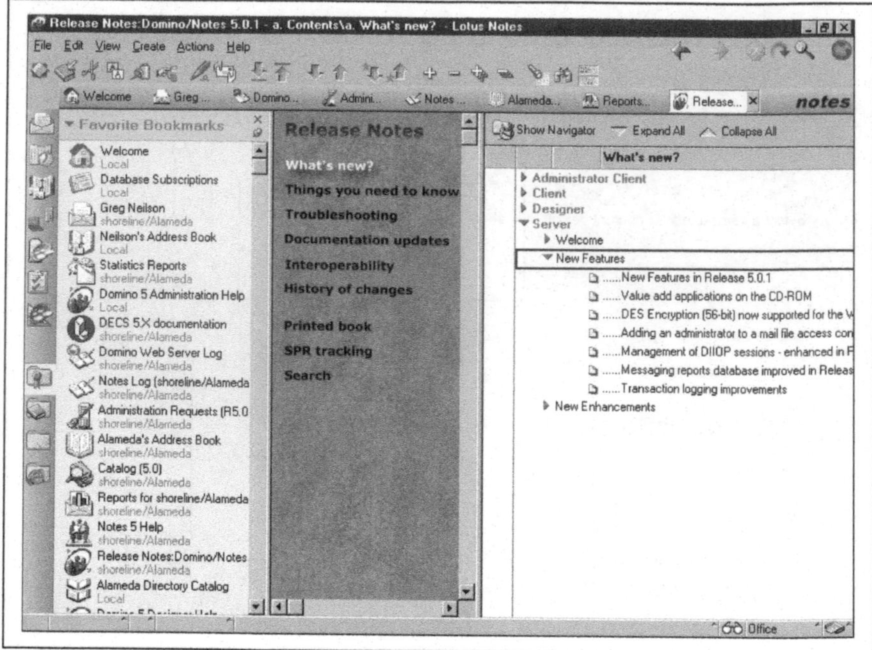

Figure 8-3: Bookmarks with the R5 Notes client

now, be aware that the created rules run as an agent on the user's home server as new mail arrives. The mail database must be using the new template or upgraded to it (*MAIL50.NTF*).

- As you learned in Chapter 3, *Domino Databases*, a new advanced database property is the ability to provide soft deletions of documents. This is intended for mail databases, although they must be created or upgraded to use the new R5 ODS structure to be able to set this property. You must create a special type of view within the database (shared, contains deleted documents) using Domino Designer to be able to see and retrieve previously deleted documents.

Basic Notes Configuration

In this section, you will learn the basics of configuring Notes for new users, including the new R5 Welcome page.

Welcome Page Interface

In this section, I'll cover how to use and customize the buttons on the top, bottom, and left side of the Notes client Welcome page. There are a great many features here that will simplify your use of Notes, impress your friends, and provide troubleshooting information unavailable from any other source. Figure 8-4 shows the initial screen of the Notes client with the default Basics Welcome page.

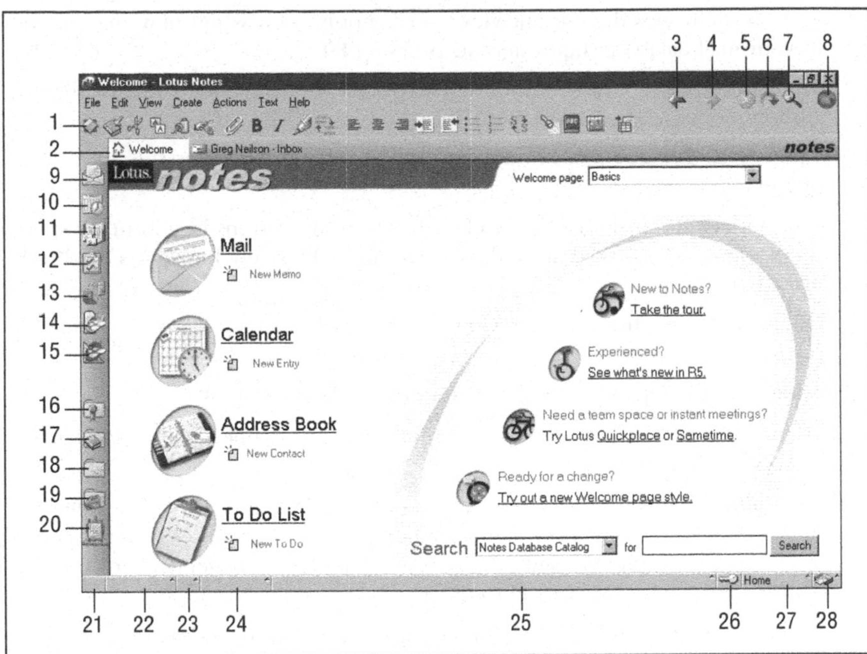

Figure 8-4: Notes R5 Welcome page (default appearance)

The Welcome page contains the following buttons:

1. SmartIcons. Disabled by default, but can be enabled by selecting File → Preferences → SmartIcons. You can also edit the SmartIcons that are displayed. I mainly use the SmartIcon on the far lefthand side, which opens an Infobox that displays the properties of the current open database or document. If you hold the mouse over a particular SmartIcon, a bubble will pop up with brief information about what the button is for.
2. Window tabs. These tabs are auto-created as more windows are opened—one for each window that is open in Notes. This functionality replaces the Windows menu from older versions of Notes, which used to confuse novice users ("Where did my window go?"). Select a window by clicking on its tab, and close a window by clicking on the "x" of its tab (it is not necessary to select the window in order to close it). This new feature also removes the old limit of nine open windows at a time within the Notes client.
3. Go Back. Part of the new browser-like behavior of Notes. As with a browser, you can easily flip back to past databases you have opened, which can be a big timesaver.
4. Go Forward. Like the Go Back button, allows you to proceed easily through the databases you have recently worked with.
5. Stop. Used to interrupt Notes when it is performing a time-consuming operation. Equivalent to pressing Ctrl-Break.

6. Refresh. Refreshes the current view—commonly used when new mail arrives in your mail database. Equivalent to pressing F9.
7. Search. Used to perform searches for people or databases from within the currently open view of a database.
8. Open URL. Brings up a window into which you can enter the URL to be opened.
9. Mail. Opens the mail database defined within the current location document. All of these icons on the far lefthand side are collectively known as the Bookmark Bar.
10. Calendar. Opens the calendar view of the mail database defined within the current location document.
11. Address Book. Opens the Personal Name and Address Book.
12. Todo. Opens the ToDo view of the mail database defined within the current location document.
13. Replicator. Opens the Replicator tab (as shown in Figure 8-7). This button is available only if the client contains replica copies of databases or has Internet mail accounts defined, since otherwise this function tended to confuse desktop users who didn't need to use it.
14. Domino Administrator. If installed, launches the Domino Administrator client. Otherwise, this button does not appear.
15. Domino Designer. If installed, launches Domino Designer. Otherwise, this button does not appear.
16. Favorite Bookmarks. When you create a bookmark, you have the option to create it within the *Favorite Bookmarks, Databases,* or *More Databases* folder. Setup Profiles, which are described in detail later in this chapter, can be used to automatically create bookmarks for the user. The user can also create his own bookmark folders.
17. Databases. (Refer to Favorite Bookmarks entry.)
18. More Bookmarks. (Refer to Favorite Bookmarks entry.)
19. Internet Explorer Links. Your saved links from your Internet Explorer browser, which you can click on to launch. Similarly, if you have Netscape Communicator installed, a bookmark for these will appear here as well.
20. Bookmark. Intended to demonstrate that you can drag and drop a database bookmark here for easy access.
21. Server communications activity. Graphically illustrates that communication activity with the server is occurring. When accessing a server via a network, this feature displays a lightning picture; when using a dialup modem, it displays a little modem icon with flashing lights to represent data transfer.
22. Change font. Available only when you are editing a rich text field within a Notes document.
23. Change character size. Available only when you are editing a rich text field within a Notes document.

24. Change paragraph style. Available only when you are editing a rich text field within a Notes document.

25. System status messages. Displays the last status message. If you click here you can see all messages, with the most recent message displayed at the bottom. This is where the user is notified when you use the broadcast server console command.

26. Database access privileges. By clicking here, you can check the access levels you have against the current open database. It lists your name, the groups you are a member of that are contained within the database ACL, and any roles within the database that are enabled for you. You will often check here when resolving issues with database access problems.

27. Location. Displays the name of the current location in use. By clicking here you can change the location from the list displayed, or edit the current location document.

28. Mail options. Click here to get a menu of options for main processing: Create, Memo/Scan, Unread, Mail/Receive, Mail/Send, Outgoing Mail/Send, and Receive Mail/Open Mail.

There are several other files that are involved in basic Notes configuration. In previous sections, we have briefly discussed the files *DESKTOP5.DSK*, *BOOKMARKS.NSF*, and *HEADLINES.NSF*. The next client database files that are included in this basic configuration are the Personal Name and Address Book (*NAMES.NSF*), *NOTES.INI* (covered in Chapter 6, *Domino Administration Tools*), and the individual user ID file.

Personal Name and Address Book

The Personal Name and Address Book (*NAMES.NSF*) file always resides on the user's workstation; it has the database title of *<lastname>'s Address Book*. It contains:

Contact documents
: Personal email contact information. Users can keep all manner of personal information here about their contacts, but for Notes to function, the only information that must be entered is the name and email address.

Group documents
: Personal distribution lists. Keep in mind that when mail is sent to a group defined locally, the list of names is expanded on the outgoing email and all can see the entire mailing list. This is in contrast to using a group defined in Domino Directory, when only the group appears in the outgoing email.

Connection documents
: Tell Notes how to connect to a given server; for example, the Domino server IP address if there is no DNS available, or the phone number if using a dialup connection.

Location documents
: Tell Notes about the current network/dialup configuration to use. Here we are assuming that we are using the default Office location, which has the user's

mail file located on a Domino server using a LAN connection. This file is automatically created when Notes is first configured for the user.

Account document

A new type of document, used to optionally create and configure additional POP3, NNTP, IMAP, LDAP or SMTP connections so that Notes can work with mail from multiple sources accounts.

NOTES.INI File

We covered the *NOTES.INI* file in Chapter 6; this file contains much of the client configuration information.

User ID File

We also need the individual user ID file locally on the client machine. This file is about 2K and contains information such as the username, password, and public and private keys. When the user changes the password (File → Tools → User ID → Set Password), this action changes the password within the ID itself, and nothing changes on the server. Therefore, when a user forgets his new Notes password, you can't reset anything on the server, so you must do one of the following:

- Use the new R5 ID recovery process (assuming you set this up beforehand) to break open the ID by one or more administrators and then reset the password.
- Send the user a copy of his ID file as originally created, with the original password used to create it. Most Domino shops typically have a defined process within their Domino administration function to keep copies of all created IDs.
- Recertify the ID file. This is done with Domino Administrator. Select the People & Groups tab, then select Recertify from the Tools menu and follow the dialogs.
- Create a new ID. This means that new public and private keys are created for the user, so that anything the user encrypted with his old ID file is now unable to be accessed by them.

Therefore, when moving a Notes user to another machine, you múst copy all these files to the new computer; otherwise, much of their tailored Notes setup will be lost.

Occasionally, a single Notes machine may be used by a number of different users. For example, a remote office machine may be used by a couple of staff members, or a developer may need to be any of a number of test users to test the application design and security. The best way to enable this is to create a Location document for each user. This specifies the mail file to use for each user. Be careful when using connection documents with client machines that will have multiple Notes users on them—the default "For user" field is for the user who created the connection document only. When you have multiple users who need to access this connection, ensure that this field contains an asterisk (*).

Remote Connection

Notes has had dialup support since the first versions. Since it predated Microsoft RAS, it uses its own X.PC protocol for dialup support. Since version 4, it has also supported RAS connections between server and client.

Another option now commonly used and one that requires no changes to the Notes client configuration is to use RAS/DUN to connect to the internal corporate network, and then use this connection via the regular Office location. With this method, users can access the Internet, and share files and printers as well as Notes from the one dialup session. When using this type of connection, from a Notes point of view, it is identical to being connected in the office via the TCPIP or SPX ports. So don't be make the mistake of thinking that this must be a modem (COM*x*) port used here in the Location document.

Setting Up the Connection

The first thing to be configured is the modem port on the client. This involves setting the port—COM1 or COM2—and then the modem type and general settings (speed, disable sound, etc.). If your modem cannot be selected from the list, you can create your own MDM file, or usually you can use the generic modem settings, configured via File → Preferences → User Preferences → Ports tab, as shown in Figure 8-5. Here we add the COM port to use (select the "Port enabled" checkbox to enable it), then select the COMx Options button, which configures the modem, as shown in Figure 8-6.

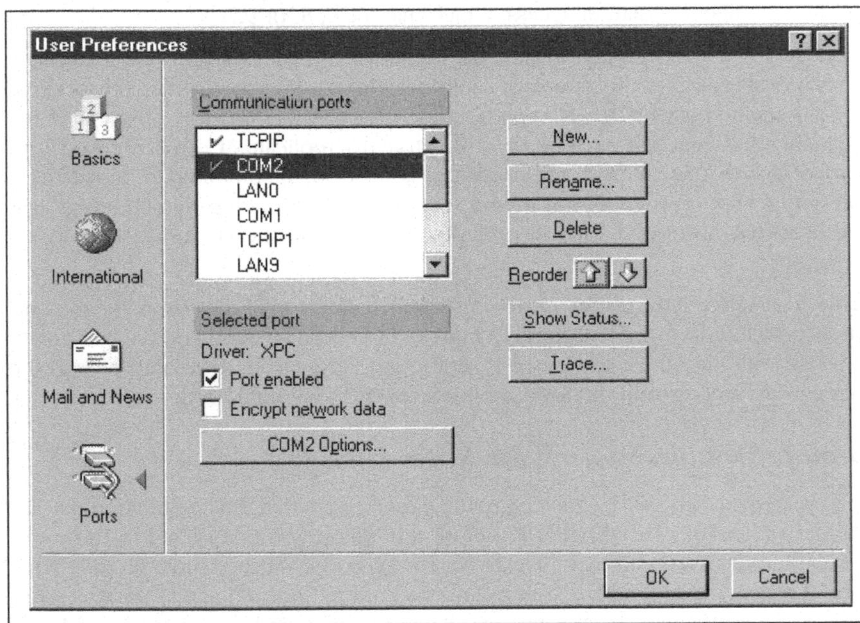

Figure 8-5: Adding a modem port

Notes Client

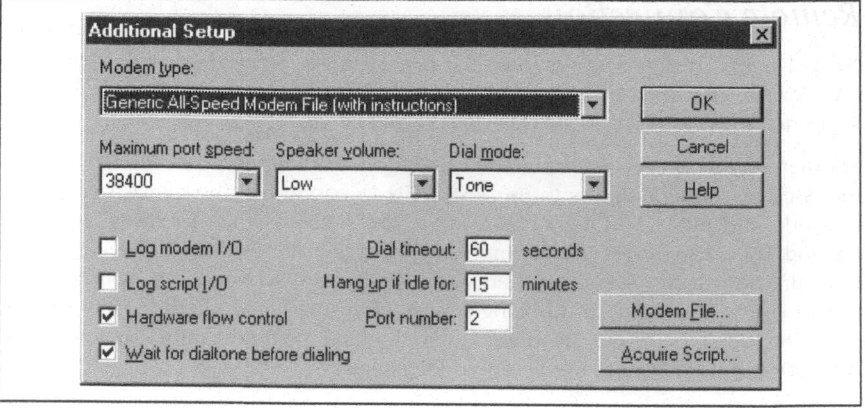

Figure 8-6: Configuring a modem port

The Connection document within the Personal Name and Address Book contains the country code, area code, and phone number of the server to call.

A Location document within the Personal Name and Address Book specifies the country/area code where the user is located. This is used by Notes to determine whether it is a local, long-distance, or international call. Users often think that they need a different location document for every city they visit, but what they really need is one document for local call access (if they have the same area code as the dialup server does), and another for long distance access. Also, here you can specify a number for dialout access, which may be 0, 8, or 9.

Users access a local replica of their mail database on their laptop. They can also have a local replica of the directory catalog if it exists in order to correctly address mail to their organization. A replica copy of Domino Directory is usually not recommended, since it is typically too large to replicate. Copying group and person records to the local address book is also not recommended, since these will not be kept updated as will the server versions, and the locally defined groups and users will always be used in preference to those in the Domino Directory on the server.

Lastly, users then have a local *MAIL.BOX*, which stores mail that users have "sent" when detached from the network. When users choose to send/receive mail or to replicate with the server, their mail is sent to the server from this database and the changes are sent to/from the local replica from the copy held on the server.

Remote Troubleshooting for Notes Dialup

This suggested process is based on the assumption that this configuration has worked successfully before (ideally before the laptop was first issued to the user). Here, educated users can make life easier for everyone—if they have no idea what they are seeing, this can be a very time-consuming (if not ultimately unsuccessful) process. Unfortunately, by the time you have been called to resolve a problem, you are probably dealing with someone who is tired and stressed from travel and now is very frustrated that they now cannot access email and applications!

Obviously the first thing you should ask is when they were last able to successfully dialup using Notes, and what has changed since then (in my experience, users will usually deny all knowledge of any changes on their machine). Assuming that this question yields no useful information, then:

- Check whether you can dial into the server successfully with a test machine in the office.
- Have the users check their phone port. If users have dialup access via another method (for example, RAS), check whether they can dial in with this port. If so, this process verifies that the phone port works (that is, this really is an analog phone port), and also that the modem is working.
- Check whether users have switched to the correct configured location within Notes. For example, the Office location would not have a COM*x* port enabled, so it would never be able to dial into a Notes server.
- Check what phone number is being called. It may be a local, long distance, or international call. Also, check whether the correct code (0, 8, or 9) is being used to dial out. You can ask the user to check this by selecting File → Mobile → Call Server and check what phone number is displayed.
- Enable the modem sound if it is disabled. You should be able to hear a dial tone and whether the modems are handshaking correctly. You can also hear if there a recorded message about the number not being able to be dialed.
- Ask user to report any messages reported on their client. You can select the message bar to see what is recorded. Also watch the server console/server log for any information.
- Ask the user to check contents of Connection and Location documents. If possible, it would probably be much quicker to have the user print this and fax them to you.
- Ask the user to check whether each operation (send mail, replicate to mail database) is not disabled by ensuring that there is a check mark in the replicator page next to each operation. Also ensure that the arrows point both ways (meaning to send and receive updates during replication). Figure 8-7 shows a typical replicator page.

Keep in mind as well that sometimes users will be impatient and not wait for replication to complete—and they may assume that something must be wrong. Of course, the longer this happens, the longer replication will eventually take to complete. One way you can convince users that something is happening is to have them check the port status of the modem (File → Preferences → User Preferences → Ports tab → modem port, COM*x*, → Show Status). If the user checks this at intervals of a few minutes, he will see that that the byte count downloaded is increasing. Given the large attachments sent around, it is not unusual to take a number of minutes to replicate mail—even with the fast modems now available.

One option you may be asked to consider for mobile users is to forward their mail to another site; for example, their personal Yahoo! or Hotmail account. This is attractive in that it involves only a simple change to their Person record in the Domino Directory (the Forwarding Address field on the Mail tab) and then the user can access their email via a browser anywhere. I have nothing against Yahoo!

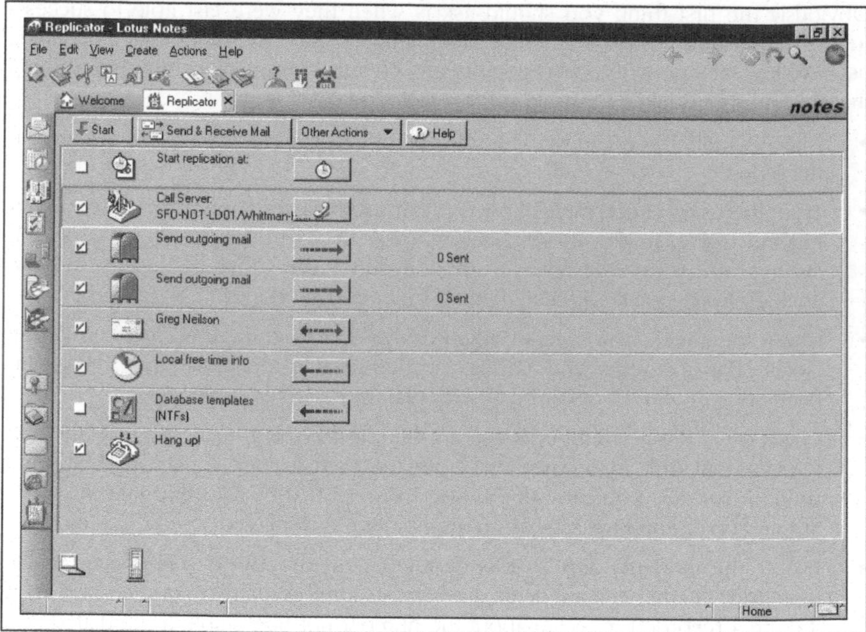

Figure 8-7: Replicator page

or Hotmail (in fact I use their services myself), but there are two things you need to think about before doing this:

- Security. You lose all control over who can access the user's email and should assume that all email sent there is likely to be read by anyone—including your competitors.
- Availability. You now have no control over the messages once they leave your corporate network. These free Internet accounts offer no defined service levels and are provided on a best effort basis. You also lose the ability to backup and restore any messages sent outside your corporate network.

Corporate email is a valuable information asset and usually needs to be treated accordingly. An alternative option is to allow access to Notes mail through the Internet via a browser. This is commonly known as "WebMail" and is discussed in detail in Chapter 4.

Setup Profiles

Setup Profiles provide the ability to tailor the initial Notes environment for a user and make changes to client configuration later as needed. When a new user is created, the Setup Profile is created via an input field in the User Registration dialog box. The created Person document within the Domino Directory has a field on the Administration tab called Setup Profile(s) that contains the name of the Setup Profile to use for that user.

Setup Profiles are defined within the Domino Directory in the Server → Setup Profiles view. They take effect when a new user has her Notes client configured to access her Domino server. Similarly, you can make changes to the Setup Profile, and these changes will be reflected in the Notes client (nearly all of these are updates to the location document in the Personal Name and Address Book) next time the user connects to her home server. Be aware that you cannot use this function to delete anything from the client configuration—only to add or change. The options available within the setup profile are:

Internet browser
: The type of browser to be used.

Directory server
: The name of the server to use to access the Domino Directory.

Catalog/Domain server
: The name of the server to use for domain searches.

Retrieve open pages
: How users retrieve web pages (from the Notes workstation, an InterNotes server, or not at all).

Default databases added as bookmarks
: Here you paste database links to the databases you want added as bookmarks. You create a database link by selecting Copy As → Database Link within an open database.

Create As new replicas on user's machine
: Here you paste database links to the databases that are to be created as new replicas on the client.

Mobile directory catalogs
: A pasted database link for each of the databases to be used.

Default Passthru server
: The name of the server to be used for passthru, and optionally the country code/area code/phone number to use.

Default Connections to Other Remote Servers
: The names of other servers to be accessed, and optionally the country code/area code/phone number to use.

Default Accounts to Internet Servers
: Creates account documents in the Name and Address book (without the name and password to use for that user) containing the name of the account, the server to access, the protocol to use (NNTP/POP3/IMAP/LDAP), and whether SSL is used.

Name Servers
: The name and addresses of secondary TCP/IP and NDS Domino name servers.

Applet Security
: Defines any trusted hosts, and then configures the access levels available for both trusted and untrusted hosts that serve Java applets.

Proxies
: The Proxy server configuration to use.

MIME
: Selects the format for Internet messages, either MIME or RTF.

Other New Features

The following sections describe two additional important new features of Notes.

Lotus Notes Minder

Lotus Notes Minder (*\lotus\notes\nminder.exe*) is a new applet that can monitor mail incoming to the users' mail database without having to continuously run the Notes client. The Notes client can use up to 40MB of memory when running, which can be a considerable load on PCs with insufficient memory. In this case, they can just run this applet and start the full Notes client only when they wish to work with incoming mail. This applet will really be of use only when the client is permanently network-attached to the Domino server, as opposed to a dialup configuration.

Typically, you would launch this applet during startup of the client machine. The running program minimizes to an icon on the Windows system tray, and uses around 7MB of RAM when running. The default activity is to poll the user's mail file (as specified in the active Location, defined in *NOTES.INI*) every 15 minutes. If the user wishes to change the default polling interval, he can select the program properties by selecting the icon with the right mouse button, and can also change the mode of notification (visual and/or audio) and temporarily disable checking of new mail. There is also the option to check the new mail summary, which brings up a dialog as shown in Figure 8-8. From here you can select a message and have the Notes client launch and open your mail database at this message.

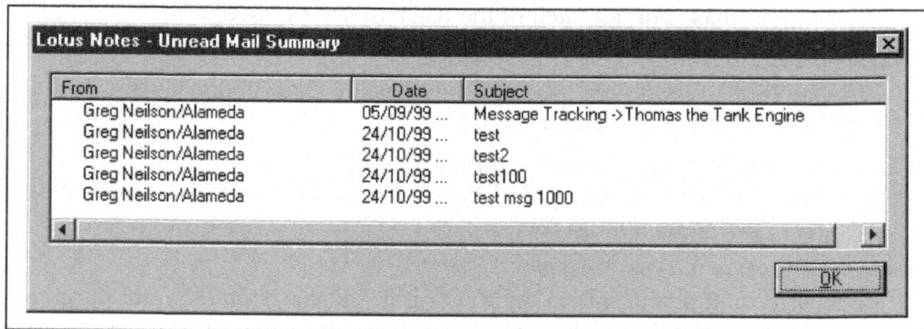

Figure 8-8: Notes Minder: Unused Mail Summary

Rules

Rules are defined under the *Rules* folder within the user mail database, as shown in Figure 8-9. Here you can create a new rule, edit or delete an existing rule, enable/disable the rule, or move each rule up or down within the hierarchy.

These rules are processed as new mail arrives on the Domino server, not on the Notes client. These rules are processed as agents on the Domino server, so you also must ensure that each mail user is authorized to run agents on the server in the Server document in the Domino Directory. Chapter 2, *Domino Directories*, covers the Domino Directory in more detail.

The available rules allow you to specify the sender, subject, body, importance, delivery priority, To, CC, BCC, Internet domains, and size to check for. Each rule can use combinations of these conditions using the AND/OR syntax as appropriate. There is an option to move or copy the incoming mail to a folder, change its importance, or delete it. For example, here you could set all incoming email from your manager or best customer to be flagged automatically as high priority within the mail database. Another option could be to move all incoming Internet newsletters to a separate folder to be read later.

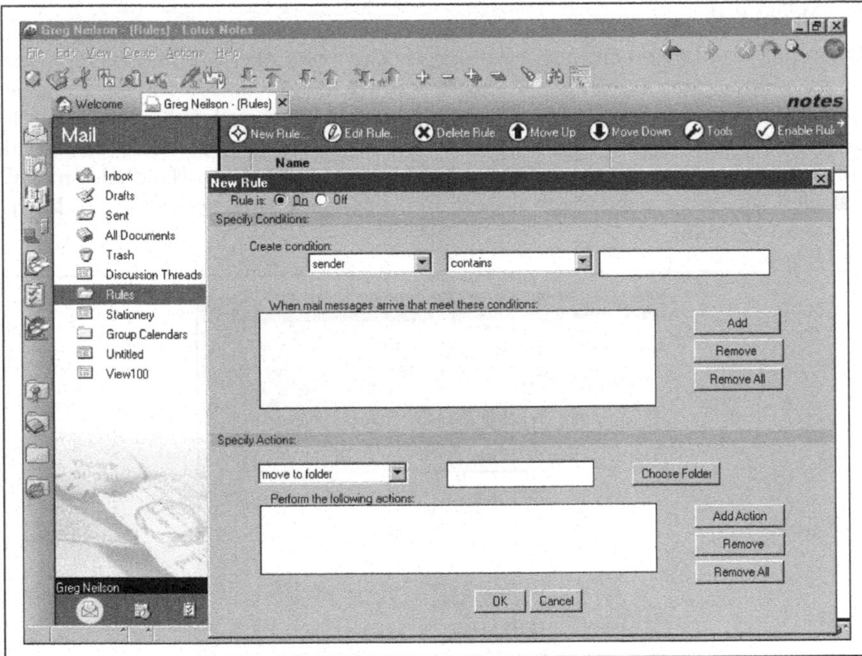

Figure 8-9: Creating a new rule within a user mailbox

EasySync: Synchronize Notes with PalmPilots

Lotus provides a separate product, EasySync, to enable PalmPilots and IBM WorkPads (rebadged PalmPilots) to synchronize with Lotus Notes. This product comes free with the WorkPad, but Palm users need to purchase a license for it. In order to work with the R5 Notes client, you need EasySync version 3.0A or later.

EasySync extends the HotSync process (which is used to synchronize the Palm with the Palm Desktop on the PC) to include five additional "conduits" to synchronize with Lotus Notes. These are:

Notes Mail
: Synchronizes the users' Notes mail database with Palm Mail.

Notes Calendar
: Synchronizes the users' Notes calendar from their mail database with the Palm Date Book.

Notes Address

Synchronizes the users' contacts from the Notes Personal Name and Address Book with the Palm Address Book.

Notes To Do

Synchronizes the users' ToDo list from the Notes Mail database with the Palm To Do List.

Notes Journal

Synchronizes the users' journal (which must be *JOURNAL.NSF*) with the Palm Memo Pad.

Any or all of these conduits can be disabled. The Notes Mail conduit has the most configuration options, as shown in Figure 8-10. Here you can see you have a great deal of control as to what is to be synchronized. Obviously, the more that is downloaded, the more memory is used on your Palm, so you should download only the items you really need. The Custom option for "Notes to Handheld" means that the contents of a specified folder from the Notes mail database can be downloaded to the Palm.

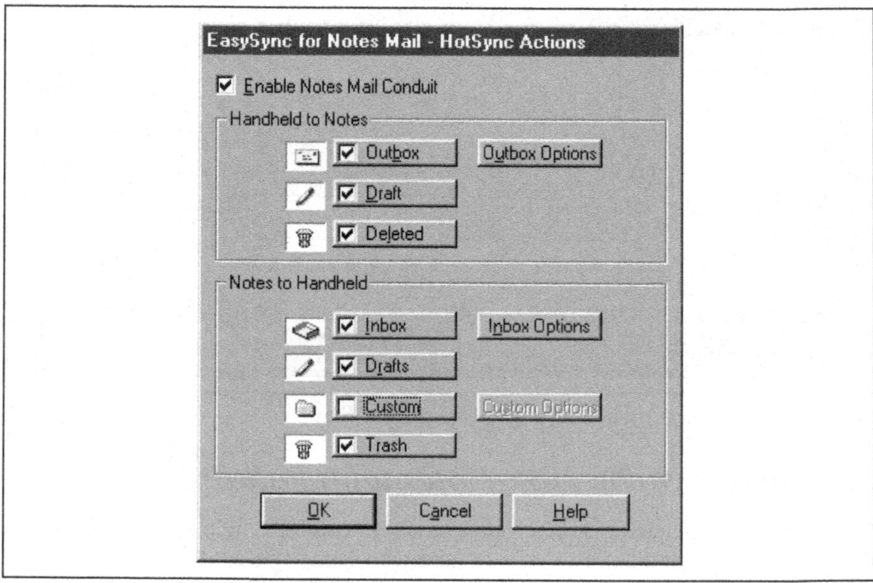

Figure 8-10: Notes Mail Conduit configuration

The remaining four conduits have a configuration screen identical to that shown in Figure 8-11. Here you have only basic controls over the process: whether to synchronize, to overwrite the data from the Notes client, or to do nothing. Slow-Sync is typically used for problem determination only, since it slows down the synchronization process further and provides detailed information about what the conduit is doing.

Generally, EasySync works well and needs little attention after the initial configuration. However, when problems do occur, it is frequently because users expect the same functionality when synchronizing with the Palm as they have with Notes

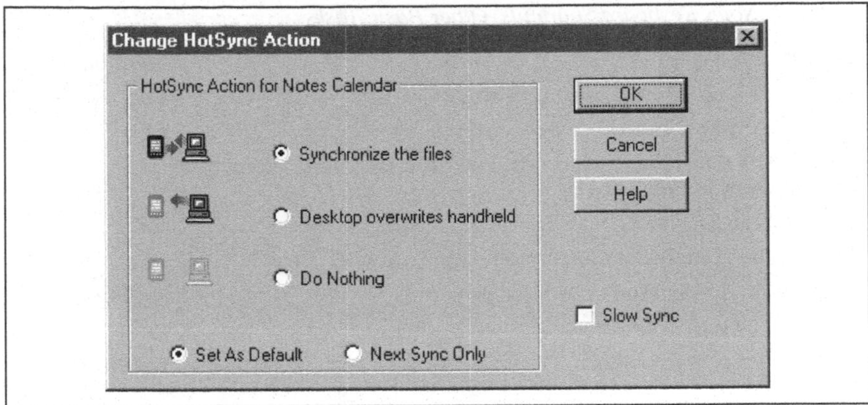

Figure 8-11: Notes Calendar Conduit configuration

replication. In order to prevent problems with this process, the best advice is to keep things simple. That is, sync a Palm with only one PC, have only a single user defined on each PC, and have only one installation of the Notes client on a PC. Keep in mind that when a user attempts to update the same data (for example, a contact) in both Notes and the Palm, the HotSync process will issue a warning message, and copy the changed item to be a duplicate of the original. In this case, the user is expected to delete the obsolete item on each platform being running HotSync again.

Common Notes Keyboard Shortcuts

Although Notes uses many GUI elements to enable the user to do their work quickly and efficiently, there are also keyboard shortcuts that are equally useful. Table 8-1 through Table 8-3 list the most commonly used keyboard shortcuts.

Table 8-1: Notes Keyboard Shortcuts, Accessing Features

Action	*Shortcut*
Access Bookmarks	Alt-B, then number of bookmark to access
Access the action bar	Alt, then number of action to access
Access the search menu	Alt-S
Access Task Buttons	Alt-W, then number of task to access
Access a web site	Alt-L then URL
Open Properties Infobox	Alt-Enter
See hidden views in a database (this works only if you have Author access or greater to the database)	Ctrl-Shift when opening the database
Open a database	Ctrl-O
Exit Notes	Alt-F4 or Ctrl-Q

Notes Client

Table 8-2: Notes Keyboard Shortcuts, Other Basic Tasks

Action	*Shortcut*
Close currently opened document or view	Esc or Ctrl-W
Context-sensitive Help	F1
Lock Notes ID (forces you to next enter the password to open the ID when using Notes)	F5
Launch Print Dialog	Ctrl-P
Refresh the contents of the currently open view	F9
Refresh all views in the open database	Shift-Ctrl-F9
Save	Ctrl-S
Stop the current operation	Ctrl-Break

Table 8-3: Notes Keyboard Shortcuts, Navigation

Action	*Shortcut*
Move to the next field in the form	Tab
Move to the next frame	F6
Move to the next task button	Ctrl-Tab
Move to the next unread document in a view	Shift-Tab
Move to the previous field in the form	Shift-Tab
Move to the previous frame	Shift-F6
Move to the previous task button	Ctrl-Shift-Tab

CHAPTER 9

DECS

Domino Enterprise Connection Services (DECS) is a new feature* as of Domino .6.3 and later; it provides real-time access to backend data resources from Domino databases. With this feature, you can specify the backend resource you wish to connect to, map fields from a database table or view into a form from a Domino database, then specify under which conditions you wish to access this hotlink between Domino and the data source. To the end user, it appears that all of the data resides in Domino. The DECS add-in dynamically works with the Domino document as it is accessed to view, create, delete, or update data from within the backend database.

DECS supports access to the following resources:

DB2

Requires DB2 version 5 or later. Optionally, if you're connecting to DB2 servers on the OS/390 or AS/400 platforms, this requires the DB2 Connect add-on (formerly known as DDCS); if you're connecting to these platforms via SNA protocols, then a communications product such as SNA Server or IBM's network Communications Server is required for an APPC connection.

Oracle

Requirements differ depending on the server platform used:

OS/2

Requires SQL*Net version 2. This version of SQL*Net must be the same as installed on the Oracle server.

Windows NT

Requires SQL*Net version 1 or 2. This version of SQL*Net must be the same as installed on the Oracle server.

* DECS used to be part of a Lotus product called NotesPump 2.5 (now called Enterprise Integrator 3.0); this function was originally called Realtime Notes Activity.

Native OS/2 server
Requires Oracle version 7.3.

Other platforms running Oracle natively
Requires Oracle version 7.2 or later.

For Oracle 7.3 on HP-UX, the fix for bug 441647 must be applied. When running Oracle 8, SQL*Net must be installed.

Sybase SQL Server
Requires the System 10 Netlib or above for OS/2 and Windows NT servers.

ODBC data sources
Requires 32-bit ODBC drivers on OS/2 or Windows NT.

EDA/SQL (middleware for data sources from SAP and J.D. Edwards, etc.)
Requires EDA/Client at Release 3.2 level or later, and must include 32-bit drivers for OS/2 and Windows NT.

Zmerge text data files
No special requirement exists.

Keep in mind that when running partitioned Domino servers, there is an architectural limitation specifying that only one partitioned server can have an active DECS task running at a time.

Configuring DECS

There are a number of steps involved in successfully creating a link between the Domino database and the backend data. By doing these one at a time, you can confirm that each step has been completed successfully, which makes problem solving much easier, since there are so many components that could be the source of a problem.

The prerequisite steps are:

1. Ensure that DECS is installed on the server, and if not, install these components. Install either the DBMS software on the server, or, if the data will be on a separate server, install the relevant client software to access this server data. Check whether the DBMS has been successfully configured by using its own client software to access the backend data. Verify that DECS can access the data source by using its LCTEST utility.
2. Create the Domino database on the server that will be used to link to the backend data.

Now you are ready to configure DECS to create the link between the Domino database and the data source using the DECS Administrator database (*DECSADM.NSF*). This involves two steps, and both steps have a wizard that you can use to assist in the configuration:

1. Create a connection to the backend database to describe how to connect to this database and also what data is available.
2. Create an activity to map fields from a form in a Domino database to the backend data and then configures how and when this link is activated.

Installing DECS

If DECS was not installed during the R5 installation, then the installation must be rerun and DECS selected for installation. If during this installation you select DECS and the Change option, you can select which DECS components to install, as shown in Figure 9-1. The first two options—DECS Domino Program Files and DECS Data Files—are mandatory for DECS to operate on the server. However, given the small amount of space savings to be made, I suggest you install all four DECS options.

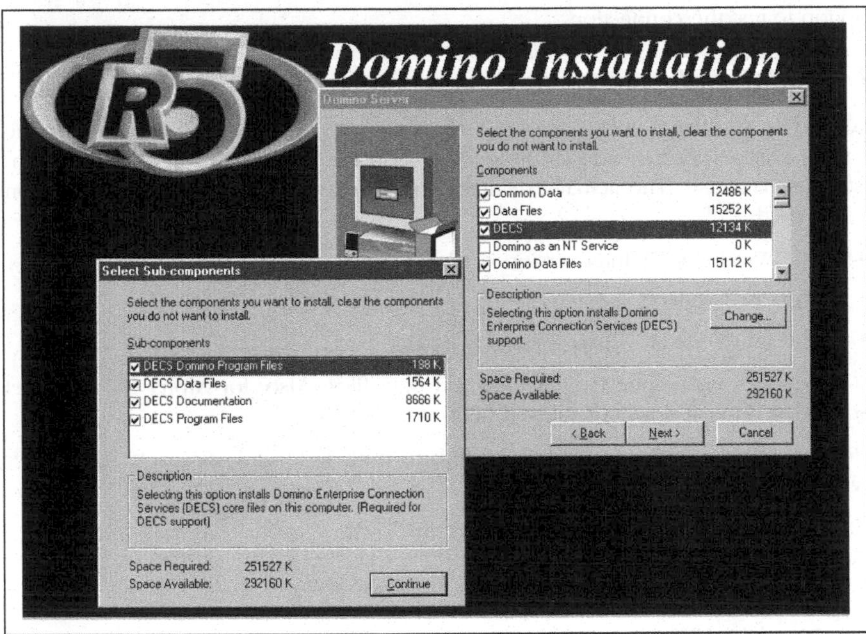

Figure 9-1: Selecting DECS to install, with the selectable subcomponents for installation

You will also need to confirm that DECS is added to the `ServerTasks=` line in *NOTES.INI*, and add the following line to install the add-in if it is not present already:

```
EXTMGR_ADDINS=decsext.dll
```

Installing the DBMS and Verifying a Successful Installation

Refer to the documentation that comes with the DBMS you are working with. Typically, this will involve connecting to a test database that comes with the DBMS and verifying that you can successfully access the data.

When you use ODBC, you configure a Data Source Name (DSN) to define the driver to use, the source of the data, and any special link configuration information. With the Windows NT platform, there are two types of DSNs used for ODBC configurations: User and System. User DSNs are stored in the NT registry under HKCU, while System DSNs are stored under HKLM. Therefore, you must use System DSNs, since these function for any logged-in user at the server, even if no user is logged in at the server.

To create a System DSN, use the ODBC applet in the Control Panel. Select the System DSN property page and select Add. This action starts a wizard, which asks you which database driver to use, the name to use for this DSN, the location of the server, how the DSN will authenticate with the server, plus some general configuration options. At the end, the wizard will list all options selected and provide the option to test the connection.

Using LCTEST

LCTEST is a utility provided by DECS to ensure it can successfully connect to the backend data source before a DECS connection is configured in the DECS Administration database. The actual executable name depends on the platform version being used:

- The Windows NT Intel version is *nlctest.exe.*
- The OS/2 version is *ilctest.exe.*
- The Windows NT Alpha version is *alctest.exe.*

LCTEST does not connect to Zmerge text data files. Also, for Alpha NT and Intel Solaris versions, it does not support EDA/SQL or DB2.

Here is the output from a successful link to both DB2 and Microsoft SQL Server (via ODBC) using LCTEST:

```
C:\Lotus\Domino>nlctest

Lotus Connector Server Connection Verification Test

Copyright 1998 Lotus Development Corporation
-------------------------------------------

This utility will verify connectivity from this
machine to the selected type of server.

At the prompt, enter the number of the test
you would like to run, or enter 0 to exit.

 0 - Exit this program
 1 - Lotus Notes
 2 - Oracle Server
 3 - ODBC
 4 - Sybase Server
 5 - EDA/SQL
 6 - DB/2

Run test number: [0] 3

ODBC Connection Verification
```

```
Copyright 1998 Lotus Development Corporation
-------------------------------------------

This utility will verify connectivity from this machine to the
specified ODBC data source.

At the prompts, enter a valid ODBC data source, username, and password

loaded library odbc32
    Data Source: DECS-Northwind
        User Id: sa
       Password: m@ddog!
 Driver Details: [N] n
Attempting to connect to DECS-Northwind...

Successfully Connected.

      Try Again: [N] n

At the prompt, enter the number of the test
you would like to run, or enter 0 to exit.

 0 - Exit this program
 1 - Lotus Notes
 2 - Oracle Server
 3 - ODBC
 4 - Sybase Server
 5 - EDA/SQL
 6 - DB/2

Run test number: [0] 6

DB2 Connection Verification

Copyright 1998 Lotus Development Corporation
-------------------------------------------

This utility will verify connectivity from this machine to the
specified DB2 server.

At the prompts, enter a valid DB2 database, username, and
password

loaded library db2cli
   Database: sample
   Username: db2admin
   Password: nine11
Attempting to connect to DB2 sample as db2admin
Successfully Connected
Successfully Disconnected

Connectivity to DB2 Verified.

Try Again? [N] n
```

Creating the Domino Database

This custom database is supplied by the developers who have written the application that uses this hotlink function. In most cases, they supply a template database, and you select File → Database → New to create the new database on the server.

Using the DECS Administrator Database

There are two stages remaining to complete the configuration of DECS, and both of these are done within the DECS Administrator database (*DECSADM.NSF*). First, define a connection to the backend database, which also lists what fields are available in the selected table or view. Then create an activity that defines the mapping of fields from Domino to this data source, and specifies under what conditions this real-time link is activated.

The DECS Administrator database is automatically created the first time the DECS task is loaded on the server. Figure 9-2 shows the navigator within this database. I'll briefly cover this in the rest of this section.

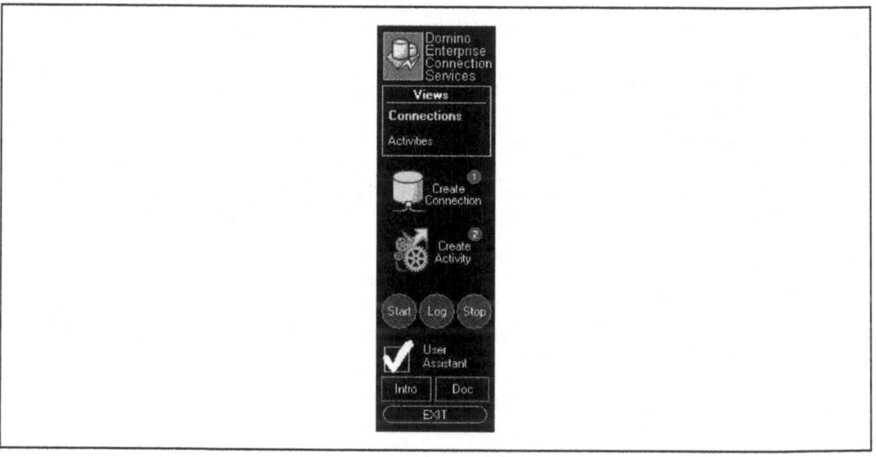

Figure 9-2: Main navigator within the DECS Administrator database

The Views section toggles between showing the Connections view or the Activities view on the righthand side. Underneath this are options to create either connections or activities. Near the bottom of the navigator is a toggle switch to turn on or off the User Assistant feature when you create activity documents. The User Assistant takes you step by step through the configuration process. If the User Assistant function is turned off, the administrator is presented with a new activity document for direct input of the configuration information. Below this are the Start/Log/Stop buttons. You can select a given activity and then either start it, stop it, or review its logged information of start and stop times. You also have the option to display an introduction to DECS or the complete DECS documentation.

Creating a Connection

When you select the option to create a connection, you are prompted to select the type of connection from a list of supported connection types.

What you're asked to enter next depends on the type of connection you have selected. For example, with DB2 you enter the name of the database, the account and password information to use to connect to the database, and specify whether you want to access a table or a view. With an ODBC data source, you are asked the name of the DSN, account and password information to access the data, and again whether you want to access a table or a view within the data source.

With this connection information specified, the DECS Administrator application connects to the database and retrieves a list of table or views, from which you select the data you want to access. DECS Administrator then retrieves a list of columns from the selected table and their data type (see Figure 9-3 and Figure 9-4).

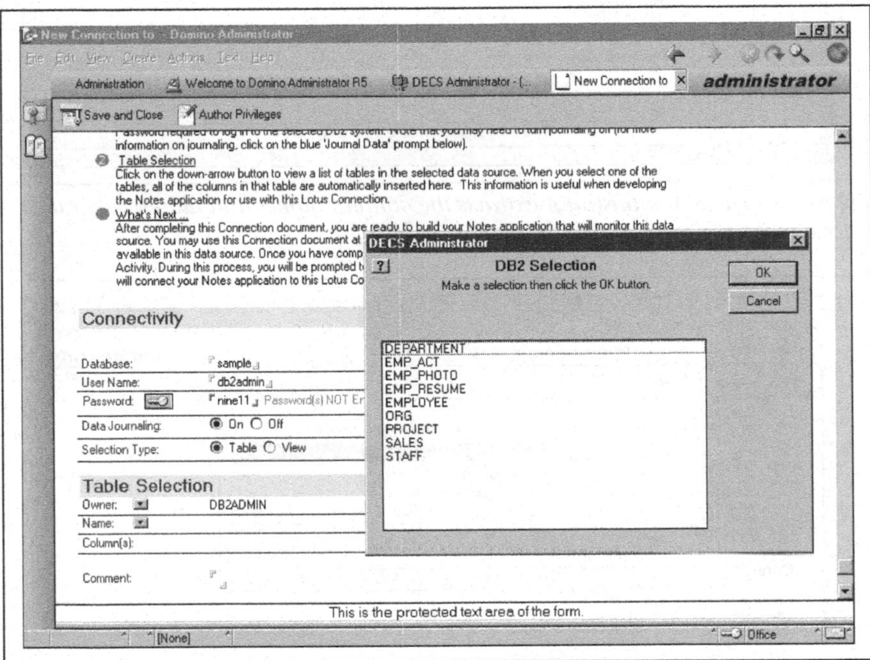

Figure 9-3: Selecting a DB2 table from the chosen database

When setting up an ODBC connection, DECS Administrator is not as helpful, and requires you to enter the name of the table you want to access (as shown in Figure 9-5). This is the fully qualified name of the table in SQL Server. After this is entered, as with DB2, the DECS Administrator is able to retrieve the list of columns in the table and the data type for each.

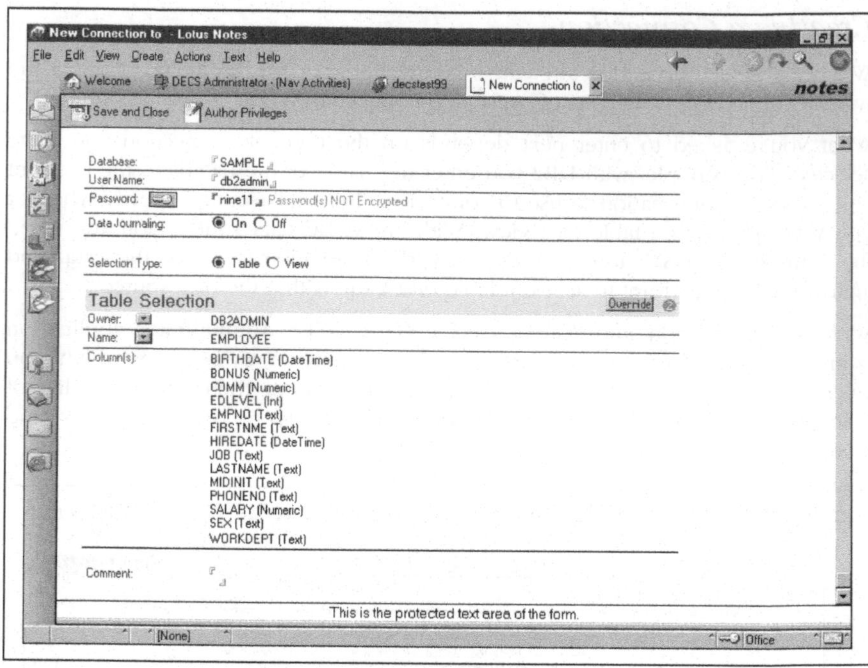

Figure 9-4: DECS Administrator extracts the column names and data type for the selected table

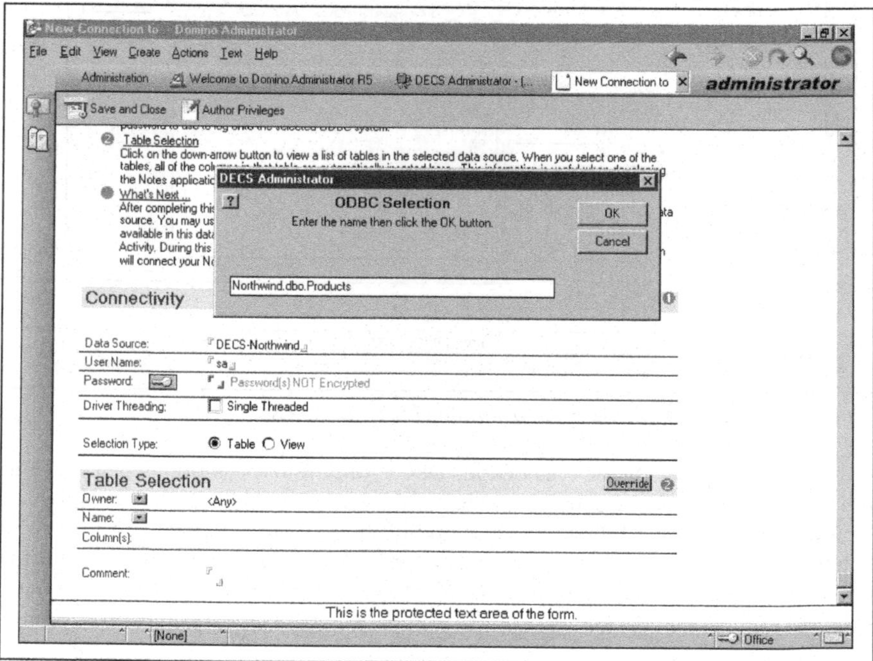

Figure 9-5: Entering the table name for an ODBC data source

Creating an Activity

When configuring the activity, you must work closely with the developers of your Domino/DECS application, since they have designed it specifically to work with the backend database in a defined way.

During the creation of this activity, you can either use the User Wizard or create the document manually. When the Activity document is in Edit mode, a drop-down button in each section of the document launches the feature of the User Wizard that corresponds to that section; for example, selecting the Domino database or mapping fields between the Domino database and the backend data source.

The steps involved in creating an activity are:

1. Select the Domino database, then the actual form within that database that will use this real-time link. This database will be provided by the Domino developer.
2. Select the DECS connection to use for this activity. You will have defined and tested this link in the previous step.
3. Map key fields (which provide uniqueness) and data fields between the Domino form and list of columns from the backend data source. This information will be provided by the application developer.
4. Select which of the Domino actions you wish to monitor (Create, Open, Update, Delete). For each of these, there are advanced options available that can run a Domino formula or run a stored procedure on the backend database. This information will be provided by the application developer.
5. Select whether the activity should autostart when the DECS task is started in Domino, or whether it should be only manually started via DECS Administrator. Typically, you will select the autostart option for production applications, though the manual start option can be useful during testing and development of the application.

The first couple of configuration tasks are straightforward. Enter the name of the Domino database and the form to use within that database. Then you are asked which configured DECS connection to use for this activity. If you are using the User Assistant, it will provide you with a list of Domino databases, then forms within that database, then DECS connections to select from.

Now you get to the real meat of configuring this activity. I am assuming that you are using the User Assistant, since it requires much less typing and reduces the risk of miskeying an entry. In the top half of Figure 9-6, I am matching the key field(s) from the backend data source to the key field(s) in the Domino document. It is the key field that uniquely identifies each Domino document and database record. There is also an option—see the checkbox in the upper lefthand corner—to use the UNID (Universal Note ID, which is a hexadecimal number that uniquely identifies a Notes document across all replicas of the database) as the unique key for Domino documents.

Then in the second half of the screen shown in Figure 9-6, match the field names from the backend database to those of the Domino form. On the far righthand side are the data fields available in the Domino form, and on the far lefthand side are the data fields available in the backend database. Match these fields one by one by selecting them with the mouse, so that the middle two columns represent the mapping of fields in order between Domino and the backend database.

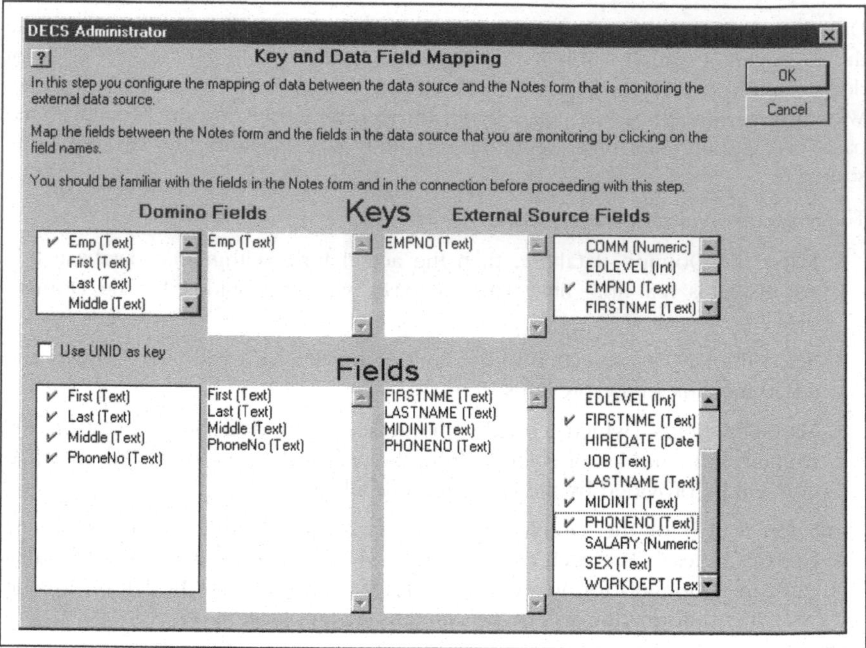

Figure 9-6: Matching key and data fields between Domino and the data source

Next, specify which Domino events you wish to have monitored. If you only want to extract data, select Open, but you also have the option to Create, Delete, or Update records in the backend data via Domino. When editing the activity document, you have the capacity (if the developer has specified this) to run a formula before any of these events occur, and you can also run any predefined triggers from the backend data source. There are also some general options that control caching of results, what to do in case of data precision loss for numeric fields, and whether trailing spaces in text fields should be trimmed.

Having completed the configuration, give this activity a name and then save it. The activity is not set to autostart by default, so if you want this option, you must manually select it. This autostart will take effect the next time the DECS task is started on the server. Don't start the activity yet, since you probably need to initialize the keys in your Domino database (see the following paragraph), and this cannot be done with the activity running. The full activity document then looks like Figure 9-7.

Before you deploy this application, you probably need to populate the Domino database with documents, since it probably currently contains none. What is needed is documents in Domino that match the keys from the backend data source. The DECS Administrator comes to your aid here; otherwise you would

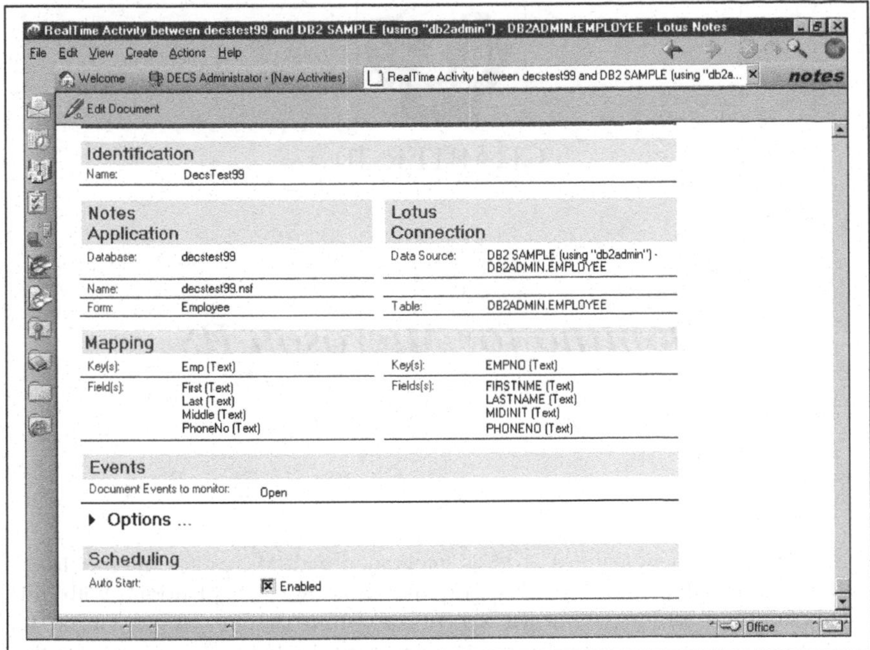

Figure 9-7: DECS activity document

have to manually or programmatically create a document in Domino for every key from the backend data source you selected. To do this, select the activity in the DECS Administrator database and then Actions → Initialize Keys. DECS knows from the activity configuration what the Domino form name is and what the key field is called within that document. It then creates a document in Domino to match every record from the selected backend database.

Now the configured DECS activity can be started manually from DECS Administrator (or the DECS task stopped and reloaded on the server).

CHAPTER 10

Domino for Microsoft IIS

One of the many new features of R5 is integration with Microsoft's Internet Information Server (IIS) 4.0 web server on the Windows NT platform. With this integration, you no longer run the HTTP stack from Domino, instead using IIS ISAPI extension mechanisms to serve Domino to web clients. The reason for this addition is that some organizations were interested in Domino's functionality, but at the same time were committed to Microsoft's IIS product and were not interested in supporting another HTTP stack in their environment. For example, IS managers may already have management tools in place to work with IIS to monitor usage, peak loads. and attempted security breaches. Using Domino for Microsoft IIS then allows these managers to keep using the tools they have purchased and/or built themselves and still provide the web functionality that Domino offers.

On the basic level, the functionality offered by IIS and Domino's `HTTP` task is the same. They serve static HTML pages, Java applets, graphics files, and support technologies such SSL, CGI, and SSI (see Chapter 5, *Domino as a Web Server*). Where they differ is in the proprietary application development extensions they provide. IIS has Active Server Pages (ASP), and Domino has its own design elements (forms, views, pages, outlines) and programming language support for its formula language and the LotusScript scripting language. Domino also has built-in replication of both data and application design, and mail-enabling of applications is very easy. ASP uses a scripting engine such as VBScript to manipulate standard and custom objects to dynamically generate HTML output for the client. Therefore, it is not a huge leap to imagine application developers now wanting to use ASP in combination with Domino replication of data and mail features in their web applications.

Most applications will work identically under this environment and the Domino HTTP stack. Obviously, all static HTML and graphics files are now served by IIS and not Domino. It is also means that some of the CGI values returned will be different, since they relate directly to the server software used to run the CGI processes, which are now IIS and not Domino.

Specific Domino HTTP features are, of course, not supported under this configuration. These include:

- Domino Internet Cluster Manager, the new clustering feature in R5 that supports load balancing and failover for web clients.
- Domino Server API (DSAPI), the API used to extend Domino functionality (like ISAPI for IIS).
- Support for the *HTTPD.CNF* configuration file. Configuration changes instead must be made within IIS.
- Support for Java Servlets. However, there are add-on products to IIS that can provide this functionality.
- Web configuration documents defined in Domino, which must be defined in IIS. These include virtual servers and virtual directories. The NT file system provides the filesystem security support here. Custom Domino web error pages are still supported.

Table 10-1 shows a brief comparison of Domino and IIS. The main differences are in the programming models used with each of the products. IIS has Active Server Pages, which can use VBScript or JScript embedded into the HTML and is processed on the server. These scripting languages can be used to invoke COM objects written in Visual C++ or Visual Basic that perform specific tasks. Domino has a number of programming options such as a formula macro-type language, LotusScript, and Java to perform tasks.

Table 10-1: Comparison of Domino and IIS

Feature	*Domino*	*IIS*
Licensing cost	Needs license	Free—comes with Windows NT/2000
Supported platforms	Windows NT/2000, OS/2, OS/390, OS/400, HP-UX, AIX, Solaris, and Linux	Windows NT/2000
Java support	Java server agents and servlets supported; Java support will be further improved due to plans to integrate Domino and WebSphere	None—requires add-on products.
Support for CGI and server-side includes	Supported	Supported
FTP server	Not included	Included
Replication of data and web content	Part of core product	None—requires add-on products
Authentication/security model	Uses own model, with optional LDAP authentication referrals	Uses Windows NT/2000
Support for FrontPage web bots	None	Supported

Table 10-1: Comparison of Domino and IIS (continued)

Feature	*Domino*	*IIS*
Mail integration for applications	Part of core product	Requires Exchange
Web server application clustering	New Internet Cluster Manager is part of the Domino Enterprise Server product	None—requires add-on products

Prerequisites

Domino for Microsoft IIS requires both NT 4.0 and IIS at Service Pack 4 or later. Also, the server ID file should not have a password, and if this ID file is not located in the server's data directory, the *NOTES.INI* for the server should have an entry for `ServerKeyFile` which points to the fully qualified location of the ID file. If you are installing a new Domino server, these steps will have been done for you automatically. Without completion of these steps, IIS will hang as it passes the URL to Domino for processing.

Last, remove the `HTTP` task from the `ServerTasks=` line in *NOTES.INI*, or else Domino and IIS will contend for the same TCP port. However, you could run both if you configured the Server document in Domino to use a different port for HTTP.

IIS Configuration

Three quick steps are required to enable IIS to invoke Domino. All of these changes are made in the Microsoft Management Console (MMC) snap-in for IIS. When this program is started, it looks like Figure 10-1. The process when configuring Windows 2000 is the same, except that it is called the Internet Services Manager, and is started from Programs → Administration Tools → Internet Services Manager. Then, the following configuration changes are needed:

1. Configure the ISAPI extension for Domino. This application mapping tells IIS to pass URLs with the .NSF extension to Domino for processing. The extension is called *NIISEXTN.DLL* on Intel NT machines and *AIISEXTN.DLL* on Alpha NT machines. To do this, select the web site to configure in the MMC, then use the right mouse button to select Properties. Then choose Home Directory → Application → Configure → dialog box as in Figure 10-2. The option to exclude the `HTTP PUT` and `HTTP DELETE` methods means that only `HTTP GET` commands are passed from IIS to Domino. `HTTP GET` commands are the regular commands issued by the browser to retrieve objects from the web server. The script engine checkbox allows the Domino extension to run without having explicit Execute access within IIS to the directory in which it resides.
2. Configure the ISAPI filter for Domino. (See Figure 10-3.) This DLL checks every incoming request and outgoing response and captures the Domino *?OpenServer* URL and passes it to Domino for processing (for example, *http://westline.alameda.com/?OpenServer*, which lists all of the Domino databases on the server). The filter is called *NIISFILT.DLL* on Intel NT machines and *AIISFILT.DLL* on Alpha NT machines. To do this, select the web site to configure in the MMC, then use the right mouse button to select Properties. Then select ISAPI Filters → Add.

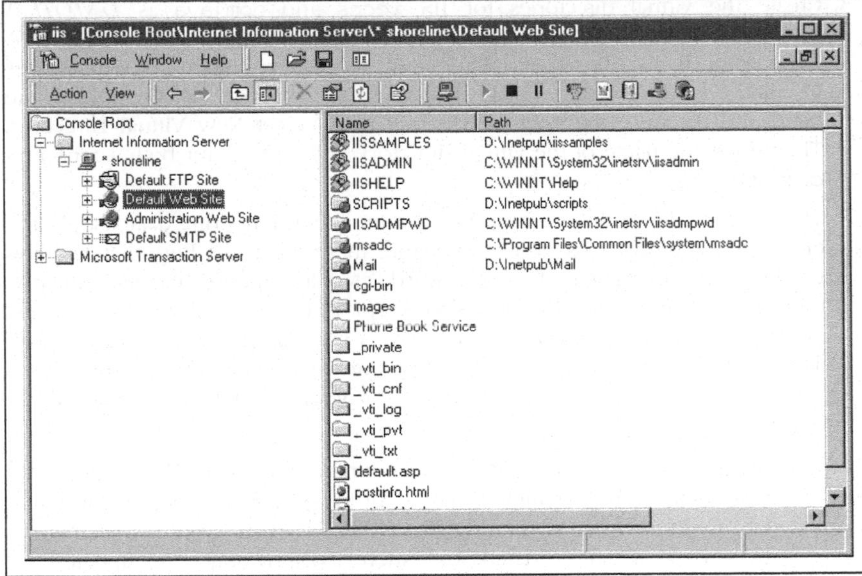

Figure 10-1: : IIS MMC snap-in

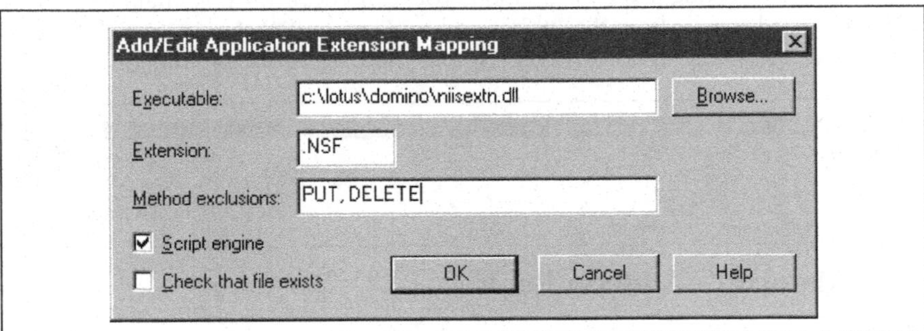

Figure 10-2: Configuring the ISAPI extension for Domino

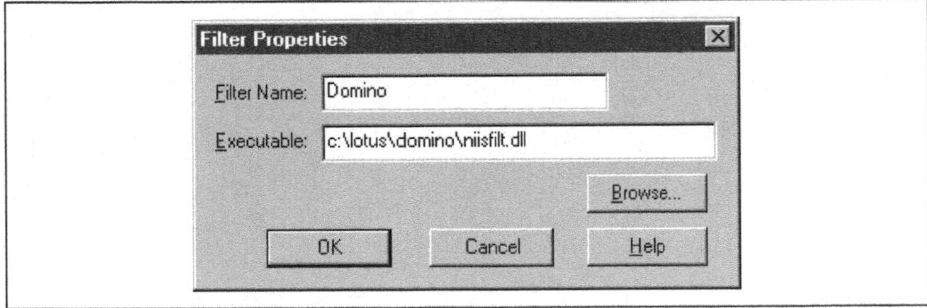

Figure 10-3: Configuring the ISAPI filter for Domino

3. Create the virtual directories for IIS `icons` and `domjava` as *D:\LOTUS\DOMINO\DATA\DOMINO\ICONS* and *D:\LOTUS\DOMINO\DATA\DOMINO\JAVA* respectively (these are the default directories, assuming Domino was installed on the *D:* drive). To do this, select the web site to configure in the MMC and then use the right mouse button to select New Virtual Directory. Then enter the name of the virtual directory and its path for both `icons` and `domjava`.

   These virtual directories are used by Domino when rendering database design elements for browser users. For example, there are icons here that Domino uses for view navigation (Back, Forward, etc.) for browser clients. Similarly, there are a number of Java applets for displaying views and editing rich text fields in a browser. These virtual directories must be given the names *ICONS* and *DOMJAVA* respectively, since these are the names that Domino uses when creating HTML to be sent to the browser client that reference these objects.

All these changes can be made while IIS is running and applied dynamically. You must also be running the Domino server. Although you can actually retrieve Domino data in IIS without it, running the Domino server ensures that maintenance activities on Domino databases, such as indexing, are updated as documents are added, updated, or deleted in Domino.

Then, after completing this configuration, you can check it by opening a Domino database by a browser from the IIS server (see Figure 10-4). For example, to open the Domino Directory we could enter the URL *http://servername/names.nsf*.

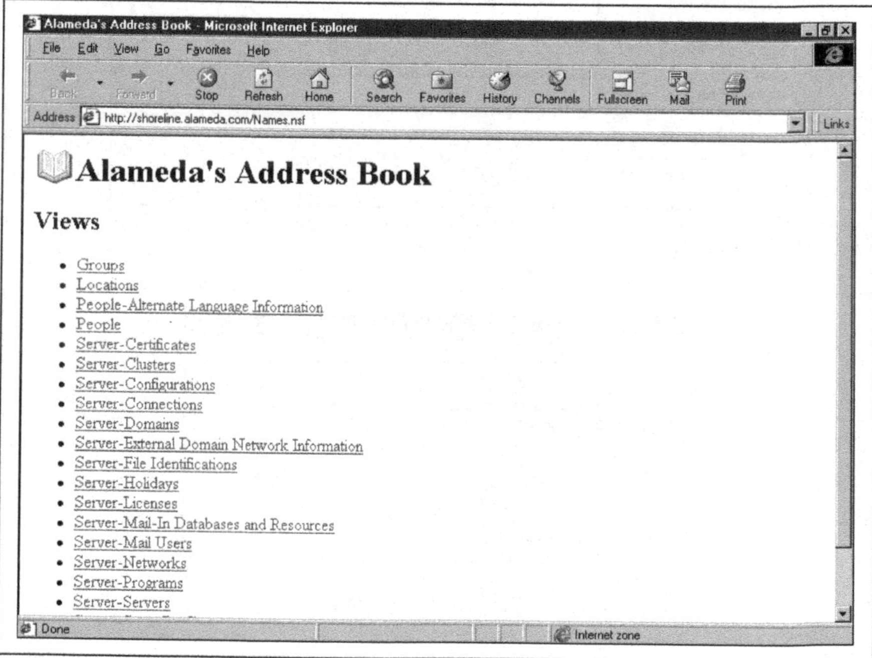

Figure 10-4: Viewing a Domino database in a browser from IIS

Table 10-2 lists the Domino configuration parameters that are supported with this configuration, and if none are supported, Table 10-2 specifies whether there are any equivalent parameters within IIS that can be used.*

Table 10-2: Domino Server Document: Supported Options and IIS MMC Equivalents[a]

Domino Server document tabs	*Domino server document field*	*Supported? or IIS equivalent*
Security	Internet server authentication	✓
Ports—Internet ports—Web	TCP/IP port number	Web site tab—TCP port
	TCP/IP port status	✓
	Authentication options—name and password	✓
	Authentication option—anonymous	✓
	All SSL settings	Directory Security tab—Secure Communications
Internet protocols	Host name	None
	Bind to host name	None
	DNS lookup	None
	Default home page	Home Directory Tab
	Allow HTTP clients to browse databases	✓
	Maximum requests over a connection	None
	Number active threads	None
	All mapping settings	Virtual directory configuration for web site
	All Enable logging settings	Web site tab—enable logging
	All log file settings	Web site tab—enable logging properties
	All log filename settings	None
	All exclude from logging settings	None
	All timeout settings	Web site tab—connection timeout

* This table was taken from an article I wrote for the IIS Administrator newsletter, an offshoot of *Windows NT Magazine*.

Table 10-2: Domino Server Document: Supported Options and IIS MMC Equivalents[a] *(continued)*

Domino Server document tabs	*Domino server document field*	*Supported? or IIS equivalent*
Internet protocols—Domino Web Engine	All HTTP Sessions Settings	✓
	All Java servlet settings	None
	All POST data settings	✓
	All character set mapping settings	✓
	Image conversion format	None
	Interlaced rendering	None
	Default lines per view page	✓
	Maximum lines per view page	✓
	Default search results limit	✓
	Maximum search results limit	✓
	Make this site accessible to crawlers	✓

[a] Copyright 1999 *Windows NT Magazine.* Reprinted with permission.

Authentication

IIS has three authentication models available, any of which can be enabled:

Anonymous access
: No credentials have been entered by the user. This is the default level of access, and a user needs to be authenticated only when anonymous access doesn't provide sufficient access for what they are attempting to do.

Basic authentication.
: User is challenged for credentials, and the user ID and password entered in the browser are sent as clear text to the server, which validates it against NT SAM. If a user doesn't use IE or if NT Challenge and Response is disabled, then this authentication method is used.

NT Challenge and Response.
: For IE only (3.0 and later), this model uses NT security to challenge for credentials and a hashed response is sent by the browser to the server to compare against NT SAM.

If the Anonymous entry in the database ACL that a user wishes to access has sufficient authority to perform what a user wants to do, then you need do nothing. If you need to have users authenticate, then this is when things get interesting. In both cases, the sequence is:

1. The account and password that the user enters are validated against NT SAM.
2. If successful, IIS passes the username to Domino. Domino then matches that username in the Domino Directory to find the Person record it applies to.
3. Domino uses the first username entry in that Person record to check against the Domino database ACL that the user has sufficient access.

The difference for Domino is the username that is passed from IIS depends on which authentication method is used. With NT Challenge and Response, the username is in the form *DOMAIN\USERNAME* (for example, `SFODOM\GNEILSON`) or *COMPUTERNAME\USERNAME* when an NT Server is running as a standalone server. With basic authentication, Domino is passed the username exactly as entered by the user, which can be either of *DOMAIN\USERNAME* or alternatively *USERNAME*. So you need to know what type of authentication will be used by IIS so you know which forms of the NT account name need to be entered in the Person record for each user. Figure 10-5 shows a sample Person record that demonstrates when both user forms are added. Note that in this example, it is a coincidence that the NT domain name and the Domino organization name are the same.

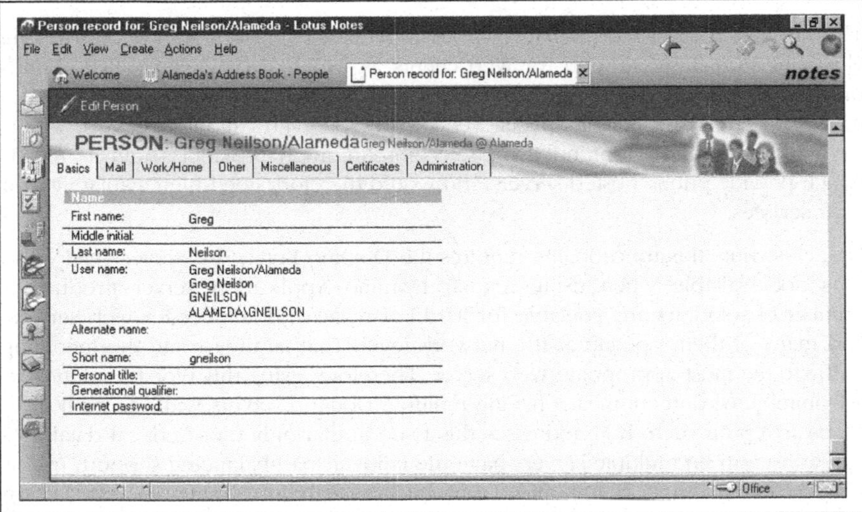

Figure 10-5: Person Record in the Domino Directory with the NT usernames added

Each Person record in the Domino Directory has an Internet password field. This is ignored when using Domino for Microsoft IIS, since all authentication is done by IIS with the NT SAM instead.

CHAPTER 11

Internet Cluster Manager (ICM)

The new Internet Cluster Manager (ICM) functionality in R5 extends the existing clustering to include support for web clients as well as Notes clients. ICM builds on the existing clustering support that has been part of Domino since 4.5. Before that, it was available in the special version of Notes 4.0 called "Notes for Public Networks," which was intended for telecommunication providers such as AT&T, which provide public hosted servers and would therefore need high availability for their services.

Like clustering, this functionality requires the Domino Enterprise Server version, so it is not available when using regular Domino Application Server product. A number of solutions are available for load balancing and failover for web servers, and many of them operate at the network level. That is, they route the incoming traffic to the most appropriate web server. Therefore, using this type of solution in a Domino environment means having multiple Domino servers with identical databases set up on each. ICM addresses this issue in that only those critical databases that are set up on multiple servers have the failover/load-balancing support. In this way, resource usage is minimized but high availability is achieved for critical applications.

Clustering Basics

A *cluster* in Domino is a group of two to six Domino servers that are part of the same Domino domain. Figure 11-1 shows Domino clustering in action. As discussed before, servers within the same Domino domain share the same Domino Directory, *NAMES.NSF*. These servers must be configured to use the TCP/IP network protocol and the same Domino Named Network (DNN). A Domino server can be a member of only one cluster at a time. Very typically, a dedicated network is set up between the servers within a cluster to handle the cluster replication alone, so as not to affect the traffic to/from clients. In this way, the server has a dedicated network card, and thus a Domino network port, for cluster replication, and another network card and Domino network port for serving clients. These dedicated network cards for cluster replication traffic are then part of the same dedicated network hub or switch. Since this is an application-level clustering, the different servers within the same cluster can be running any of the supported operating system platforms, providing load balancing and failover support for critical applications.

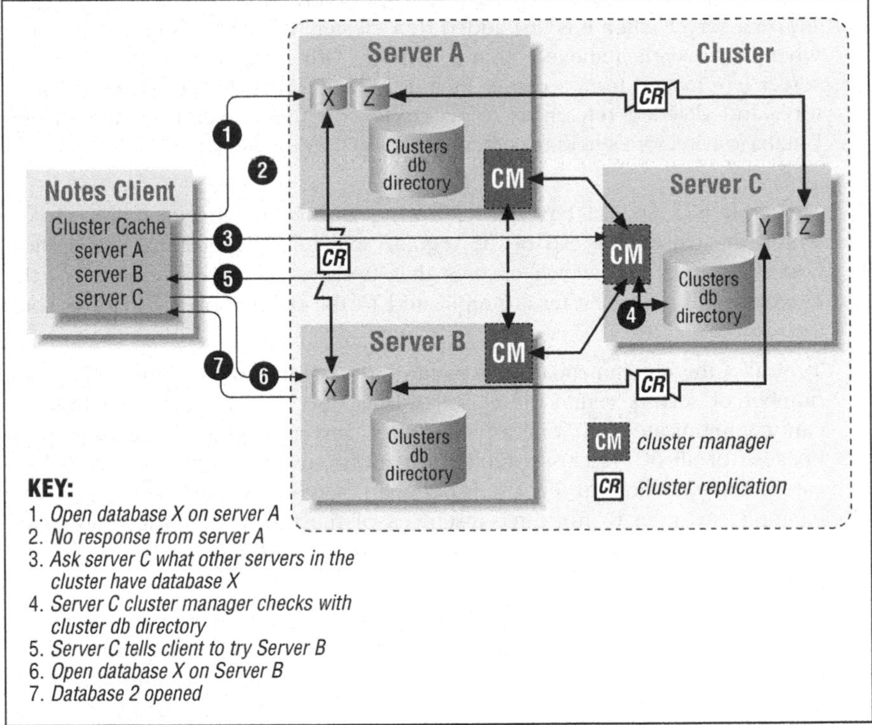

Figure 11-1: Clustering architecture

The components of clustering are as follows:

Cluster Manager
This task runs on all of the servers within the cluster and monitors the status of the other servers within the cluster. This task sends probes to the other servers in the cluster to measure the other servers' availability. It is the Cluster Manager task that refers the Notes client to another server when it is not able to open a database within the cluster.

Cluster Database Directory
This directory contains the details of all databases within the cluster, and a replica copy is stored on every server within the cluster. The Cluster Manager refers to the Cluster Database Directory in order to determine which servers the Notes client should be referred to. In order to make use of clustering, more than one copy of the mission-critical databases must be located on servers within the cluster. These replica copies must be created as needed by the system administrator. Clustering can also be used for mail databases. In this way, only important databases have multiple copies within the cluster.

Cluster Database Directory Manager

This task runs on each server within the cluster and keeps the Cluster Database Directory updated.

Cluster Administrator

This task starts the Cluster Database Directory Manager and Cluster Database Directory tasks (**CLDBDIR** and **CLREPL** respectively), and adds them to *NOTES.INI* on a server when it is first added to a cluster. This task also removes these when a server is removed from a cluster. Other tasks performed when a server is removed from a cluster include deleting the Cluster Database Directory, and deleting references to databases on this server from the Cluster Database Directories held on other servers within the cluster.

Cluster Replicator

This task is a special type of replication that occurs between the servers within the cluster. Instead of the regular scheduled replication, this replication is event-driven, which ensures that updates made to one copy of the database within the cluster are replicated to the other replica copies as soon as possible.

Typically, the recommendation is to run as many instances of this task as the number of servers within the cluster minus one. In this way, each instance can communicate with one of the other servers within the cluster. It is because of all of the cluster replication traffic that it is common for a dedicated network link to be used between servers within the cluster. For example, in order to run three instances of the Cluster Replicator task, add **CLREPL** three times to the **ServerTasks=** line in *NOTES.INI.*

Notes client cluster cache

The Notes client must be using 4.5 or later to be able to work with clustering. The first time Notes connects to a clustered server, it stores within its cluster cache the names of the other servers within the cluster. This cluster cache is used to contact other servers within a cluster to locate other copies of a database when one cannot be opened.

It is important to understand when the failover to other servers within the cluster actually happens. It is triggered when the Notes client cannot access a server or a database on a server it knows is part of a cluster. It also occurs when composing and sending mail, inviting others, and performing free time lookups. Otherwise, if a user is in a database that is no longer available, it must be closed and reopened so that another server within the cluster can be located.

It is suggested that the regular replication (with the **REPLICA** task) also be configured by Connection documents between the servers within the replica. In this way, the databases will be kept up to date if for any reason the Cluster Replication task is stopped on any of the servers within the cluster. Keep in mind that cluster replication does not make use of selective replication, which may produce different replication results from regular replication.

Other servers outside of the replica can use replication with the cluster as a whole, rather than with individual servers. That is, the **REPLICATE** command and the Connection document in the Domino Directory can specify the name of the cluster to replicate with instead of a server. This too requires that the server be running 4.5

or later, and like the Notes client, that the server keeps a cluster cache of the names of servers within the cluster to contact.

The server availability is calculated approximately once per minute, and its value is [100 – (current response time / optimum response time)]. With the *NOTES.INI* statement `Server_Availability_Threshold`, you can set the value of server availability below which the server's `BUSY` state is triggered. When a server is `BUSY`, it will attempt to redirect database open requests to other servers in the cluster, but if none are available, the server will perform the open request.

When the *NOTES.INI* parameter of `Server_Restricted` is set to 1 or 2, the server is in a `RESTRICTED` state and will not perform any further database open requests. Users who have open sessions on the server can continue to work with the open database, but other users should be redirected to other servers in the cluster.

ICM Overview

The ICM extends the Domino clustering concept by making it available to HTTP/HTTPS clients. It regularly probes the Domino servers within the cluster and uses the information contained within the Cluster Database Directory to determine to which server each client request should be referred. Figure 11-2 shows an example of the ICM in action.

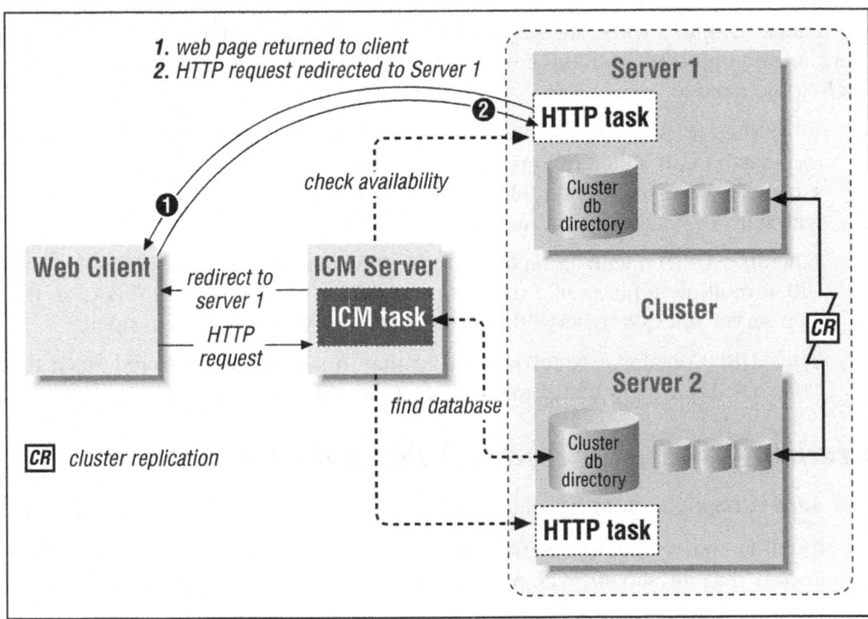

Figure 11-2: ICM example

As for regular clustering, the server running ICM must be running the Domino Enterprise Server version, and must be part of the same domain as the clustered servers.

The ICM server can be located within or outside of the cluster. Having it outside of the cluster can assist in reliability in ensuring that the ICM server is lightly loaded and therefore more likely to be available. It also means that the ICM server must use the Cluster Database Directory on one of the servers within the cluster. If the ICM server is to be located within the cluster, it is recommended that it be on the most lightly loaded server in the cluster, or on the server with the most hardware.

Whether or not you choose to locate the ICM within or outside of the cluster, for redundancy, you can configure multiple ICMs. The usual way to make this work is to configure the DNS with the same alias for multiple machines with the same address. Because of DNS round-robin, these multiple servers will be alternately contacted.

When the ICM is used, the web client contacts the ICM with a URL that requests a database to be opened; for example, *http://<ICMservername>/Names.nsf*. The ICM is able to check with the Cluster Database Directory for servers that contain the database being requested, and from the results of its regular polling, is able to determine the best choice of server to serve the request. The client is then redirected to this server. Any URLs that are created by the server within the cluster and sent back to the web user refer to the ICM rather than to themselves.

When using ICM with a 4.*x* Domino web server, the URLs do not refer to the ICM; generated URLs will keep referring the user back to the same 4.*x* server.

All regular Domino URLs are supported (*?OpenDatabase*, *?OpenView*, etc.), but there are a couple of warnings for using ICM that in most circumstances are not likely to be needed:

- When the URL contains a path, the ICM may not be able to determine the correct database if different servers within the cluster have a database in the same path with different replica IDs. If this happens, the user is presented with a list of databases and must choose the correct database.
- When the URL contains a replica ID, the ICM may not be able to resolve this URL if multiple replicas of a database are on the same server. In this case, the web server selected to serve the user determines which replica to open.
- If the URL contains a NoteID, the ICM may not work as expected since the NotesIDs have the potential to be different in different replicas.

Creating a Cluster and Configuring the ICM

The steps to configure ICM are as follows:

1. Install Domino Enterprise Server on all servers that will be part of the cluster. Ensure that all servers within the cluster that will be serving web browser clients are running the `HTTP` task.
2. Determine the critical application databases that are needed on multiple servers within the cluster. Make the replica copies of each database as needed on the other servers in the cluster. It is good practice to ensure that the ACLs on these database are identical on each replica to make sure the users have the correct access for each replica in the cluster. Selecting the database ACL property "Enforce a consistent Access Control List" across all replicas of this database will ensure that this is the case.

3. (Optional) Create Connection documents between each of the servers within the proposed cluster for regular database replication.
4. Add the servers to the cluster.

   Add multiple Cluster Replicators (the **CLREPL** task) on each server as needed on the **ServerTasks=** line within *NOTES.INI*.

   If a dedicated network port has been set up for cluster replication on each server, add the line **Server_Cluster_Default_Port=*PortName*** to *NOTES.INI* on each server and restart each server.
5. (Optional) Run Cluster Analysis to validate that clustering has been set up properly. This step is not essential for the setup process, but its checks can make certain that everything within the cluster is fine, and save you from tearing your hair out later.
6. Determine which server(s) will be running the **ICM** task. Configure the ICM section of their Server documents within the Domino Directory. Add the **ICM** task to the *NOTES.INI* for these servers.
7. Start the **ICM** task on the server(s).

In the following sections, I will discuss adding the servers to the cluster, running the cluster analysis, and configuring the **ICM** task in more detail.

Adding the Servers to the Cluster

Figure 11-3 shows the process for adding the servers to the cluster. This procedure can be done either from Domino Administrator, using the Configuration tab → All Server Documents view, or from the Servers view in the Domino Directory. Select the Add to Cluster button and the Cluster Name dialog is launched.

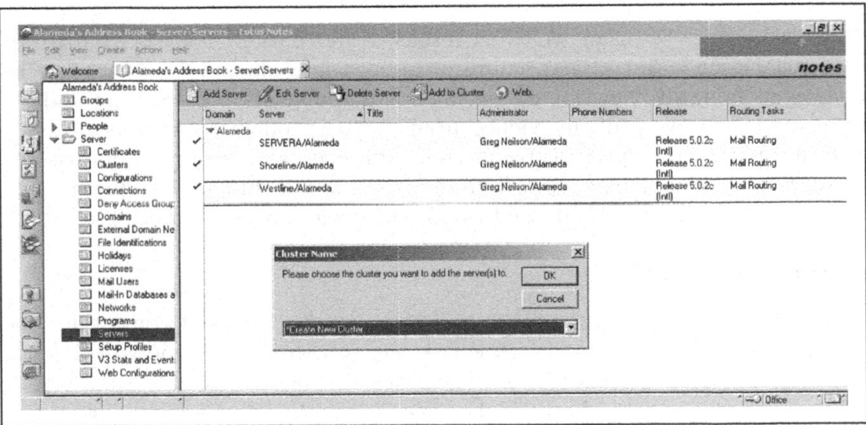

Figure 11-3: Adding the servers to the cluster

If a cluster already exists within the domain, the name of the cluster can be selected from the list, or a new cluster can be created. You are then prompted for a name for the cluster and asked whether you want this done in the foreground or in the background with the **AdminP** task. The **AdminP** task may take longer to complete the setup, but the same configuration changes are done by either choice.

Running Cluster Analysis

Cluster Analysis is a useful tool to ensure that a cluster has been set up correctly. Launch it from Domino Administrator on the Server → Analysis tab, then select Tools → Cluster Analysis. The launches the dialog shown in Figure 11-4, which enables you to choose which cluster analysis tests to perform.

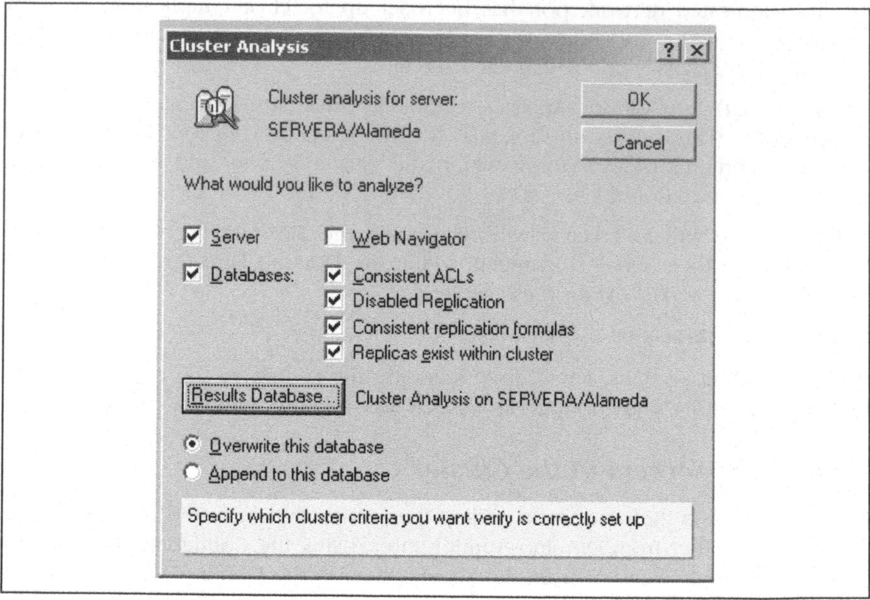

Figure 11-4: Cluster Analysis test selection

The Cluster Analysis agent writes its results to the Cluster Analysis database as shown in Figure 11-5. Each test returns a pass or fail result, and you can select the documents from this view for the details on what tests were carried out and the results obtained. As you can deduce from the large number of errors obtained from this run, there appears to be an issue with network connectivity in that one server is not able to communicate with the others in the cluster. Once these issues are resolved, this tool can be rerun to verify the environment is correctly set up.

Configuring ICM

Now you need to configure the ICM section in the Server document for the server(s) that will be running the `ICM` task. Figure 11-6 is an example of the ICM section. You can open the server document directly from the Domino Directory, or select the Configuration tab within Domino Administrator and locate the Server document to edit either the Current Server document or All Server Documents view.

Many of these fields can be left at the defaults. The Port settings are straightforward, but the Basics and Configuration sections require more explanation:

Cluster Name

The default setting is blank, which means that the cluster name of this server will be used. You need to enter a name here only if the ICM will be running on a server outside of the cluster.

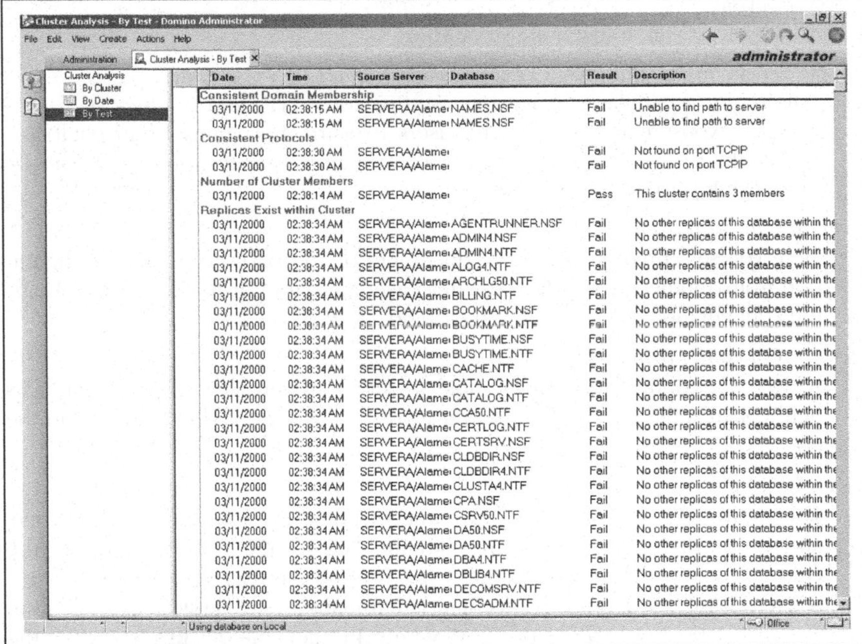

Figure 11-5: Cluster Analysis results

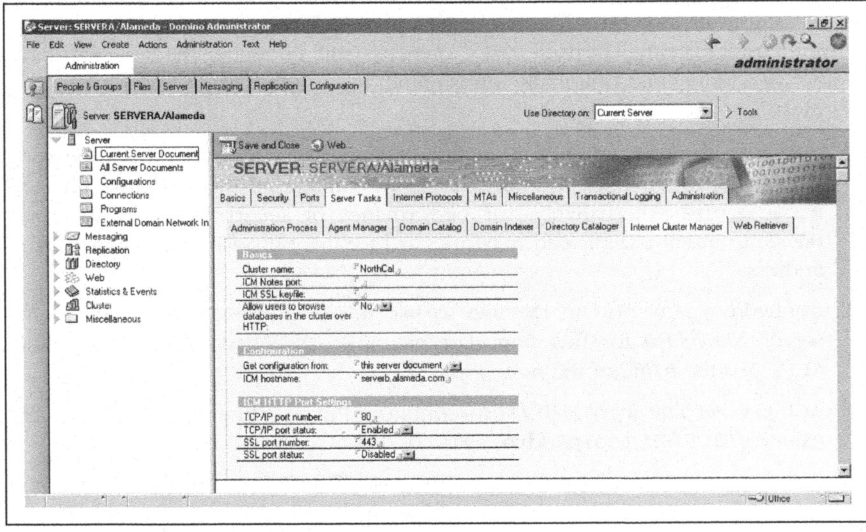

Figure 11-6: ICM section of the Server document

ICM Notes port

This setting is the Domino port used for communication with web browser clients. The default setting is blank, which makes all ports available for client communication.

ICM SSL keyfile
: This is the keyfile to use for SSL by ICM.

Allow users to browse databases in the cluster over HTTP
: This setting is similar to the server setting for HTTP, and is often seen as a security exposure in allowing the users to learn the names of all databases within the cluster by issuing the URL *http://<ICMservername>/?OpenServer*. The default is to not permit this.

Get configuration from
: Here you select either this server document or an option to get the configuration from another server. In the latter case, the name of the server that holds the configuration is listed in the next field.

Obtain ICM configuration from
: If the "Get configuration from" field is set to another server document, this field contains the name of the server to use. Otherwise it is not present in the document.

ICM hostname
: This is the fully qualified domain name of this ICM or IP address that users are to use when communicating with the `ICM`. Domino web servers in the cluster then use this when creating URLs to send the user back to the ICM for referral within the cluster. If this field is left blank (the default), servers within the cluster do not include the ICM within the generated URLs and thus the `ICM` is no longer being used.

If you are running the `ICM` and `HTTP` tasks on the same server, since they both use port 80, they will contend for access to this port. Therefore you can either change the ports used for either of these tasks, or better still, configure the server to have another IP address, and optionally a hostname, to use for ICM. In order to do this, you must:

1. Configure the new IP address at the operating system level. Most operating systems allow multiple IP addresses to be configured on the same physical network card. Alternatively, for performance or security reasons you may decide to install a dedicated network card for this purpose and assign it an IP address.
2. Configure a new port in Domino to use this IP address. Add a line to the server *NOTES.INI* for this port. For example, *`TCPICM`*`=TCP,0,15,0`, where *`TCPICM`* is the name of the new port.
3. Add another line in *NOTES.INI* to configure the IP address for this port. For example, *`TCPICM`*`_TcpIpAddress=10.0.0.1`
4. Use the name of this new port—in this case, TCPICM—in the ICM Notes port field of the `ICM` section of the Server document.
5. To ensure that the `HTTP` and `ICM` tasks can then work on the same machine with port 80, you need to make a small change for HTTP in the Server document. Under the Internet Protocols → HTTP tab, enter the IP address or hostname to use for HTTP. Then, enable the "Bind to host name" field.

CHAPTER 12

R4/R5 Coexistence and Migration

Many IT Managers using R4.*x* were initially interested and excited about the new features offered in R5, but the later-than-expected release of R5, combined with the planned systems "lock-downs" for Y2K in late 1999, meant that in many cases a deployment wasn't practical. Now, R5 is a mature product ready for enterprise use, and finally, there are resources available to assist with the upgrade.

There are two main references you should consult in your planning and testing of the upgrade process. The Lotus manual *Moving to Notes and Domino R5* has a great deal of information in Chapters 1–10. Also, an IBM redbook, *Lotus Notes and Domino Take Center Stage: Upgrading from R4 to R5*, contains practical information about planning and performing the upgrade. You can download this information in PDF (Adobe Acrobat) format from *http://www.redbooks.ibm.com*.

Upgrade Considerations

When planning your upgrade, you should consider carefully the following factors:

Upgrades from R4.1 to R5 are supported
: Most likely, your implementation will be running 4.5*x* or 4.6*x*. The recommendation from Lotus is that before you upgrade, you move to the latest version in your current installed codestream (4.5.7g and 4.6.6c at the time of writing). Appendix G, *Domino Updates: QMRs and QMUs*, covers the general area of QMRs and QMUs in more detail.

Changes to supported server platforms
: The Domino server is no longer supported on the Novell NetWare platform for R5, so if you were using this for R4, select another server operating system.

Changes to supported client platforms
: The Notes R5 client runs only on PowerPC Macintoshes and machines running Windows 95/98/NT/2000. Therefore, if you have clients running

Windows 3.1, OS/2, or Unix, you need to consider how you will support these clients. As I see it, you have three options, ranked from easiest to hardest in the following list:

- Use the browser support in Domino to access mail and applications. This will work only if your custom applications have been designed to work this way (mail and discussion databases that come with the Domino product will work fine). Keep in mind that this method uses a different authentication model—it checks against a password field of the Person record in the Domino Directory, whereas regular Notes users are authenticated against the ID file that is located on their local machine.
- Migrate clients to a 32-bit Windows platform and upgrade the clients to Notes R5 at the same time. This approach has the advantage of requiring only one set of upgrades to the client at a time. For example, an upgrade to Office 2000 may be part of this client install process as well.
- Consider a thin-client solution such as Citrix to provide access for these other platforms.

Native SMTP support

In a typical R4 environment, dedicated machines run the **SMTPMTA** task, which receives incoming Internet mail into Notes and also sends outgoing Internet mail from Notes using SMTP. All the other Domino servers run the standard mail **ROUTER** task, and mail to/from the Internet is sent to the server(s) running **SMTPMTA** first. With R5, the mail **ROUTER** task can now handle SMTP mail natively, so potentially every server can send and receive SMTP mail.

You now have to decide how you want your mail environment to look after the R5 upgrade. This may not be your decision alone, since the network security folks may insist that only certain servers be exposed (and visible) to the Internet to receive mail. For example, for a server to receive mail for your *company.com* Internet domain, the DNS name server needs a record for the server and an MX record that specifies that the server can receive mail. Since these servers are now public knowledge (by being listed in DNS), you can be potentially open to a denial of service attack from the Internet, which in the worst case could crash all of your mail servers.

Native MIME support

Notes/Domino used to have a proprietary internal storage format called "CD" for messages. Messages sent to and from the Internet had to be converted (sometimes with a loss of fidelity) to and from MIME format before transmission. With R5, MIME support has been added for servers and clients. This means that the message integrity is preserved, and all of the processing in changing message formats doesn't need to be done. You should be aware for coexistence of the R4/R5 environment which servers and clients are still running R4, since they need to be accommodated. For example, the Person record for R4 clients needs to be updated in the Domino Directory to specify that incoming messages should be in Notes format; otherwise they may see apparently corrupt incoming messages, particularly those containing attachments, which may be left in MIME format. R4 servers during the transition to R5 will still need a server to send, receive, and perform conversions for Internet mail.

ODS changes

Many of the R5 improvements are related to the new ODS (On Disk Structure), which is the internal structure used for Domino Databases. These enhancements include the new maximum database size, in-place database compaction, fast server restarts, transaction logging, and all the advanced database properties. Therefore, at some stage, as part of the R5 implementation process, you must run the `COMPACT` task to change the ODS version for R5. The internal database format is transparent to clients who access these databases via a server (and not locally).

Transaction logging has two modes of operation: circular and archival. Transactional logging is an optional feature, but if you use it, you must determine what type of logging to use. Alternatively, you could implement circular logging immediately (since the changes involved are much smaller) and possibly consider archival logging at a later date.

Circular logging reuses the logs as needed. The main benefits in using it are write performance (it is quicker to write to the sequential log file than to a Domino database) and server startup after a failure, where the last committed transactions can be applied to the server and Domino can then restart, rather than using the old method, whereby Domino had to check the integrity of every database on the server that it considered might be open.

Archival logging keeps all logs since the last backup. It has all of the benefits of the circular logging, and allows a database to be restored from a backup, and then the contents of the logs rolled forward to provide a point-in-time recovery of the database. This requires backup software that can work with these transaction logs, and a change in the restore process to (a) restore database from backup, then (b) apply the changes from all of the logs taken since that backup. It also requires system administrators be familiar with these changes in backups and that the backup/restore documentation is changed accordingly.

Suggested Upgrade Sequence

Lotus has suggested a sequence for the upgrade that provides immediate benefits from R5 while ensuring that the clients remain operational and unexposed to features that are not available to them. It is also suggested that you upgrade all of your existing environment to R5 before attempting to implement new R5 features. These suggestions are intended to reduce the implementation risks of moving to R5.

This plan assumes you have a medium-to-large environment as well as servers set up for dedicated purposes, such as hub servers, which are the focal point in the architecture for mail routing and database replication for the spoke servers. It is typical to separate servers hosting mail databases from those running applications. This simplifies the environment and ensures that applications with heavy resource usage (such as frequent, long-running, backend server agents) don't detract from the system performance of mail users on the same server.

The suggested upgrade sequence is:

1. Upgrade hub servers
2. Upgrade mail servers

3. Upgrade application servers
4. Upgrade Notes client
5. Upgrade applications
6. Upgrade mail templates
7. Implement new R5 features as required

Upgrading the hub servers first means that the performance benefits from the new ODS version and multiple *MAIL.BOX* databases (which reduce contention on the server for mail processing) can be gained immediately. This is a relatively low-risk upgrade, because the users will not be directly affected by this work. Administrators then should use Domino Administrator to perform administration tasks for this environment.

When the first server in a domain is upgraded, so too is the design of the Domino Directory. This is needed for R5 servers to function. R4 servers can use this directory and R4 clients can view the contents of the upgraded Domino Directory (although many of the form types look rather strange).

The next stage in the upgrade is the mail servers. Note the detailed steps in the Lotus manual that are required when converting R4 servers that were running the `SMTPMTA` task—the inbound and outbound queues need to be cleared before the server is stopped and upgraded to R5. You have the option to upgrade user mail files to the new ODS version now, or this can wait until later.

Next, application servers can be upgraded. This does not mean that the application design can be upgraded to use R5 features at this time—these are the last two steps in the process.

The R5 Client is then rolled out. Although there is a temptation to cut corners and not provide user training, you would be well advised to run an education session for an hour or two to explain the new features of the client. These are intuitive once you understand the new paradigm, but can be intimidating to the user community at large. You need to understand in detail how the R5 client works with the R4 mail design and ensure that your users understand any interim impacts. For example, the bookmarks to open calendars and ToDos will not work as expected, since these open database elements are not present in the R4 mail template. Similarly, server-based Directory Catalogs do not perform the same level of functionality using the type-ahead for mail addressing with R4 clients that they provide for R5 clients.

Next, the applications can be upgraded to using R5 features. If you have applications that only serve browser users, this can of course happen earlier, but if you need to support a mixed Notes/browser audience, it is best if you wait until now. There are a great number of new features here that make web development much easier, and at the same time make sure the Notes experience and the browser experience are similar for the users. For example, there is native frame support in Notes R5, which can be graphically designed using Domino Designer, in contrast to R4.*x*, where frames had to be constructed manually.

The mail template should not be upgraded until all clients are using the R5 Notes client and all servers have been upgraded to R5. This enables features like Rules and Mail signatures for users to operate as designed.

Lastly, one of the compelling features in R5 is the scalability improvement of being able to support more users with less hardware. There is a new function in R5 called the Decommission Server agent, which can be run to quickly provide a checklist of server resources that need to be moved from the target server to the destination server in order to decommission a server from your environment.

CHAPTER 13

Domino Server Tasks and Console Commands

In this chapter, I discuss how to specify which component tasks Domino loads at startup and how to configure Domino to run scheduled maintenance tasks. This type of configuration is usually done once as the server is commissioned, with occasional changes as needed.

There is also a set of commands that you can issue at the Domino server console to dynamically control the operation of the server. These commands are typically used to diagnose and resolve issues with Domino operations, make dynamic configuration changes to the Domino server, or to override scheduled operations and make things such as mail routing or database replication happen immediately.

Domino Server Tasks

A few lines in *NOTES.INI* define which server tasks are started when the server starts up, and also which scheduled tasks are to run at various times during the day.

The `ServerTasks=` line lists the tasks to start as the server starts up. The scheduled tasks are listed in the `ServerTasksAt0=` to `ServerTasksAt23=` lines. These specifications use the 24-hour clock, where 0 is midnight and 23 is 11:00 P.M.

Another option for scheduling tasks is the Program document in the Domino Directory. The Program document is described in Chapter 2, *Domino Directories*.

By default, the following tasks are configured to start, depending on how the server has been configured:

- When the Quick and Easy Configuration setup option is selected, the tasks set to start at startup are `Router`, `Replica`, `Update`, `AMgr`, `AdminP`, `CalConn`, `Event`, `Sched`, `Stats`, and `Maps`. Then other tasks are added depending on which other client audience options are selected:
  - — Web Browsers adds `HTTP` and `DIIOP`
  - — Internet Mail Packages adds `IMAP` and `POP3`

— News Readers adds NNTP

— Enterprise Connection Services adds DECs

- When the Advanced Configuration setup option is selected, the tasks set to start at startup are AdminP, AMgr, Update, Replica, Router, and Maps. Other tasks, such as CalConn, Event, Sched, and Stat, are optionally added if selected. Other tasks are added if they are selected by name. These are:

  — HTTP, DIIOP

  — IMAP, POP3

  — LDAP

  — NNTP

  — DECS

- When the server has been upgraded from 4.x, you are not required to run the setup application after the code has been installed. This means that the original list of startup tasks is retained. Because the Reports task no longer exists in R5 and has been replaced by the Collect task, you must remove it. You also must remove the SMTPMTA statement, since this function has been added to the Router process.

Then, for the scheduled tasks in *NOTES.INI*, these entries are added as part of the original installation:

```
ServerTasksAt1=Catalog,Design
ServerTasksAt2=UpdAll,Object Collect mailobj.nsf
ServerTasksAt3=Object Info -Full
ServerTasksAt5=Statlog
```

You should also be aware that after you reinstall or upgrade your Domino server code, these entries are usually added again to *NOTES.INI*, if they had been removed.

Here is a list of all of the Domino server tasks, their functions, and the specific console commands they accept:

`AdminP`

The Administration Process automates many administration tasks. This task has the following commands available to modify its behavior while it is running:

`tell adminp process all`

Instructs the admin process to process all new and modified immediate/interval/daily/delayed requests.

`tell adminp process daily`

Instructs the admin process to process all new and modified daily requests.

`tell adminp process delayed`

Instructs the admin process to process all new and modified delayed requests.

`tell adminp process interval`

Instructs the admin process to process all immediate and interval requests.

Server Tasks

`tell adminp process new`
: Instructs the `admin` process to process all new requests.

`tell adminp process people`
: Instructs the `admin` process to process all new and modified requests to update Person records within the Domino Directory.

`tell adminp process time`
: Instructs the `admin` process to process all new and modified requests to delete mail files that become unlinked.

`tell adminp show databases`
: Lists the databases that an administration server manages, and also lists databases that do not have an administration server configured.

`AMgr`

The Agent Manager runs scheduled and triggered agents in Domino databases. This task has the following commands available to modify its behavior while it is running:

`tell amgr pause`
: Pauses the agent manager service, so no new agents can be scheduled for execution on the server.

`tell amgr resume`
: Resumes the agent manager service, so new agents can be scheduled for execution on the server.

`tell amgr schedule`
: Displays the scheduled agents that are to run today, and also the database in which they reside.

`tell amgr status`
: Displays the status of the agent manager, and also configuration information of the agent manager from the server document in the Domino Directory.

`Billing`

Collects the configured usage information for billing.

`Calconn` *(Calendar Connector)*

Used to request free/busy time information for users whose mail databases reside on other servers.

`Catalog`

Maintains the Domain Catalog, which helps users to find and locate Domino databases and files of interest to them within the Domino domain.

`Chronos`

Performs updates of database full text indexes for databases that are configured to be updated hourly or daily. This task is autostarted by Domino and does not need to be added to *NOTES.INI* in order to run. You can cause this task to run immediately by issuing the commands `load chronos daily` or `load chronos hourly`.

`Cladmin` *(Cluster Administration Process)*

Ensures correct operation of the Domino application-level cluster.

`Cldbdir` *(Cluster Database Directory Manager)*
Maintains the cluster database directory.

`Clrepl` *(Cluster Replicator)*
Replicates between servers in a cluster in real time. Cluster replication is event-driven, whereas standard replication is schedule-driven. This task has the following commands available to modify its behavior while it is running:

`tell clrepl log`
Instructs the cluster replication tasks to immediately log information into the server log database, rather than wait for the defined log interval. Use this command when cluster replication is encountering problems—you can view the log entries for the errors and ensure that the problem is resolved before the next cluster replication attempt.

`Collect`
Collects server activity statistics from one or more servers. This task has the following command available to modify its behavior while it is running:

`tell collector collect`
Runs the Domino server statistic collection on every server specified and creates statistic reports.

Server Tasks

`Compact` *(Database Compaction)*
Reorganizes the disk usage by each database in order to free up unused space. The `Compact` task can be invoked with the following commands (the various options can be combined as needed):

`load compact` *`[database]`*
Compacts the database or specified subdirectory.

`load compact` *`[database]`* `-S` *`X`*
Compacts databases with greater than *X*% free space.

`load compact` *`[database]`* `-D`
Compacts databases and deletes any built view indexes.

`load compact` *`[database]`* `-R`
Compacts databases and changes the ODS version to R4 from R5. Used when backing out of an upgrade from R4 to R5.

`load compact` *`[database]`* `-M`
For R4 databases, sets a maximum size of 4GB and compacts the database.

`load compact` *`[database]`* `-b`
Compacts databases in place. Can be used only if the database internal format is not being changed due to a change in one if the advanced database properties. It recovers unused space within the database, but does not reduce the file size of the database.

`load compact` *`[database]`* `-B`
Compacts databases in place. It recovers unused space within the database, and does reduce the file size of the database.

`load compact [database] -c`

Uses copy-style compaction of the database, rather than in-place compaction.

`load compact [database] -L`

When using copy-style compaction, allows access to the database while the compaction is in process. Compaction ends for the database if a user accesses the database.

`load compact [database] -i`

When using copy-style compaction, ignores any errors that occur during compaction.

`load compact [database] -f`

Compacts the database and changes the format of the database to disable support for document table bitmap optimization.

`load compact [database] -F`

Compacts the database and changes the format of the database to enable support for document table bitmap optimization.

`load compact [database] -H`

Compacts the database and changes the format of the database to enable support for maintenance of the specialized response hierarchy used by the @AllChildren and @AllDesendants view selection formulae.

`load compact [database] -h`

Compacts the database and changes the format of the database to disable support for maintenance of the specialized response hierarchy used by the @AllChildren and @AllDesendants view selection formulae.

`load compact [database] -T`

Compacts the database and changes the format of the database to enable transactional logging.

`load compact [database] -t`

Compacts the database and changes the format of the database to disable transactional logging.

`load compact [database] -U`

Compacts the database and changes the format of the database to maintain unread marks.

`load compact [database] -u`

Compacts the database and changes the format of the database to disable maintaining unread marks.

`load compact [database] -A`

Doesn't compact the database; archives documents to another database, and then deletes those documents from this database if archiving is set up for the database.

`load compact [database] -a`

If archiving is set up for the database, archives documents to another database and then deletes these documents from this database and compacts the database.

`Convert`

Used to update the mail databases to a new mail template design, typically used when upgrading the server to from R4 to R5. The Convert task can be invoked with the following commands:

`load convert [-r]` *`mailfilepath currenttemplatename newtemplatename`*

Converts the mail databases in the given *`mailfilepath`* from the *`currenttemplatename`* (* can be used to match all existing templates) to the *`newtemplatename`*. The new mail template for R5 is called *MAIL50.NTF*. The `-r` option is used to recursively process subdirectories below the given *`mailfilepath`*.

`load convert -l` *`mailfilelist`*

Produces a list of primary mail databases (but not replicas) on the server and writes the list to the file specified in *`mailfilelist`*. This option is used to produce a list of mail database files, which would be used with the `-f` option as shown in the next entry.

`load convert -f` *`mailfilelist currenttemplatename newtemplatename`*

Updates the mail databases listed in the *`mailfilelist`* from the *`currenttemplatename`* (* can be used to match all previous templates) to the *`newtemplatename`*. The new template in R5 is called *MAIL50.NTF*.

`load convert -m` *`mailfilepath`*

Changes the mail databases specified within the *`mailfilepath`* to able be used for IMAP mail access.

`DECS` *(Domino Enterprise Connection Services)*

Enables hot linking between documents within a Domino database and backend data sources such as DB2 or Oracle.

`Design`

Updates database designs from their template.

`DIIOP`

An object request broker; allows browser clients running Java applets to access backend Notes database objects via the IIOP protocol. This task has the following commands available to modify its behavior while it is running:

`tell diiop show users`

Shows all active users connected to the server by DIIOP.

`tell diiop drop all`

Drops all user connections using DIIOP immediately.

`Dircat`

Maintains small copies of the Domino Directory called the Directory Catalog, which can be used for user lookup for mobile/laptop users. This task is usually not started via an entry in *NOTES.INI*; when you enable a schedule on the Directory Cataloger tab in the Server Document this task is launched automatically.

`Event` *(Event Monitor)*

Tracks of specific events that have occurred on the Domino server

Server Tasks

`Fixup`

Fixes suspected corrupt Domino databases. These options can be combined as needed:

`load fixup [`*database*`] -F`

When `fixup` runs against multiple databases, by default it checks only documents with the last modified date since its last run. This parameter then forces the `fixup` task to check all documents in all databases being checked.

`load fixup [`*database*`] -i`

Checks only new documents in the database since the last run of `fixup`.

`load fixup [`*database*`] -J`

Runs `fixup` against databases that have transaction logging enabled. If this parameter isn't used, `fixup` doesn't check these databases.

`load fixup -L`

When used without specifying the database to check, logs every database suspected of being corrupted. The default is to log only when a database problem is found and needs to be corrected.

`load fixup [`*database*`] -N`

Changes the way that `fixup` operates when a corrupted document within a database is encountered. When this parameter is specified, any corrupted documents found are not deleted. A typical use of this is to allow documents to be copied to another database before `fixup` deletes them in an effort to retrieve documents from a corrupted database.

`load fixup [`*database*`] -Q`

Instructs `fixup` to be less thorough in its checking for corrupted documents in the database.

`load fixup [`*database*`] -U`

Changes unread document lists to the older R4 format. (Lotus recommends that you do this only when requested by Lotus Support.)

`load fixup [`*database*`] -V`

Specifies to not check views for corruption.

`HTTP` *(Domino web server)*

Serves regular HTML/CGI and converts Domino elements into HTML/Java applets as required. This task has the following commands available to modify its behavior while it is running:

`tell http restart`

Refreshes the configuration for the `HTTP` task without having to unload and reload the task into the server memory.

`tell http show file access`

Shows filesystem access on the server for HTTP clients.

`tell http show security`

Displays SSL configuration information for the web server.

`tell http show users`
: Shows the current list of session-based users that are connected and authenticated to Domino.

`tell http show virtual servers`
: Displays the configured virtual web servers defined on the Domino server.

`ICM` *(Internet Cluster Manager)*
: Manages access to clustered servers for HTTP (web) clients.

`IMAP`
: Facilitates access to Domino mail databases by IMAP clients.

`LDAP`
: Facilitates access to the Domino Directory by LDAP clients. This task has the following commands available to modify its behavior while it is running:

`tell ldap reloadschema`
: Updates the schema for LDAP to reflect customizations made to the Domino Directory.

`tell ldap exportschema`
: Creates or updates the schema database (*SCHEMA50.NSF*) to reflect schema changes in the Domino Directory.

Server Tasks

`Maps`
: Extracts information from Connection documents to produce the graphical replication and routing information in Domino Administrator.

`MTC` *(Message Tracking Collector)*
: Monitors the work of the `Router` process (which delivers mail in Domino) and keeps records as required as to what mail was sent to whom. This allows users and administrators to query mail status. This task does not need to be explicitly started; if mail tracking is enabled on the server by a Configuration document, then Domino will start this task automatically as the `Router` task is started.

`tell mtc process`
: Collects information now for message tracking, rather than waiting for the message tracking interval.

`tell mtc interval` *`value`*
: Changes the collection interval used for message tracking information by the `MTC` task.

`tell mtc compact`
: Compacts the message tracking store database now.

`tell mtc reindex`
: Reindexes the message tracking store database now.

`tell mtc purge` *`value`*
: Purges collected message tracking information older than *`value`* days from the message tracking database now.

`NNTP`

Enables the Domino server to be used as a newsgroup server. This task has the following commands available to modify its behavior while it is running:

`tell nntp newgroup` *`newsgroupname`*
Creates a new newsgroup called *`newsgroupname`*.

`tell nntp newgroup delete` *`groupname1, groupname2`*
Deletes the specified newsgroups.

`tell nntp newgroup` *`newsgroupname pathname`*
Tells the `NNTP` task to add a new newsgroup to its cache using the specified database.

`tell nntp print cache list`
Displays the current newsgroups and their corresponding databases.

`tell nntp print config`
Shows the configuration information for the NNTP server.

`tell nntp reset` *`servername`*
Resets the newsfeed from the specified server, so the next newsfeed will be considered an initial newsfeed.

`tell nntp show config`
Shows the configuration information for the NNTP server.

`tell nttp show groups`
Shows the currently configured newsgroups on the server, and the path of each relative to the data directory on the server.

`Object` *(Object Store Manager)*

Works with single-object store mail databases, if enabled. The `Object` task can be invoked as follows:

`load object create` *`sharedmaildb.nsf`*
Creates a new shared mail database with the name *`sharedmaildb.nsf`*.

`load object link` *`usermaildb.nsf sharedmaildb.nsf`*
Links messages already present within *`sharedmaildb.nsf`* into the shared mail database.

`load object link -nocompact` *`usermaildb.nsf sharedmaildb.nsf`*
Links messages already present within *`sharedmaildb.nsf`* into the shared mail database. The `-nocompact` option means that *`usermaildb.nsf`* is not compacted (which reclaims unused space in databases) even if there are more than five messages linked into *`sharedmaildb.nsf`*.

`load object link -relink` *`usermaildb.nsf sharedmaildb.nsf`*
Links a user's mail database to a different *`sharedmaildb.nsf`*.

`load object unlink` *`usermaildb.nsf`*
Unlinks messages for the given *`usermaildb.nsf`*.

`load object unlink` *`sharedmaildb.nsf`*
Unlinks messages for the given *`sharedmaildb.nsf`*.

`load object set -never` *`usermaildb.nsf`*
Sets *`usermaildb.nsf`* to never use shared mail.

`load object reset -never usermaildb.nsf`
: Removes the setting to never use shared mail for *usernmildb.nsf*.

`load object set -always usermaildb.nsf sharedmaildb.nsf`
: Ensures all replicas of the *usermaildb.nsf* use the shared mail database *sharedmaildb.nsf*.

`load object reset -always usermaildb.nsf`
: Removes the setting that makes sure all replicas of *usermaildb.nsf* use the shared mail database.

`load object collect -nodelete`
: Checks which old messages are ready to be deleted, but does not actually delete them.

`load object collect usermaildb.nsf`
: Deletes obsolete messages from the *usermaildb.nsf*.

`load object collect sharedmaildb.nsf`
: Deletes obsolete messages from the *sharedmaildb.nsf*.

`load object collect -force sharedmaildb.nsf`
: The `-force` option is used after a user mail database has been deleted, and you wish to reclaim the space used for linked messages in *sharedmaildb.nsf* that were referred to only from that user mail database.

`load object info usermaildb.nsf`
: Checks whether the *usermaildb.nsf* contains any messages that use a shared mail database.

`POP3`
: Facilitates access to Domino mail databases by POP3 clients.

`Replica`
: Allows Domino servers to replicate database updates with each other.

`Router`
: Delivers mail to databases on this server and forwards it to other servers as required. This task has the following commands available to modify its behavior while it is running:

`tell router delivery stats`
: Shows the current mail routing delivery statistics.

`tell router compact`
: Shuts down the mail routing process on the server, and compacts the *MAIL.BOX* database. If more than one *MAIL.BOX* is on the server (for example, *MAIL1.BOX* and *MAIL2.BOX* if the server is configured to have two), each of these databases is compacted in turn. When the compaction activity is complete, the router process is resumed.

`tell router show queues`
: Shows the current number of waiting mail items in the queues for each destination mail server.

`tell router use databasename`

Enables the use of shared mail on this server. It also changes the value of `SHARED_MAIL` to 2 in *NOTES.INI*. `databasename` is the name of the database used for the shared mail database, and a new database link called *MAILOBJ.NSF* is created in the server data directory, which points to `databasename`.

`RunJava ISpy`

Allows us to configure probes between servers to periodically check that servers can be accessed to send mail or that they can communicate via a TCP port. Note that this task name is case-sensitive—it must be specified in this way (with an uppercase `IS` and lowercase `py`)—otherwise, the Java VM within Domino will not be able to find the appropriate Java classes to load.

`Sched` *(Schedule Manager)*

Tracks free/busy time for all who have their mail database on that server. This task has the following commands available to modify its behavior while it is running:

`tell sched stats`

Displays the number of user appointments and resources reservations in the free time database.

`tell sched show username`

Displays when `username` is busy according to the schedule in that given user's mail database.

`tell sched validate`

For every mail user on the server, checks whether free/busy time is recorded in the free time database.

`tell sched validate username`

For `username`, checks whether free/busy time is recorded in the free time database.

`SMTP`

Listens for incoming SMTP mail. Usually you need not configure this task to start; it is started automatically once the `SMTP Listener` task is enabled on the Server document within the Domino Directory.

`Statlog`

Records database usage information into the Domino Log file, *LOG.NSF*.

`Stats`

Produces statistics for a Domino server.

`Updall` *(Indexer)*

Maintains changed views and full text indices as the data changes within the Domino database.

`load updall [database] -A`

Performs an incremental update of an R4 site search database.

`load updall [database] -B`

Performs a full update of an R4 site search database.

`load updall` *`database`* `-C`
: Rebuilds the full text indexes and any unused views in the database.

`load updall [`*`database`*`] -F`
: Updates full text indexes but not views.

`load updall [`*`database`*`] -H`
: Updates full text indexes that are configured to be updated immediately.

`load updall [`*`database`*`] -L`
: Updates full text indexes that are configured to be updated immediately, hourly, or daily.

`load updall [`*`database`*`] -M`
: Updates full text indexes that are configured to be updated immediately or hourly.

`load updall [`*`database`*`] -R`
: Rebuilds all full text indexes and all views in the database.

`load updall` *`database`* `-T` *`view`*
: Rebuilds the out-of-date view in the database.

`load updall` *`database`* `-T` *`view`* `-R`
: Rebuilds the view in the database whether or not it is out of date.

`load updall [`*`database`*`] -V`
: Updates view but not full text indexes.

`load updall [`*`database`*`] -X`
: Displays the number of user appointments and resource reservations in the free time database.

`Web`
: Converts HTML web pages into Notes documents for retrieval by Notes clients. This task has the following commands available to modify its behavior while it is running:

`tell web help`
: Lists the available options for the web task: `tell web quit`, `load web`, `tell web help`, and `tell web refresh`.

`tell web refresh`
: Refreshes the web navigator task settings while the task is running.

Domino Server Console

The Domino server console is a DOS-like window on NT and OS/2 servers in which you can view server messages and enter commands. For those platforms, switch to this open window to access it at the server. On the AS/400 platform, issue the command `WRKDOMCSL` *`servername`* (work with Domino Console) to access the Domino console. On the OS/390 platform, you have the option to use telnet or the OS/390 operator console with the as-is DOMCON package, which is downloadable from *http://www.s390.ibm.com/products/domino/domcon/dmcmain.html.*

On the Unix platforms (AIX, HP/UX, Linux, and Solaris), there is a new character console in R5 that can be used to access the server console. This function works

Server Tasks

only on the Domino server itself, so to do this remotely requires telnet access to the server. Also, you have to be listed as an Administrator for that server within the Domino Directory. The steps to use this function in Unix are:

- Change to the data directory for the server (`cd ~/notes/data`).
- Execute the cconsole program (`/opt/bin/cconsole`).
- Enter the location of your ID file, then enter your password.

There are three special commands available on the Unix platforms to work with this character console:

`done`
: Exits the console program.

`live on`
: Turns on live update of server messages on the console.

`live off`
: Turns off live update of server messages on the console. You might do this so that commands you enter and any responses made by Domino are not lost in a sea of updated messages issued by the running server.

These console commands on all platforms are also logged in the *LOG.NSF* database on the server. So if the output messages from the commands you enter get scrolled off the screen because of other messages from the server, you can open the Miscellaneous Events view of this database to review the output messages. The documents in this view are listed in chronological order, with the most recent log messages therefore at the bottom of the view (see Figure 13-1).

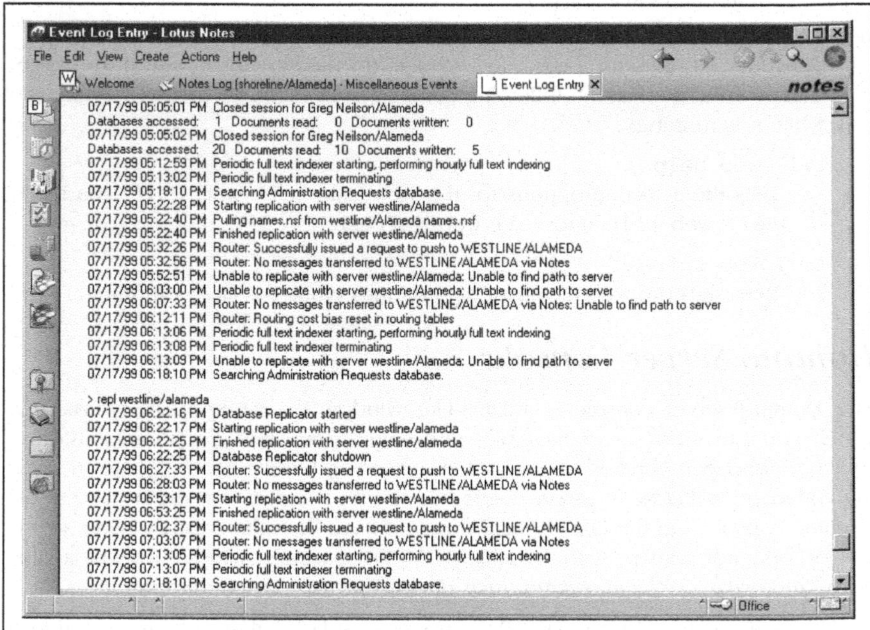

Figure 13-1: Viewing old console messages in the server's log database (LOG.NSF)

As discussed in Chapter 6, *Domino Administration Tools*, Domino Administrator has an option on the Server tab to access the console of the current server being administered. You are more likely to use this in day-to-day operations than you are to use the server itself. Another advantage of using this mode of operation is that the Domino Administrator client has a built-in list of server commands, which means that you don't need to always work from memory on the command names and their correct syntax (see Figure 13-2).

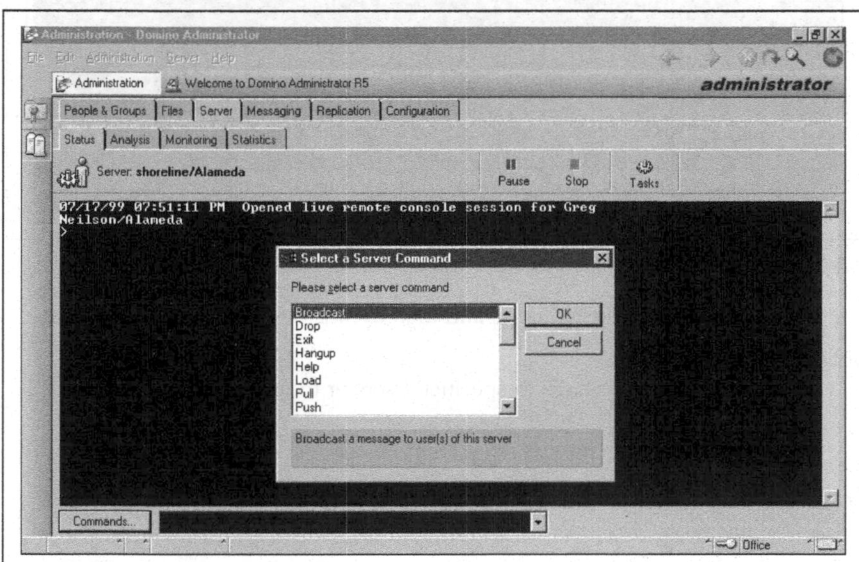

Figure 13-2: Accessing the server console via the Domino Administrator client

The Domino server console supports redirection for both input and output with the > and < operators. You can create a text file of server commands, then issue the name of the file on the server console to run the command listed in this batch file of server commands. The default location of this file is *\LOTUS\DOMINO*, so if another location is specified, then the fully qualified filename of this file must be entered at the server console. A use for this could be when you wish to push changes now from a hub server to all the spoke servers in the company, rather than wait until the replication schedule. You could have a text file on the hub server that contains a series of `PUSH` commands to each server, and run this just by typing the name of this command file.

You can also redirect the console output into a file. If you use Domino Administrator, you can see that under the hood, this is how it gets some of the server information about task and user status. Figure 13-3 shows examples of both types of command redirection (the meaning of the actual commands listed will be explained later in this chapter).

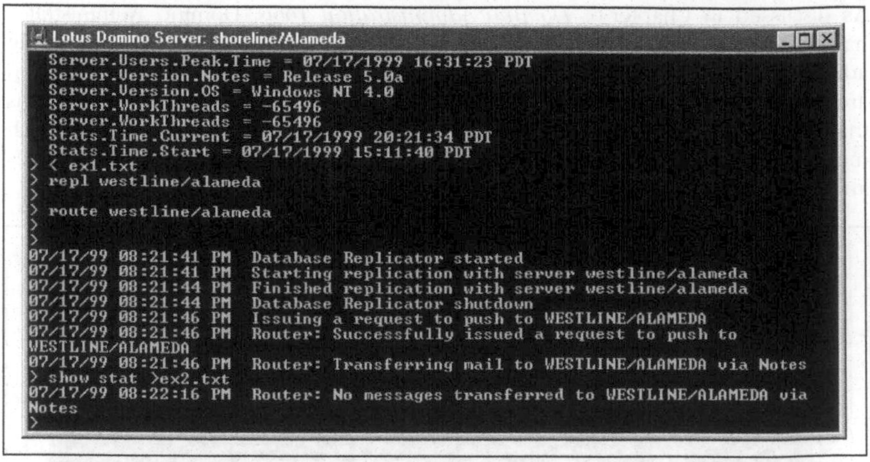

```
Lotus Domino Server: shoreline/Alameda
  Server.Users.Peak.Time = 07/17/1999 16:31:23 PDT
  Server.Version.Notes = Release 5.0a
  Server.Version.OS = Windows NT 4.0
  Server.WorkThreads = -65496
  Server.WorkThreads = -65496
  Stats.Time.Current = 07/17/1999 20:21:34 PDT
  Stats.Time.Start = 07/17/1999 15:11:40 PDT
> < ex1.txt
> repl westline/alameda
>
> route westline/alameda
>
>
07/17/99 08:21:41 PM  Database Replicator started
07/17/99 08:21:41 PM  Starting replication with server westline/alameda
07/17/99 08:21:44 PM  Finished replication with server westline/alameda
07/17/99 08:21:44 PM  Database Replicator shutdown
07/17/99 08:21:46 PM  Issuing a request to push to WESTLINE/ALAMEDA
07/17/99 08:21:46 PM  Router: Successfully issued a request to push to
WESTLINE/ALAMEDA
07/17/99 08:21:46 PM  Router: Transferring mail to WESTLINE/ALAMEDA via Notes
> show stat >ex2.txt
07/17/99 08:22:16 PM  Router: No messages transferred to WESTLINE/ALAMEDA via
Notes
>
```

Figure 13-3: Redirection of input and output with the Domino server console

The basic commands are listed here, and then each is described in further detail:

`broadcast`
: Sends a broadcast message to specified users or to all users.

`dbcache`
: Displays, disables, or flushes the Domino database cache.

`drop`
: Drops the server sessions for specified users or all users.

`exit`
: Stops the Domino server.

`help`
: Lists all Domino servers available.

`load`
: Starts a task on the server.

`platform`
: Works with the collection of operating system statistics by Domino.

`pull`
: Starts replication now from the specified server.

`push`
: Starts replication now to the specified server.

`quit`
: Stops the Domino server.

`replicate`
: Starts replication now from/to the specified server.

`restart`
: Stops and restarts the Domino server or the specified communication port.

`route`
: Starts mail routing with the specified server.

`set`
: Makes changes to the Domino server configuration.

`show`
: Displays information about the Domino server.

`start port`
: Enables the given Domino port for network connections.

`stop port`
: Disables the given Domino port for network connections.

`tell`
: Issues a command to a Domino server task.

`trace`
: Tests the connection to another server.

---

broadcast (b)

This is a broadcast message from the server console to either nominated users or to all connected users to the server. This message is displayed in the status bar of the Notes client with no warning sound, so it can be very easy to for users to miss the message.

Syntax

```
broadcast message
broadcast message users
```

Command options

`message`
: The message you wish to send. For messages containing spaces, enclose the entire message in quotation marks to ensure that it is processed as the message content.

`users`
: Defines which users receive the message. If this parameter is not specified, the command applies to all connected users. If a name is a specified, it should be enclosed in quotes.

Examples

```
> b "Please close all open Domino databases for scheduled maintenance"
07/11/99 09:16:06 PM  BROADCAST from shoreline/Alameda: Please close all
open Domino databases for scheduled maintenance
> b "Please call the help desk on xtn5555" "Greg Neilson/Alameda"
07/11/99 09:16:41 PM  BROADCAST from shoreline/Alameda: Please call the
help desk on xtn5555 [Greg Neilson/Alameda]
```

dbcache

Domino uses the database cache to keep open the most recently used databases for performance reasons. However, sometimes you may need to work with one of the databases within the cache (perhaps to restore from backup). You can use these commands to view the contents of the database cache, disable the use of the cache, and flush out the contents of the database cache.

Syntax

```
dbcache show
dbcache disable
dbcache flush
```

Command options

`show`
: Displays the current opened databases in the database cache.

`disable`
: Disables the server from using the database cache.

`flush`
: Flushes out the open databases that were in the database cache.

Examples

This is the output from a **dbcache show** command to display which databases are currently open in the cache:

```
> dbcache show

Database Cache is limited to 121 entries
    Database
C:\Lotus\Domino\Data\mtdata\mtstore.nsf
C:\Lotus\Domino\Data\admin4.nsf
C:\Lotus\Domino\Data\mail\sneilson.nsf
```

drop (dr)

This command can be used to close user sessions either for all users or for the nominated users. Typically you would use this command only in preparation for an unscheduled shutdown of the Domino server.

Syntax

```
drop all
drop username
```

Command options

`all`
: Drops all user sessions from the server.

`username`
: Drops the nominated user sessions from the server. More than one username can be entered at once, each of which should be enclosed in double quotes.

Examples

This is output from a command to drop all user sessions from the server:

```
> dr all
07/11/99 09:06:24 PM  Closed session for Greg Neilson/Alameda
Databases accessed:    2   Documents read:    2   Documents written:    1
07/11/99 09:06:24 PM  Closed session for Greg Neilson/Alameda
Databases accessed:    1   Documents read:    0   Documents written:    0
```

exit (e)

Closes down the Domino server.

Syntax

```
exit [password]
```

Command options

password
If the SET SECURE command has been run to provide a password for operation of the Domino server, then this password needs to be provided in order to shut down the server.

See Also

quit, restart server

help (he)

Displays the list of server commands and their main parameters. Unfortunately, this list is too long for a single screen and quickly scrolls to the end. To use this list, you can either view the console output in the server log database (*LOG.NSF*) or redirect the server output into a file.

Syntax

```
help
```

load (l)

Starts a Domino server task. Three particular tasks, `convert`, `compact`, and `object`, have a number of optional command-line parameters. For the `compact` task, if a database or subdirectory is not specified, this command applies to all databases on the server. The `object` task works with the optional shared mail feature, and is further described in Chapter 4, *Mail*. The `convert` task is used when upgrading to a new release of the server code—say from R4 to R5—and updates the specified mail databases to use the new design template.

Syntax

```
load program [options]
```

Command options

`program`

See the list of server tasks at the start of this chapter.

---

platform (pl)

Works with operating system statistic collection on the Windows NT (Intel) and Solaris (Sparc) platforms. You must have the collection of platform statistics enabled (by having the *NOTES.INI* parameter `PLATFORM_STATISTICS_ENABLED=1`) to be able to use these commands.

Syntax

```
platform time [secs]
platform reset
platform run
platform wait
```

Command options

`time [minutes]`

When this command is run without a time parameter, it displays the current statistic collection sampling rate. The default is one minute. Otherwise, this sets the statistic collection sampling rate to the value (in minutes) entered.

`reset`

Issued at the start of a monitoring session, this command resets the statistic counters for the operating system platform.

`run`

Resumes the collection of platform statistics.

`wait`

Temporarily pauses the collection of platform statistics.

---

pull (pul)

Starts database replication from the specified server to the local server. Typically, a Connection document defines the scheduled replication between servers, and this command is used to manually override it.

Syntax

```
pull server [database]
```

Command options

`server`

The name of the remote server you wish to pull database changes from to the local server. The remote server name should be the full hierarchical name, and enclosed in quotes if there any spaces in it.

`database`

Optionally, the name of the database on the local server into which you wish to pull changes from the server. The database on the other server must be a replica copy (that is, have the same replica ID) in order for replication to occur.

If the database parameter is not listed, then the server prepares a list of databases with identical replica IDs on both servers, and then pulls the changes in each from the other server.

Examples

`pul Westline/Alameda` pulls changes from the remote server named *Westline/Alameda* to the local server for all databases having the same replica ID.

`pul Shoreline/Alameda names.nsf` pulls changes from the remote server named *Shoreline/Alameda* to the local server for the *NAMES.NSF* database.

See Also

`push, replicate, route`

---

push (pus)

Starts database replication from the local server to the specified server. Typically, a Connection document defines the scheduled replication between servers, and this command is used to manually override it.

Syntax

```
push server [database]
```

Command options

`server`

The name of the remote server you wish to push database changes to from the local server. The server name should be the full hierarchical name, and enclosed in quotes if there any spaces in it.

`database`

Optionally, the name of the database on the local server out of which you wish to push changes to the remote server. The database on the remote server must be a replica copy (that is, have the same replica ID) in order for replication to occur.

If the database parameter is not listed, the server prepares a list of databases with identical replica IDs on both servers, and then pushes the changes in each to the other server.

Examples

`pus Westline/Alameda` pushes changes from this local server to the remote server *Westline/Alameda* for all databases having the same replica ID.

`pus Shoreline/Alameda names.nsf` pushes changes from the local server to the remote server *Shoreline/Alameda* for the *NAMES.NSF* database.

See Also

`pull, replicate, route`

quit (q)

Closes down the Domino server.

Syntax

```
quit [password]
```

Command options

`password`

If the `SET SECURE` command has been run to provide a password for operation of the Domino server, this password needs to be provided in order to shut down the server.

See Also

`exit, restart server`

replicate (rep)

Starts database replication from this server to/from the specified remote server. Typically, a Connection document defines the scheduled replication between servers, and this command is used to manually override it. The process works in two stages: the local server pulls any changes from the remote server, and then the remote server has the option to pull any changes from the local server. The remote server refers to the replication schedule, and performs a pull now only if this manual replication doesn't fall within the timeframe the server replicates to this server.

Syntax

```
replicate server [database]
```

Command options

`server`

The name of the remote server you wish to push/pull database changes to or from. The server name should be the full hierarchical name, and enclosed in quotes if there any spaces in it.

`database`

An optional parameter specifying which database to replicate. If this parameter is not present, the server attempts to replicate every database that has a common replica ID between the two servers.

Examples

This example replicates the Domino Directory between the two servers with the command `rep Westline/Alameda names.nsf`:

```
> rep westline/alameda names.nsf
07/18/99 12:10:43 AM  Database Replicator started
07/18/99 12:10:43 AM  Starting replication with server westline/alameda
07/18/99 12:10:43 AM  Pulling names.nsf from westline/alameda names.nsf
07/18/99 12:10:44 AM  Replicator added 1 document(s) to names.nsf from
westline/alameda names.nsf
```

```
07/18/99 12:10:44 AM  Pushing names.nsf to westline/alameda names.nsf
07/18/99 12:10:44 AM  Replicator added 1 document(s) to westline/alameda
names.nsf from names.nsf
07/18/99 12:10:44 AM  Replicator updated 6 document(s) in westline/
alameda
names.nsf from names.nsf
07/18/99 12:10:44 AM  Finished replication with server westline/alameda
07/18/99 12:10:44 AM  Database Replicator shutdown
```

See Also

`pull, push, route`

---

restart

Stops or starts the Domino server or one of its network ports.

Syntax

```
restart server [password]
restart port portname
```

Command options

`server`

Performs an orderly shutdown of the server and then restarts it.

Note that this does not work when Domino is configured as a Windows NT/2000 service. In this case, you must stop and start the service to restart the Domino server.

`port` *`portname`*

Specifies which port is to be restarted. The currently enabled ports for Domino are defined in the `Ports=` line in *NOTES.INI*. The default ports available to be configured (others can be defined if needed) are `TCPIP`, `LAN0ip`, `VINES`, `SPX`, `Appletalk`, `LAN1-LAN8` (NetBIOS), and `COM1-COM5`.

`password`

If the `SET SECURE` command has been run to provide a password for operation of the Domino server, this password must be provided in order to shut down the server.

Examples

`restart server` shuts down and restarts the Domino server.

`restart port tcpip` stops and restarts the TCP/IP port for Domino network communications.

See Also

`exit, quit, start port, stop port, show allports`

---

route (ro)

Starts mail routing with a given server. Typically, a Connection document will define the scheduled mail routing a server, and this command is used to manually override the scheduled mail routing. If there is no mail to route at this server (that is, *MAIL.BOX* is empty) this command is ignored.

Syntax

```
route servername
```

Command options

`servername`
: The name of the server we wish to send mail to, using the hierarchical name format.

Examples

`route Westline/Alameda` sends any outstanding mail that was destined for that server.

See Also

`replicate, push, pull`

---

set (se)

Makes dynamic changes to the Domino server configuration.

Syntax

```
set configuration variable = value [password]
set secure password
set secure password newpassword
set stat statisticname
```

Command options

`configuration variable = value`
: This command specifies the variable from *NOTES.INI* to be changed and its new value to use. As well as making the dynamic change in the Domino, the *NOTES.INI* file is also updated with this new value. It can also be used to add configuration variables to *NOTES.INI*.

Note that if the server console has been secured via a `SET SECURE` command, this password needs to be supplied in order to change this variable.

`secure password`
: Sets a password for the Domino server that must be entered to shut down the server or dynamically change any of the parameters. However, this usage is not entirely foolproof—it adds an entry to *NOTES.INI* called `SERVER_CONSOLE_PASSWORD` and stores the password there in a hashed format. This line can be deleted from *NOTES.INI* to remove the use of the password. So physical security of the server, ensured by placing it in a secured room with limited access, is probably a better idea.

If the same command is run again with the current password, the password is deleted from use.

`newpassword`
: Used to change the password from the previous password to this new value.

`stat` *`statisticname`*

Resets the value of the counter statistic to `0`. The ***`statisticname`*** parameter must be provided. You can obtain a complete set of statistics from the output of the **`show stat`** console command. However, the vast majority of the server statistics cannot be reset; if you attempt to reset them, the console will return the message "*`statistic`* `cannot be reset`." The only statistics that can be reset are those for the server. These are:

- SERVER.BUSYTIMEQUERY.RECEIVEDCOUNT
- SERVER.OPENREQUEST.MAXUSERS
- SERVER.OPENREQUEST.PREV4CLIENT
- SERVER.OPENREQUEST.RESTRICTED
- SERVER.OPENREQUEST.V4CLIENT
- SERVER.TRANS.TOTAL

Examples

This example resets the **`SERVER.TRANS.TOTAL`** statistic:

```
> set stat  Server.Trans.Total
07/17/99 08:29:00 PM  SERVER.TRANS.TOTAL was set to zero.
```

The following example checks the value of the `LOG_REPLICATION` configuration value, then sets it to `5` (which displays the most information when replicating), then checks the value again:

```
> show configuration log_replication
LOG_REPLICATION=1
> set configuration log_replication=5
> show configuration log_replication
LOG_REPLICATION=5
```

See Also

`show configuration`

show (sh)

This command has many options available and is used to display information about the Domino server. Note that much of this information is available graphically from the Server tab in Domino Administrator.

Syntax

```
show allports
show cluster
show configuration setting
show directory [*log | *nolog]
show diskspace [location]
show memory
show performance
show port portname
show schedule
show server
```

Server Tasks

```
show stat [statisticname]
show tasks
show transactions
show users
```

Command options

`allports`
: Lists all ports defined on the server as enabled or disabled ports.

`cluster`
: If the server is part of a Domino cluster, displays current information such as the name of the cluster, which servers are defined in the cluster, and their availability state and index (out of 100). This command can be abbreviated as:

```
SH CL
```

`configuration` *`setting`*
: Displays the current value of a given setting from *NOTES.INI*. This command can be abbreviated as:

```
SH CO setting
```

`directory [*log | *nolog]`
: Lists all files in the server's *DATA* directory, what database version they are (R4 or R5), whether the database uses transactional logging, and the date and time of the last update. This command can be abbreviated as:

```
SH DIR
```

The `*log` option displays only files that use transactional logging, while the `*nolog` option displays only files that do not use transactional logging.

`diskspace [`*`location`*`]`
: Shows how much free space is available on the given drive (NT and OS/2) and filesystem (Unix variants). If the drive is unspecified, the default is to use the drive/file system that has the Domino program directory. The disk space is displayed in bytes. This command can be abbreviated as:

```
SH DIS
```

`memory`
: The command displays the amount of available memory, which includes the virtual memory allowed. In OS/2, this is the remaining free space on the drive that houses the swap file; in NT, this is the sum of the maximum specified sizes for paging files (assuming there is sufficient free space available on the disk(s)). This command can be abbreviated as:

```
SH ME
```

`performance`
: Toggles on or off the display of performance data to the Domino each minute. This display shows the number of transactions per minute and the number of users on the server. This command can be abbreviated as:

```
SH PE
```

`port` *`portname`*
: Shows communication statistics for that configured port. This command can be abbreviated as:

```
SH PO portname
```

`schedule [`*`taskname`*` | `*`servername`*`]`

Displays the list of currently scheduled tasks and when they are scheduled to run next. If a task name is given, the next time that task is scheduled to run is displayed. For mail routing and replication, if a destination servername is given, then the next time this is scheduled to run is listed.

This uses information from Connection (for mail routing and database replication) and Program documents to determine the scheduled tasks. It does not include those from the **`ServerTasksAtx=`** lines in *NOTES.INI*. This command can be abbreviated as:

```
SH SC
```

`server`

Shows information about the server, including the name, whether transaction logging is enabled, whether shared mail is enabled, whether there is any mail still to be sent somewhere, and some measures of the peak server load since starting. This command can be abbreviated as:

```
SH SE
```

`stat [`*`statisticname`*`]`

If a statistic name is entered, then the current value of that statistic is displayed. Also, a group of statistics can be entered with `*` as the wildcard character; for example, **`show stat database.*`**. If no statistic name is entered, all of the currently defined statistics and their values are listed. In this case, since there are likely to be over 200 values displayed—and perhaps more depending on how many tasks are running on the server at that time—this information will scroll through the console window too quickly to read. In this case, you can either review the output in the server log, or redirect the output to a file setting from *NOTES.INI*. This command can be abbreviated as:

```
SH ST [statisticname]
```

`tasks`

Lists the currently executing Domino server tasks and their status. This command can be abbreviated as:

```
SH TA
```

`transactions`

Lists statistics of Domino NRPC transaction types performed on the server. For each command, lists the transaction count and the minimum, maximum, total time, and average time to complete the command in milliseconds. This command can be abbreviated as:

```
SH TR
```

`users`

Lists the current user sessions on the server, the databases they have open, and how long since the database was last used. This command can be abbreviated as:

```
SH US
```

Examples

Output example from the SHOW SCHEDULE command:

```
> show schedule
westline/Alameda          Replication          07/24/99 08:00:00 AM
westline/Alameda          Mail Routing         07/24/99 08:00:00 AM
compact                   Run Program          07/24/99 11:30:00 PM
```

Output example from the SHOW TRANSACTION command:

Function	Count	Min	Max	Total	Average
ILLEGAL	3	0	0	0	0
OPEN_DB	25	0	541	1373	54
GET_SPECIAL_NOTE_ID	2	0	10	10	5
OPEN_NOTE	3	10	30	60	20
CLOSE_DB	20	0	20	20	1
POLL_DEL_SEQNUM	7	0	20	20	2
SERVER_AVAILABLE_LITE	53	0	0	0	0
START_SERVER	65	0	902	2635	40
REGISTER_MONITOR_RQST	3	0	20	20	6
MONITOR_GETEVENTS_RQST	12	0	70	80	6
FINDDESIGN_NOTES	3	0	20	20	6

This is an example of the SHOW CLUSTER command:

```
> sh cl
Cluster Information
 Cluster name: Cluster1, Server name: shoreline/Alameda
 Server cluster probe timeout: 1 minute(s)
 Server cluster probe count: 72
 Server availability threshold: 0
 Server availability index: 100 (state: AVAILABLE)
 Cluster members (2)...
        server: shoreline/Alameda, availability index: 100
        server: westline/Alameda, availability index: 100
```

See Also

`set configuration, set statisics`

start port

This command enables the network port for communications in Domino.

Syntax

start port *portname*

Command options

portname

The currently enabled ports for Domino are defined in the `Ports=` line in *NOTES.INI*. The default ports that are available to be configured (others can be defined if needed) are `TCPIP`, `LAN0ip`, `VINES`, `SPX`, `Appletalk`, `LAN1-LAN8` (NetBIOS), and `COM1-COM5`.

Examples

`start port tcpip` enables the TCP/IP port to be used for Domino network communications.

See Also

`show allports, stop port, restart port`

---

stop port

This command disables the network port for communications in Domino.

Syntax

```
stop port portname
```

Command options

`portname`
: The currently enabled ports for Domino are defined in the `Ports=` line in *NOTES.INI*. The default ports that are available to be configured (others can be defined if needed) are `TCPIP`, `LAN0ip`, `VINES`, `SPX`, `Appletalk`, `LAN1-LAN8` (NetBIOS), and `COM1-COM5`.

Examples

`stop port tcpip` disables this port from being used for Domino communications.

See Also

`show allports, start port, restart port`

---

tell (t)

Used to issue a command to a running Domino server task. Every task responds to the `quit` command, but some tasks have special options available to control their operation.

Syntax

```
tell task quit
tell task [options]
```

Command options

`task` `quit`
: Stops the *task*.

---

trace (tr)

Used to test whether a server can successfully connect to another. There is also an option to specify which port to use to test the connection.

Server Tasks

Syntax

```
trace servername
trace portname!!!servername
```

Command options

servername
The name of the server you wish to test the connection to.

portname
The name of the server communication port you optionally wish to use to connect to the other server.

Examples

Output from a successful invocation of `trace servername`:

```
> trace westline/alameda
Determining path to server WESTLINE/ALAMEDA
Enabled Ports:  TCPIP
Checking normal priority connection documents only...
Local network connection document found for westline/Alameda
  Verifying address 'westline.alameda.com' for WESTLINE/ALAMEDA on TCPIP
    Requesting IP Address for westline.alameda.com from DNS
    DNS returned address 10.0.0.11 for westline.alameda.com
  Connected to server WESTLINE/ALAMEDA
```

See Also

`show allports, start port, stop port, restart port`

CHAPTER 14

NOTES.INI

The *NOTES.INI* file contains many configuration parameters for both the Domino server and Notes client. You will rarely need to enter changes within *NOTES.INI* file directly, since most of the configuration is done within the Domino Directory for Domino Servers, and within either the Personal Name and Address Book or the File → Preferences → User Preferences dialog for Notes clients .

With R5, the location of *NOTES.INI* changed. It can be found in the following locations:

- For Notes clients, the Notes program directory (*C:\LOTUS\NOTES*)
- For NT servers, the Domino program directory (*C:\LOTUS\DOMINO*)
- For Unix servers, the Domino data directory (*/LOCAL/NOTESDATA*)
- For partitioned servers, the data directory for each partition

NOTES.INI parameters can be set by a Configuration document within the Domino Directory. This is explained in more detail in Chapter 2, *Domino Directories*. For the parameters listed in this chapter that can be configured with a Configuration document, you can select the parameter name and bring up a help dialog that explains the parameter and its meanings. All the other parameters can still be added; however, you must know the name of the parameter you are working with as well as the value you wish to set it to, and type these manually in the fields supplied on the document.

A sample *NOTES.INI* file from a Domino server is shown in Example 14-1.

Notice that some of the statements in Example 14-1 are not listed in this chapter, since their usage is not explained either within the product documentation or the Lotus knowledge base. Lotus does not want you changing these statements, so you should change them only if you are sure of the consequences.

Example 14-1: Sample NOTES.INI for a Domino server

```
[Notes]
Directory=C:\Lotus\Domino\Data
KitType=2
SetupDB=Setup.nsf
UserName=Greg Neilson
NotesProgram=C:\Lotus\Domino
InstallType=4
CONSOLE_Lotus_Domino_Server=80 25 7 113 111 765 442
WinNTIconPath=C:\Lotus\Domino\Data\W32
Timezone=8
DST=1
$$HasLANPort=1
WWWDSP_SYNC_BROWSERCACHE=0
WWWDSP_PREFETCH_OBJECT=0
EnablePlugins=1
Preferences=2147486833
AltNameLanguage=en
ContentLanguage=en
WeekStart=2
ViewWeekStart=2
NavWeekStart=2
XLATE_CSID=52
SPELL_LANG=2057
Region=en
Passthru_LogLevel=0
Console_LogLevel=2
VIEWIMP1=Lotus 1-2-3 Worksheet,0,_IWKSV,,.WKS,.WK1,.WR1,.WRK,.WK3,.WK4,,4,
VIEWIMP3=Structured Text,0,_ISTR,,.LTR,.CGN,.STR,,1,
VIEWIMP4=Tabular Text,0,_ITAB,,.PRN,.RPT,.TXT,.TAB,,1,
VIEWEXP1=Lotus 1-2-3 Worksheet,0,_XWKS,,.WKS,.WK1,.WR1,.WRK,,4,
VIEWEXP3=Structured Text,0,_XSTR,,.LTR,.CGN,.STR,,1,
VIEWEXP4=Tabular Text,1,_XTAB,,.LTR,.RPT,.CGN,.TAB,,1,
EDITIMP1=ASCII Text,0,_ITEXT,,.TXT,.PRN,.C,.H,.RIP,,1,
EDITIMP2=MicrosoftWord RTF,0,_IRTF,,.DOC,.RTF,,2,
EDITIMP3=Lotus 1-2-3 Worksheet,0,_IWKSE,,.WKS,.WK1,.WR1,.WRK,.WK3,.WK4,,4,
EDITIMP4=Lotus PIC,0,_IPIC,,.PIC,,8,
EDITIMP5=CGM Image,0,_IFL,,.GMF,.CGM,,8,
EDITIMP6=TIFF 5.0 Image,0,_ITIFF,,.TIF,,18,
EDITIMP7=BMP Image,0,_IBMP,,.BMP,,18,
EDITIMP8=Ami Pro,0,_IW4W,W4W33F/V0,.SAM,,2,
EDITIMP9=HTML File,0,_IHTML,,.HTM,.HTML,,1,
EDITIMP17=WordPerfect 5.x,0,_IW4W,W4W07F/V1,.DOC,.WPD,,2,
EDITIMP21=WordPro 96/97,0,_IW4W,W4W12F/V0,.LWP,,2,
EDITIMP22=PCX Image,0,_IPCX,,.PCX,,18,
EDITIMP28=Binary with Text,0,_ISTRNGS,,.*,,1,
EDITIMP29=WordPerfect 6.0/6.1,0,_IW4W,W4W48F/V0,.WPD,.WPT,.DOC,,2,
EDITIMP30=Excel spreadsheet,0,_IW4W,W4W21F/V4C,.XLS,,4,
EDITIMP31=Word for Windows,0,_IW4W,W4W49F/V0,.DOC,,2,
EDITIMP32=GIF Image,0,_IGIF,,.GIF,,18,
EDITIMP33=JPEG Image,0,_IJPEG,,.JPG,,18,
EDITEXP1=ASCII Text,2,_XTEXT,,.TXT,.PRN,.C,.H,.RIP,,1,
EDITEXP2=MicrosoftWord RTF,2,_XRTF,,.DOC,.RTF,,4,
```

```
EDITEXP3=CGM Image,2,_XCGM,,.CGM,.GMF,,8,
EDITEXP4=TIFF 5.0 Image,2,_XTIFF,,.TIF,,18,
EDITEXP5=Ami Pro,2,_XW4W,W4W33T/V0,.SAM,,2,
EDITEXP14=WordPerfect 5.1,2,_XW4W,W4W07T/V1,.DOC,,2,
EDITEXP21=WordPerfect 6.0,2,_XW4W,W4W48T/V0,.DOC,,2,
EDITEXP22=WordPerfect 6.1,2,_XW4W,W4W48T/V1,.WPD,.WPT,.DOC,,2,
EDITEXP23=Word for Windows 6.0,2,_XW4W,W4W49T/V0,.DOC,,2,
DDETimeout=10
NAMEDSTYLE0=03004261736963000000000000000000000000000000000000000000000000000
0000000000001010100000A0000000000000100A0050A0000006400A0050A0000000000000000
00000000000000000000000000000000000000000000000000000000000000000000000000940
4000000000000
NAMEDSTYLE0_FACE=Default Sans Serif
NAMEDSTYLE1=030042756C6C657400000000000000000000000000000000000000000000000000
0000000000001010100000A00000000000000008070A000000640008070A0000000000000000
0000000000000000000000000000000000000000000000000000000000000000000000000004940
4000000000000
NAMEDSTYLE1_FACE=Default Sans Serif
NAMEDSTYLE2=0300486561646C696E6500000000000000000000000000000000000000000000000
0000000000001010101 0B0C0000000000000100A0050A0000006400A0050A0000000000000000
00000000000000000000000000000000000000000000000000000000000000000000000000940
4000000000000
NAMEDSTYLE2_FACE=Default Sans Serif
DefaultMailTemplate=mail50.ntf
ServerTasks=Router,Replica,Update,Amgr,AdminP,CalConn,Event,Sched,Stats,HTTP,
DIIOP,IMAP,POP3,LDAP,NNTP,DECS,maps,Cldbdir,Clrepl,collect, RunJava Ispy
ServerTasksAt1=Catalog,Design, Compact
ServerTasksAt2=UpdAll,Object Collect mailobj.nsf
ServerTasksAt3=Object Info -Full
ServerTasksAt5=Statlog
TCPIP=TCP, 0, 15, 0
LAN0ip=NETBIOS, 0, 15, 0
VINES=VINES, 0, 15, 0
SPX=NWSPX, 0, 15, 0
AppleTalk=ATALK, 0, 15, 0
LAN1=NETBIOS, 1, 15, 0
LAN2=NETBIOS, 2, 15, 0
LAN3=NETBIOS, 3, 15, 0
LAN4=NETBIOS, 4, 15, 0
LAN5=NETBIOS, 5, 15, 0
LAN6=NETBIOS, 6, 15, 0
LAN7=NETBIOS, 7, 15, 0
LAN8=NETBIOS, 8, 15, 0
COM1=XPC,1,15,0,
COM2=XPC,2,15,0,
COM3=XPC,3,15,0,
COM4=XPC,4,15,0,
COM5=XPC,5,15,0,
Ports=TCPIP
DisabledPorts=LAN0ip,VINES,SPX,AppleTalk,LAN1,LAN2,LAN3,LAN4,LAN5,LAN6,LAN7,L
AN8,COM1,COM2,COM3,COM4,COM5
LOG_REPLICATION=1
```

Example 14-1: Sample NOTES.INI for a Domino server (continued)

```
LOG_SESSIONS=1
KeyFilename=server.id
CertificateExpChecked=server.id 28/07/99
CertifierIDFile=C:\Lotus\Domino\Data\cert.id
MailServer=CN=shoreline/O=Alameda
ServerKeyFileName=server.id
Domain=Alameda
Admin=CN=Greg Neilson/O=Alameda
EXTMGR_ADDINS=decsext
TemplateSetup=55
Setup=59
ServerSetup=50
DESKWINDOWSIZE=-4 -4 808 608
MAXIMIZED=1
CleanSetup=1
PhoneLog=2
Log=log.nsf, 1, 0, 7, 40000
TRANSLOG_AutoFixup=1
TRANSLOG_UseAll=0
TRANSLOG_Style=0
TRANSLOG_Performance=2
TRANSLOG_Status=0
MTEnabled=1
SCHEDULE_VERSION=3
WebAdminSetup=5
DominoConfigLevel=3
SERVER_CLUSTER_ON=1
FileDlgDirectory=C:\Lotus\Domino
CONSOLE_NSERVICE=80 25 7 132 132 784 463
shared_mail=2
```

The **SHOW CONFIGURATION** command can be issued at the Domino console to display the current value of a specific parameter. The **SET CONFIGURATION** statement can be used to update *NOTES.INI* and also dynamically update the Domino configuration. There is an example of this in Chapter 13, *Domino Server Tasks and Console Commands.*

You will often see entries in your *NOTES.INI* file commencing with a $. These entries are environment variables in custom applications that use *NOTES.INI* to store information. For example, when a user first starts using a custom application, the application may prompt for such information as phone extension or manager's name, which is then stored in *NOTES.INI* and retrieved as needed by the application. However, there is now a better method for this—the profile document—which was added in 4.5, and which allows for the user configuration information to be stored in a special document within the Domino database. Older applications may continue to use the old environment settings, but newer applications should make use of profile documents instead. One of the dangers with environment variables is that they are used for such things as the last sequence number used in an application. But if the Notes client needs to be reinstalled or if the user moves to a new workstation, this stored value would be lost and there would be the possibility of duplicate sequence numbers within the Domino applications.

Admin

Description The username of the server administrator.

Syntax `ADMIN=`*`canonicalusername`*

Values `ADMIN=CN=Greg Neilson/O=ALAMEDA`

Usage

Applies to Domino servers. Equivalent to the Administrators field on the Server document within the Domino Directory.

AdminPInterval

Description

The interval in minutes the Administration Process uses for processing requests.

Syntax `AdminPInterval=`*`minutes`*

Values

The server first checks the Interval field in the Server Tasks → Administration Process tab of the Server document in the Domino Directory. If this field is empty, the value of this parameter within *NOTES.INI* is checked.

The default is 60 minutes.

Usage

Applies to Domino servers.

Can be configured using a Configuration document in the Domino Directory.

See also `AdminPModifyPersonDocumentsAt`

AdminPModifyPersonDocumentsAt

Description

The hour of the day the Administration Process updates Person documents in the Domino Directory.

Syntax `AdminPModifyPersonDocumentsAt=`*`time`*

Values

The time format used is the military format—0 represents midnight and 23 represents 11:00 P.M.

The server first checks for the contents of the "Execute once a day tasks at" field in the Server Tasks → Administration Process tab of the Server Document in the Domino Directory. If this field is blank, it checks for this parameter in *NOTES.INI*.

The default is 0, which corresponds to midnight.

The time specified should be when users are not attempting to access Domino, since it is resource-intensive, and when administrators are not updating the Domino Directory, since this could cause replication conflicts for the updated Person records.

Usage Applies to Domino servers.

Can be configured using a Configuration document in the Domino Directory.

See also `AdminPInterval`

Allow_Access

Description Lists who is authorized to access the Domino server.

Syntax

```
AllowAccess=names
```

Values

This parameter can have multiple names and groups specified, each separated by a comma. A single `*` allows all defined users with the Domino Directory to access the server. This wildcard can also be used for all users underneath specific certifiers by specifying, say, `*/ALAMEDA`.

The server first checks the contents of the Allow Access field within the Security tab of the Server document within the Domino Directory. If that field is empty, the value of this parameter within *NOTES.INI* is checked.

The default is to allow all defined users access to the server.

Usage Applies to Domino servers.

See also `Deny_Access`

Allow_access_<port>

Description

Lists who is authorized to use this defined port to access a Domino server.

Syntax `Allow_Access_port=names`

Values

The port parameter can be any enabled port on the server, such as TCPIP, LAN0-8, etc. The enabled ports on the server are specified in the `PORTS` parameter in *NOTES.INI.*

This names parameter can have multiple names and groups specified, each separated by a comma. A single `*` allows all defined users with the Domino Directory to access the server. This wildcard can also be used for all users underneath specific certifiers by specifying, for example, `*/ALAMEDA`.

The default is to allow all defined users access to the port.

Usage Applies to Domino servers.

See also `Deny_Access_portname`

AllowBookmarkFocus

Description

Extends the functionality of the user preference "Show extended accelerators" to allow the user to navigate bookmarks.

Syntax `AllowBookmarkFocus=1`

Values

When present, this means that the user can type Alt-B to access the bookmarks, then can use Up Down, Home, End, PgUp, and PgDn keys.

Usage Applies to Notes clients.

Allow_Passthru_Access

Description

Lists the users, servers, and groups that can access this server via passthru.

Syntax `Allow_Passthru_Access=names`

Values

This parameter can have multiple names and groups specified, each separated by a comma. A single `*` allows all defined users with the Domino Directory to access the server. This wildcard can also be used for all users underneath specific certifiers by specifying, say, `*/ALAMEDA`.

Equivalent to the "Access this server" field in the Security tab of the Server document in the Domino Directory. If there is any conflict between the entries, the Server document value takes precedence.

The default is to allow no access.

Usage Applies to Domino servers.

See also

```
Allow_Passthru_Callers
Allow_Passthru_Clients
Allow_Passthru_Targets
Passthru_Hangup_Delay
Passthru_LogLevel
```

NOTES.INI

Allow_Passthru_Callers

Description

Lists the users, servers, and groups that can cause this server to make a phone call to connect to another server to enable passthru access.

Syntax `Allow_Passthru_Callers=names`

Values

This parameter can have multiple names and groups specified, each separated by a comma. A single * allows all defined users with the Domino Directory to access the server. This wildcard can also be used for all users underneath specific certifiers by specifying, for example, `*/ALAMEDA`.

Equivalent to the Cause calling field in the Security tab of the Server document in the Domino Directory. If there is any conflict between the entries, the Server document value takes precedence.

The default is to allow no access.

Usage Applies to Domino servers.

See also

`Allow_Passthru_Access`
`Allow_Passthru_Clients`
`Allow_Passthru_Targets`
`Passthru_Hangup_Delay`
`Passthru_LogLevel`

Allow_Passthru_Clients

Description

Lists the users, servers, and groups that can use a passthru server to access this server.

Syntax `Allow_Passthru_Clients=names`

Values

Can have multiple names and groups specified, each separated by a comma. A single * allows all defined users with the Domino Directory to access the server. This wildcard can also be used for all users underneath specific certifiers by specifying, for example, `*/ALAMEDA`.

Equivalent to the "Route through" field in the Security tab of the Server document in the Domino Directory. If there is any conflict between the entries, the Server document value takes precedence.

The default is to allow no access.

Usage Applies to Domino servers.

See also

```
Allow_Passthru_Access
Allow_Passthru_Callers
Allow_Passthru_Targets
Passthru_Hangup_Delay
Passthru_LogLevel
```

Allow_Passthru_Targets

Description Lists the servers this server can connect to via passthru.

Syntax `Allow_Passthru_Targets=`*`servernames`*

Values

Can list multiple servers, each separated by a comma.

Equivalent to the Destinations allowed field in the Security tab of the Server document in the Domino Directory. If there is any conflict between the entries, the Server document value takes precedence.

The default is to allow passthru connections to all servers.

Usage Applies to Domino servers.

See also

```
Allow_Passthru_Access
Allow_Passthru_Caller
Allow_Passthru_Clients
Passthru_Hangup_Delay
Passthru_LogLevel
```

NOTES.INI

AMgr_DisableMailLookup

Description

When a mail-triggered agent is to run, the agent manager looks up the mail server of the user who last modified it, and runs it only if this server is the mail server for the user. This parameter disables this mail lookup.

Syntax `AMgr_DisableMailLookup=`*`value`*

Values

0 Perform mail lookup when running mail-triggered agents

1 Perform no mail lookup when running mail-triggered agents

The default is to perform the mail lookup when running mail-triggered agents.

Usage Applies to both Domino servers and Notes clients.

See also

```
AMgr_DocUpdateAgentMinInterval
AMgr_DocUpdateEventDelay
```

AMgr_NewMailAgentMinInterval
AMgr_NewMailEventDelay
AMgr_SchedulingInterval
AMgr_UntriggeredMailInterval
AMgr_WeekendDays

AMgr_DocUpdateAgentMinInterval

Description

Controls the minimum time in minutes between running the same document update-triggered agent event by the agent manager.

Syntax `AMgr_DocUpdateAgentMinInterval=minutes`

Values The default value is 30 minutes.

Usage

Applies to both Domino servers and Notes clients.

Can be configured using a Configuration document in the Domino Directory.

See also

AMgr_DisableMailLookup
AMgr_DocUpdateEventDelay
AMgr_NewMailAgentMinInterval
AMgr_NewMailEventDelay
AMgr_SchedulingInterval
AMgr_UntriggeredMailInterval
AMgr_WeekendDays

AMgr_DocUpdateEventDelay

Description

Controls the delay in minutes after a document update-triggered agent occurs before the agent is scheduled by the agent manager.

Syntax `AMgr_DocUpdatEventDelay=minutes`

Values The default is 5 minutes.

Usage Applies to both Domino servers and Notes clients.

Can be configured using a Configuration document in the Domino Directory.

See also

AMgr_DisableMailLookup
AMgr_DocUpdateAgentMinInterval
AMgr_NewMailAgentMinInterval
AMgr_NewMailEventDelay
AMgr_SchedulingInterval
AMgr_UntriggeredMailInterval
AMgr_WeekendDays

AMgr_NewMailAgentMinInterval

Description

Controls the minimum time in minutes between running the same new mail-triggered agent event by the agent manager.

Syntax `AMgr_NewMailAgentMinInterval=`*`minutes`*

Values The default is 0 minutes.

Usage Applies to both Domino servers and Notes clients.

Can be configured using a Configuration document in the Domino Directory.

See also

AMgr_DisableMailLookup
AMgr_DocUpdateAgentMinInterval
AMgr_DocUpdateEventDelay
AMgr_NewMailEventDelay
AMgr_SchedulingInterval
AMgr_UntriggeredMailInterval
AMgr_WeekendDays

AMgr_NewMailEventDelay

Description

Controls the delay in the minutes after new mail arrives and the new mail-triggered agent is scheduled by the agent manager.

Syntax `AMgr_NewMailEventDelay=`*`minutes`*

Values The default is 1 minute.

Usage Applies to both Domino servers and Notes clients.

Can be configured using a Configuration document in the Domino Directory.

See also

AMgr_DisableMailLookup
AMgr_DocUpdateAgentMinInterval
AMgr_DocUpdateEventDelay
AMgr_NewMailAgentMinInterval
AMgr_SchedulingInterval
AMgr_UntriggeredMailInterval
AMgr_WeekendDays

AMgr_SchedulingInterval

Description

Controls the delay in minutes between running the scheduler for the agent manager.

Syntax `AMgr_SchedulingInterval=`*`minutes`*

Values

The default is 1 minute, and the maximum allowable value is 60 minutes.

Usage Applies to both Domino servers and Notes clients.

See also

```
AMgr_DisableMailLookup
AMgr_DocUpdateAgentMinInterval
AMgr_DocUpdateEventDelay
AMgr_NewMailAgentMinInterval
AMgr_NewMailEventDelay
AMgr_UntriggeredMailInterval
AMgr_WeekendDays
```

AMgr_UntriggeredMailInterval

Description

Controls the delay in minutes between running the check for untriggered mail by the agent manager.

Syntax `AMgr_UntriggeredMailInterval=`*`minutes`*

Values

The default value is 60 minutes. This value can be anywhere in the range of 1 minute to 1440 minutes.

Usage Applies to both Domino servers and Notes clients.

See also

```
AMgr_DisableMailLookup
AMgr_DocUpdateAgentMinInterval
AMgr_DocUpdateEventDelay
AMgr_NewMailAgentMinInterval
AMgr_NewMailEventDelay
AMgr_SchedulingInterval
AMgr_WeekendDays
```

AMgr_WeekendDays

Description

Controls what the agent manager uses as weekend days. Agents can be configured not to run on the weekend, so this parameter can be used to control the days of the week these agents are not scheduled to run.

Syntax `AMgr_WeekendDays=`*`days`*

Values

Domino considers the week starts on Sunday, so 1 corresponds to Sunday and 7 corresponds to Saturday. The days of the week considered to be weekend days are entered separated by a comma.

The default values are 7,1 (Saturday and Sunday)

Usage Applies to both Domino servers and Notes clients.

Can be configured using a Configuration document in the Domino Directory.

See also

```
AMgr_DisableMailLookup
AMgr_DocUpdateAgentMinInterval
AMgr_DocUpdateEventDelay
AMgr_NewMailAgentMinInterval
AMgr_NewMailEventDelay
AMgr_SchedulingInterval
AMgr_UntriggeredMailInterval
AMgr_WeekendDays
```


AppleTalkNameServer

Description

Used with the AppleTalk protocol in the Domino network, and specifies the name of the secondary AppleTalk server. The secondary server is used when the user's primary Domino server is unavailable.

Syntax `AppleTalkNameServer=`*`servername@appletalkzone`*

Usage Applies to Notes clients.

Can be configured using the Notes client by selecting File → Preferences → User Preferences → Ports tab → AppleTalk port → Options.

AutoLogoffMinutes

Description

Controls the time in minutes before an inactive Notes client is automatically logged off. The logoff, which can be done manually with the F5 key, acts as a security measure, preventing unauthorized use of an unattended Notes client. When the user next uses the Notes client, he is prompted to enter his password.

Syntax `AutoLogoffMinutes=minutes`

Values There is no default value for this parameter.

Usage Applies to Notes clients.

Can be configured using the Notes client by selecting File → Preferences → User Preferences → Basics tab. Then enter a number in the field Lock ID after *x* minutes of inactivity.

BatchRegFile

Description

Specifies the filename to use for batch registration of users by the Domino Administrator, so the administrator is not prompted for a filename when creating users from a text file.

Syntax `BatchRegFile=filename`

Usage Applies to Administration clients.

See Also `BatchRegSeparator`

BatchRegSeparator

Description

Specifies the separator character to use when registering users in Domino Administrator from a text file.

Syntax `BatchRegSeparator=char`

Values The default separator character is a semicolon.

Usage Applies to Administration clients.

See Also `BatchRegFile`

BillingAddinOutput

Description

Controls the location to where billing information is logged—to a Domino database and/or a binary file.

Syntax `BillingAddinOutput=value`

Values

0 Log to the billing database (*BILLING.NSF*)

1 Log to a binary file (*BILLING.NBF*); default

9 Log to both the billing database and binary file

Usage Applies to Domino servers.

See also

```
BillingAddinRuntime
BillingAddinWakeup
BillingClass
BillingSuppressTime
```

BillingAddinRuntime

Description

Controls for how many seconds the billing task runs to process billing records.

Syntax `BillingAddinRuntime=`*seconds*

Values The default value is 10 seconds.

Usage Applies to Domino servers.

Can be configured using a Configuration document in the Domino Directory.

See also

```
BillingAddinOutput
BillingAddinWakeup
BillingClass
BillingSuppressTime
```

BillingAddinWakeup

Description

Controls how often in seconds the billing task wakes up and processes billing records.

Syntax `BillingAddinWakeup=`*seconds*

Values The default value is 60 seconds.

Usage Applies to Domino servers.

Can be configured using a Configuration document in the Domino Directory.

See also

```
BillingAddinOutput
BillingAddinRuntime
BillingClass
BillingSuppressTime
```

BillingClass

Description

Controls which classes of Domino server activity you wish to track for billing purposes.

Syntax `BillingClasses=classes`

Values

Valid values are **`Agent`**, **`Database`**, **`Document`**, **`HttpRequest`**, **`Mail`**, **`Replication`**, and **`Session`**. Each billing class should be separated by a comma in this parameter. There is no default.

Usage

Applies to Domino servers. Note that each additional class added to this list means additional work for the server in tracking it.

Can be configured using a Configuration document in the Domino Directory.

See also

```
BillingAddinOutput
BillingAddinRuntime
BillingAddinWakeup
BillingSuppressTime
```

BillingSuppressTime

Description

Controls how often billing data for the session and database classes are written during billing data collection. As this number decreases, the amount of billing workload on the Domino server increases.

Syntax `BillingSuppressTime=minutes`

Values The default is 15 minutes.

Usage Applies to Domino servers.

Can be configured using a Configuration document in the Domino Directory.

See also

```
BillingAddinOutput
BillingAddinRuntime
BillingAddinWakeup
BillingClass
```

CDP_Command

Description

CDP settings are used to control applications that are opening and closing when using OLE. Applications that use variables other than CDP_NEW, CDP_OPEN, CDP_EDIT, CDP_SAVE, CDP_CLOSE, CDP_SHOWITEM, CDP_SHOWACTIVEITEM, or CDP_EXIT use DIP and must be entered on separate lines.

Syntax `CDP_Command=value`

Usage Applies to both Domino servers and Notes clients.

CertificateExpChecked

Description

Specifies the name of the ID file in use and the last date in which the ID file was checked for expiring certificates.

Syntax `CertificateExpChecked=IDfile date`

Usage Applies to both Domino servers and Notes clients.

CertifierIDFile

Description The location of the certifier ID file.

Syntax `CertifierIDFile=IDFilePath`

Usage Applies to Domino servers.

COM<portnumber>

Description

Specifies the COM port configurations used for modem communication within Notes/Domino.

Syntax

```
COMportnumber=driver, unit_ID, max_sessions, buffer_size, flags, modem_
speed, modem_volume, modem_filename, dial_timer, hangup_timeout
```

Values Table 14-1 defines the meanings for each of these values.

Table 14-1: COM Port Definition Values

Value	Meaning
driver	Driver name
unit_ID	Unit ID
max_sessions	Maximum number of concurrent sessions

Table 14-1: COM Port Definition Values (continued)

Value	*Meaning*
buffer_size	Buffer size in KB
flags	Configuration flags—secured channel, log modem I/O, enable RTS/CTS
modem_speed	Modem speed
modem_volume	Modem volume (off, low, medium, high) and dialing mode (tone or pulse)
modem_filename	Name of .MDM modem command file
dial_timer	Connection timeout in seconds
hangup_timeout	Idle hang-up time in minutes

The following example is a part of a *NOTES.INI* file, with COM2 enabled and the remaining COM ports not configured:

```
COM1=XPC,1,15,0,
COM2=XPC,2,15,0,,12292,38400,16,gen_all.mdm,60,15
COM3=XPC,3,15,0,
COM4=XPC,4,15,0,
COM5=XPC,5,15,0,
```

Usage Applies to both Domino servers and Notes clients.

Can be configured using the Notes client by selecting File → Preferences → User Preferences → Ports tab → each COM port in turn → Options.

Config_DB

Description

Specifies the location of the statistics and events database (*EVENTS5.NSF*).

Syntax `Config_DB=databasename`

Values The default value is *EVENTS5.NSF*.

Usage Applies to Domino servers.

Console_Loglevel

Description

Controls the level of output displayed on the Notes status bar when tracing a connection.

Syntax `Console_Loglevel=value`

Values

0 No information

1 Only errors

2 Summary progress information

3 Detailed progress information

4 Full trace information

The default level is 2.

Usage Applies to Notes clients.

See also

```
Log
Log_AgentManager
Log_Dircat
Log_Replication
Log_Sessions
Log_Tasks
Log_Update
Log_View_Events
Passthru_LogLevel
PhoneLog
RTR_Logging
```

Country_Language

Description Specifies which language to use for the user interface.

Syntax `Country_Language=`*`value`*

Values The default is en-US, or US-English.

Usage Applies to both Domino servers and Notes clients.

Can be configured using a Configuration document in the Domino Directory.

Can be configured using the Notes client by selecting File → Preferences → User Preferences → International tab → Content Language button.

Create_File_Access

Description Lists who is able to create Domino databases on the server.

Syntax `Create_File_Access=`*`names`*

Values

Can have multiple names and groups specified, each separated by a comma. A single `*` allows all defined users with the Domino Directory to access the server. This wildcard can also be used for all users underneath specific certifiers by specifying, for example, `*/ALAMEDA`.

The server first checks the contents of the Create New databases field within the Security tab of the Server document within the Domino Directory. If that field is empty, the value of this parameter within *NOTES.INI* is checked.

The default is to allow all users who can access the server to create databases on it.

Create_Replica_Access

Description Controls who can create database replicas on the server.

Syntax `Create_Replica_Access=names`

Values

Can have multiple names and groups specified, each separated by a comma. A single `*` allows all defined users with the Domino Directory to access the server. This wildcard can also be used for all users underneath specific certifiers by specifying, say, `*/ALAMEDA`.

The server first checks the contents of the Create Replica Databases field within the Security tab of the Server document within the Domino Directory. If that field is empty, the value of this parameter within *NOTES.INI* is checked.

The default is to allow no users to create replicas.

Usage Applies to Domino servers.

CTF

Description Configures the international character set used for import/export.

Syntax `CTF=filename`

Values The default value is *L_CPWIN.CLS*.

Usage Applies to Notes clients.

Can be configured using the Notes client by selecting File → Preferences → User Preferences → International tab → Import/Export character set button.

DDE_Timeout

Description

The wait time in seconds that Notes will wait for a DDE application to respond to a DDE request.

Syntax `DDE_Timeout=seconds`

Values The default is 10 seconds.

Usage Applies to Notes clients.

Debug_AMgr

Description

Enables the capturing of debug information from the running of the Agent Manager task, which is written to the server console and the log database.

Syntax `Debug_AMgr=`*`debugoptions`*

Values The debug options can be one or more of:

`c` Agent Manager control information

`e` Agent Manager event information

`l` Agent Manager loading information

`m` Agent Manager memory warning information

`p` Agent Manager performance information

`r` Agent manager run report information

`s` Agent Manager scheduling information

`v` Verbosely list information about agent loading, scheduling, and queues

`*` Enable all options

Usage

Applies to both Domino servers and Notes clients. The **DEBUG_OUTFILE** option must be set on a Notes client, since it doesn't have a console to write this debug information to.

See Also

`Log_AgentManager`
`DEBUG_OUTFILE`

DEBUG_OUTFILE

Description

When used in combination with the **Debug_Amgr** parameter that is used to product debug information from the **Agent Manager** task, this parameter redirects the output to a text file.

Syntax `DEBUG_OUTFILE=`*`filename`*

Values The debug information is redirected to the filename specified.

Usage

Applies to both Domino servers and Notes clients when debugging in the **Agent Manager** task.

See also `Debug_AMgr`

DECSTranslation

Description

Allows a tradeoff of a performance gain in DECS against a growing level of assumption about the data. Translation with Unicode is always done, so if this is present, this value is used.

Syntax `DECSTranslation=value`

Values

0 Don't do character set translation between character sets except Unicode. Use this when data is mostly ASCII characters compatible with the internal Domino format used for database (LMBCS).

1 Don't do translation between character sets between non-LMBCS data. This again is used when the data and Notes are in compatible character sets.

2 Always translate between character sets. This is the default value.

Usage Applies to Domino servers running the **DECS** task.

DECSNativeText

Description Overrides the character set on the Domino server.

Syntax `DECSNativeText=value`

Values

There are more than 250 character sets supported. Refer to Appendix D of the *LotusScript Extension for Domino Connectors* manual (*LSXLCDOC.NSF*) for a complete list. The character set value given to this parameter is the name of the character set in the manual with the *LCSTREAMFMT_* prefix removed. For example, *LCSTREAMFMT_ASCII* is listed as:

```
DECSNativeText=ASCII
```

Usage Applies to Domino servers running the **DECS** task.

Default_Index_Lifetime_Days

Description

This controls the default lifetime for view indices if none are specified by the developer. If the index is inactive for the number of days specified in this parameter, it is purged.

Syntax `Default_Index_Lifetime_Days=days`

Values The default is 45 days.

Usage Applies to Domino servers.

Can be configured using a Configuration document in the Domino Directory.

Deny_Access

Description Lists who are denied access to the Domino server.

Syntax `Deny_Access=names`

Values

Can have multiple names and groups specified, each separated by a comma. A single * allows all defined users with the Domino Directory to access the server. This wildcard can also be used for all users underneath specific certifiers by specifying, for example, `*/ALAMEDA`.

The server first checks the contents of the "Not access this server" field within the Security tab of the Server document within the Domino Directory. If that field is empty, the value of this parameter within *NOTES.INI* is checked.

The default is not to deny access to any user.

Usage Applies to Domino servers.

See also `Allow_Access`

Deny_Access_<portname>

Description

Lists who is denied access to use this defined port to access a Domino server.

Syntax `Deny_Access_portname=names`

Values

The port parameter can be any enabled port on the server, such as TCPIP, LAN0-9, etc. The enabled ports on the server are specified in the `PORTS` parameter in *NOTES.INI*.

This names parameter can have multiple names and groups specified, each separated by a comma. A single * allows all defined users with the Domino Directory to access the server. This wildcard can also be used for all users underneath specific certifiers by specifying, for example, `*/ALAMEDA`.

The default is not to deny anyone access to any port on the Domino server.

Usage Applies to Domino servers.

See also `Allow_Access_portname`

Desktop

Description Configures the location of the Notes Desktop file (*DESKTOP.DSK*).

Syntax `Desktop=location`

Values The default desktop location is the Notes data directory.

Usage Applies to Notes clients.

Directory

Description Configures the location of the data directory.

Syntax `Directory=location`

Values

This is as configured during the Domino server or Notes client install. For new servers it is by default *\LOTUS\DOMINO\DATA* and for new clients it is by default *\LOTUS\NOTES\DATA*.

Usage Applies to both Domino servers and Notes clients.

Can be configured using the Notes client by selecting File → Preferences → User Preferences → Basics tab → "Local database folder" field.

Domain

Description

Specifies the Domino domain in which a server is configured; for a Notes client, specifies which domain is the user's mail server.

Syntax `Domain=domain`

Usage Applies to both Domino servers and Notes clients.

For Domino Servers, the value here is the same as appears under the "Domain name" field within the Server document in the Domino Directory. For Notes Clients, the value is the same as appears under the Domain field in the user's Person document within the Domino Directory.

DominoAsynchronizeAgents

Description

Controls how agents triggered from web browser clients are executed.

Syntax `DominoAsynchonizeAgents=value`

Values

0 Run only one agent at a time (the default).

1 Allow more than one agent to run at the same time.

Usage Applies to Domino servers running the `HTTP` task.

DominoNoDirLinks

Description

Controls whether web browser clients are allowed to access directory links.

Syntax `DominoNoDirLinks=value`

Values

0 Allow web browser clients to access directory links (default).

1 Web browser clients are not allowed to access directory links.

Usage Applies to Domino servers running the HTTP task.

DST

Description Controls whether a server or client observes Daylight Saving Time.

Syntax `DST=`*`value`*

Values

0 Daylight Saving Time is not observed.

1 Daylight Saving Time is observed (default).

Usage Applies to both Domino servers and Notes clients.

Should not be needed with R5—the default is to use the underlying operating system values for Daylight Saving Time and remove this complexity from Notes/Domino. Otherwise, during the Daylight Savings period, the creation and modified time of documents on the server are time-stamped an hour behind the system time.

See also

```
DSTlaw
DST_Begin_Date
DST_End_Date
```

NOTES.INI

DSTlaw

Description Configures when Daylight Saving Time is observed.

Syntax

```
DSTlaw=startmonth, startweek, startday, endmonth, endweek, endday
```

Values

The months are specified as the numbers 1 to 12 for January to December.

The weeks are numbered 1 to 4. A negative number such as –1 starts backwards and denotes the last week in the month.

The days of the week are 1 (Sunday) to 7 (Saturday).

The default values are 4, 1, 1, 10, –1, and 1, which means that Daylight Saving starts on the Sunday of first week of April, and ends on the Sunday of the last week in October.

Usage Applies to both Domino servers and Notes clients.

Should not be needed with R5—the default is to use the underlying operating system values for Daylight Saving Time and remove this complexity from Notes/Domino.

See also

DST
DST_Begin_Date
DST_End_Date

DST_Begin_Date

Description Start date of when Daylight Saving Time should be observed.

Syntax `DST_Begin_Date=`*`date`*

Values The date should be specified in *dd/mm/yyyy* format.

Usage Applies to Domino servers.

Should not be needed with R5—the default is to use the underlying operating system values for Daylight Saving Time and remove this complexity from Notes/Domino.

See also

DST
DSTlaw
DST_End_Date

DST_End_Date

Description End date of when Daylight Saving Time should be observed.

Syntax `DST_End_Date=`*`date`*

Values The date should be specified in *dd/mm/yyyy* format.

Usage Applies to Domino servers.

Should not be needed with R5—the default is to use the underlying operating system values for Daylight Saving Time and remove this complexity from Notes/Domino.

See also

DST
DSTlaw
DST_Begin_Date

EditExp<number>

Description Controls document-level file exporting.

Syntax `EditExpnumber=parm1, parm2, parm3, parm4, parm5 . .`

Values Table 14-2 describes each of the values in detail.

Table 14-2: Document-Level File Export Values

Values	Meaning
1	Program name and file type.
2	Append options: 0 No append option. 1 Append option offered through a dialog box. 2 Automatically write to a temporary file to avoid the 64K limit.
3	Export routine name.
4	Not used.
5 and onwards	File extensions to use in the selection of a file type in the File Import dialog.

By default, a Notes client contains the following entries:

```
EDITEXP1=ASCII Text,2,_XTEXT,,.TXT,.PRN,.C,.H,.RIP,,1,
EDITEXP2=MicrosoftWord RTF,2,_XRTF,,.DOC,.RTF,,4,
EDITEXP3=CGM Image,2,_XCGM,,.CGM,.GMF,,8,
EDITEXP4=TIFF 5.0 Image,2,_XTIFF,,.TIF,,18,
EDITEXP5=Ami Pro,2,_XW4W,W4W33T/V0,.SAM,,2,
EDITEXP14=WordPerfect 5.1,2,_XW4W,W4W07T/V1,.DOC,,2,
EDITEXP21=WordPerfect 6.0,2,_XW4W,W4W48T/V0,.DOC,,2,
EDITEXP22=WordPerfect 6.1,2,_XW4W,W4W48T/V1,.WPD,.WPT,.DOC,,2,
EDITEXP23=Word for Windows 6.0,2,_XW4W,W4W49T/V0,.DOC,,2,
```

Usage Applies to Notes clients.

See also

```
EditImp
ViewExp
ViewImp
```

NOTES.INI

EditImp<number>

Description Controls document-level file importing.

Syntax `EditImpnumber=parm1, parm2, parm3, parm4, parm5 . . .`

Values Table 14-3 describes each of the values in detail.

Table 14-3: Document-Level File Import Values

Values	Meaning
1	Program name and file type
2	Not used, always 0
3	Import routine name
4	Not used
5 and onwards	File extensions to use in the selection of a file type in the File Import dialog

By default, a Notes client contains the following entries:

```
EDITIMP1=ASCII Text,0,_ITEXT,,.TXT,.PRN,.C,.H,.RIP,,1,
EDITIMP2=MicrosoftWord RTF,0,_IRTF,,.DOC,.RTF,,2,
EDITIMP3=Lotus 1-2-3 Worksheet,0,_IWKSE,,.WKS,.WK1,.WR1,.WRK,.WK3,.
WK4,,4,
EDITIMP4=Lotus PIC,0,_IPIC,,.PIC,,8,
EDITIMP5=CGM Image,0,_IFL,,.GMF,.CGM,,8,
EDITIMP6=TIFF 5.0 Image,0,_ITIFF,,.TIF,,18,
EDITIMP7=BMP Image,0,_IBMP,,.BMP,,18,
EDITIMP8=Ami Pro,0,_IW4W,W4W33F/V0,.SAM,,2,
EDITIMP9=HTML File,0,_IHTML,,.HTM,.HTML,,1,
EDITIMP17=WordPerfect 5.x,0,_IW4W,W4W07F/V1,.DOC,.WPD,,2,
EDITIMP21=WordPro 96/97,0,_IW4W,W4W12F/V0,.LWP,,2,
EDITIMP22=PCX Image,0,_IPCX,,.PCX,,18,
EDITIMP28=Binary with Text,0,_ISTRNGS,,.*,,1,
EDITIMP29=WordPerfect 6.0/6.1,0,_IW4W,W4W48F/V0,.WPD,.WPT,.DOC,,2,
EDITIMP30=Excel spreadsheet,0,_IW4W,W4W21F/V4C,.XLS,,4,
EDITIMP31=Word for Windows,0,_IW4W,W4W49F/V0,.DOC,,2,
EDITIMP32=GIF Image,0,_IGIF,,.GIF,,18,
EDITIMP33=JPEG Image,0,_IJPEG,,.JPG,,18,
```

See also

EditExp
ViewExp
ViewImp

EmptyTrash

Description

Controls how documents marked for deletion (and moved to the trash folder) are purged from the Domino server.

Syntax `EmptyTrash=value`

Values

0 Prompt user before database is closed (default).

1 Always empty trash folder before database is closed.

2 Empty the trash folder manually.

Usage Applies to Notes clients.

Can be configured using the Notes client by selecting File → Preferences → User Preferences → Basics tab → change the value for the Empty Trash folder field.

EnableBiDiNotes

Description

Controls whether support for BiDirectional languages (such as Arabic and Hebrew) is enabled at the Domino server.

Syntax `EnableBiDiNotes=value`

Values

0 Turns BiDirectional support off (default).

1 Turns BiDirectional support on.

Usage Applies to Notes clients.

ExtMgr_Addins

Description

Defines the Domino add-ins for the Extension Manager, which are loaded into server memory. DECS and other Domino add-ins use the Extension Manager to change Domino server behavior on the fly.

Syntax `ExtMgr_Addins=value1, value2,. . .`

Values Each value represents an add-in to load.

Usage Applies to Domino servers.

FileDlgDirectory

Description

Keeps track of the last directory used for file open operations (such as attach, import, and export) so that this same directory is used as a default the next time a file open dialog is created.

Syntax `FileDlgDirectory=path`

Values The default location is the Notes data directory.

Usage Applies to Notes clients.

Fixup_Tasks

Description

Controls how many **Fixup** tasks are launched as the server is started. The **Fixup** task runs database consistency checks and fixes.

Syntax `FixupTasks=value`

Values The default is two tasks per installed processor on the server.

Usage Applies to Domino servers.

NOTES.INI

FT_DOMAIN_IDXTHDS

Description

Controls the numbers of threads to launch to perform indexing for the Domain Search feature. As more threads are created, this speeds the indexing process but also consumes more system resources, which could slow server responsiveness for users.

Syntax `FT_DOMAIN_IDXTHDS=value`

Values The default is two threads per CPU.

Usage Applies to Domino servers.

FT_Intl_Setting

Description

Changes the way full text search works with Japanese language to ensure that Notes search works properly.

Syntax `FT_Intl_Setting=1`

Values

The value `1` makes full text searches all case-sensitive, ignores the word stop file, and turns off stemming.

Usage Applies to Notes clients.

FT_LIBNAME

Description

Uses an updated full text search engine (new in 5.0.3). This new engine is faster than the original engine, but once it is enabled, it forces the rebuilding of the full-text index for every database on the server.

Syntax `FT_LIBNAME=ftgtr34`

Values

The value of `ftgtf34` is the only value applicable for this search engine.

Usage Applies to Domino servers.

FT_NO_COMPWINTITLE

Description

Determines whether the domain indexer computes the document title for every document that is indexed. Determining the document title for every document in the database can be very CPU-intensive.

Syntax `FT_NO_COMPTITLE=1`

Values

The value `1` means that the domain indexer does not compute the document title for documents being indexed.

Usage Applies to Domino servers.

FTG_Index_Limit

Description

Overrides the default full text index size, which is of use when indexing databases with large file attachments.

Syntax `FTG_Index_Limit=`*`size`*

Values

The size specified is the maximum size of full text index files. The default value is 6MB.

Usage Applies to Domino servers.

HTTPFormulaCache

Description

Controls whether the `HTTP` process can cache formulae to improve performance.

Syntax `HTTPFormulaCache=`*`value`*

Values

0 Disables the formula cache (default)

1 Enables the formula cache

Usage Applies to Domino servers running the `HTTP` task.

See also `HTTPFormulaCacheSize`

HTTPFormulaCacheSize

Description

Controls the size of the formula cache, in KB. Each formula cached uses one of these cache buffers.

Syntax `HTTPFormulaCacheSize=size`

Values

If HTTP formula caching is enabled, the default formula cache size is 1K.

Usage Applies to Domino servers running the `HTTP` task.

See also `HTTPFormulaCache`

IMAILExactSize

Description

Controls whether the IMAP service can report an estimated size of a MIME message or whether the exact message size is to be returned.

Syntax `IMAILExactSize=value`

Values

0 IMAP reports estimated message size (default)

1 IMAP reports exact message size

Usage Applies to Domino servers running the `IMAP` task.

See also

```
POP3ExactSize
IMAPAddress
IMAP_Config_Update_Interval
IMAPGreeting
IMAPRedirectSSLGreeting
IMAP_Session_Timeout
IMAPMaxSessions
IMAPSSLGreeting
```

IMAPAddress

Description Defines the IP address to use for an IMAP server using partitioning.

Syntax `IMAPAddress=address`

Values

The address can be either the IP address of the server or the fully qualified name of server.

Usage

Applies to Domino servers running the IMAP task and using partitioning.

See also

LDAPAddress
NNTPAddress
POP3Address
IMAILExactSize
IMAP_Config_Update_Interval
IMAPGreeting
IMAPRedirectSSLGreeting
IMAP_Session_Timeout
IMAPMaxSessions
IMAPSSLGreeting

IMAP_Config_Update_Interval

Description

Controls how often the IMAP process checks the Domino Directory for any configuration changes to apply.

Syntax `IMAP_Config_Update_Interval=`*minutes*

Values

The time in minutes the IMAP process waits before checking the Domino Directory again for changes.

The default is two minutes.

Usage Applies to Domino servers running the IMAP task.

See also

IMAPAddress
IMAILExactSize
IMAPGreeting
IMAPRedirectSSLGreeting
IMAP_Session_Timeout
IMAPMaxSessions
IMAPSSLGreeting

IMAP_Greeting

Description

Allows customization of the message sent to IMAP clients (TCP/IP only—those using SSL use a separate message).

Syntax `IMAP_Greeting=`*text*

Values

The default greeting is:

```
* OK Domino IMAP4 Server V5.0 ready Mon, 22 August 1999 11:35:12 -0800
```


NOTES.INI

Usage Applies to Domino servers running the `IMAP` task.

See also

```
IMAPAddress
IMAILExactSize
IMAP_Config_Update_Interval
IMAPRedirectSSLGreeting
IMAP_Session_Timeout
IMAPMaxSessions
IMAPSSLGreeting
```

IMAPRedirectSSLGreeting

Description

Allows customization of the message sent to clients who are attempting to connect over TCP/IP when the port is configured to redirect to SSL.

Syntax `IMAPRedirectSSLGreeting=`*`text`*

Values

The default redirection greeting is:

```
IMAP Server configured for SSL Connections only. Please reconnect using
the SSL Port portnumber.
```

Usage

Applies to Domino servers running `IMAP` that are configured for to redirect to SSL connections.

See also

```
IMAPAddress
IMAILExactSize
IMAP_Config_Update_Interval
IMAPGreeting
IMAP_Session_Timeout
IMAPMaxSessions
IMAPSSLGreeting
```

IMAP_Session_Timeout

Description

Controls how long in minutes the server waits before dropping idle IMAP client sessions.

Syntax `IMAP_Session_Timeout=`*`time`*

Values The default is 30 minutes.

Usage Applies to Domino servers running the `IMAP` task.

See also

IMAPAddress
IMAILExactSize
IMAP_Config_Update_Interval
IMAPGreeting
IMAPRedirectSSLGreeting
IMAPSSLGreeting
NoMsgCache

IMAPMaxSessions

Description

Configures the maximum number of IMAP sessions that can be established on the server. New for 5.0.3.

Syntax

`IMAPMaxSessions=`*value*

Values

A value of 0 means that there is no limit on the number of IMAP sessions that can be established (the default). Otherwise, the value here is the maximum number of IMAP sessions that can be established on the server.

Usage

Applies to Domino servers running the `IMAP` task.

See also

IMAPAddress
IMAILExactSize
IMAP_Config_Update_Interval
IMAPGreeting
IMAPRedirectSSLGreeting
IMAP_Session_Timeout
IMAPSSLGreeting

IMAPSSLGreeting

Description

Allows customization of the message sent to IMAP clients when using SSL.

Syntax

`IMAPSSLGreeting=`*text*

Values

The default greeting is:

```
* OK Domino IMAP4 Server V5.0 ready Mon, 22 August 1999 11:35:12 -0800
```

Usage

Applies to Domino servers running the `IMAP` task configured for SSL connections.

See also

`IMAPAddress`
`IMAILExactSize`
`IMAP_Config_Update_Interval`
`IMAPGreeting`
`IMAPRedirectSSLGreeting`
`IMAP_Session_Timeout`

InstallType

Description Identifies type of product installed.

Syntax `InstallType=`*`value`*

Values

0 Domino Designer (includes Notes)

1 Domino Administrator (includes Notes)

2 Domino Designer and Domino Administrator (includes Notes)

3 Domino Mail Server

4 Domino Enterprise Server

5 Domino Application Server

6 Notes client

Usage Applies to both Notes clients and Domino servers.

ITASK_Print_Hostname

Description

Configures the `NNTP` task to use hostnames instead of IP addresses when performing status reporting or logging.

Syntax `ITASK_Print_Hostname=`*`value`*

Values

`ITASK_Print_Hostname=1` enables hostname lookups for NNTP logging and status reporting.

The default is to use IP addresses for NNTP logging and status reporting.

Usage Applies to Domino servers running the `NNTP` task.

JavaUserClasses

Description

Specifies the location of the Java VM classpath. The classpath is used for Java to locate class files to load.

Syntax `JavaUserClasses=path`

Usage Applies to both Domino servers and Notes clients.

KeyFilename

Description

Identifies the location of the ID file in use for both the user (on a Notes client) and server (on a Domino server). If you have both installed into the same directories, use the `ServerKeyFileName` parameter for the location of the server ID.

Syntax `KeyfileName=filename`

Usage Applies to both Domino servers and Notes clients.

See also `ServerKeyFileName`

KillProcess

Description

Controls whether the cleanup shutdown procedures are enabled to clean up all processes from a crashed Domino server partition.

Syntax `KillProcess=value`

Values

0 Disables the cleanup shutdown procedure

1 Enables the cleanup shutdown procedure (default)

Usage Applies to Domino servers using partitioning.

Can be configured using a Configuration document in the Domino Directory.

See also

`TCPPort_PortMappingnumber`
`TCPPort_TCPIPAddress`

KitType

Description

Identifies whether the installed product is a Notes client or Domino server.

Syntax `KitType=value`

Values

1 Notes client

2 Domino server

Usage Applies to both Domino servers and Notes clients.

LAN<number>

Description

Configures network ports for use with the Notes client or the Domino server.

Syntax `LAN<number>=port_driver, unit_ID, notused, buffersize`

Values

The port driver can be any of the following: ATALK, NETBIOS, NWSPX, TCP, VINES, and XPC as appropriate for the network transport.

The *unit_ID* is the adapter number that the port driver is to use, starting from 0.

The *buffersize* is specified in bytes.

Usage Applies to both Domino servers and Notes clients.

Can be configured on a Domino server using the Ports tab in the Server document within the Domino Directory and on a Notes client by selecting File → Preferences → User Preferences → Ports tab.

LDAPAddress

Description Defines the IP address to use for an LDAP server using partitioning.

Syntax `LDAPAddress=address`

Values

The address can be either the IP address of the server or the fully qualified name of server.

Usage

Applies to Domino servers running the LDAP task and using partitioning

See also

```
IMAPAddress
LDAPAddress
NNTPAddress
POP3Address
LDAP_CountryCheck
LDAP_Enforce_Schema
LDAPReferrals
LDAP_Strict_RFC_Adherence
```

LDAP_CountryCheck

Description

Controls how the LDAP server works with entries that don't contain country attributes; works only when the client searches for users underneath a country attribute. This parameter is mainly intended for clients using Outlook Express, which by default uses a country attribute value as a search base when a country is not explicitly specified by the user.

Syntax `LDAP_CountryCheck=value`

Values

0 Do not strictly use directory tree location for entries without country attributes (default)

1 Strictly use directory tree location for entries without country attributes

Usage Applies to Domino servers running the **LDAP** task.

See also

`LDAPAddress`
`LDAP_Enforce_Schema`
`LDAPReferrals`
`LDAP_Strict_RFC_Adherence`

LDAP_Enforce_Schema

Description

Controls whether schema checking is enforced for LDAP add and modify operations.

Syntax `LDAP_Enforce_Schema=value`

Values

1 Check that LDAP update/add request conforms to Domino directory schema before allowing the update to process.

Usage Applies to Domino servers running the **LDAP** task.

See also

`LDAPAddress`
`LDAP_CountryCheck`
`LDAPReferrals`
`LDAP_Strict_RFC_Adherence`

LDAPReferrals

Description

Controls how many referrals (a URL to an LDAP server that may have the information requested) can be sent to a client.

Syntax `LDAPReferrals=value`

Values

The default is to return only one referral. Microsoft Internet Explorer clients fail if more that one referral is returned to them.

Usage Applies to Domino servers running the **LDAP** task.

See also

```
LDAPAddress
LDAP_CountryCheck
LDAP_Enforce_Schema
LDAP_Strict_RFC_Adherence
```

LDAP_Strict_RFC_Adherence

Description

Configures adherence to RFCs 2251-4 to ensure the LDAP client name is the same as their fully qualified distinguished name.

Syntax `LDAP_Strict_RFC_Adherence=1`

Values The value of `1` means that the RFCs 2251-4 are strictly enforced.

Usage Applies to Domino servers running the **LDAP** task.

See also

```
LDAPAddress
LDAP_CountryCheck
LDAP_Enforce_Schema
LDAPReferrals
```

Location

Description

Identifies the name of the currently selected location within the Notes client.

Syntax `Location=`*`name`*

Usage Applies to Notes clients.

Log

Description

Controls how logging operates and also where the log database is located.

Syntax `LOG=`*`filename, option, filler, days, size`*

Values Table 14-4 shows the available values.

Table 14-4: Log Parameters

Values	*Meaning*
Filename	Filename of log database, usually *LOG.NSF*
Option	Available options are: 1 Log to Domino console 2 Force database fixup when opening the log file 4 Full document scan
Filler	Not used, always 0
Days	Number of days to keep log documents
Size	Size of log text (in words) in event documents

Usage Applies to both Domino servers and Notes clients.

See also

```
Console_Loglevel
Log_AgentManager
Log_Dircat
Log_MailRouting
Log_Replication
Log_Sessions
Log_Tasks
Log_Update
Log_View_Events
Passthru_LogLevel
PhoneLog
RTR_Logging
```

NOTES.INI

Log_AgentManager

Description

Controls whether the start of execution of an agent is written to the server console and log database.

Syntax `Log_AgentManager=`*`value`*

Values

0 Disable logging of agent execution events (default)

1 Log agent execution events (both partially and completely successful agents)

2 Log agents execution agents (completely successful only)

Usage Applies to Domino servers.

Can be configured using a Configuration document in the Domino Directory.

See also

```
Console_Loglevel
Debug_Amgr
Log
Log_Dircat
```

Log_MailRouting
Log_Replication
Log_Sessions
Log_Tasks
Log_Update
Log_View_Events
Passthru_LogLevel
PhoneLog
RTR_Logging

Log_Dircat

Description

Controls whether additional information is to be logged for the DIRCAT server task.

Syntax `LOG_DIRCAT=1`

Values

The value of 1 logs the DIRCAT start, which directories it uses, and when it completes.

The default is to log only when the DIRCAT task starts.

Usage Applies to Domino servers running the DIRCAT task.

See also

Console_Loglevel
Log
Log_AgentManager
Log_MailRouting
Log_Replication
Log_Sessions
Log_Tasks
Log_Update
Log_View_Events
Passthru_LogLevel
PhoneLog
RTR_Logging

Log_MailRouting

Description Controls the level of logging for mail routing activity on the server.

Syntax `Log_MailRouting=`*`value`*

Values

10 Log errors and warnings only

20 Log errors, warnings, and transfer and delivery output (default)

30 Log errors, warnings, transfer and delivery output, and information about transfer threads and processes

40 Log errors, warnings, transfer and delivery output, and detailed information about transfer threads and processes

Usage Applies to Domino servers.

Can be configured using a Configuration document in the Domino Directory.

See also

```
Console_Loglevel
Log
Log_AgentManager
Log_Dircat
Log_MailRouting
Log_Sessions
Log_Tasks
Log_Update
Log_View_Events
Passthru_LogLevel
PhoneLog
RTR_Logging
```

Log_Replication

Description Controls the level of logging used for server replication activity.

Syntax `Log_Replication=`*`value`*

Values

0 Don't log replication events

1 Log server replication events (default)

2 Log replication at the database level

3 Log replication at the element level (views, documents)

4 Log replication at the field level

5 Log replication summary information

Usage Applies to Domino servers.

Can be configured using a Configuration document in the Domino Directory.

See also

```
Console_Loglevel
Log
Log_AgentManager
Log_MailRouting
Log_Dircat
Log_Sessions
Log_Tasks
Log_Update
Log_View_Events
```

```
Passthru_LogLevel
PhoneLog
RTR_Logging
```

Log_Sessions

Description Controls the level of session logging.

Syntax `Log_Sessions=value`

Values

0 Do not log individual sessions

1 Log individual sessions (default)

Usage Applies to Domino servers.

Can be configured using a Configuration document in the Domino Directory.

See also

```
Console_Loglevel
Log
Log_AgentManager
Log_Dircat
Log_MailRouting
Log_Replication
Log_Tasks
Log_Update
Log_View_Events
Passthru_LogLevel
PhoneLog
RTR_Logging
```

Log_Tasks

Description Controls the level of logging of server task information.

Syntax `Log_Tasks=value`

Values

0 Don't send task status information to the console and log file

1 Send task status information to the console and log file

Usage Applies to Domino servers.

Can be configured using a Configuration document in the Domino Directory.

See also

```
Console_Loglevel
Log
Log_AgentManager
Log_Dircat
Log_MailRouting
```

```
Log_Replication
Log_Sessions
Log_Update
Log_View_Events
Passthru_LogLevel
PhoneLog
RTR_Logging
```

Log_Update

Description

Controls the level of logging of the index updating for the server console and log database.

Syntax `Log_Update=`*`value`*

Values

0 Records Indexer start and shutdown.

1 Records Indexer start and shutdown and the database name being updated (default).

2 Records Indexing start and shutdown and the database name being updated. Also displays the view name being updated.

Usage Applies to Domino servers.

See also

```
Console_Loglevel
Log
Log_AgentManager
Log_Dircat
Log_MailRouting
Log_Replication
Log_Sessions
Log_Tasks
Log_View_Events
Passthru_LogLevel
PhoneLog
RTR_Logging
```

NOTES.INI

Log_View_Events

Description

Controls the level of logging when views are rebuilt in the server log file.

Syntax `Log_View_Events=`*`value`*

Values

0 Don't log when views are rebuilt (default)

1 Log when views are rebuilt

Usage Applies to Domino servers.

Can be configured using a Configuration document in the Domino Directory.

See also

```
Console_Loglevel
Log
Log_AgentManager
Log_Dircat
Log_MailRouting
Log_Replication
Log_Sessions
Log_Tasks
Log_Update
Passthru_LogLevel
PhoneLog
RTR_Logging
```

MailAllowPriorityTime

Description

Configures the time window in which the server can route low priority mail.

Syntax `MailAllowPriorityTime=`*`start-end`*

Values The start and end hours are entered in 24-hour format.

The default window is 00:00–06:00.

Usage Applies to Domino servers.

Can be configured using a Configuration document in the Domino Directory.

MailCharSet

Description

Controls the character set used by the Domino server to messages to POP3.

Syntax `MailCharSet=`*`value`*

Values Table 14-5 shows the possible values of **`MailCharSet`**.

Table 14-5: MailCharSet Values and Their Meanings

MailCharSet Value	*Mime Name*	*Character Set Group*	*Language: Encoding Character Set*
18	x-sjis	Japanese	ShiftJS
24	euc-kr	Korean	EUC-KR
26	big5	Taiwanese	Big5, Codepage 950
27	gb2312	Simplified Chinese	PRC Chinese: GB, GBK

Table 14-5: MailCharSet Values and Their Meanings (continued)

MailCharSet Value	*Mime Name*	*Character Set Group*	*Language: Encoding Character Set*
32	iso-8859-1	Western	ISO Latin-1 (8859)
33	iso_8859-2	Central European	ISO Latin-2 (8859-2)
34	iso-8859-3	Turkish	ISO Latin-3 (8859-3)
35	iso-8859-4	Baltic Rim	ISO Latin-4 (8859-4)
36	iso-8859-5	Cyrillic	ISO 8859-5
37	iso-8859-6	Arabic	ISO 8859-6
38	iso-8859-7	Greek	ISO 8859-7
39	iso-8859-8	Hebrew	ISO 8859-8
40	iso-8859-9	Turkish	ISO Latin-5 (8859-9)
80	cp1250 windows-1250 (NT)	Central European	Codepage 1250
81	cp1251 windows-1251 (NT)	Cyrillic	Codepage 1251
82	usascii	Western	Codepage 1252
82	us-ascii	Western	Codepage 1252
83	cp1253 windows-1253 (NT)	Greek	Codepage 1253
84	cp1254 windows-1254 (NT)	Turkish	Codepage 1254
85	cp1255 windows-1255	Hebrew	Codepage 1255
86	cp1256 windows-1256	Arabic	Codepage 1256
87	cp1257 windows-1257	Baltic Rim	Codepage 1257
96	x-mac-roman	Western	Mac Script Roman
144	cp874 windows-874 (NT)	Thai	Codepage 874
3277	iso-2022-jp	Japanese	ISO-2022-JP
3301	x-euc-jp	Japanese	EUC-J
3302	x-euc-tw	Taiwanese	EUC-TW
3308	koi8-r	Cyrillic	KOI8

If this value is not specified, the server checks for a parameter called `WWWDSP_Codepage`; otherwise, it defaults to us-ascii as the default code page.

Applies to Domino servers running the `POP3` task.

MailClusterFailover

Description

Controls whether user mail databases can use the failover functionality provided by clustering. If this is enabled (and there is a another replica copy of their mail database somewhere in the cluster), then when the user's home server fails or is overworked, the client opens the replica copy of their mail database on another server.

Syntax `MailClusterFailover=1`

Usage Applies to Domino servers running clustering.

Can be configured using a Configuration document in the Domino Directory.

See also

```
Server_Availability_Threshold
Server_Cluster_Default_Port
Server_MaxSessions
Server_MaxUsers
Server_Restricted
```

MailCompactDisabled

Description

Controls whether or not the server mailbox files (*MAIL.BOX**) are compacted when the `Compact` task runs on the server.

Syntax `MailCompactDisabled=`*`value`*

Values

0 Mailboxes are compacted (default)

1 Mailboxes are not compacted

Usage Applies to Domino servers.

MailConvertMIMEonTransfer

Description

Controls whether the `Router` task does conversions for MIME messages.

Syntax `MailConvertMIMEonTransfer=`*`value`*

Values

0 Router doesn't do conversions for MIME messages (default)

1 Router does do conversions for MIME messages

Usage Applies to Domino servers.

MailDisablePriority

Description

Controls whether to ignore mail priority and treat all mail as having the same priority.

Syntax `MailDisablePriority=1`

Values

The value of `1` causes the server to ignore mail priority. The default is to recognize mail priority.

Usage Applies to Domino servers.

Can be configured using a Configuration document in the Domino Directory.

Mail_Disable_Implicit_Sender_Key

Description

Controls whether to encrypt an encrypted message with the sender's public key.

Syntax `Mail_Disable_Implicit_Sender_Keys=`*`value`*

Values

0 Doesn't encrypt the encrypted message with the sender's public key (default)

1 Encrypts the encrypted message with the sender's public key

Usage Applies to Notes clients.

Mail_Log_To_MiscEvents

Description

Controls whether mail events are logged to the Miscellaneous Events view of the Log database.

Syntax `Mail_Log_To_MiscEvents=`*`value`*

Values

0 Doesn't display mail events in the Miscellaneous Events view of the log database (default)

1 Displays mail events in the Miscellaneous Events view of the log database

Usage Applies to both Domino servers and Notes clients.

Can be configured using a Configuration document in the Domino Directory.

MailMaxThreads

Description

Configures the maximum number of mail threads (or processes for platforms that don't support threading) that the `Router` task can launch to transfer mail.

Syntax `MailMaxThreads=`*`value`*

Usage Applies to Domino servers.

Can be configured using a Configuration document in the Domino Directory.

MailServer

Description Identifies the server that contains the user's mail database.

Syntax `MailServer=`*`server`*

Usage Applies to both Domino servers and Notes clients.

Mail_Skip_NoKey_Dialog

Description

Controls whether an encryption failure dialog is displayed to the user when Notes can't locate the public key.

Syntax `Mail_Skip_NoKey_Dialog=`*`value`*

Values

0 Shows the dialog when Notes can't locate the public key (default)

1 Doesn't show the dialog when Notes can't locate the public key

Usage

Applies to Notes clients. In the dialog, selecting the option "Don't show signature or encryption failures again and continue sending" enables this parameter in future.

Mail_System

Description Specifies the mail system to use when the Notes client is setup.

Syntax `MailSystem=`*`value`*

Values

0 Notes mail

1 cc:Mail or a non-Lotus mail system

Usage Applies to Notes clients.

MailTimeout

Description

Configures the number of days before the server returns undelivered mail to the sender.

Syntax `MailTimeout=`*`days`*

Values The default is one day.

Usage Applies to Domino servers.

Can be configured using a Configuration document in the Domino Directory.

See also `MailTimeoutMinutes`

MailTimeoutMinutes

Description

Configures the number of minutes before the server returns undelivered mail to the sender. Is used instead of **`MailTimeout`** when configuring for a period of less than a day.

Syntax `MailTimeoutMinutes=`*`minutes`*

Values The default is one day (1440 minutes).

Usage Applies to Domino servers.

See also `MailTimeout`

Map_Retry_Delay

Description

Configures the retry delay after an unsuccessful attempt to contact another server.

Syntax `Map_Retry_Delay=`*`minutes`*

Usage Applies to Domino servers.

Memory_Quota

Description

For OS/2 servers, the maximum virtual memory in MB that the Domino server can use.

Syntax `Memory_Quota=`*`size`*

Values

The minimum size is 4MB; without this setting, the Domino server uses all available memory.

Usage Applies to OS/2 Domino servers.

Can be configured using a Configuration document in the Domino Directory.

MinNewMailPoll

Description

Controls how often clients can poll the server to check whether new mail has arrived. This can override the client setting ("Check for new mail every *x* minutes" in the Preferences dialog on the Mail and News tab) to reduce the load on the server caused by this polling activity.

Syntax `MinNewMailPoll=`*`minutes`*

Usage Applies to Domino servers.

See also `NewMailInterval`

Move_Mail_File_Expiration_Days

Description

Configures the number of days that the Notes client updates mail file-related change requests; after this period has expired the change requests become obsolete.

Syntax `Move_Mail_File_Expiration_Days=`*`days`*

Usage Applies to Domino servers.

MTEnabled

Description Defines whether message tracking is enabled.

Syntax `MTEnabled=1`

Values

0 Message tracking is disabled (default).

1 Message tracking enabled.

Usage Applies to Domino servers.

Equivalent to the Message Tracking field (enabled/disabled) on the Router/SMTP tab in the Configuration document within the Domino directory.

MTMaxResponses

Description

Configures the maximum number of responses that can be returned from a message-tracking query. If this number is reached, a warning message is displayed on the Administrator panel status line.

Syntax `MTMaxResponses=number`

Values

The maximum number of responses that can be returned from a query is 100.

Usage Applies to Domino servers.

Names

Description

Lists the Domino directories to search when addressing and routing mail messages.

The ability to use multiple secondary name and address book is often called using "cascading name and address books." A better solution to use instead is the Directory Assistance feature.

Syntax `Names=values`

Values

The default is to search only the primary Domino directory for the domain, which has the filename *NAMES.NSF*. The *.NSF* extension does not need to be used for the domino directories in this parameter.

Remote directories (on other servers) can also be specified by using the canonical name of the server separated by *!!!* and the database name; for example, *CN=shoreline/O=alameda!!!Names*.

Multiple directories are separated by a comma. This line has a maximum length of 256 characters.

Usage Applies to both Domino servers and Notes clients.

Name_Change_Expiration_Delay

Description

Configures the number of days a name-change request remains active; after this period has expired, the change request becomes obsolete.

Syntax `Name_Change_Expiration_Delay=days`

Values

The minimum value is 14 days; the maximum value is 60 days; the default is 21 days.

Usage Applies to Domino servers.

Can be configured using a Configuration document in the Domino Directory.

NetwareNDSName

Description

Configures the NDS name of the Domino server to allow the server to autologin to NDS at startup.

Syntax `NetwareNDSName=name`

Values

Novell NetWare NDS uses an X.500-based directory in a similar manner to Domino. Keep in mind that NetWare uses a period rather than the slash character in its fully qualified name format. For example: *cn=shoreline.o=alameda.*

Usage

Applies to Domino servers that are configured to work within NetWare NDS networks.

Can be configured using a Configuration document in the Domino Directory.

See also

```
NWNDSPassword
NWNSDUserid
```

New_DNParse

Description

Enables a new method in R5 to parse mail addresses that can accommodate X.400 addresses. This method is disabled by default to ensure compatibility with earlier versions of Notes/Domino. Using this parameter enables the parsing of X.400 addressing.

Syntax `New_DNParse=1`

Usage Applies to Domino servers.

NewMailInterval

Description

Specifies how often the Notes client polls the Domino server for new mail messages.

Syntax `NewMailInterval=`*`minutes`*

Values The default is 1 minute.

Usage Applies to Notes clients.

Can be configured on a Notes client by selecting File → Preferences → User Preferences → Mail and News tab → Check for new mail every *x* minutes.

See also `NewMailTune, MinNewMailInterval`

NewMailTune

Description Configures the tune played when new mail arrives.

Syntax `NewMailTune=`*`wavefile`*

Usage Applies to Notes clients.

Can be configured on a Notes client by selecting File → Preferences → User Preferences → Mail and News tab → enabling audio notification → sound to play from the list.

See also `NewMailInterval`

NNTPAddress

Description

Defines the IP address to use for an NNTP server using partitioning.

Syntax `NNTPAddress=`*`address`*

Values

The address can be either the IP address of the server or the server's fully qualified name.

Usage

Applies to Domino servers running the `NNTP` task and using partitioning

See also

```
IMAPAddress
LDAPAddress
POP3Address
NTTP_Delete_Delays
NNTP_Delete_Days_Expired
```

`NNTP_Initial_Feed_All`
`NNTP_Initial_Feed_Days`
`NTTP_Previous_`*`X_servername`*
`NNTP_Prohibit_NEWNEWS_Command`
`NNTP_PullAsServer`

NNTP_Delete_Delays

Description

Controls when inactive articles are deleted from newsgroups created by the Domino server.

Syntax `NNTP_Delete_Days=`*`days`*

Values The default is five days.

Usage Applies to Domino servers running the `NNTP` task.

See also

`NNTPAddress`
`NNTP_Delete_Days_Expired`
`NNTP_Initial_Feed_All`
`NNTP_Initial_Feed_Days`
`NTTP_Previous_`*`X_servername`* `NNTP_Prohibit_NEWNEWS_Command`
`NNTP_PullAsServer`

NNTP_Delete_Days_Expired

Description

Controls when newsgroup articles marked as expired are deleted from newsgroups created by the server.

Syntax `NNTP_Delete_Days_Expired=`*`days`*

Values The default is five days.

Usage Applies to Domino servers running the `NNTP` task.

See also

`NNTPAddress`
`NTTP_Delete_Delays NNTP_Initial_Feed_All`
`NNTP_Initial_Feed_Days`
`NTTP_Previous_`*`X_servername`*
`NNTP_Prohibit_NEWNEWS_Command`
`NNTP_PullAsServer`

NNTP_Initial_Feed_All

Description

If this parameter is enabled, all articles are transferred during the initial newsfeed.

Syntax `NNTP_Initial_Feed_All=1`

Values

The initial newsfeed default setting transfers articles published within the last three days.

Usage Applies to Domino servers running the NNTP task.

See also

NNTPAddress
NTTP_Delete_Delays
NNTP_Delete_Days_Expired
NNTP_Initial_Feed_Days
NTTP_Previous_*X_servername*
NNTP_Prohibit_NEWNEWS_Command
NNTP_PullAsServer

NNTP_Initial_Feed_Days

Description

Controls how many past days of articles are transferred during the initial newsfeed.

Syntax `NNTP_Initial_Feed_Days=`*days*

Values

The initial newsfeed default setting transfers articles published within the last three days.

Usage Applies to Domino servers running the NNTP task.

See also

NNTPAddress
NTTP_Delete_Delays
NNTP_Delete_Days_Expired
NNTP_Initial_Feed_All
NTTP_Previous_*X_servername*
NNTP_Prohibit_NEWNEWS_Command
NNTP_PullAsServer

NNTP_Previous_<X_servername>

Description

Identifies the date and time of the most recent newsfeed for each defined feed connection.

Syntax `NNTP_Previous_`*X_servername*`=` *yymmdd hhmmss GMT*

Values *X* should be 0 for a pull feed and 1 for a push feed.

Usage Applies to Domino servers running the NNTP task.

See also

NNTPAddress
NTTP_Delete_Delays
NNTP_Delete_Days_Expired
NNTP_Initial_Feed_All
NNTP_Initial_Feed_Days
NNTP_Prohibit_NEWNEWS_Command
NNTP_PullAsServer

NNTP_Prohibit_NEWNEWS_Command

Description

If this parameter is present, it prevents remote NNTP servers from pulling new articles from this Domino server.

Syntax `NNTP_Prohibit_NEWNEWS_Command=1`

Values `ADMIN=CN=Greg Neilson/O=ALAMEDA`

Usage Applies to Domino servers running the `NNTP` task.

See also

NNTPAddress
NTTP_Delete_Delays
NNTP_Delete_Days_Expired
NNTP_Initial_Feed_All
NNTP_Initial_Feed_Days
NTTP_Previous_*X_servername*
NNTP_PullAsServer

NNTP_PullAsServer

Description

If this parameter is present, the `NNTP` task pulls news from remote NNTP servers without using reader mode. Otherwise, the `NNTP` task uses reader mode.

Syntax `NNTP_PullAsServer=1`

Usage Applies to Domino servers running the `NNTP` task.

See also

NNTPAddress
NTTP_Delete_Delays
NNTP_Delete_Days_Expired
NNTP_Initial_Feed_All
NNTP_Initial_Feed_Days
NTTP_Previous_*X_servername*
NNTP_Prohibit_NEWNEWS_Command

NoDesignMenu

Description Controls whether the Design menu is hidden for Notes clients.

Syntax `NoDesignMenu=value`

Values

0 Shows the Design menu (default)

1 Hides the Design menu

Usage Applies to Notes clients.

NoExternalApps

Description

Controls whether certain workstation features are disabled to guard against mail virus attacks. These features include OLE, DDE, the `@Command`, launching file attachments, `@DbLookup`, `@DbColumn`, and `@Mailsend` formulas.

Syntax `NoExternalApps=value`

Values

0 Enables these workstation features (default)

1 Disables these workstations features

Usage Applies to Notes clients.

NOTES.INI

No_Force_Activity_Logging

Description

Configures whether the *Statlog* scheduled task automatically enables activity logging on all server databases. Regardless of this setting, database activity is still logged in the Database Usage view in the server's log database.

Syntax `No_Force_Activity_Logging=value`

Values

0 Allows automatic activity logging on all databases (default)

1 Prevents automatic activity logging on all databases

Usage Applies to Domino servers.

Can be configured using a Configuration document in the Domino Directory.

NoMailMenu

Description

If this parameter is present, the Mail menu in Notes doesn't appear in the Note client, and the user's mail system is changed to None.

Syntax `NoMailMenu=1`

Usage Applies to Notes clients.

NoMsgCache

Description

If this parameter is present, it disables the per-user message cache for IMAP clients. This feature can reduce memory used in supporting IMAP clients.

Syntax `NoMsgCache=1`

Usage Applies to Domino servers running the `IMAP` task.

See also

`IMAPAddress`
`IMAILExactSize`
`IMAP_Config_Update_Interval`
`IMAPGreeting`
`IMAPRedirectSSLGreeting`
`IMAP_Session_Timeout`
`IMAPSSLGreeting.`

NSF_Buffer_Pool_Size

Description

Configures the maximum size of the NSF buffer pool, which is used when the Domino server buffers I/O. Lotus recommends you leave this for Domino to configure automatically.

Syntax `NSF_Buffer_Pool_Size=`*`bytes`*

Values

The maximum size available is 256MB. For Macintosh clients, the maximum size is 16MB.

Usage

`NSF_Buffer_Pool_Size_MB` is the same parameter, but uses MB instead of bytes as its value.

Applies to both Domino servers and Notes clients.

Can be configured using a Configuration document in the Domino Directory.

NSF_DbCache_Disable

Description Specifies whether the database cache is enabled or disabled.

Syntax `NSF_DbCache=value`

Values

0 Enables the database cache (default)

1 Disables the database cache

Usage Applies to Domino servers.

See also `NSF_DbCache_MaxEntries`

NSF_DbCache_MaxEntries

Description

Defines the maximum number of databases that can be held in the server's cache.

Syntax `NSF_DbCache_MaxEntries=value`

Values

The minimum number of cache entries is 25. The default number of cache entries is the greater of 25 or the `NSF_Buffer_Pool_Size` divided by 300K.

Usage Applies to both Domino servers and Notes clients.

See also `NSF_DbCache_Disable`

NWNDSPassword

Description

Configures the NDS password to allow the Domino server or Notes user to autologin to NDS at startup.

Syntax `NWNDSPassword=password`

Values The password is not hashed and appears in clear text.

Usage

Applies to Domino servers and Notes clients that are configured to work within NetWare NDS networks.

See also

`NetwareNDSName`
`NWNSDUserid`

NOTES.INI

NWNDSUserid

Description

Configures the NDS name of the Domino server or Notes user to allow an autologin to NDS at startup.

Syntax `NWNDSUserid=`*`name`*

Values

Novell NetWare NDS uses an X.500-based directory in a similar manner to Domino. Keep in mind that NetWare uses a period rather than the slash character in its fully qualified name format. For example: *cn=gneilson.o=alameda.*

Usage

Applies to Domino servers and Notes clients that are configured to work within NetWare NDS networks.

See also

```
NetwareNDSName
NWNDSPassword
NWNSDUserid
```

ODBCThreadSafeDrivers

Description

Configures whether ODBC drivers can be considered thread-safe when running in a multithreaded application.

Syntax `ODBCThreadSafeDrivers=`*`value`*

Values

ALL All ODBC drivers are thread-safe

NONE No OBDC drivers are thread-safe

Otherwise, specific driver names can be listed, each separated by a comma.

Usage Applies to Domino servers.

ORBThreads

Description

Configures the number of threads to use with the DIIOP Object Request Broker to process requests.

Syntax `ORBThreads=`*`value`*

Values The default is 10 threads.

Usage Applies to Domino servers running the `DIIOP` task.

Passthru_Hangup_Delay

Description

Configures how long a passthru server waits to hang up after the last dialup session ends.

Syntax `Passthru_Hangup_Delay=`*`seconds`*

Values The default is 120 seconds.

Usage Applies to Domino servers.

See also

```
Allow_Passsthru_Access
Allow_Passthru_Callers
Allow_Passthru_Clients
Allow_Passthru_Targets
Passthru_LogLevel
```

Passthru_LogLevel

Description

Configures the amount of trace information recorded for network connections, including passthru. This information is sent to the Miscellaneous Events view of the log database.

Syntax `Passthru_LogLevel=`*`value`*

Values

0 Record nothing

1 Record errors only

2 Record summary progress information

3 Record detailed progress information

4 Record full trace information

5 Record full trace information and driver messages

Usage Applies to both Domino servers and Notes clients.

Can be configured using the Notes client by selecting File → Preferences → User Preferences → Ports tab → highlight the port to trace → Trace option → levels of tracing activity required.

See also

```
Allow_Passsthru_Access
Allow_Passthru_Callers
Allow_Passthru_Clients
Allow_Passthru_Targets
Console_Loglevel
Log
Log_AgentManager
```

NOTES.INI

```
Log_Dircat
Log_Replication
Log_Sessions
Log_Tasks
Log_Update
Log_View_Events
PhoneLog
RTR_Logging
```

PhoneLog

Description Controls whether phone calls are logged to the log database.

Syntax `PhoneLog=value`

Values

0 Record nothing

1 Record all calls except those with a busy signal

2 Record all calls (default)

Usage Applies to both Domino servers and Notes clients.

Can be configured using a Configuration document in the Domino Directory.

See also

```
Console_Loglevel
Log
Log_AgentManager
Log_Dircat
Log_Replication
Log_Sessions
Log_Tasks
Log_Update
Log_View_Events
Passthru_LogLevel
RTR_Logging
```

PLATFORM_STATISTICS_ENABLED

Description

Enables a newly added feature in Domino in 5.0.2 to collect statistics for the Windows NT and Solaris Sparc operating systems.

Syntax `PLATFORM_STATISTICS_ENABLED=value`

Values

0 Collection of operating system statistics is not enabled (default).

1 Collection of operating system statistics is enabled.

Usage Applies to Domino servers.

POP3Address

Description Defines the IP address to use for a POP3 server using partitioning.

Syntax `POP3Address=`*`address`*

Values

The address can be either the IP address of the server or the fully qualified name of the server.

Usage

Applies to Domino servers running the `POP3` task and using partitioning.

See also

```
IMAPAddress
LDAPAddress
NNTPAddress
POP3_Config_Update_Interval
POP3_Disable_Cache
POP3DNSLookup
POP3_Domain
POP3_Enable_Cache_Stats
POP3ExactSize
POP3_MarkRead
POP3_Message_Stat_Cache_NumPerUser
POP3NotesPort
```


POP3_Config_Update_Interval

Description

Configures how often in minutes the `POP3` task updates its configuration information.

Syntax `POP3_Config_Update_Interval=`*`minutes`*

Values The default is every 2 minutes.

Usage Applies to Domino servers running the `POP3` task.

See also

```
POP3Address
POP3_Disable_Cache
POP3DNSLookup
POP3_Domain
POP3_Enable_Cache_Stats
POP3ExactSize
POP3_MarkRead,
POP3_Message_Stat_Cache_NumPerUser
POP3NotesPort
```

POP3_Disable_Cache

Description Controls whether per-user caching is supported for POP3 clients.

Syntax `POP3_Disable_Cache=value`

Values

0 Disables caching (default)

1 Enables caching

Usage Applies to Domino servers running the `POP3` task.

See also

```
POP3Address
POP3_Config_Update_Interval
POP3_Disable_Cache
POP3DNSLookup
POP3_Domain
POP3ExactSize
POP3_MarkRead
POP3_Message_Stat_Cache_NumPerUser
POP3NotesPort
```

POP3DNSLookup

Description

Controls whether the Domino server performs a reverse DNS lookup to find the hostname for the POP3 client's IP address.

Syntax `POP3DNSLookup=value`

Values

0 Don't lookup hostname (default)

1 Lookup hostname

Usage Applies to Domino servers running the `POP3` task.

See also

```
POP3Address
POP3_Config_Update_Interval
POP3_Disable_Cache
POP3_Domain
POP3_Enable_Cache_Stats
POP3ExactSize
POP3_MarkRead
POP3_Message_Stat_Cache_NumPerUser
POP3NotesPort
```

POP3_Domain

Description

Identifies the Internet domain to use as the gateway to send mail for local addresses. If this setting is used, it overrides the DNS MX values.

Syntax `POP3_Domain=`*`name`*

Usage Applies to Domino servers running the `POP3` task.

See also

```
POP3Address
POP3_Config_Update_Interval
POP3_Disable_Cache
POP3DNSLookup
POP3_Enable_Cache_Stats
POP3ExactSize
POP3_MarkRead
POP3_Message_Stat_Cache_NumPerUser
POP3NotesPort
```

POP3_Enable_Cache_Stats

Description Enables or disables POP3 caching statistics.

Syntax `POP3_Enable_Cache_Stats=`*`value`*

Values

0 Disable POP3 cache statistics (default)

1 Enable POP3 cache statistics

Usage Applies to Domino servers running the `POP3` task.

See also

```
POP3Address
POP3_Config_Update_Interval
POP3_Disable_Cache
POP3DNSLookup
POP3_Domain
POP3ExactSize
POP3_MarkRead
POP3_Message_Stat_Cache_NumPerUser
POP3NotesPort
```

POP3ExactSize

Description

Configures whether the POP3 can return an estimated size of the message or instead must return the exact size of the message. Computing the exact size can

NOTES.INI

consume significant CPU cycles of the server and also delay the response to the user.

Syntax `POP3ExactSize=value`

Values

0 POP3 STAT returns estimated size (default)

1 POP3 STAT returns exact size

Usage Applies to Domino servers running the `POP3` task.

See also

```
IMAILExactSize
POP3Address
POP3_Config_Update_Interval
POP3_Disable_Cache
POP3DNSLookup
POP3_Domain
POP3_Enable_Cache_Stats
POP3_MarkRead
POP3_Message_Stat_Cache_NumPerUser
POP3NotesPort
```

POP3_MarkRead

Description

Controls whether POP3 downloaded messages are marked as read or unread on the Domino server.

Syntax `POP3_MarkRead=value`

Values

0 Mark the downloaded POP3 messages as unread (default)

1 Mark the downloaded POP3 message as read.

Usage Applies to Domino servers running the `POP3` task.

See also

```
POP3Address
POP3_Config_Update_Interval
POP3_Disable_Cache
POP3DNSLookup
POP3_Domain
POP3_Enable_Cache_Stats
POP3ExactSize
POP3_Message_Stat_Cache_NumPerUser
POP3NotesPort
```

POP3_Message_Stat_Cache_NumPerUser

Description

Configures how many POP3 message statistics can be cached per user. Caching statistics consumes server resources (CPU and memory).

Syntax `POP3_Message_Stat_Cache_NumPerUser=`*number*

Values The default value is 50 statistics per user.

Usage Applies to Domino servers running the `POP3` task.

See also

```
POP3Address
POP3_Config_Update_Interval
POP3_Disable_Cache
POP3DNSLookup
POP3_Domain
POP3_Enable_Cache_Stats
POP3ExactSize
POP3_MarkRead
POP3NotesPort
```

POP3NotesPort

Description

Configures which port to use to serve POP3 client connections on a partitioned Domino server.

Syntax `POP3NotesPort=`*port*

Values

The port can be any enabled port on the server that uses the TCP port driver.

Usage

Applies to Domino servers running the `POP3` task on a partitioned server.

See also

```
POP3Address
POP3_Config_Update_Interval
POP3_Disable_Cache
POP3DNSLookup
POP3_Domain
POP3_Enable_Cache_Stats
POP3ExactSize
POP3_MarkRead
POP3_Message_Stat_Cache_NumPerUser
```

NOTES.INI

<portname>_MaxSessions

Description

Configures the maximum sessions available on a configured Domino network port.

Syntax `portname_MaxSessions=number`

Usage Applies to Domino servers.

Ports

Description Defines the enabled ports on the server or workstation.

Syntax `Ports=names`

Values

The ports can be given any name. Those that are predefined are TCPIP, AppleTalk, SPX, VINES, COM1-COM5, and LAN0-LAN8.

Usage Applies to both Domino servers and Notes clients.

Can be configured using the Notes client by selecting File → Preferences → User Preferences → Ports tab. On a Domino server, this can be configured using the Port tab in the Server document in the Domino Directory.

ProgramMode

Description

This value identifies the type of license the Notes client is using to run with—either as defined in the first setup or if the user has switched IDs to a Mail ID.

Was used for R4 and is no longer used in R5.

Syntax `ProgramMode=value`

Values

0 Full Notes license (default)

1 Notes Mail license

8 Desktop license

Usage Applies to Notes clients.

Repl_Error_Tolerance

Description

Configures the number of replication errors of the same type that can occur between a pair of databases before the server stops replicating.

Syntax `Repl_Error_Tolerance=value`

Values The default value is 2.

Usage Applies to Domino servers.

See also

```
Repl_Push_Retries
ReplicationTimeLimit
Replicators
```

Repl_Push_Retries

Description

Configures the number of times to retry a failed replication push to an R3 server, since R3 doesn't support simultaneous replication of the same database with multiple users and/or servers.

Syntax `Repl_Push_Retries=number`

Usage Applies to Domino servers.

Can be configured using a Configuration document in the Domino Directory.

See also

```
Repl_Error_Tolerance
ReplicationTimeLimit
Replicators
```

NOTES.INI

ReplicationTimeLimit

Description

Configures the time limit for replication between this server and another.

Syntax `ReplicationTimeLimit=minutes`

Values The default is no time limit for replication.

Usage Applies to Domino servers.

This entry is equivalent to the "Replication Time Limit" field on the Connection document within the Domino Directory.

See also

```
Repl_Error_Tolerance
Repl_Push_Retries
Replicators
```

Replicators

Description

Configures the number of replicator tasks that can run concurrently.

Syntax `Replicators=number`

Values The default value is 1.

Usage

Applies to Domino servers. This value should generally not exceed the number of processors in the server – 1.

Can be configured using a Configuration document in the Domino Directory.

See also

```
Repl_Error_Tolerance
Repl_Push_Retries
ReplicationTimeLimit
```

ReportSSLHandshakeErrors

Description

Configures whether to report errors encountered during SSL handshaking.

Syntax `ReportSSLHandshakeErrors=1`

Values

When present, this enables the reporting of SSL handshake errors to the server console and the log database.

Usage Applies to Domino servers using SSL.

See Also `TraceSSLHandshake`

ReportUseMail

Description

Configures how the reporter task sends statistics to other servers—either via the network or as mail messages sent by the router task. The option for mail messages can be useful for sending statistics over a dialup connection to another server.

Syntax `ReportUseMail=value`

Values

0 Use the router to send statistics

1 Use the network to send statistics (default)

Usage Applies to Domino servers.

Can be configured using a Configuration document in the Domino Directory

RouterAllowConcurrentXFERToAll

Description

Configures whether the router task can use multiple threads to transfer mail to remote domains over slower network links. New with 5.0.3.

Syntax `RouterAllowConcurrentXFERToAll=value`

Values

0 Disables multiple mail router threads (default).

1 Enable multiple threads when sending to remote domains.

Usage Applies to Domino servers.

RTR_Logging

Description Enables or disables monitoring of cluster replication.

Syntax `RTR_Logging=value`

Values

0 Disable monitoring (default)

1 Enable monitoring

Usage Applies to Domino servers within a cluster.

See also

```
Console_Loglevel
Log
Log_AgentManager
Log_Dircat
Log_Replication
Log_Sessions
Log_Tasks
Log_Update
Log_View_Events
Passthru_LogLevel
PhoneLog
```

Sched_Purge_Interval

Description

Configures how many days to keep busy-time schedule information.

Syntax `Sched_Purge_Interval=days`

Values The default is 7 days. A value of 0 means to never purge.

Usage Applies to Domino servers.

NOTES.INI

See Also

```
Schedule_Check_Entries_When_Validating
Schedule_No_CalcStats
Schedule_No_Validate
```

Schedule_Check_Entries_When_Validating

Description

Configures whether the Schedule Manager checks entries in the busy-time database on a user-by-user basis.

Syntax `Schedule_Check_Entries_When_Validating=value`

Values

0 Disables validation (default)

1 Enables validation

Usage Applies to Domino servers.

See also

```
Sched_Purge_Interval
Schedule_No_CalcStats
Schedule_No_Validate
```

Schedule_No_CalcStats

Description

Controls whether the Schedule Manager performs an hourly update and calculation of schedule statistics.

Syntax `Schedule_No_CalcStats=value`

Values

0 Enables the hourly update and calculation of statistics (default)

1 Disables the hourly update and calculation of statistics

Usage Applies to Domino servers.

See also

```
Sched_Purge_Interval
Schedule_Check_Entries_When_Validating
Schedule_No_Validate
```

Schedule_No_Validate

Description

Configures whether the Schedule Manager performs a daily busy-time validation. This checks every mail database on the server to confirm that their busy-time calendar information is stored within the free time database.

Syntax `Schedule_No_Validate=value`

Values

0 Enables daily busy-time validation (default)

1 Disables daily busy-time validation

Usage Applies to Domino servers.

See also

```
Sched_Purge_Interval
Schedule_Check_Entries_When_Validating
Schedule_No_CalcStats
```

SecureMail

Description

Controls whether to force mail to be signed and encrypted, removing these options from dialog boxes.

Syntax `SecureMail=value`

Values

0 Sign and encrypt sent mail, removing the option to sign or send mail from dialog boxes.

1 User dialog boxes prompt user to determine whether to sign or encrypt mail as it is being sent (default)

Usage Applies to Notes clients.

The option to sign and/or encrypt mail can be configured on the Notes client by selecting File → Preferences → User Preferences → Mail and News tab. There are checkboxes on the page to sign and to encrypt sent mail.

Server_Availability_Threshold

Description

Used within a clustered Domino environment to determine the level at which the server is considered to be busy, and thus at what point requests would be passed on to other servers in the cluster. This feature can be used to balance the work-load amongst the servers.

This threshold is compared against a server's availability index; when the availability index is below this threshold value, the server is considered busy and requests are passed to other servers within the cluster.

Syntax `Server_Availability_Threshold=value`

Values

The threshold can be any number between 0 (which means that workload balancing is disabled) and 100 (which means that the server is considered busy and the Cluster Manager will try to redirect the request to other servers within the cluster).

Usage Applies to Domino servers within a cluster.

Can be configured using a Configuration document in the Domino Directory.

See also

```
MailClusterFailover
Server_Cluster_Default_Port
Server_MaxSessions
Server_MaxUsers
Server_Restricted
```

Server_Cluster_Default_Port

Description

Configures the port to use for cluster replication traffic to other servers in the cluster. The ports available are configured using the `Ports` parameter in *NOTES.INI* or the Ports section of the Server document in the Domino Directory.

Syntax `Server_Cluster_Default_Port=name`

Usage Applies to Domino servers within a cluster.

Can be configured using a Configuration document in the Domino Directory.

See also

```
MailClusterFailover
Server_Availability_Threshold
Server_MaxSessions
Server_MaxUsers
Server_Restricted
```

Server_Console_Password

Description

Contains the server console password if one is enabled by using the `SET SECURE` command.

Syntax `Server_Console_Password=password`

Values

The password is not stored in clear text, but is encrypted. If the password is later forgotten, this entry can be removed from *NOTES.INI*; when the server is next started, a password will not be required.

Usage Applies to Domino servers.

ServerKeyFileName

Description

Identifies the name of the server ID file. Before R5, when a Notes client and Domino server on the same machine used the same *NOTES.INI* file, this parameter was needed to ensure that a logged-on user and the server used a different ID file. Otherwise, if a user switched IDs at the server, when the server next started it would attempt to start using the ID of that person since this would change the value of the `KeyFileName` parameter within *NOTES.INI*. This parameter can still be used in R5 if the Notes client and server code is installed into the same directory.

Syntax `ServerKeyFileName=filename`

Usage Applies to Domino servers.

Server_Max_Concurrent_Trans

Description

Sets a limit on the maximum number of concurrent transactions on the server.

Syntax `Server_Max_Concurrent_Trans=value`

Values

For partitioned servers, Lotus recommends the sum of these for all defined Domino servers on the same machine to be 20 or less.

Usage Applies to Domino servers.

Server_MaxSessions

Description

Controls the maximum number of concurrent sessions that can be established with this Domino server.

Syntax `Server_MaxSessions=number`

Usage Applies to Domino servers.

Can be configured using a Configuration document in the Domino Directory.

See also

```
MailClusterFailover
Server_Availability_Threshold
Server_Cluster_Default_Port
Server_MaxUsers
Server_Restricted
```

Server_MaxUsers

Description

Controls the maximum number of users that can access a server. After this number is reached, the server refuses to accept new database open requests.

Syntax `Server_MaxUsers=`*`number`*

Values A value of 0 provides unlimited access to the server.

Usage Applies to Domino servers.

Can be configured using a Configuration document in the Domino Directory.

See also

```
MailClusterFailover
Server_Availability_Threshold
Server_Cluster_Default_Port
Server_MaxSessions
Server_Restricted
```

ServerName

Description The full hierarchical name of the server.

Syntax `ServerName=`*`name`*

Usage Applies to Domino servers.

Equivalent to the Server Name field in the Server document within the Domino Directory.

ServerNoReplRequests

Description

Stops the server from accepting any replication requests from other servers. Any other server that replicates with this server must use pull-push replication.

Syntax `ServerNoReplRequests=`*`value`*

Values

0 Accepts replication requests from other servers (default)

1 Doesn't accept replication requests

Usage Applies to Domino servers.

ServerPullReplication

Description

Controls whether all scheduled replication from this server must be pull-push only.

Syntax `ServerPullReplication=value`

Values

0 Scheduled replication runs normally (default)

1 Only pull-push replication is enabled from this server.

Usage Applies to Domino servers.

Can be configured using a Configuration document in the Domino Directory.

ServerPushReplication

Description

Controls whether all replication from this server must be push-pull only.

Syntax `ServerPushreplication=value`

Values

0 Scheduled replication runs normally (default)

1 Only push-pull replication is enabled from this server.

Usage Applies to Domino servers.

Server_Restricted

Description

Enables or disables a server. A disabled server does not accept new open database requests from clients. This parameter can be used within a clustered Domino environment to stop users from accessing one of the servers.

Syntax `Server_Restricted=value`

Values

0 Server access is not restricted (default).

1 Server access is restricted now, but after the server is restarted it will not be restricted.

2 Server access is persistently restricted, meaning this status will continue after the server is restarted.

Usage Applies to Domino servers.

Can be configured using a Configuration document in the Domino Directory.

See also

```
MailClusterFailover
Server_Availability_Threshold
Server_Cluster_Default_Port
Server_MaxSessions
Server_MaxUsers
```

Server_Session_Timeout

Description

Configures the timeout for when the Domino server drops inactive connections.

Syntax

`Server_Session_Timeout=minutes`

Values

The default is 4 hours (240 minutes), and Lotus recommends that the minimum value be 15 minutes; otherwise the server workload in having to reestablish sessions slows down the server.

Usage

Applies to Domino servers.

Can be configured using a Configuration document in the Domino Directory.

Server_Show_Performance

Description

Controls whether server performance events are displayed on the Domino server console.

Syntax

```
Server_Show_Performance=value
```

Values

0 Records performance events in the Domino log database (default)

1 Displays performance events on the Domino server console

Usage

Applies to Domino servers.

Can be configured using a Configuration document in the Domino Directory.

ServerTasks

Description

Configures the Domino server tasks that start when the server is started.

Syntax

`ServerTasks=task, task, . . .`

Values

Refer to Chapter 13 for a list of Domino server tasks.

Usage Applies to Domino servers.

ServerTasksAt<Time>

Description Schedules tasks to run each hour on the Domino server.

Syntax `ServerTasksAttime=task, task . . .`

Values

The time is specified in 24-hour format, so it ranges from 0 (midnight) to 23 (11 P.M.).

Refer to Chapter 13 for a list of server tasks that can be scheduled.

Usage Applies to Domino servers.

The Program document in the Domino Directory can also be used to schedule tasks; however, it has broader scheduling capabilities, as it is able to schedule by day of the week as well as by hour of the day.

Setup

Description Identifies the revision number of the installed Notes/Domino code.

Syntax `Setup=value`

Usage Applies to both Domino servers and Notes clients.

NOTES.INI

SetupDB

Description

Identifies the setup database application to configure the Domino server.

Syntax `SetupDB=database`

Values

For Windows NT servers on the Intel platform, this setup database is called *SETUP.NSF*. For all other platforms, the database is *SETUPWEB.NSF*. The server can be started in HTTP Server mode by adding the `HTTPSSetup` argument to start the server. The server will not enter the HTTP server setup mode without this parameter.

Usage Applies to Domino servers.

SetupServerAddress

Description

Configures the address of the server to contact during the initial setup of the client software. This means that the user doesn't need to enter this information.

Syntax `SetupServerAddress=address`

Values

The DNS name (when using TCP/IP) or the phone number to use (when using dialup support over XPC or DUN/RAS).

Usage Applies to Notes clients.

SetupServerName

Description

Configures the name of the server to contact during the initial setup of the client software. This means the user doesn't need to enter this information.

Syntax `SetupServerName=name`

Usage Applies to Notes clients.

Shared_Mail

Description

Configures whether the shared mail feature is enabled on the server. Refer to Chapter 4, *Mail*, for a discussion on how shared mail works.

Syntax `Shared_Mail=value`

Values

0 Shared mail not used (default)

1 Shared mail used for new mail delivered to this server

2 Shared mail used for new mail delivered to this server and mail transferred through this server.

Usage Applies to Domino servers.

Can be configured using a Configuration document in the Domino Directory.

Show_Task_Detail

Description

Configures whether to add the name of the executing transaction to the session message.

Syntax `Show_Task_Detail=value`

Values

0 Turns off adding the name of the executing transaction (default)

1 Adds name of executing transaction

Usage Applies to Domino servers.

Can be configured using a Configuration document in the Domino Directory.

SMIME_Strong_Algorithm

Description

Configures the encryption method for MIME messages to recipients whose public keys are longer than 512 bits, but don't have the "strong encryption" flag in their certificates.

Syntax `SMIME_Strong_Algorithm=value`

Values Table 14-6 lists the available values for this parameter.

Table 14-6: S/MIME Encryption Values for the SMIME_Strong_Algorithm Parameter

Value	*Meaning*
RC2_40	Use RC2 algorithm with a 40-bit key
RC2_56	Use RC2 algorithm with a 56-bit key
RC2_64	Use RC2 algorithm with a 64-bit key
RC2_80	Use RC2 algorithm with an 80-bit key
RC2_128	Use RC2 algorithm with a 128-bit key
RC5_5	Use RC2 algorithm with a 5-bit key
RC5_7	Use RC2 algorithm with a 7-bit key
RC5_10	Use RC2 algorithm with a 10-bit key
RC5_16	Use RC2 algorithm with a 16-bit key
DES	Use DES algorithm
3DES	Use triple DES algorithm

Usage Applies to Notes clients.

See also `SMIME_Weak_Algorithm`

SMIME_Weak_Algorithm

Description

Configures the encryption method for MIME messages to recipients whose public keys are less than 512 bits.

Syntax `SMIME_Weak_Algorithm=value`

Values Table 14-7 lists the available values for this parameter.

Table 14-7: S/MIME Encryption Values for the SMIME_Weak_Algorithm Parameter

Value	*Meaning*
RC2_40	Use RC2 algorithm with a 40-bit key
RC2_56	Use RC2 algorithm with a 56-bit key
RC2_64	Use RC2 algorithm with a 64-bit key
RC2_80	Use RC2 algorithm with an 80-bit key
RC2_128	Use RC2 algorithm with a 128-bit key
RC5_5	Use RC2 algorithm with a 5-bit key
RC5_7	Use RC2 algorithm with a 7-bit key
RC5_10	Use RC2 algorithm with a 10-bit key
RC5_16	Use RC2 algorithm with a 16-bit key
DES	Use DES algorithm
3DES	Use triple DES algorithm

Usage Applies to Notes clients.

See also `SMIME_Strong_Algorithm`

SMTP_Config_Update_Interval

Description

Controls how often the Domino server checks for updates to its SMTP configuration by Configuration documents within the Domino Directory. If the configuration information has been updated, it rereads all SMTP settings.

Syntax `SMTP_Config_Update_Interval=`*`minutes`*

Values The default interval is every two minutes.

Usage Applies to Domino servers.

See also

```
SMTPDebug
SMTPDebugIO
SMTPGreeting
SMTPMaxForRecipients
SMTPMTA_Space_Repl_Char
SMTPSaveImportErrors
SMTPStrict821AddressSyntax
SMTPStrict821LineSyntax
SMTPTimeoutMultiplier
```

SMTPDebug

Description

Configures whether to log SMTP information and what level of logging to use.

Syntax `SMTPDebug=value`

Values

0 No SMTP logging (default)

1 Log SMTP errors

2 Log SMTP protocol commands

Usage Applies to Domino servers using SMTP.

See also

```
SMTP_Config_Update_Interval
SMTPDebugIO
SMTPGreeting
SMTPMaxForRecipients
SMTPMTA_Space_Repl_Char
SMTPSaveImportErrors
SMTPStrict821AddressSyntax
SMTPStrict821LineSyntax
SMTPTimeoutMultiplier
```


SMTPDebugIO

Description

Configures whether to log all data received by SMTP. This can be a huge amount of data recorded, so it should be enabled only for short periods of time when resolving any issues with SMTP processing.

Syntax `SMTPDebugIO=value`

Values

0 No logging (default)

1 Log all data received by SMTP

Usage Applies to Domino servers using SMTP.

See also

```
SMTP_Config_Update_Interval
SMTPDebug
SMTPGreeting
SMTPMaxForRecipients
SMTPMTA_Space_Repl_Char
SMTPSaveImportErrors
SMTPStrict821AddressSyntax
SMTPStrict821LineSyntax
SMTPTimeoutMultiplier
```

SMTPGreeting

Description Allows customization of the message sent to SMTP clients.

Syntax `SMTP_Greeting=text`

Values

The default greeting is:

```
hostname ESMTP Service V5.0 ready Mon, 22 August 1999 11:35:12 -0800
```

Usage Applies to Domino servers running using SMTP.

See also

```
SMTP_Config_Update_Interval
SMTPDebug
SMTPDebugIO
SMTPMaxForRecipients
SMTPMTA_Space_Repl_Char
SMTPSaveImportErrors
SMTPStrict821AddressSyntax
SMTPStrict821LineSyntax
SMTPTimeoutMultiplier
```

SMTPMaxForRecipients

Description

Configures the number of addresses that can be added when SMTP adds received headers to messages received.

Syntax `SMTPMaxForRecipients=number`

Values The default is 0.

Usage Applies to Domino servers running SMTP.

See also

```
SMTP_Config_Update_Interval
SMTPDebug
SMTPDebugIO
SMTPGreeting
SMTPMTA_Space_Repl_Char
SMTPSaveImportErrors
SMTPStrict821AddressSyntax
SMTPStrict821LineSyntax
SMTPTimeoutMultiplier
```

SMTPMTA_Space_Repl_Char

Description

Configures the character that SMTPMTA uses to replace spaces in Domino user names.

Syntax `SMTPMTA_Space_Repl_Char=value`

Values

Can be either an underscore (_) or a period (.). The default is the underscore.

Usage Applies to Domino servers running the SMTPMTA task.

See also

SMTP_Config_Update_Interval
SMTPDebug
SMTPDebugIO
SMTPGreeting
SMTPMaxForRecipients
SMTPSaveImportErrors
SMTPStrict821AddressSyntax
SMTPStrict821LineSyntax
SMTPTimeoutMultiplier

SMTPSaveImportErrors

Description

Configures whether SMTP mail import errors are recorded. This option should be used only sparingly during resolution of specific problems with SMTP processing, since it can consume large amounts of disk space.

Syntax `SMTPSaveImportErrors=value`

Values

0 Doesn't record any errors (default)

1 If an incoming message has errors and cannot be written to the server *MAIL.BOX*, the data stream is written to a temporary directory and the name of the file is logged.

2 All incoming messages are written to a temporary directory, and the name of the file is logged.

Usage Applies to Domino servers running SMTP.

See also

SMTP_Config_Update_Interval
SMTPDebug
SMTPDebugIO
SMTPGreeting
SMTPMaxForRecipients

NOTES.INI

```
SMTPMTA_Space_Repl_Char
SMTPStrict821AddressSyntax
SMTPStrict821LineSyntax
SMTPTimeoutMultiplier
```

SMTPStrict821AddressSyntax

Description

Controls whether to strictly enforce the RFC821 standard and ensure that the MAIL FROM and RCPT TO fields are properly formed and contain < and >.

Syntax `SMTPStrict821AddressFormat=`*`value`*

Values

0 RFC821 standard not enforced (default)

1 RFC821 standard is enforced

Usage Applies to Domino servers running SMTP.

See also

```
SMTP_Config_Update_Interval
SMTPDebug
SMTPDebugIO
SMTPGreeting
SMTPMaxForRecipients
SMTPMTA_Space_Repl_Char
SMTPSaveImportErrors
SMTPStrict821LineSyntax
SMTPTimeoutMultiplier
```

SMTPStrict821LineSyntax

Description

Controls whether to strictly enforce the RFC821 standard and ensure that all protocol text is terminated by a CRLF sequence.

Syntax `SMTPStrict821LineSyntax=`*`value`*

Values

0 RFC821 standard for CRLF not enforced; an LF is accepted as a line terminator (default)

1 RFC821 standard for CRLF is enforced

Usage Applies to Domino servers running SMTP.

See also

```
SMTP_Config_Update_Interval
SMTPDebug
SMTPDebugIO
SMTPGreeting
```

SMTPMaxForRecipients
SMTPMTA_Space_Repl_Char
SMTPSaveImportErrors
SMTPStrict821AddressSyntax
SMTPTimeoutMultiplier

SMTPTimeoutMultiplier

Description

This value is used to multiply the standard timeouts for each SMTP protocol exchange, so as to increase all SMTP timeout periods.

Syntax `SMTPTimeoutMultiplier=value`

Values The default value is 1.

Usage Applies to Domino servers.

See also

SMTP_Config_Update_Interval
SMTPDebug
SMTPDebugIO
SMTPGreeting
SMTPMaxForRecipients
SMTPMTA_Space_Repl_Char
SMTPSaveImportErrors
SMTPStrict821AddressSyntax
SMTPStrict821LineSyntax

SSLCipherSpec

Description

Configures which SSL-compliant cipher to use when encrypting files.

Syntax `SSLCipherSpec=value`

Values

The ciphers can be any or all of the following as defined in Table 14-8. The leading zeroes are required. Multiple ciphers can be specified with no spaces or commands between them.

Table 14-8: SSL Cipher Values

Value used	Cipher
01	SSL_RSA_WITH_NULL_MD5
02	SSL_RSA_WITH_NULL_SHA
03	SSL_RSA_EXPORT_WITH_RC4_40_MD5
04	SSL_RSA_WITH_RC4_128_MD5
05	SSL_RSA_WITH_RC4_128_SHA

NOTES.INI

Table 14-8: SSL Cipher Values (continued)

Value used	*Cipher*
06	SSL_RSA_EXPORT_WITH_RC2_CBC_40_MD5
09	SSL_RSA_WITH_DES_CBC_SHA
0A	SSL_RSA_WITH_3DES_EDE_CBC_SHA

Usage Applies to Domino servers using SSL.

This is equivalent to the Ports → Internet Ports → Web tab of the Server document within the Domino Directory.

SwapPath

Description

Identifies the location of the server swap file in OS/2. Domino then uses this to compile statistics for the *Server.Path.Swap* statistic.

Syntax `SwapPath=path`

Values The default location that Domino checks is *C:\OS2\SYSTEM.*

Usage Applies to Domino servers running on OS/2.

Can be configured using a Configuration document in the Domino Directory.

<TCPPort>_PortMapping<number>

Description

Identifies the TCP/IP port for each partitioned server that shares the same IP address as the port mapping server. This entry appears in the *NOTES.INI* for the port mapping server only.

Syntax `TCPPort_PortMappingnumber=servername, IP address:port`

Values

The TCPPort name must use the TCP driver and be enabled in the Ports entry in *NOTES.INI.* Only the numbers 00 to 04 are supported as server definitions, meaning there is a limit of five partitioned servers when using port mapping. The server name must be the fully qualified hierarchical name. An example could be:

```
TCPIP_PortMapping00=cn=westline/o=alameda,10.0.0.2:15000
TCPIP_PortMapping01=cn=shoreline/o=alameda,10.0.0.2:15001
```

Usage Applies to Domino servers using partitioning with port mapping.

See also

```
KillProcess
TCPPort_TCPIPAddress
```

<TCPPort>_TCPIPAddress

Description Identifies the TCP/IP address and port for a Domino server.

Syntax `TCPPort_TCPIPAddresss=0,`*`IP address:port`*

Values

The TCPPort name must use the TCP driver and be enabled in the Ports entry in *NOTES.INI*.

Usage Applies to Domino servers using partitioning.

See also

`KillProcess`
`TCPPort_PortMappingnumber`

TimeZone

Description Identifies the time zone for the server or client.

Syntax `Timezone=`*`number`*

Values

A value of 0 represents GMT. Each time zone then moves westward around the globe. For example, U.S. Pacific Standard Time is 8.

Usage Applies to both Domino servers and Notes clients.

With R5 using the time zone of the underlying operating system by default, the value for this parameter is less important now than it once was.

TraceSSLHandshake

Description Specifies whether to trace the SSL handshaking process.

Syntax `TraceSSLHandshake=1`

Values

0 Disables tracing of SSL handshaking to the server console (default).

1 Enables tracing of SSL handshaking to the server console and the log database.

Usage Applies to Domino servers using SSL.

See also `ReportSSLHandshakeErrors`

TRANSLOG_MaxSize

Description Configures the maximum size in MB of the transaction logging file.

Syntax `TRANSLOG_MaxSize=`*`value`*

Values

The default is approximately three times the amount of server RAM.

Usage Applies to Domino servers that use transaction logging.

Equivalent to "Maximum log space" field in the Transaction Logging tab of the Server document within the Domino directory.

See also

```
TRANSLOG_MaxSize
TRANSLOG_Path
TRANSLOG_Performance
TRANSLOG_Status
TRANSLOG_Style
TRANSLOG_UseAll
```

TRANSLOG_Path

Description

Configures the path to the log files used for transactional logging. To make the most of the transactional logging feature, the logs should be on a separate disk for both performance and redundancy to the Domino databases that have logging enabled.

Syntax `TRANSLOG_MaxSize=`*`path`*

Values

The default location is */logdir* subdirectory underneath the Domino data directory.

Usage Applies to Domino servers that use transactional logging.

Equivalent to the "Log path" field in the Transaction Logging tab of the Server document within the Domino directory.

See also

```
TRANSLOG_MaxSize
TRANSLOG_Performance
TRANSLOG_Status
TRANSLOG_Style
TRANSLOG_UseAll
```

TRANSLOG_Performance

Description

Configures transaction logging to be optimized for either faster runtime performance or restart performance.

Syntax `TRANSLOG_Performance=`*`value`*

Values

1 Favor runtime. More changes are made in memory, and fewer changes to the logs to improve server performance during normal operations

2 Standard. A compromise between the other two options (default).

3 Favor restart recovery time. Fewer changes are made in memory and more changes are written to the logs. This speeds up the recovery process at the expense of slower regular performance.

Usage Applies to Domino servers that use transactional logging.

Equivalent to the "Runtime/Restart performance" field in the Transaction Logging tab of the Server document within the Domino directory.

See also

```
TRANSLOG_MaxSize
TRANSLOG_Path
TRANSLOG_Status
TRANSLOG_Style
TRANSLOG_UseAll
```

TRANSLOG_Status

Description Configures whether transactional logging is enabled on the server.

Syntax `TRANSLOG_Status=`*`value`*

Values

0 Disables transactional logging (default)

1 Enables transactional logging

Usage Applies to Domino servers.

Equivalent to the "Transaction logging" field in the Transaction Logging tab of the Server document within the Domino directory.

See also

```
TRANSLOG_MaxSize
TRANSLOG_Path
TRANSLOG_Performance
TRANSLOG_Style
TRANSLOG_UseAll
```

TRANSLOG_Style

Description Configures how the server uses transaction log files.

Syntax `TRANSLOG_Style=`*`value`*

Values

0 Circular logging (default). Log files are reused as necessary. This value specifies the database can be restored only later as at the last full backup.

1 Archive logging. Log files are kept until the next full backup. This option is needed to be able to perform a point-in-time recovery as at the last backup, followed by replay of log activity of Domino databases.

Usage Applies to Domino servers that use transactional logging.

Equivalent to the "Logging style" field in the Transaction Logging tab of the Server document within the Domino directory.

See also

```
TRANSLOG_MaxSize
TRANSLOG_Path
TRANSLOG_Performance
TRANSLOG_Status
TRANSLOG_UseAll
```

TRANSLOG_UseAll

Description

Configures whether the server can use all available space on the log device for transactional logging.

Syntax `TRANSLOG_UseAll=`*`value`*

Values

0 Use either the default size or that specified within the *TRANSLOG_MaxSize* (default)

1 Use all available space on the log device

Usage Applies to Domino servers that use transactional logging.

Equivalent to the "Use all available space on log device" field in the Transaction Logging tab of the Server document within the Domino directory

See also

```
TRANSLOG_MaxSize
TRANSLOG_Path
TRANSLOG_Performance
TRANSLOG_Status
TRANSLOG_Style
```

Update_No_BRP_Files

Description Controls whether the **Fixup** task creates .BRP files.

Syntax `Update_No_BRP_Files=1`

Values

The value of 1 means that the `Fixup` task will not create a .BRP file when an error is encountered with a view index.

Usage Applies to Domino servers.

Update_No_Fulltext

Description Turns full text indexing on or off for the server.

Syntax `Update_No_Fulltext=value`

Values

0 Enables full text indexing (default)

1 Disables full text indexing

Usage

Applies to Domino servers; can be used for servers that carry only user mail databases to stop users creating a full text index of their mail database on the server.

Can be configured using a Configuration document in the Domino Directory.

Updaters

Description

Configures the number of `Update` tasks that can concurrently run on the server.

Syntax `Updaters=number`

Values The default is to run one `Update` task at a time.

Usage Applies to Domino servers.

Can be configured using a Configuration document in the Domino Directory.

See also

`Update_Supression_Limit`
`Update_Suppression_Time`

Update_Suppression_Limit

Description

Configures an override to the value in the `Update_Suppression_Time` parameter when this number of duplicate requests to updates views and indexes is received.

Syntax `Update_Suppression_Limit=value`

Usage Applies to Domino servers.

Can be configured using a Configuration document in the Domino Directory.

See also

Updaters
Update_Suppression_Time

Update_Suppression_Time

Description

Configures the delay between full text indexing and view updating, even if immediate indexing is scheduled as a task.

Syntax `Update_Suppression_Time=minutes`

Values The default is 5 minutes.

Usage Applies to Domino servers.

Can be configured using a Configuration document in the Domino Directory.

See also

Updaters
Update_Supression_Limit

UpgradeApps

Description

Configures the installed migration applications from cc:Mail, Exchange, and LDIF. These are not installed by default when installing the Administration client, and must be individually selected.

Syntax `UpgradeApps=file1, file2, . . .`

Usage Applies to the Administration client.

UseFontMapper

Description

Configures whether the font mapper is enabled to attempt to map the font face name in a CGM metafile and those installed on the Notes workstation.

Syntax `UseFontMapper=value`

Values

0 Disables the font mapper

1 Enables the font mapper (default)

Usage Applies to Notes clients.

ViewExp<number>

Description Controls how view-level file exporting is carried out.

Syntax `ViewExpnumber=parm1, parm2, parm3, parm4, parm5 . . .`

Values Table 14-9 describes each of the following values in detail.

Table 14-9: View-Level File Export Parameters

Value	Meaning
1	Program name and file type
2	Append options 0 No append option 1 Append option offered through a dialog box 2 Automatically write to a temporary file to avoid the 64K limit
3	Export routine name
4	Not used
5 and onwards	File extensions to use in the selection of a file type in the File Export dialog

By default, a Notes client will contain the following entries:

```
VIEWEXP1=Lotus 1-2-3 Worksheet,0,_XWKS,,.WKS,.WK1,.WR1,.WRK,,4,
VIEWEXP3=Structured Text,0,_XSTR,,.LTR,.CGN,.STR,,1,
VIEWEXP4=Tabular Text,1,_XTAB,,.LTR,.RPT,.CGN,.TAB,,1,
```

Usage Applies to Notes clients.

See also

```
EditExp
EditImp
ViewImp
```

ViewImp<number>

Description Controls how view-level file importing is carried out.

Syntax `ViewImpnumber=parm1, parm2, parm3, parm4, parm5 . . .`

Values Table 14-10 describes each of the following values in detail.

Table 14-10: View-Level File Import Values

Value	Meaning
1	Program name and file type
2	Not used, always 0
3	Import routine name
4	Not used
5 and onwards	File extensions to use in the selection of a file type in the File Import dialog

By default, a Notes client will contain the following entries:

```
VIEWIMP1=Lotus 1-2-3 Worksheet,0,_IWKSV,,.WKS,.WK1,.WR1,.WRK,.WK3,.
WK4,,4,
VIEWIMP3=Structured Text,0,_ISTR,,.LTR,.CGN,.STR,,1,
VIEWIMP4=Tabular Text,0,_ITAB,,.PRN,.RPT,.TXT,.TAB,,1,
```

Usage Applies to Notes clients.

See also

EditExp
EditImp
ViewExp

WebAdmin_Disable_Force_GUI

Description

Configures whether OS/2 browser users are forced to the plain interface when using the web administration tool.

Syntax `WebAdmin_Disable_Force_GUI=`*`value`*

Values

0 OS/2 browser must use the Plain interface (default)

1 OS/2 browser can use the Dropdown, Button, or Plain interface

Usage Applies to Domino servers running the `HTTP` task.

WebAdmin_Expire_Cache

Description

Configures whether the client browser reloads web administration tool elements from its cache or from the Domino server. This is intended to correct an issue with Netscape browsers not using updated elements for changes in user preferences.

Syntax `WebAdmin_Expire_Cache=`*`value`*

Values

0 Reload the Web Administration tool from browser cache (default)

1 Reload the Web Administration tool from the Domino server

Usage Applies to Domino servers running the `HTTP` task.

WebAgentTimeLimit

Description

Configures the execution time limit for agents triggered by web clients.

Syntax `WebAgentTimeLimit=`*`time`*

Values The default is not to limit web-triggered agents.

Usage Applies to Domino servers running the `HTTP` task.

Window_Title

Description Configures the titlebar text for both the server and client.

Syntax `Window_Title=`*`text`*

Usage Applies to both Domino servers and Notes clients.

WinInfoboxPos

Description Retains the last used position of the Infobox by the user.

Syntax `WinInfoboxPos=`*`value1, value2`*

Values The default original location is 85,193.

Usage Applies to Notes clients.

WinSysFontnumber

Description

When the font mapper is not enabled, these lines list the installed Windows system fonts to which the CGM font numbers are mapped. The CGM fonts are identified by number within CGM metafiles.

Syntax `WinSysFontnumber=`*`cvalue1, value2, value3`*

Usage Applies to Notes clients.

XPC_Console

Description Turns the display of modem input/output on or off.

Syntax `XPC_Console=`*`value`*

Values

0 Displays the modem input/output console (default)

1 Hides the console

Usage

Applies to both NT Domino servers and NT/Windows 95/Windows 98 Notes clients.

APPENDIX A

Domino/Windows NT Integration

Since Domino 4.5, there have been a number of Domino/Windows NT integration features in the product. These features are intended to improve the interaction between Domino and NT, which is the most common operating platform used for Domino servers.

There are two performance changes that Lotus recommends you make on NT to work with Domino, assuming that you are using a dedicated NT server for Domino, and not intending to use that server for file and print sharing as well. You can make the changes via the NT Control Panel, or you can make the changes to the registry directly. However, all the standard Microsoft warnings about editing the registry apply.

First, you must change the way the Server service performs. In the Control Panel, select Network → Services tab → Server service → Properties button. Here you should change the optimization to "Maximize Throughput for Network Applications." If you want to edit the registry manually, change the value of HKLM\System\CurrentControlSet\Control\Session Manager\LargeSystemCache to 0. This setting means NT assigns memory to provide for an unlimited number of network connections, but at the same time doesn't set aside much memory for caching (which would be used for file and print sharing).

Secondly, you should remove the performance boost to the foreground application. This setting is great for user workstations in giving the active application they are working with a higher priority than others on the workstation—but on servers, it robs performance from Domino (and thus its network users) to boost the priority for an administrator working at the server. Select Control Panel → System → Performance tab. Change the Application Performance setting, "Performance boost for the foreground application" to None. If you want to edit the registry manually, change

HKLM\System\CurrentControlSet\Control\PriorityControl\Win32PrioritySeparation to 0.* Both of these changes require the server to be rebooted to take effect.

Like any application server, it is recommended that you do not install Domino on a Domain Controller. The processing of NT domain logons by these DCs can be very processor-intensive, particularly for larger domains, which in turn can seriously affect the performance of Domino on the server. Therefore, if the server is to be within an NT domain, the server should be a member server within the domain.

Performance Monitor

By default, when Domino is installed on Windows NT, a set of counters are provided for use with NT's Performance monitor. These are most of the statistics from the `SHOW STATS` server console command. As an example, on a test server I executed the `SHOW STATS` command and the output consisted of nearly 400 values (this number will change depending on the tasks running on the server). However, some of these "counters" are actually static configuration information such as OS platform and status information of each of the server tasks. When I then went into NT's Performance Monitor on the same server, there were only 274 available statistic counters. These were grouped as listed in Table A-1.

Table A-1: Example Statistics Available Within the Performance Monitor

Group	*Number of Statistic Counters*
Agent.*	8
Calendar.*	6
Database.*	115
DIIOP.*	4
Disk.*	10
Domino.*	60
Mail.*	12
Mem.*	5
Monitor.*	2
NET.*	11
Replica.*	9
Server.*	32

When adding these counters to a Performance Monitor chart or log, they have the counter object name of *Lotus Notes*, and the counter is called *Notes Statistics*. The actual Domino statistic counters themselves appear under the Instance heading. Figure A-1 contains a sample performance monitor chart.

* I should point out that the second edition of *Inside Windows NT*, by David Solomon, says that this parameter actually has no effect on NT Server. I don't doubt his information, since he was granted access to the NT code and developers when he was writing the book. However, this information is not widely known and Domino will complain with a warning message to the console if you do not make this configuration change.

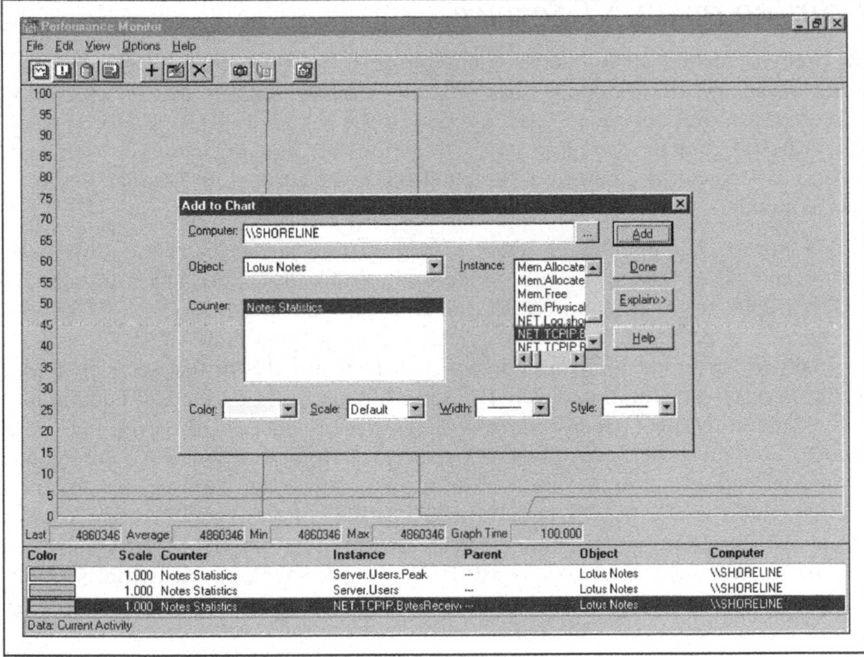

Figure A-1: Performance Monitor with Domino counters

In Figure A-1, the chart is graphing the peak number of Domino users since it was last started (*Server.Users.Peak*), the current number of active users (*Server.Users*) and the number of bytes received by Domino on the TCP/IP network port (*NET.TCPIP.BytesReceived*). As you can probably see, if you attempt to graph any more than 10 counters at a time, the graph becomes too unwieldy to be of any use, so you need to be selective in which counters to choose to graph.

You also have the option to view basic NT counters as well to check (for example) whether the system requires more memory (Page Faults/sec), or has I/O bottlenecks (Average Disk Queue Length), or whether the processor(s) are overloaded (%ProcessorTime).

One advantage to using NT's Performance Monitor over regular statistical monitoring is that it has the ability to create a log file of performance counters, which can be viewed later to monitor for peak usage times. However, you must be careful with the disk space used in creating this log, since at the designated save interval (the default interval is 15 seconds), it saves the value of every Notes counter to the log file.

It should be noted that Performance Monitor doesn't need to be running on the same machine that is running Domino. You can see from the previous screenshot that the computer to capture the statistics from can be either selected from a list of servers in the domain or directly entered. By running Performance Monitor on a remote machine, this can save resources on a running production Domino server if there are already performance issues.

Domino as an NT Service

An optional feature allows the Domino server to be run as an NT service. The main advantage this offers is that Domino can start when the NT server is rebooted, without requiring a user to logon at the server and start it. More importantly, if you start the Domino Server from the NT Start menu rather than as a service, when your account user is logged off at the server, the Domino server is also stopped.

This feature is not installed by default; during installation, select the Customize option and select "Domino as an NT Service" to install it. This action installs the wrapper code that acts as an NT service and starts the Domino server. However, the service is not configured to start automatically by default—it is set to start manually, so in order to change this you must change this in the Services applet within Control Panel on the server. The service name will be called something like *Lotus Domino Server (LotusDominoData)*. The information in the parentheses is used to distinguish between multiple instances of Domino if you have configured partitioning for Domino; it is derived from the unique data path for that instance (in this case it is *C:\LOTUS\DOMINO\DATA*). This option to run as a service will run as expected only if the Domino server does not have a password; otherwise, the service will start, but Domino will be waiting for a password before starting. The current default is to create server IDs without a password, so this will most likely be an issue for older servers.

Since this is a service, you can start and stop Domino via the Services applet in Control Panel, or via the command line. You can also stop the service from a remote machine using NT's Server Manager tool. The service name has spaces within it, so you need to enclose the name in quotes as follows:

```
net stop "Lotus Domino Server (LotusDominoData)"
net start "Lotus Domino Server (LotusDominoData)"
```

Stopping and starting Domino from the command line is sometimes done to allow non-Domino-aware backup programs to backup the Domino databases without any contention issues against the running server. However, in this case you would do better to install a Domino-aware backup solution that can work with open Domino databases and can work with database transaction logs.

Log Domino Events to NT's Event Viewer

The "Log Domino Events to NT's Event Viewer" option sends Domino events as they are raised to NT's event viewer. This option is enabled when an event is created by selecting this notification method, as is seen in Figure A-2. With this option enabled, an administrator may need to view the NT event log only to monitor the health of both NT and Domino on the server. Any scripts written to monitor for specific events in NT can then be modified to monitor for Domino events as well. Also, system management tools that are not Domino-aware but monitor the NT Event log can be configured to monitor for Domino events.

When a Domino event is raised, a record is added to the NT Application Log, as shown in Figure A-3. Depending on how many of these events you expect to be sent to the NT event viewer, you might wish to change the maximum log size for

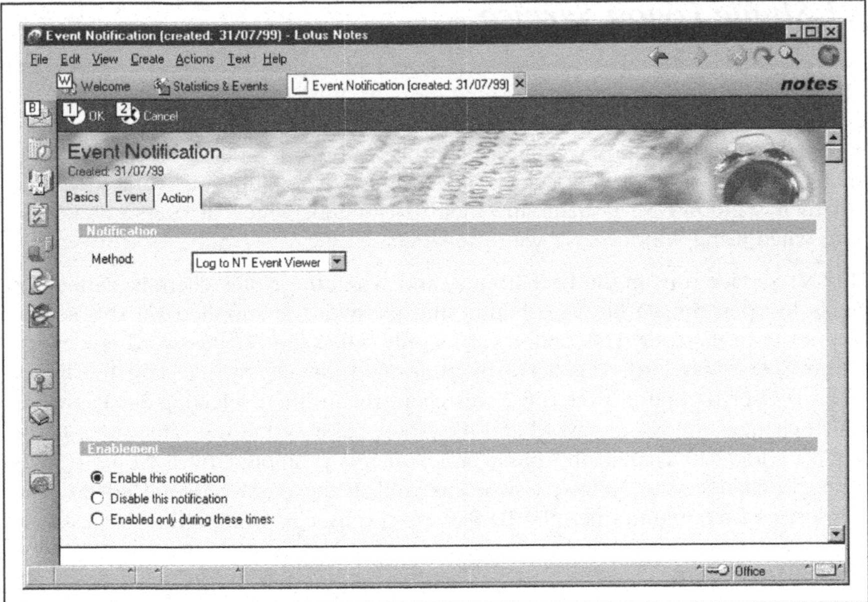

Figure A-2: Configuring an event to be sent to NT's event viewer

the Application log to be more than the 512KB default, and also to change how the log wraps when it reaches that maximum size. The default is to overwrite events older than seven days. Both of these options can be changed in the Event Viewer by selecting Log → Log Settings from the menu.

Event Viewer - Application Log on \\SHORELINE

Log View Options Help

Date	Time	Source	Category	Event	User	Co
31/07/99	16:45:30	NotesEvent	None	1	N/A	
31/07/99	14:50:35	Quincy	None	4097	N/A	
31/07/99	14:24:09	JET	General	8	N/A	
31/07/99	14:24:07	ZipToA	None	105	N/A	
31/07/99	14:24:03	IomegaAccess	None	105	N/A	
30/07/99	1:23:21	IISInfoCtrs	None	1003	N/A	
30/07/99	1:23:21	IISInfoCtrs	None	1003	N/A	
30/07/99	1:23:21	IISInfoCtrs	None	1003	N/A	
30/07/99	1:23:21	IISInfoCtrs	None	1003	N/A	
30/07/99	1:23:21	IISInfoCtrs	None	1003	N/A	
30/07/99	1:23:21	IISInfoCtrs	None	1003	N/A	
30/07/99	1:23:21	IISInfoCtrs	None	1003	N/A	
30/07/99	1:23:21	IISInfoCtrs	None	1003	N/A	

Figure A-3: Application Log with Domino events

Refer to Chapter 7, *Monitoring Domino*, for more information about configuring Domino events.

NT Single Logon Service

"NT Single Logon Service" is an optional installable component of the Notes client when installing on Windows NT (and not on Windows 95/98). Although this works on the Windows NT Server platform, running it makes sense only on the Windows NT workstation machines. What this feature attempts to do is remove the irritation that users experience in having to logon to multiple network services—first their Windows NT domain and then to Domino, which of course they don't have when using Windows NT with Exchange.

This NT service runs in the background, and when the Notes client is started and needs to open the ID file to continue, the password is supplied via this service and not from the user. This option works only when the NT password is identical to the Notes password. This action is performed initially by selecting the File → Tools → User ID option from the Notes client menu, then selecting Set Password, which changes the NT password and the Notes password at the same time. If you use NT's tools to change the password, you are prompted by a Notes pop-up dialog to change your Notes password as well. If the passwords are not in sync, this service isn't able to open the ID file and the user is prompted for a password as usual.

User Manager Extensions

User Manager has an extensible API that Domino uses to add a Notes menu option to User Manager (Exchange provides a similar menu option). This means you can configure the system to create/delete users for Windows NT and Domino at the same time, thus reducing the cost of administration. In practice, this feature isn't widely used and appears to have been developed mainly in answer to marketing comparisons with Exchange's NT integration. The main reason for this (in my opinion) is the current process Domino uses is not as transparent as it should be. Most medium-to-large IT shops use an automated process to create NT users (using batch files with the `NET USER` command, or with a Perl script), and, similarly, use text files to register users within Domino. However, it is worth discussing this feature so that you can determine whether this could be of use to you.

Before this can be used to add or delete users and groups, you should configure the degree of interaction you want between NT and Domino when working with User Manager. The menu options under the new Notes menu are:

Notes Synchronization Options
: Controls which synchronization options are in effect, as shown in Figure A-4. You have the option to select any or all of synchronization for the creation of Users and Groups, deletion of Users and Groups, or synchronization of existing users. If only some operations are enabled, the relevant configuration menu option for that operation is then disabled. For example, if User/Group registration is disabled, the Add Selected NT User/Group to Notes, Registration Setup, and the Mail/ID Registration Options are disabled (grayed) from this menu.

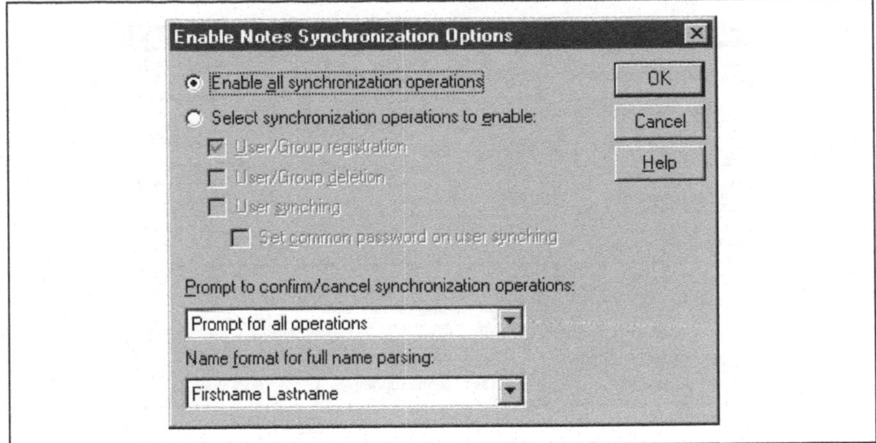

Figure A-4: Notes Synchronization Options

Add Selected NT Users/Group to Notes

One or more users are first selected in User Manager, and then, if this option is selected, they can be set up in Domino. Typically this option is used when Domino is installed into an environment in which the NT domain users have already been created.

Synch Selected NT Users with Notes

This option changes the NT password for the selected user(s) and changes the Internet password field in the Person document that corresponds to this user to the same. There are four conditions that must be met for this user synchronization to occur between the selected NT account(s) and the Person documents in the Domino Directory:

- NT Account name must match the `Short Name` field in the Person document.
- NT Full Name must match an entry in the `User Name` field in the Person document.
- NT Last Name must match the `Last Name` field in the Person document.
- If there is an entry in the Person document for `Network Account Name`, it must match the NT Account name.

Note that this option does not change the password in the user's ID file—if this needs to be done, it must be done separately. This option is of use only if your NT users access Domino via a browser and require authentication.

Registration Setup

These settings are the regular settings you see when creating a new user in Domino. (See Figure A-5.) Note that these settings are not saved, so they need to be re-entered each time you launch User Manager. Refer to the User Registration section of Chapter 2, *Domino Directories*, for more information about the meaning for any of these fields.

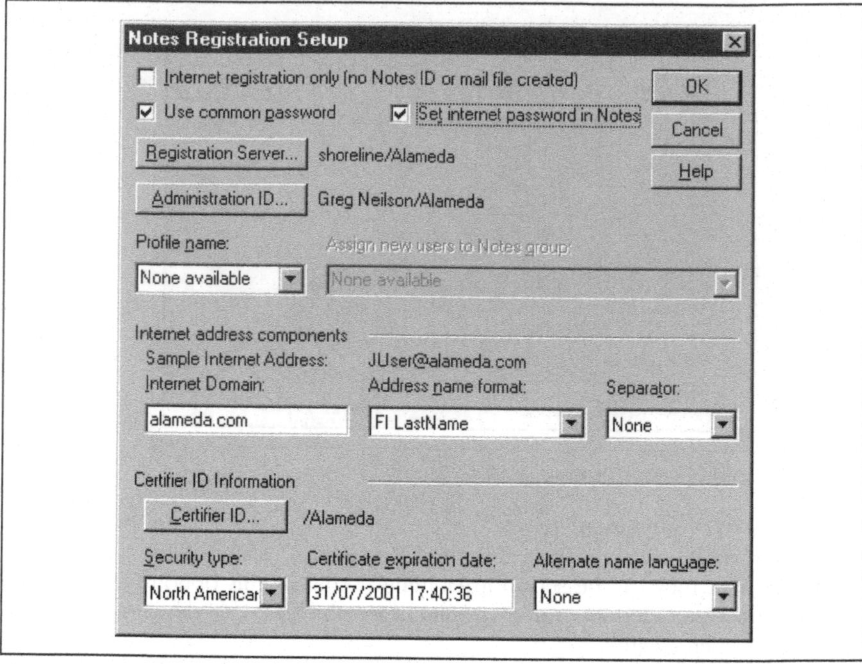

Figure A-5: Registration setup

Mail/ID Registration options

These settings are the regular settings you see when creating a new user in Domino as shown in Figure A-6. Note that these settings are not saved, so they need to be re-entered each time you launch User Manager. Refer to the User Registration section of Chapter 2 for more information about the meaning for any of these fields.

Delete/User Synch Options

These options specify what to do when an NT user is deleted. (See Figure A-7.) You have the following options:

- Don't delete the user's mail database
- Delete only the user's mail database as configured on their person record
- Delete all replicas of a user's mail database

The decision factor here is more of a busness issue than a technical one; after people leave a company, it quite often happens that other staff within the same department later need to access that person's mail to retrieve important business information. If you delete the database, then you may have to spend the time later to restore that mail database from a tape backup. However, if you don't delete the mail database at this time, you must manually delete that database later when it is no longer needed. A quick way to check for these mail databases with deleted Person documents is to check the Notes log database output overnight when the schedule validation process runs on the server. This checks every mail database on the server and complains about each database that doesn't have a matching Person record within the Domino Directory.

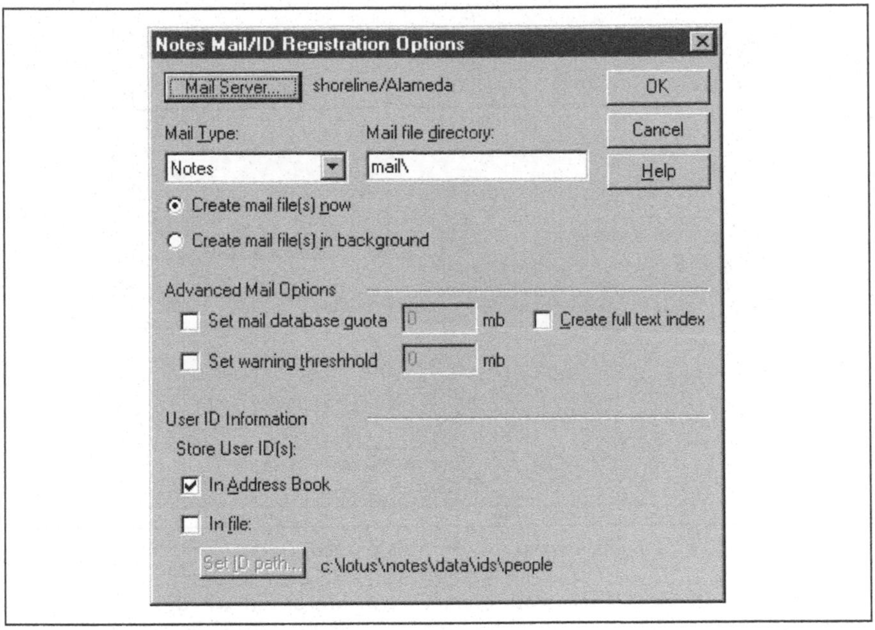

Figure A-6: Mail/ID Registration setup

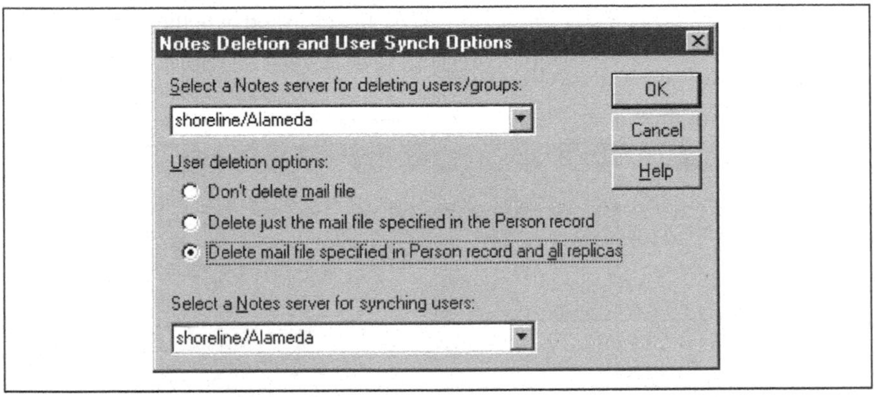

Figure A-7: Delete/User Synch options

Note that these settings are not saved, so they need to be re-entered each time you launch User Manager.

Register Notes Users Now

This menu option is normally disabled. It is enabled when you create NT users but when prompted to create the Domino users now, select "No."

After you complete the setup for the User Manager/Domino integration, you can create new users. As you register new users, after you enter the user details in User Manager and press the Add button, an additional dialog box is presented. This is shown in Figure A-8 with the details of the user to be created in Domino.

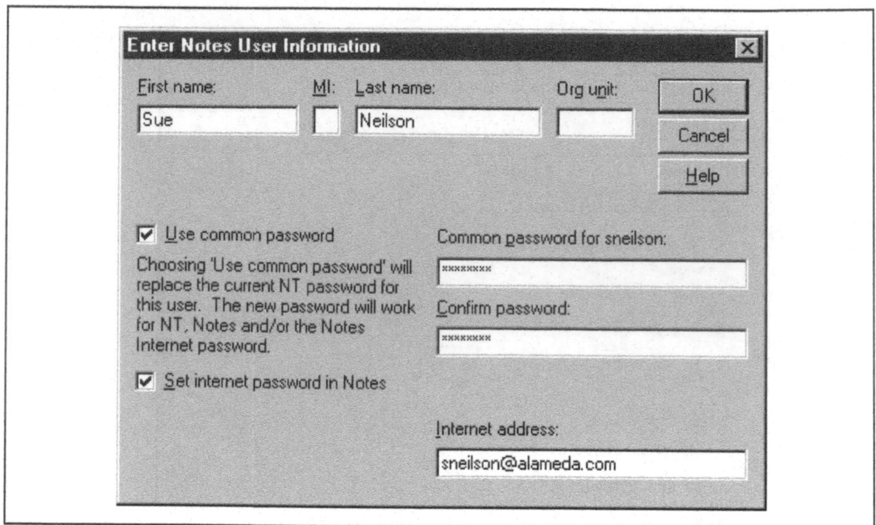

Figure A-8: Adding a new Domino user in NT's User Manger

Then, after all of the NT users are created, you are asked whether you want to create the Domino users at that time. You can elect to create these later by selecting the "Register Notes Users Now" menu option.

Similarly, when you create a group in NT, you are asked whether you want to create that group in Domino, and have the option to create Domino users for the members within that NT group (see Figure A-9).

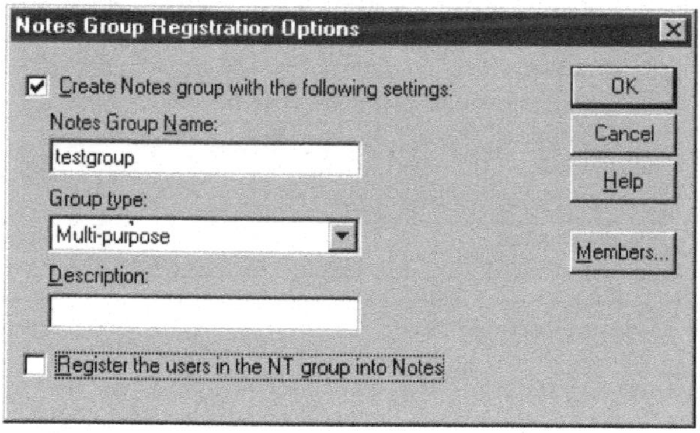

Figure A-9: Adding a new Domino group in NT's User Manager

Windows 2000 Support

Generally speaking, Lotus has made an assessment that most of their customers will be waiting at least six months after the release of Windows 2000 before planning to move to it in any significant way.

In the 5.0.3 QMR, which is scheduled for release after the release of Windows 2000, Lotus will support running this version of Notes and Domino on Windows 2000. It is expected that the current NT integration features discussed earlier in this appendix (including Domino for IIS, as described in Chapter 10, *Domino for Microsoft IIS*) will work as is, with any limitations in that version highlighted in the release notes. Lotus has no current plans to support any 4.x releases on Windows 2000. Keep in mind that there is no Windows 2000 support for those machines that used to run NT 4.0 on the Alpha platform.

In a later feature release that Lotus is not yet specifying (but which appears to be around six to nine months later), Lotus will release a version that is certified for Windows 2000. Some of the planned contents of that release include:

- Directory synchronization with Windows 2000 Active Directory
- Domino User Manager Extensions to enable user and group creation for both Domino users and groups and Windows 2000 users and groups
- Support for Windows Installer, the new method that Microsoft is promoting for software distribution
- ADSI Service Provider for Domino. (ADSI allows administrators to query/update directory information with scripting languages such as JScript or VBScript)
- MMC snap-in for Domino administration
- Support for Windows 2000 Unicode
- Coexistence with Windows 2000 Kerberos-based security
- Windows 2000 logo compliance

It is important to understand what Lotus means by supported and certified platforms. I have extracted these comments from the Lotus Knowledgebase article 142703 in a discussion of the support for the then-new Windows NT 4.0 support, which is relevant here for Windows 2000 as well:

> If a platform is categorized as "certified" for a specific release, Lotus has tested this configuration and is committed to continued testing of this configuration. If a platform is "supported" for a specific release, Lotus is committed to assisting both vendors and customers in understanding the Lotus Notes product dependencies.

So in essence, this means that the supported version will probably work fine in most circumstances, but Lotus will be reserving the right to advise customers to change to a certified platform if any serious problems are encountered.

APPENDIX B

Using InstallShield's Silent Installation Option

The Notes client and Domino Server on the Windows 95/98/NT/2000 platforms use InstallShield as their installation tool. This allows you to "record" some installation options as entered online and "playback" that installation using what InstallShield refers to as a *silent installation*.

The first step is to record an installation. To do this, start the install with the regular Notes *SETUP.EXE* installation program and use the `-r` input parameter. This records your selected answers and input during installation (user name, installation directories, installable options, whether or not to reboot after installation, etc.) and writes them to the file *SETUP.ISS*. This file will be located in the system directory; by default, this is *\WINDOWS* for Windows 95/98 and *\WINNT* for Windows NT/2000.

The following is a sample *SETUP.ISS* file for a Notes Client installation that has taken the default installation options:

```
[InstallShield Silent]
Version=v5.00.000
File=Response File
[File Transfer]
OverwriteReadOnly=NoToAll
[DlgOrder]
Dlg0=SdWelcome-0
Count=7
Dlg1=SdLicense-0
Dlg2=SdRegisterUser-0
Dlg3=SdAskDestPath-0
Dlg4=SdSetupType-0
Dlg5=SdSelectFolder-0
Dlg6=SdFinishReboot-0
[SdWelcome-0]
Result=1
[SdLicense-0]
```

```
Result=1
[SdRegisterUser-0]
szName=Alameda Corp
szCompany=Alameda Corp
Result=1
[SdAskDestPath-0]
szDir=D:\Lotus\Notes
szDir1=D:\Lotus\Notes\Data
Result=1
[SdSetupType-0]
svSetupType=Notes Client
bCustomize=0
Result=1
[SdSelectFolder-0]
szFolder=Lotus Applications
Result=1
[Application]
Name=Notes
Version=5.0
Company=Lotus
Lang=0009
[SdFinishReboot-0]
Result=1
BootOption=0
```

Copy the Notes client code to a file share on the network. You must delete or rename the executable *LotusProductRegistration.exe*, which displays the user registration panels from the regular installation process and would otherwise be launched during a silent install.

Last, make any necessary changes you want to the *SETUP.ISS* file to tailor the installation, and make this file available on the network. This could be anywhere, although the logical place would be the same location as the Notes code. You can also make a number of different versions of this *SETUP.ISS* file for different installation options if you wish. These can be given any name, since the filename to use during the silent installation is an input parameter.

The syntax to use for the silent installation is:

```
setup -s -f1installationoptionsfile [-f2logfile]
```

Domino 5.0.1b introduced a new optional parameter that can be used to determine whether a reboot occurs at the end of the install. The updated syntax is:

```
setup [reboot|noreboot] -s -f1installationoptionsfile [-
f2logfile]
```

The `-s` option tells setup that this is a silent installation. The `-f1` parameter is the location of the setup options (the *SETUP.ISS file*), and the optional `-f2` parameter is the location of the installation log file. If the `-f2` parameter is not present, the default is to write *SETUP.LOG* to the system directory. Note that there are no spaces between `-f1` and `-f2` and the filenames.

As an example, assuming the shared Notes code was installed onto the *Y:\ NOTESR5* directory, a batch file could be created to install the Notes client containing the following statement:

```
y:\notesr5\setup -s -f1y:\notesr5\setup.iss -f2c:\temp\notes.log
```

This batch file could then be run by SMS or whatever method you have available for software distribution in your environment.

You should check the final log file for the successful completion of the installation, or use it to determine the cause of any problems encountered. For example, in SMS a job can be created to extract this file from every client machine. A successful log file looks like this:

```
[InstallShield Silent]
Version=v5.00.000
File=Log File
[Application]
Name=Notes
Version=5.0
Company=Lotus
Lang=0009
[ResponseResult]
ResultCode=0
```

The most important line is the last line, since the `ResultCode` tells you whether the installation was successful (0 is a successful installation). The possible values for this `ResultCode` are listed in Table B-1.

Table B-1: InstallShield Resultcode Values

ResultCode	*Meaning*
0	Successful installation
–1	General error
–2	Invalid mode
–3	Required data not found in the *SETUP.ISS* file
–4	Not enough memory available
–5	File does not exist
–6	Cannot write to the response file
–7	Unable to write to the log file
–8	Invalid path to the response file
–9	Not a valid list type
–10	Data type is invalid
–11	Unknown error during setup
–12	Dialogs are out of order
–51	Cannot create the specified folder
–52	Cannot access the specified file or folder
–53	Invalid option selected

The uninstall process also makes use of InstallShield. The exact command line that will be executed resides in the registry at HKLM\SOFTWARE\Microsoft\Windows\CurrentVersion\Uninstall\Lotus Notes\UninstallString and typically contains a string such as `C:\WINNT\IsUninst.exe -fc:\notes\uninst.isu`. This means that the uninstall process could similarly be automated by a batch file that runs the previous command.

One last warning: the Notes install process is typically a two-phase process. The first phase installs the code, and the second phase configures Notes for the user (the user name and default Notes server, and optionally any Internet mail connectivity). All we have automated here is the first phase of the installation process. For new installations, the second phase of the installation still needs to be done later and cannot be automated. However, for upgrades this has already been done, and after this automated process has completed, the user can access Notes without requiring any further intervention.

If you encounter any problems using InstallShield with your Notes installation, Lotus will refer to you InstallShield for assistance. Therefore, you should probably check out *http://support.installshield.com* for any issues you have in this area.

APPENDIX C

Domino for AS/400

The AS/400 has quickly become the second most popular server platform for running Domino, behind Windows NT. The primary reasons for this are due to the reliability and scalability of the AS/400 platform, and also the ease of backend data integration for line of business applications already running on the AS/400 platform. Some IT managers are finding they can consolidate many PC-based Domino servers into a single AS/400 running multiple Domino partitions.

Because of the interest in the AS/400 as a Domino platform, IBM has introduced a range of dedicated AS/400s specifically to run Domino. These machines have had changes made to their OS/400 operating system to make them more suitable for the interactive tasks required when running a Domino server, since the AS/400 is usually optimized for batch processing.

There are two aspects unique to Domino on the AS/400 platform: a series of special AS/400 commands used to work with the Domino server, and directory synchronization with the AS/400's System Distribution Directory (SDD).

Directory Synchronization

The AS/400 has a System Distribution Directory (SDD) used to describe users on the AS/400. This feature provides one-way or two-way synchronization with the Domino Directory, thus allowing mail users on the AS/400 (using software such as OfficeVision/400) to address and send mail to Domino users and vice versa.

Directory Synchronization is configured via the Directory Synchronization Configuration Database (*NNDIRSYNC.NSF*), which resides on the Domino AS/400 server. It is here that the synchronization is configured and enabled/disabled/suspended; however, all the work to do the configuration is done via a series of jobs on the AS/400 with the QNNDI* prefix. You can use selection criteria to select only certain users to be sent to the Domino Directory. The *Directory Synchronization Log Database* (*NNDILOG.NSF*) contains log messages for the synchronization process. Check this log database if the synchronization process is not producing the results you expect.

AS/400-Specific Domino Commands

The AS/400 uses a series of standard verbs and nouns, which when added together are used to create commands on the platform. These verbs and nouns are three-letter "words," typically with the vowels missing. For example, *WRK* is for work, and *CRT* is used for create. *DOM* is as the noun for the Domino server.

Note that the F4 key lists all available options for each command. Also, keep in mind when working with the AS/400 IFS (Integrated File System), that like Unix it uses forward slashes (/) instead of backslashes (\) on PCs. You can use FTP to copy database and template files to/from the Domino data directory on the AS/400.

Following is a list of some AS/400-specific Domino commands:

`GO CMDDOM`
: Lists all of the available AS/400 commands for working with Domino.

`STRDOMSVR` *`servername`*
: Starts the named Domino server.

`ENDDOMSVR` *`servername`* `*CNTRLD | *IMMED`
: Stops the named Domino server. It can be stopped immediately or via a controlled shutdown. Unless it is an emergency shutdown, the controlled shutdown is preferable.

`WRKDOMCSL` *`servername`*
: Displays the named Domino console and allows commands to be entered.

`DSPDOMCSL` *`servername`*
: Displays the Domino console for the named server, but there is no capability to enter commands.

`CFGDOMSVR` *`servername`* `*FIRST | *ADD | *REMOVE`
: Performs the initial configuration of the Domino server after installation, either as the first server in the Domino network or as an additional server. The remove option is used to uninstall Domino.

To edit the *NOTES.INI* file for Domino on the AS/400, use the **`Edit File`** command with a format similar to the following:

```
EDTF STMF('/lotus/domino/data/notes.ini')
```

APPENDIX D

Domino on Linux

At LotusSphere in January 1999, Jeff Papows made the exciting commitment that Domino would be supported on Linux before the end of the year. In mid-November 1999, Domino 5.0.2 was released and included a Linux version.

Domino on Linux is *not* Open Source (and therefore not free!). It is still a licensed product that you must pay for; however, you can download and use an evaluation version from Lotus's web site for trial purposes.

Not surprisingly, the Linux implementation looks and feels very similar to the other Unix implementations of Domino. However, for those of us used to the ease of installing on OS/2 or Windows NT, there is a *little* more work required to install and configure Domino on Linux. Also, keep in mind that this is for the server component only; there is no Notes client code available for Linux or any of the other Unix platforms.

System Requirements

As of 5.0.2, Domino is certified by Lotus to run on Red Hat 6.0 for Intel x86 and Caldera 2.2 for Intel x86. Other versions are being tested and will be certified later. Running Domino on custom builds of the Linux kernel is not supported by Lotus.

The minimum RAM required is 64MB, with 128MB recommended. The minimum disk space required is 750MB with 1GB recommended. Only the TCP/IP and X.PC (for dialup support) protocols are supported. Lotus recommends that your swap space be a minimum of three times the physical memory in the server.

DECS support was not released as part of this version, but should be available at a later time for download. Also note that if you intend to use IIOP on the Linux server, that Domino cannot use the default ports of 63148 and 63149. Instead you must configure the port to use an unused port between 1024 and 60999. This change is made in the server document in the Domino Directory under the Ports tab, Internet Ports, then the IIOP section.

The 5.0.2 release notes make an interesting point about the scalability on Domino with Red Hat. Apparently with Red Hat 6.0, there are limitations that only allow about 200 Domino sessions, which includes users and tasks etc. This is resolved in Red Hat 6.1, which has increased the number of tasks per user from 256 to 2000.

Installing Domino on Linux

The following steps are necessary to get Domino running under Linux:

- The first step is to install the Linux operating system on your PC. I installed Red Hat 6.0 and selected the Server option, which correctly auto-sensed all of my PC hardware—within 15 minutes I had an operational Linux server. If you intend to use the Domino's Internet services such as HTTP and SMTP, ensure your server doesn't have Apache and/or Sendmail running, since these would contend for the same TCP/IP port. You can use the commands:

  ```
  ps -ef | grep httpd
  ```

  or:

  ```
  ps -ef | grep sendmail
  ```

  to check whether either of these are currently running. Check the documentation for your Linux distribution on how to configure these daemons to not autostart when the server is booted.

  If either of these daemons are running, the previous commands return the numeric process ID of the running process. You can either restart the server after the configuration is changed to not autostart these processes, or use the command:

  ```
  kill -9 <process id>
  ```

  to manually stop these processes for now.

- Copy the Domino executable to the Linux server. In my case, I had downloaded the code to another Windows 2000 server machine, so I configured the FTP server option and copied the file into the default FTP location (*D:\INETPUBS\FTPROOT*). Then I was able to issue the FTP commands from the Linux server to copy the file.

- Expand the Domino executable with the command:

  ```
  tar -xvf cx66rna.tar
  ```

  This is the filename of the North American version—if you have downloaded the International version, the filename is *CW66XIE.TAR*. Expanding this file creates a subdirectory called *linux* under the current directory and expands the files under this new subdirectory.

- Create the user account that Domino uses to run. This can be done with the `adduser` *`username`* command. This also creates a group of the same name and places the user in it. Then use the `passwd` *`username`* command to set the password for this account. The usual account name to create in this case is called "notes," but be careful. The release notes for Domino 5.0.2 say that with R5 Unix servers, "These defaults no longer work and the server will not start up." These did work when I installed and configured the server, but beware.

- Run the installation program, called *INSTALL*, which is located under the *linux* directory. In most cases, you can proceed with the defaults. Just to leave you in no doubt that this is a licensed product, you are presented with the license agreement in four languages and have to confirm your acceptance of it. The main things you are asked to configure are:

  — Domino server version (Mail, Application or Enterprise)

  — Location of program files (default is */OPT/LOTUS*)

  — Location of data directory (default is */LOCAL/NOTESDATA*)

  — Unix user for Domino (default is *notes*)

  — Unix group for Domino (default is *notes*)

  After confirming your selections, the files are expanded and copied into the desired locations.

- Change to the Notes user and launch the HTTP server in order to configure Domino. To do this, enter these commands:

  ```
  su - notes
  /opt/lotus/bin/http httpsetup
  ```

- From a browser (either locally or from another on the network), launch this URL to start the Domino configuration application:

  ```
  http://Linuxservername:8081
  ```

  This action configures Domino and tells it whether it is a new organization and domain, or whether it is joining an existing domain and which server to get the Domino Directory from. If you are joining an existing domain, you should copy the ID file onto the Linux, since the alternative is to leave the ID file as attachment in the Domino Directory. This means the server ID has to have a password (you can't attach it to the Domino Directory without it), which needs to be entered each time the server starts.

- Then, to launch the Domino server, enter these commands:

  ```
  su - notes
  cd /local/notesdata
  /opt/lotus/bin/server
  ```

For more information about Linux, O'Reilly has a range of books on the subject. The IBM redbook *Lotus Domino R5 on IBM RS/6000: Installation, Customization, and Administration* has some detailed information about running Domino on a Unix platform, so much of the same information is applicable here for the Linux implementation. You can download the book in PDF format from *http://www.redbooks.ibm.com*. There is also a new redbook planned for later in the year that will specifically cover running Domino on the Linux platform.

APPENDIX E

TCP/IP Ports

TCP/IP is by far the most common network protocol used to access Domino. Frequently, when configuring intermediate network components such as routers and/or firewalls, you need to know which ports are in use so that you can utilize network resources while still ensuring the security of the network. Table E-1 lists the default ports used by Domino.

Table E-1: Default TCP and SSL Port Numbers Used by Domino

Protocol	*TCP Port*	*SSL Port*
Notes RPC	1352	N/A
HTTP/HTTPS	80	443
LDAP	389	636
NNTP	119	563
IMAP	143	993
POP3	110	995
SMTP inbound	25	465
SMTP outbound	25	465
IIOP	63148	63149

The Notes RPC protocol is used by Domino to listen to requests from Notes clients and other Domino servers. The 1352 port is a well-known port for Lotus Domino that has been assigned by IANA, so generally speaking, it should not conflict with other applications on your network. There are a couple of ways to change this port, depending on whether this is a network-wide change between all servers and clients, or whether it is for only parts of the network.

To change the port that a Domino server uses to listen for incoming requests from Notes clients, add a line to the *SERVICES* file on the Domino server as follows:

```
Lotusnotes        newportnumber/tcpip # comment
```

The *SERVICES* file resides in *\WINNT\SYSTEM32\DRIVERS\ETC* directory in Windows NT, or within the */ETC* directory on the Unix platforms. To make this universal on your network, make the same change on all clients as well. The *SERVICES* file on Windows 95/98 machine resides in the *\WINDOWS* directory.

Alternatively, you can modify some of the Domino servers in your network to use this new TCP/IP port. For the other servers and clients, you then need to configure the connection details for this new port. For Notes clients, this means setting up a Connection document in the Personal Name and Address Book for each of the server(s) using the nonstandard ports that you need to connect to. Then, in the Destination Server field on the Advanced tab, enter the hostname, or the fully qualified name or IP address, of the server followed by the port it uses to listen for incoming requests. So for example, any of `shoreline:5000`, `shoreline.alameda.com:5000`, or `10.0.0.2:5000` would be suitable, although for ease of maintenance, it would be preferable to not use the IP address and instead make use of DNS for name resolution. Refer to Chapter 8, *Supporting the Notes Client* for more information about configuring Notes clients and the Personal Address Book.

Then, for each server that has connections for replication and/or routing to this server, you need to enter the Optional Network Address field on the Basics tab of the appropriate Connection document in the Domino Directory. This field should contain the server hostname, or fully qualified name or IP address, followed by the port it uses to listen for incoming requests. Refer to Chapter 2, *Domino Directories*, for more information about the Domino Directory and Connection documents.

All the other protocols are configured on the Server document for each server in the Domino Directory on the Ports page on the Internet ports tab. For the majority of these protocols, you can configure which port to use, whether it is enabled or disabled, and whether anonymous or name and password authentication is enabled. However, for the mail protocols (IMAP, POP, SMTP outbound), anonymous access doesn't make sense here and is not applicable. For more information about the server document in the Domino Directory, see Chapter 2.

Keep in mind that if you change the configuration of Domino and don't use the well-defined ports for these services, you need to ensure all the clients are configured correctly to use the modified port. They would be configured to use the regular well-defined ports by default.

You can check which ports are currently being listened to by the Domino server by viewing the server output from the `SHOW TASKS` command. For LDAP, IMAP, POP3, NNTP, SMTP and HTTP, the console output shows which ports are being listened to on the server. Unfortunately, IIOP does not report which ports are being used for this task. Refer to Chapter 8, *Supporting the Notes Client*, for more information about using this command.

Using NotesConnect to Test Connectivity

NotesConnect is a very useful tool to test network connectivity for Domino servers. Typically, when resolving network access problems, you are limited to using the *ping* utility at the operating system level. However, in many secure network environments, routers and firewalls are configured not to respond to ping packets. Even if you were able to use ping to check basic connectivity between machines, this tells you little about whether you are able to successfully connect using the ports we want to use for Domino services.

NotesConnect is a tool written by IRIS employee Bob Lomme and can be downloaded from *http://notes.net/sandbox.nsf/Download*. It runs on 32-bit Windows machines (95/98/NT).

Once the *NCONNECT.EXE* file is downloaded, you have a self-extracting executable that contains the releases notes and two versions of the utility: *NPING.EXE* and *NPINGCL.EXE* (the GUI and command line versions). Place the extracted executables in *\LOTUS\NOTES* for Notes clients or *\LOTUS\DOMINO* to run on the Domino server, since it needs to access the *NOTES.INI* file and some of the Notes/Domino DLLs to function.

Figure E-1 and Figure E-2 show a successful and unsuccessful connection to a Domino server. You can select the server name, how many times to connect, and what port to use. The well-known ports for Domino are already configured in the GUI version of the tool, so you do not have to know them beforehand. However, you have the option to attempt to connect on any port you choose.

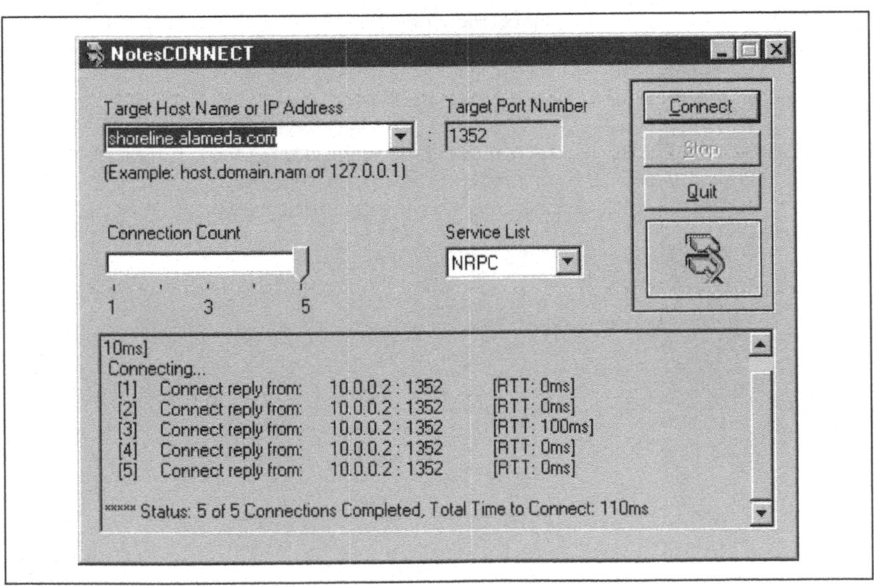

Figure E-1: NotesConnect—successful connection

You can also run *NPINGCL.EXE* from the command line. Its syntax is as follows:

```
npingcl servername [port] [times]
```

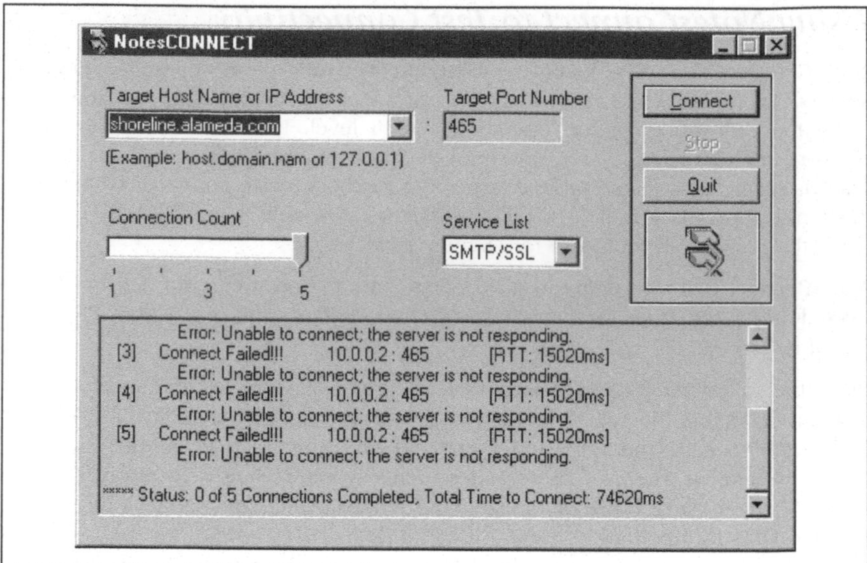

Figure E-2: NotesConnect—unsuccessful connection

By default, it uses the Notes RPC (NRPC)—port 1352—and attempts to connect five times to the server. Here is some sample output from the tool:

```
C:\Lotus\Notes>npingcl shoreline.alameda.com
***** DNS Lookup:         shoreline.alameda.com           [RTT: 20ms]
 Connecting to:           shoreline.alameda.com [10.0.0.2]
    [1]  Reply from:      10.0.0.2 : 1352 [RTT: 0ms]
    [2]  Reply from:      10.0.0.2 : 1352 [RTT: 100ms]
    [3]  Reply from:      10.0.0.2 : 1352 [RTT: 0ms]
    [4]  Reply from:      10.0.0.2 : 1352 [RTT: 100ms]
    [5]  Reply from:      10.0.0.2 : 1352 [RTT: 0ms]
***** Status: 5 of 5 Connections Completed, Total Time to Connect:
[220ms]
```

APPENDIX F

Web Links

This appendix lists a selection of web sites, discussion forums, and e-zines that may be of interest to the reader.

Web Sites

http://notes.net
: The IRIS web site. In the rest of this appendix, I have separately listed some of the most interesting areas on their site, but keep in mind that there are still many areas I have not mentioned. These include a history and future vision of Notes/Domino, as well as an assortment of links to other interesting Domino web sites.

http://notes.net/doc
: View the product documentation for Domino online and/or download them in PDF format to view with Adobe Acrobat Reader.

http://notes.net/down.nsf/welcome
: Download the quarterly fixes for Notes and Domino for your chosen platform, and also some useful tools available in the IRIS sandbox such as NotesConnect and NotesView.

http://www.redbooks.ibm.com
: These "redbooks" (the name comes from their red cover) are supervised by IBM's International Technical Support Organization (ITSO), and written by experienced IBM staff, business partners, and customers. A redbook will typically look at an area of technology very closely—such as Domino clustering, for example—and discuss the findings of the team in using the product. It will describe in detail the configurations, what worked, and what didn't. You can view these online or download them in PDF format. If you do use any of the redbooks, please remember to submit your feedback form (which can be found as the last page in the book). The ITSO is continually looking for these to assist in getting annual funding within IBM.

http://www.support.lotus.com

The Lotus support site, which you can search to find resolutions to your problems and questions.

http://www.lotus.com/home.nsf/welcome/r5home

The home page for Domino R5. Much of the material here is for marketing purposes, but the Reviewer's Guide is an excellent overview of the new features in R5.

http://www.as400.ibm.com/domino/index.htm

The home page for Domino on the AS/400. You'll find a great deal of information about running Domino on an AS/400, particularly in being able to size an AS/400 for your expected system load.

htp://www.notes411.com

A good portal site for all matters related to Notes/Domino.

http://www.searchdomino.com

A new Domino portal site that contains some original content and indexes a number of other Domino-related sites for searching.

http://www.keysolutions.com/notesfaq

The maintainers of this site have taken FAQs (frequently asked questions) from the discussion forums, listed in the next sections, and categorized them by version and subject area.

http://www.notesbench.org

Here you can find performance and capacity information from the various server vendors in running Domino.

Discussion Forums and Usenet Newsgroups

http://notes.net/cafe.nsf

A discussion forum hosted by IRIS, monitored by their developers. You can lurk here as you please, but need to register to be able to append to the forums. This is definitely the discussion forum of choice for Domino since it is moderated and appends are likely to get expert attention.

comp.groupware.lotus-notes
comp.groupware.lotus-notes.admin
comp.groupware.lotus-notes.apps
comp.groupware.lotus-notes.misc
comp.groupware.lotus-notes.programmer

The Usenet newsgroups that cover Lotus Notes/Domino. These are unmoderated and appenders appear to habitually cross-post to many of these newsgroups at once, so there is no need to monitor all these forums to keep updated.

E-zines

http://notes.net/today.nsf

The monthly magazine *IRIS Today*, which features in-depth articles about various features of Domino and includes interviews with the developers about how certain features have come into being and why.

http://www.dominopower.com

The monthly magazine *DominoPower*, which often has articles of interest for the Domino system administrator. It also has a daily news page that highlights news items relating to Domino. You can also subscribe here to their weekly email newsletter, which often contains a useful tip, hint, or undocumented feature of Domino.

http://www.dominopro.com

The new *Domino Professional* magazine, which offers articles of interest for system administrators and also keeps track of Domino news items. One particularly interesting feature is the "Ask Ben" column, where readers can submit their own questions. The questions are answered by Ben Malekzedah, who spent a number of months inside Lotus during the development of R5 and knows much about the way in which the new R5 features were designed and implemented.

APPENDIX G

Domino Updates: QMRs and QMUs

Lotus releases regular updates to Domino as *QMRs* and *QMUs*. A QMR (Quarterly Maintenance Release) is the scheduled update released at the end of each quarter. A QMU (Quarterly Maintenance Update) is released as needed between the QMRs to fix any urgent bugs that are encountered. You can tell which is which by checking the numbering of the version of the Domino release. A QMR ends with a number, and a QMU ends with a letter—for example, Domino 5.01 was a QMR and 5.01a was a QMU.

Since some functionality had to be dropped from the original 5.0 release in order for the code to be ready to ship, there are often many new enhancements as well as bug fixes in each QMU for Domino R5.

Lotus ships CDs with the updated code to their business partners and those customers in their Passport maintenance program, but these can take some time to be pressed and mailed, so an alternative is to download the *Incremental Installer* package for the release(s) you wish to install from *http://www.notes.net/qmrdown.nsf/QMRWelcome*. So that you don't have to download the complete new version, these packages consist of patches to take either Notes or Domino from one version to another for a given platform. For example, a complete download of 5.0.1 for Windows NT was 77MB, but the Incremental Installer file to take that version to 5. 0.1a from 5.0.1 was only 23MB—still a significant download, but a savings of 54MB!

The Incremental Installer runs in three stages, and cannot be run while Notes or Domino is running. It starts by checking the location of the executable code and the data files to be updated. Then it checks whether the installed version in these directories is exactly the same as the "before" version that the package was created to install against. If that is acceptable, then the Notes/Domino code and templates are updated.

Version 5.0 was originally available online around March 30, 1999; 5.0a came very soon after and fixed a number of critical stability issues (mostly memory leaks and bug fixes).

Version 5.0a.0a was a special version for the OS/390 platform only.

Version 5.0.1 introduced a number of new features as listed in Table G-1 and Table G-2. There were also many improvements to the Domino Designer product, but these are not listed here since they are not likely to be of interest for system administrators. This version also introduced the first Solaris version of Domino R5.

Table G-1: Version 5.0.1 Notes Client Changes

Feature	*Description*
Updated attachment viewers	Capability to view Microsoft Office 2000 documents.
Improved JavaScript support	Support for additional JavaScript methods and events.
Improved certificate handling	X.509 certificates that are PKCS #12 compliant can be imported into the Notes ID file. Different X.509 certificates can be used for encryption and signing messages.
Administration client—optionally add *admin* to ACL of migrated mail database	New feature within the Domino Upgrade Services, within the Domino Administrator, which enables the administrator be added to the ACL (as manager) of the migrated user mail database. Another new option allows the existing password for the user to be overwritten by a random password.
Administration client—enhanced Internet Address Tool	Enables the administration to select multiple people within the Domino Directory to have their Internet address field set.

Table G-2: Version 5.0.1 Domino Server Changes

Feature	*Description*
API changes for transaction logging	A new function is provided to check the state of a logged database (this will be more likely to be of use for third-party vendors who provide backup solutions to work with Domino transaction logging). If a failure is experienced during a transaction logging restart, then a list of "dirty" databases is written to the Domino server console. When a server is next restarted after transaction logging is turned off, a restart recovery is run to clean up the databases.
DES support for International versions	56-bit DES encryption is now available for use with the web server for International (non-U.S.) versions of Domino.

Table G-2: Version 5.0.1 Domino Server Changes (continued)

Feature	*Description*
Database for LDAP schema customization	The Domino LDAP Schema database (*SCHEMA50.NSF*) displays schema information about the Domino Directory and is automatically updated as the schema for the Domino Directory is modified.
Updated *REPORTS.NTF* database template included	This template had shipped in the R5 betas, but until now had not been part of the released R5 product.

Version 5.0.1.01 was a special version for AS/400 only.

Version 5.0.1a provided bug fixes, but also offered the first R5 Macintosh client for Notes (and Notes Designer), and also the first R5 version of Domino for OS/2 Warp Server.

Version 5.0.1b provided a series of bug fixes, but was also the first version of R5 for the HP/UX platform.

Version 5.0.2 was released in mid-November 1999, and was the first version to support Linux; Red Hat 6.0 (and later) for Intel and Caldera 2.2 Intel are supported. Later versions support additional Linux distributions (that is, it could run on SuSe 6.2 and TurboLinux with additional libraries installed, but it was not considered supported on these platforms). Also, 64-bit mode support for Solaris 7.0 was added in this version.

Version 5.0.2 introduced a number of new features as listed in Tables G-3 and G-4.

Table G-3: Version 5.0.2 Notes Client Changes

Feature	*Description*
Contact management for web mail clients	The Mail template *MAIL50.NTF* has been extended to support contact details (users and groups) in the user's mail file when accessed via a browser.
Sametime Integration	If you have Sametime Connect installed and have a Sametime server installed, you can now see whether the sender and recipients are online and have an instant messaging conversation with them. Also, if SameTime is installed, a new bookmark icon is created to launch it from Notes.
Calendar printing enhancements	Support for additional printing formats for Calendar information: To Do list printing and a trifold option that can print three panels on a page.

Table G-4: Version 5.0.2 Domino Server Changes

Feature	*Description*
XML Support	XML support added via a new *?ReadViewEntries* URL. This lists the entries within the view using XML. Further XML support will be added in future releases.

Table G-4: Version 5.0.2 Domino Server Changes (continued)

Feature	*Description*
Windows NT and Solaris Sparc statistics now available for performance monitoring	Domino can now track OS performance counters for the Windows NT Intel and Sun Solaris Sparc platforms. These can be written to the server console or viewed in the Domino Administrator Statistics and Events view.
LDAP Schema checking	A new option allows the enforcement of LDAP schema checking. When enabled, this means that when adding or modifying the Domino directory via LDAP, the updates are only completed if the LDAP request conforms to the directory schema. There were also a number of LDAP schema changes made in this release.
Java VM	Updated to 1.1.8 for the Windows NT and Alpha platforms.

Versions 5.0.2a QMU introduced support for COM (Microsoft's Component Object Model) access to Domino server resources.

Versions 5.0.2b and 5.0.2c QMUs were bug fixes that introduced no new features.

Version 5.0.3 introduced a number of new features as listed in Table G-5 and Table G-6. Support for Windows 2000 was also added.

Table G-5: Version 5.0.3 Notes Client Changes

Feature	*Description*
Calendar printing enhancements	Support for additional printing formats for Calendar information: To Do list printing, and a trifold option that can print three panels on a page.

Table G-6: Version 5.0.3 Domino Server Changes

Feature	*Description*
DECS	Support for updated database drivers. DECS now supported on Linux.
Multiple threading for mail to remote domains	New *NOTES.INI* parameter `RouterAllow-ConcurrentXFERToAll` allows the `ROUTER` task to use multiple threads when sending mail to remote domains over slower network links.
New full text searching engine	When the parameter `FT_LIBNAME=ftgtr34` is added to *NOTES.INI*, this new engine is used. This new engine is intended to be faster when searching large databases. When this parameter is first added, the full text search index for each database is recreated.

QMRs & QMUs

Table G-6: Version 5.0.3 Domino Server Changes (continued)

Feature	*Description*
IMAP session limiting	New parameter **IMAPMaxSessions** in *NOTES.INI* defines maximum number of IMAP client sessions supported on the server. A value of 0 means that there is no limit. Also, support added for a number of other IMAP clients.

QMR 5.0.4 was released mid-June and included the first Global release of Notes/Domino instead of the former North American and International versions. This is discussed further in Chapter 1, *Notes and Domino Overview*. A new *NOTES.INI* parameter, **PercentAvailSysResources**, can be used either with partitioned servers or for clients running from a Terminal Server. This parameter is a number between 2 and 100 and denotes the percentage of physical memory to be used for that server or client instance.

A couple of useful tips for using these Incremental Installer packages to installing QMUs and QMRs:

- The 32-bit Windows versions of the packages allow you to rerun the Incremental Installer to back out of the upgrade. The backup versions of key files in the data directory and the program directory have an .IIB file extension. This can take up a lot of disk space, so these files can be deleted once you are satisfied with the upgraded code.
- These Incremental Installers do not always work as expected—often, for no apparent reason, they will complain about an installed file not matching the expected checksum and then exit. Check the contents of the *UPGRADE.LOG* file in the program directory; this file lists files that cannot be found or matched. You can try renaming or deleting the original files that the Incremental Installer is complaining about and then rerunning the Installer.

Glossary

This is a short glossary of Domino- and Notes-specific terminology. It does not include those terms in wide use that describe Internet protocols for web and mail technology.

ACL
: Access Control List. An ACL is created on every database to determine who can and cannot access the database and what type of access they can have with the database.

agent
: A program that performs an automated task. This can run on the either the Notes client or the Domino server. Notes client agents can be written using simple actions (which require no programming skill), Notes formula language, JavaScript, or LotusScript. Domino server agents can be written using simple actions, Notes formula language, LotusScript, or Java.

bookmark
: A new term to describe an element of the R5 Notes client. A bookmark is typically a shortcut to a Domino object, usually a database.

calendar
: A calendar is a type of view within a Domino database. Therefore, calendering information is stored within a user's mail database, which they view and update using calendar views.

certifier ID
: A file used to create new server IDs and user IDs. Also used to create certifiers for child containers of this organization/organizational unit.

clustering
: As well as the operating system level clustering that is provided with AIX and Windows NT, Domino also supports application-level clustering for use with failover and load balancing. R5 now introduces support for clustering for Domino browser clients.

cross-certification

The process by which servers and users can trust the identity of other users and servers created from certifiers from a different organization. The cross-certificates are stored in the Domino Directory or the Personal Name and Address Book when done at a per-user level.

DECS

Domino Enterprise Connection Services. This was originally a component of the NotesPump add-on (which has now been renamed Enterprise Integrator) that provided real-time access to backend databases from Domino databases. This is now part of R5 and was available for download for Domino 4.6.3 and above.

directory assistance

A feature that allows Domino to refer to directory information from other Domino domains and also LDAP directories. This is implemented by a Directory Assistance database, which used to be called the Master Name and Address book in R4.*x*.

directory catalog

A new feature in R5 that creates a smaller version of the Domino Directory for quick lookups by both servers and laptop users.

DNN (Domino Named Network)

A group of servers within the same Domino domain that share the same network protocol can have their network ports configured to be in the same Notes Named Network. Domino routes mail automatically between these servers without requiring any special configuration.

domain

A domain is a group of servers and users that use the same Domino Directory.

Domino Directory

The database (*NAMES.NSF*) that is shared within a Domino domain. In earlier releases this was known as the Public Name and Address Book.

ECL

Execution Control List. These define on the Notes client what access Java, JavaScript and LotusScript can have, depending on who signs the design database. These are used to provide a "sandbox" type of environment so that trusted applications can execute as needed, but untrusted applications do not perform unauthorized changes on the workstation (for example, to prevent mail bomb type of viruses).

event

In terms of server monitoring, an event is the occurrence of any activity on the Domino server. We then configure the monitoring for specific events of interest to us as administrators.

flat

The standard naming scheme used before R3 that comprised a flat namespace for Notes users. This is still used by some of the early adopters of Notes, but there are more and more features of Notes/Domino that are unavailable to companies using a flat naming scheme. The R5 Domino Administration client is not able to create new flat users, so if flat naming is retained, an R4 client must be used to create the user.

hierarchical

Describes the X.500-like naming standard that has been used since R3 to identify users and servers. At the top of the hierachy, it comprises a Country (C) and an Organization (0), then optionally up to four levels of Organizational Units (OUs). Within these containers are servers and users, which are identified by their Common Name (CN).

LotusScript

A BASIC-like programming language used in Notes/Domino. It can be used to write agents that run on the Domino server and the Notes client.

memo

An older term used inter-changeably with mail within Notes client user interface.

MTA

Message Transfer Agent. This is used to transfer and convert messages between Domino different mail systems, for example, the cc:Mail MTA and the X.400 MTA.

NOTES.INI

A text file used to contain much of the configuration information for both the Domino server and the Notes client.

NRPC

Notes RPC (Remote Procedure Call) is the proprietary protocol used between Domino servers and Notes clients.

NS4

The file extension used in R5 to keep databases in the old ODS format and thus compatible with the previous version.

NSF

The file extension used for Notes and Domino databases.

NTF

The file extension used for Notes and Domino database templates.

ODS

The On Disk Structure is the internal database format used for Notes and Domino. R5 introduces an updated ODS that allows larger database size, in place compaction, and support for transaction logging.

partitioning

Domino can be configured to execute multiple instances on the same server hardware. All instances share the same program code, but each instance has its own data directories.

passthru

A feature that allows access from a Notes client through one or more Domino servers to another Domino server that is not one same network. This is typically used when a Notes client dials into one server and accesses another.

personal name and address book

This database (*NAMES.NSF*) resides on the Notes client and defines how the client connects to server resources and keeps personal contact information and distribution lists.

port

Notes/Domino gives each port a name to describe each of its network protocols on each network adapter.

replica

A copy of a database that shares the same replica ID—an internal hexadecimal number within the database such as 882567BD:001181B4. Replication can only be carried out between databases that are replica copies of each other.

replication

The process by which database content updates (adds, changes, deletes) are propagated with another replica copy.

role

A feature within the database ACL that allows developers additional granularity over the regular Notes/Domino access types. Developers can define specific roles with their application, then check to see whether a given user is a member of a defined role.

routing

The processing by which mail is transferred from the sender to the recipient.

shared mail

An optional feature that allows (for instance) storage for mail messages on the same server. Otherwise, each recipient keeps their own copy of the message within their own mail database.

statistic

Statistics are the status of a given server component, which is continually updated as the server runs.

subscription

A new Notes R5 feature that allows it to regularly monitor changes in database content on Domino servers, and displays these on the Notes welcome page.

template

A special type of database that contains design information and optionally data documents as well that can be used as a basis to create new databases.

view

A collection of documents within a database that meet a given criteria.

X.PC

The proprietary dialup protocol used between Notes clients and Domino servers. It can also be used between Domino servers.

Index

Symbols

A

B

C

D

E

F

G

H

I

J

K

L

M

N

Q

R

S

T

U

V

W

X

Y

Z

About the Author

Greg Neilson has over 11 years of IT experience. He has worked with Lotus Notes/Domino since 1993 and has deployed it on various platforms including Windows NT, OS/2, AS/400, AIX, Solaris and Linux. He is certified as a CLP Domino R5 Principal System Administrator, a CLP Domino R5 Principal Application Developer, and also has an MCNE and MCSE+I.

Currently, he works as a Senior Notes Architect for a large IT services company in Australia and is a Contributing Editor for *Microsoft Certified Professional* magazine. He has also written about Domino for magazines such as *Microsoft Certified Professional Magazine, Windows NT Magazine, IIS Administrator* newsletter, and also *NEWS/400 Magazine.*

In his spare time he works toward completing his MBA and plays the guitar.

Colophon

Our look is the result of reader comments, our own experimentation, and feedback from distribution channels. Distinctive covers complement our distinctive approach to technical topics, breathing personality and life into potentially dry subjects.

The animal on the cover of *Lotus Domino Administration in a Nutshell* is a Dalmatian dog, a medium-sized, short-haired breed. Dalmatians are mostly white, with distinctive round black or liver (brown) spots, which develop only after birth. The dogs have an average life span of 11 to 13 years, and grow to almost two feet tall at the shoulder.

Dalmatians are active dogs, originally bred to run long distances with horse-drawn carriages ("coaching"), and famous as the traditional dogs of firemen. The breed received its official name in the mid-eighteenth century (from the Croatian province of Dalmatia), but there is evidence of similar animals as long ago as 3000 B.C.

The 1956 book *The Hundred and One Dalmatians,* by Dodie Smith (popularized by Disney), greatly increased demand for these distinctive animals as pets.

Nancy Kotary was the production editor and copyeditor for *Lotus Domino Administration in a Nutshell.* Mary Sheehan was the proofreader. Colleen Gorman and Jane Ellin provided quality control. Pamela Murray wrote the index.

Hanna Dyer designed the cover of this book, based on a series design by Edie Freedman. The cover image is an original illustration created by Susan Hart. Emma Colby produced the cover layout with QuarkXPress 3.32 using Adobe's ITC Garamond font.

Alicia Cech and David Futato designed the interior layout based on a series design by Nancy Priest. Mike Sierra implemented the design in FrameMaker 5.5.6. The text and heading fonts are ITC Garamond Light and Garamond Book. The illustrations that appear in the book were produced by Robert Romano using Macromedia FreeHand 8 and Adobe Photoshop 5. This colophon was written by Nancy Kotary.

Whenever possible, our books use a durable and flexible lay-flat binding. If the page count exceeds this binding's limit, perfect binding is used.

9 781565 927179

Lightning Source UK Ltd.
Milton Keynes UK
UKOW01f1147250917
309832UK00008B/1252/P